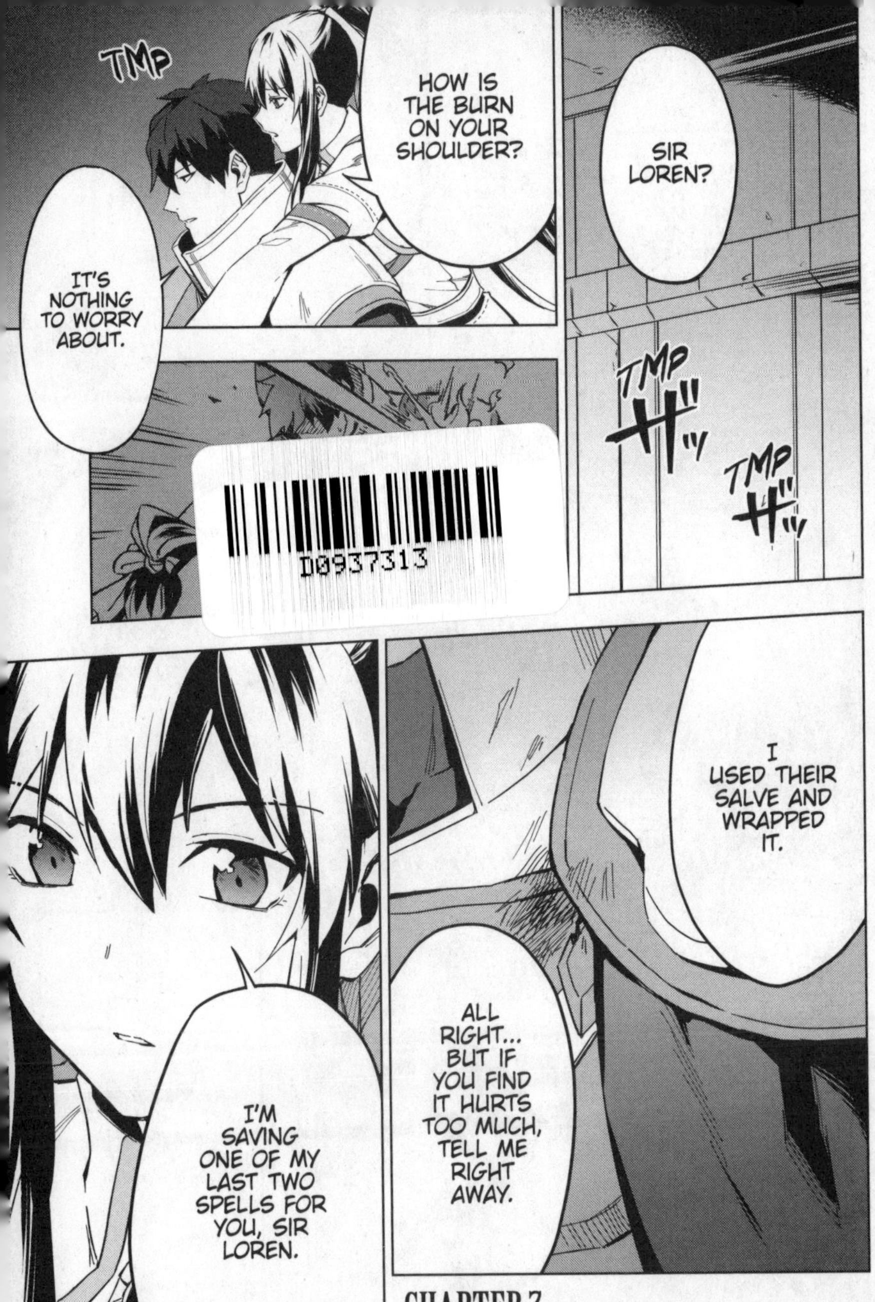
SIR LOREN?
TMP
ザッ
TMP
ザッ
HOW IS THE BURN ON YOUR SHOULDER?
TMP
IT'S NOTHING TO WORRY ABOUT.
I USED THEIR SALVE AND WRAPPED IT.
ALL RIGHT... BUT IF YOU FIND IT HURTS TOO MUCH, TELL ME RIGHT AWAY.
I'M SAVING ONE OF MY LAST TWO SPELLS FOR YOU, SIR LOREN.

CHAPTER 7

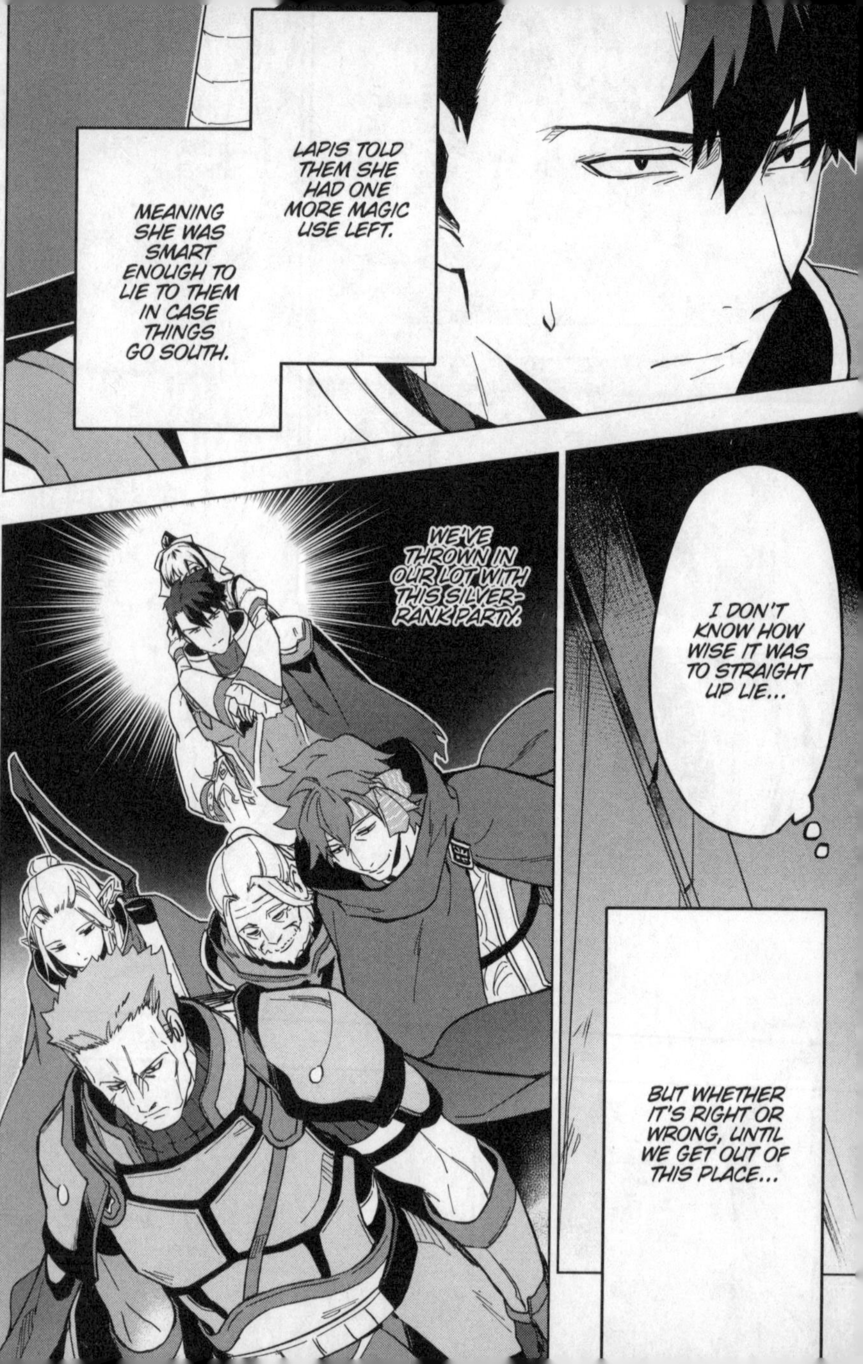
LAPIS TOLD THEM SHE HAD ONE MORE MAGIC USE LEFT.
MEANING SHE WAS SMART ENOUGH TO LIE TO THEM IN CASE THINGS GO SOUTH.
I DON'T KNOW HOW WISE IT WAS TO STRAIGHT UP LIE...
BUT WHETHER IT'S RIGHT OR WRONG, UNTIL WE GET OUT OF THIS PLACE...
WE'VE THROWN IN OUR LOT WITH THIS SILVER-RANK PARTY.

CHAPTER 7 SEARCHING TOGETHER

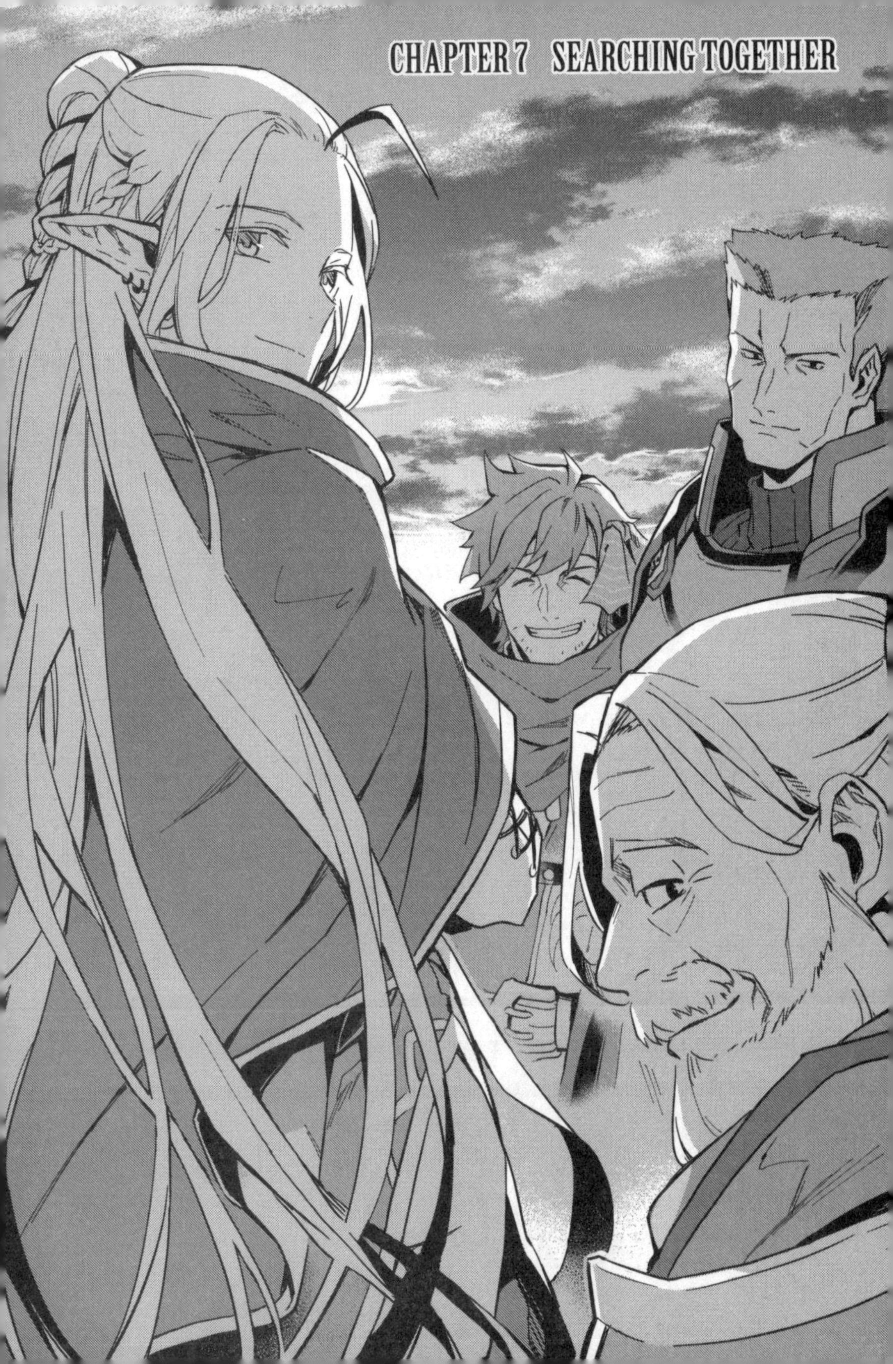

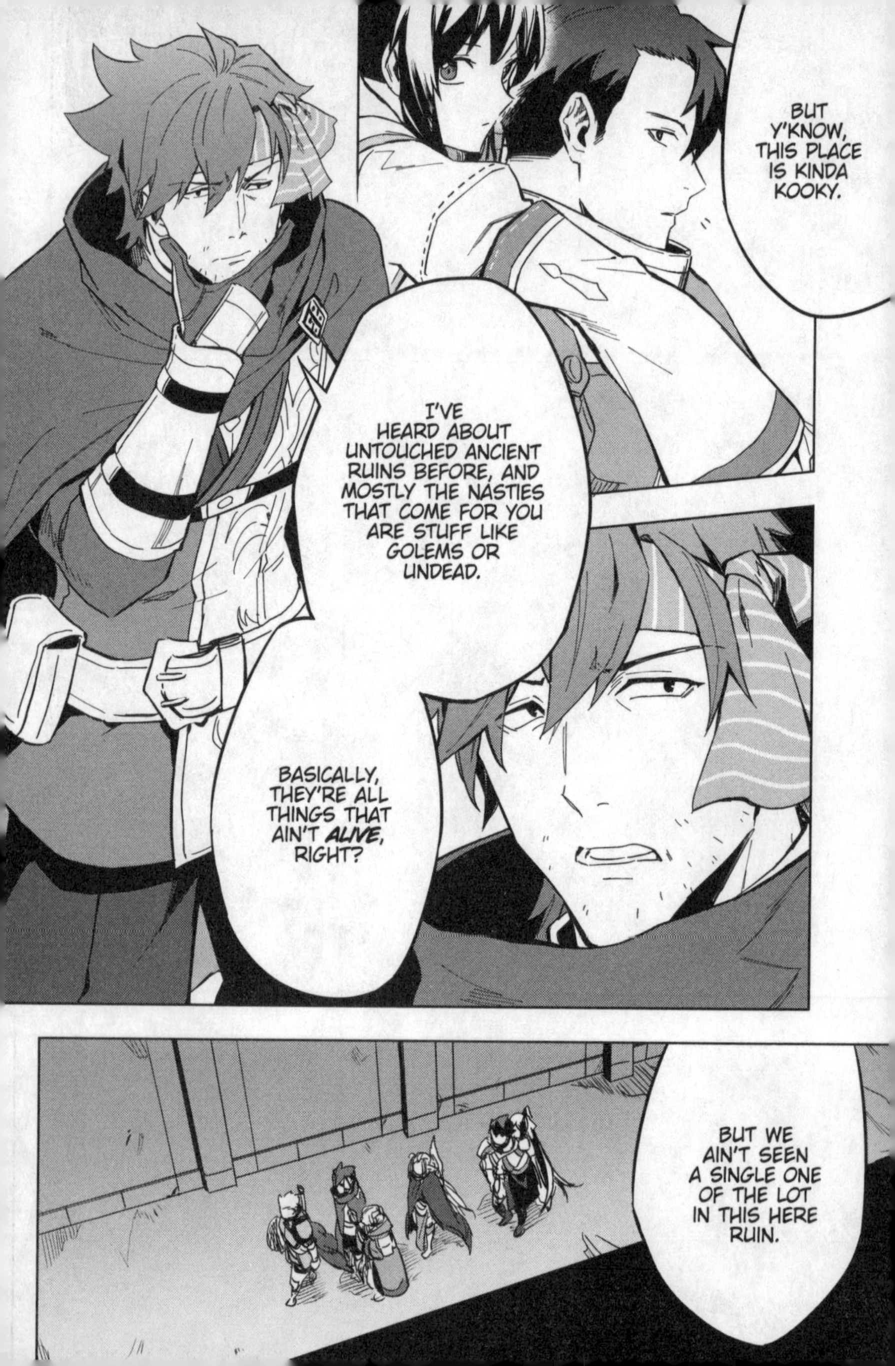
BUT Y'KNOW, THIS PLACE IS KINDA KOOKY.
I'VE HEARD ABOUT UNTOUCHED ANCIENT RUINS BEFORE, AND MOSTLY THE NASTIES THAT COME FOR YOU ARE STUFF LIKE GOLEMS OR UNDEAD.
BASICALLY, THEY'RE ALL THINGS THAT AIN'T *ALIVE*, RIGHT?
BUT WE AIN'T SEEN A SINGLE ONE OF THE LOT IN THIS HERE RUIN.

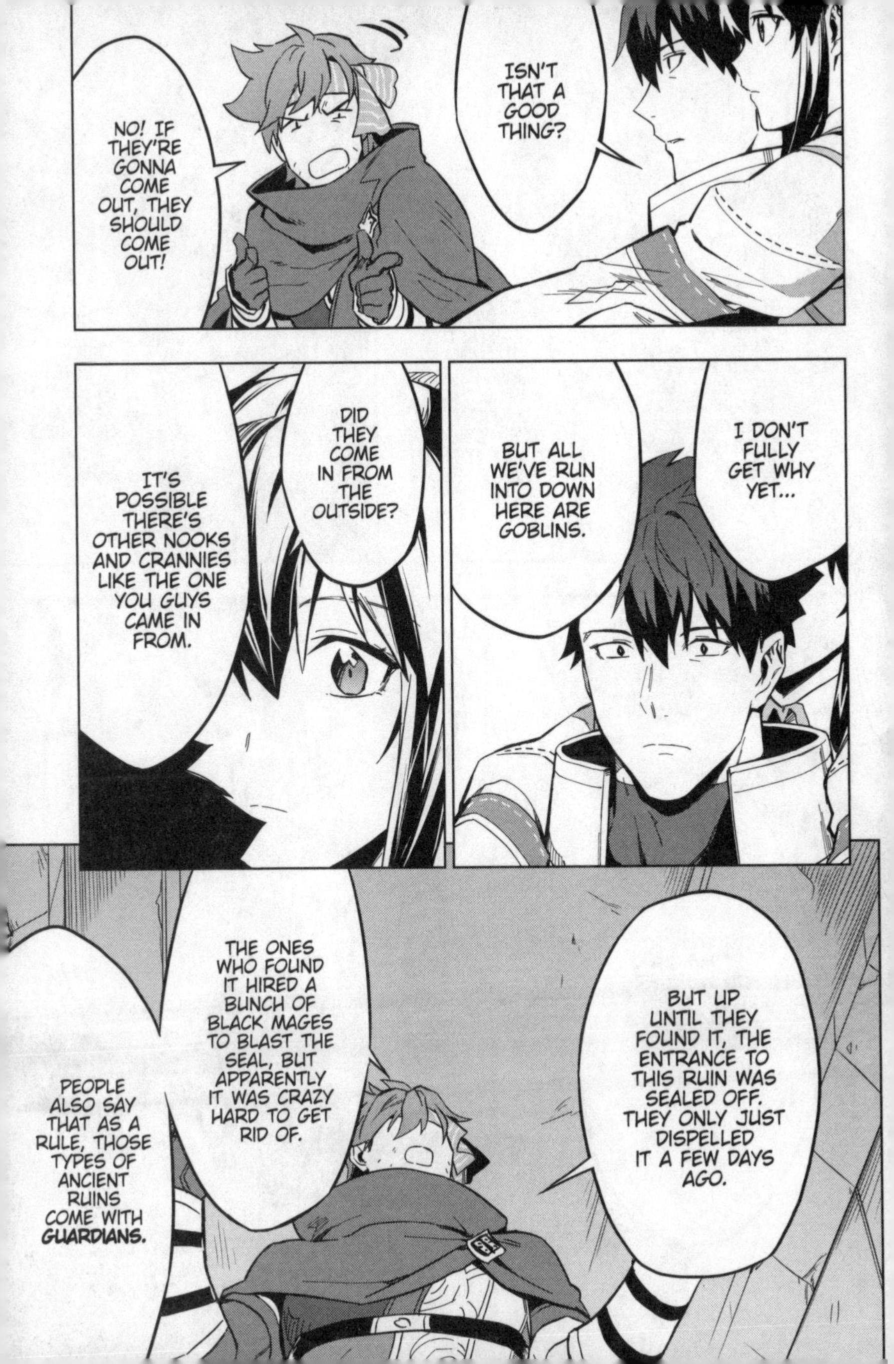
ISN'T THAT A GOOD THING?
NO! IF THEY'RE GONNA COME OUT, THEY SHOULD COME OUT!
I DON'T FULLY GET WHY YET...
BUT ALL WE'VE RUN INTO DOWN HERE ARE GOBLINS.
DID THEY COME IN FROM THE OUTSIDE?
IT'S POSSIBLE THERE'S OTHER NOOKS AND CRANNIES LIKE THE ONE YOU GUYS CAME IN FROM.
BUT UP UNTIL THEY FOUND IT, THE ENTRANCE TO THIS RUIN WAS SEALED OFF. THEY ONLY JUST DISPELLED IT A FEW DAYS AGO.
THE ONES WHO FOUND IT HIRED A BUNCH OF BLACK MAGES TO BLAST THE SEAL, BUT APPARENTLY IT WAS CRAZY HARD TO GET RID OF.
PEOPLE ALSO SAY THAT AS A RULE, THOSE TYPES OF ANCIENT RUINS COME WITH **GUARDIANS.**

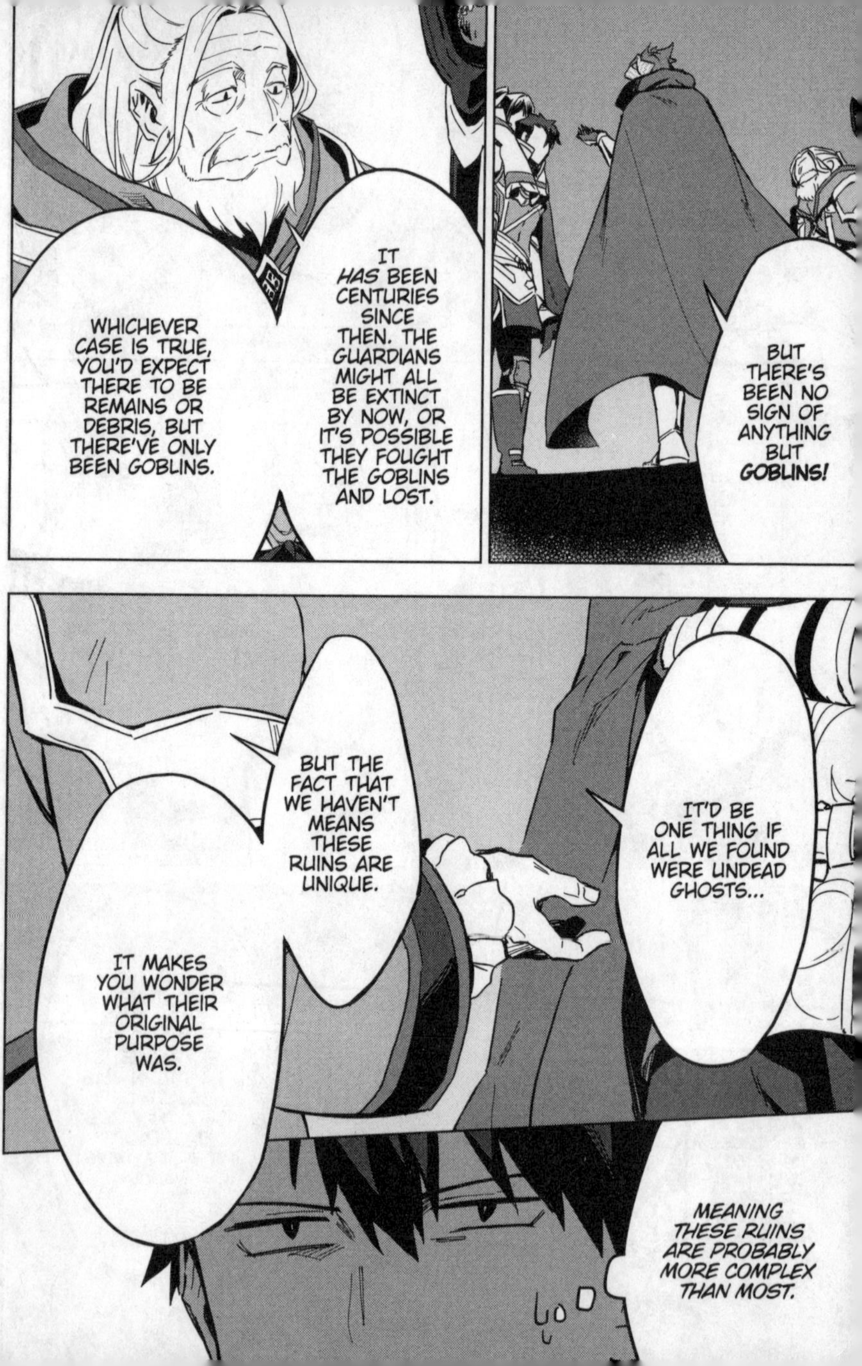
BUT THERE'S BEEN NO SIGN OF ANYTHING BUT **GOBLINS!**
IT *HAS* BEEN CENTURIES SINCE THEN. THE GUARDIANS MIGHT ALL BE EXTINCT BY NOW, OR IT'S POSSIBLE THEY FOUGHT THE GOBLINS AND LOST.
WHICHEVER CASE IS TRUE, YOU'D EXPECT THERE TO BE REMAINS OR DEBRIS, BUT THERE'VE ONLY BEEN GOBLINS.
IT'D BE ONE THING IF ALL WE FOUND WERE UNDEAD GHOSTS...
BUT THE FACT THAT WE HAVEN'T MEANS THESE RUINS ARE UNIQUE.
IT MAKES YOU WONDER WHAT THEIR ORIGINAL PURPOSE WAS.
MEANING THESE RUINS ARE PROBABLY MORE COMPLEX THAN MOST.

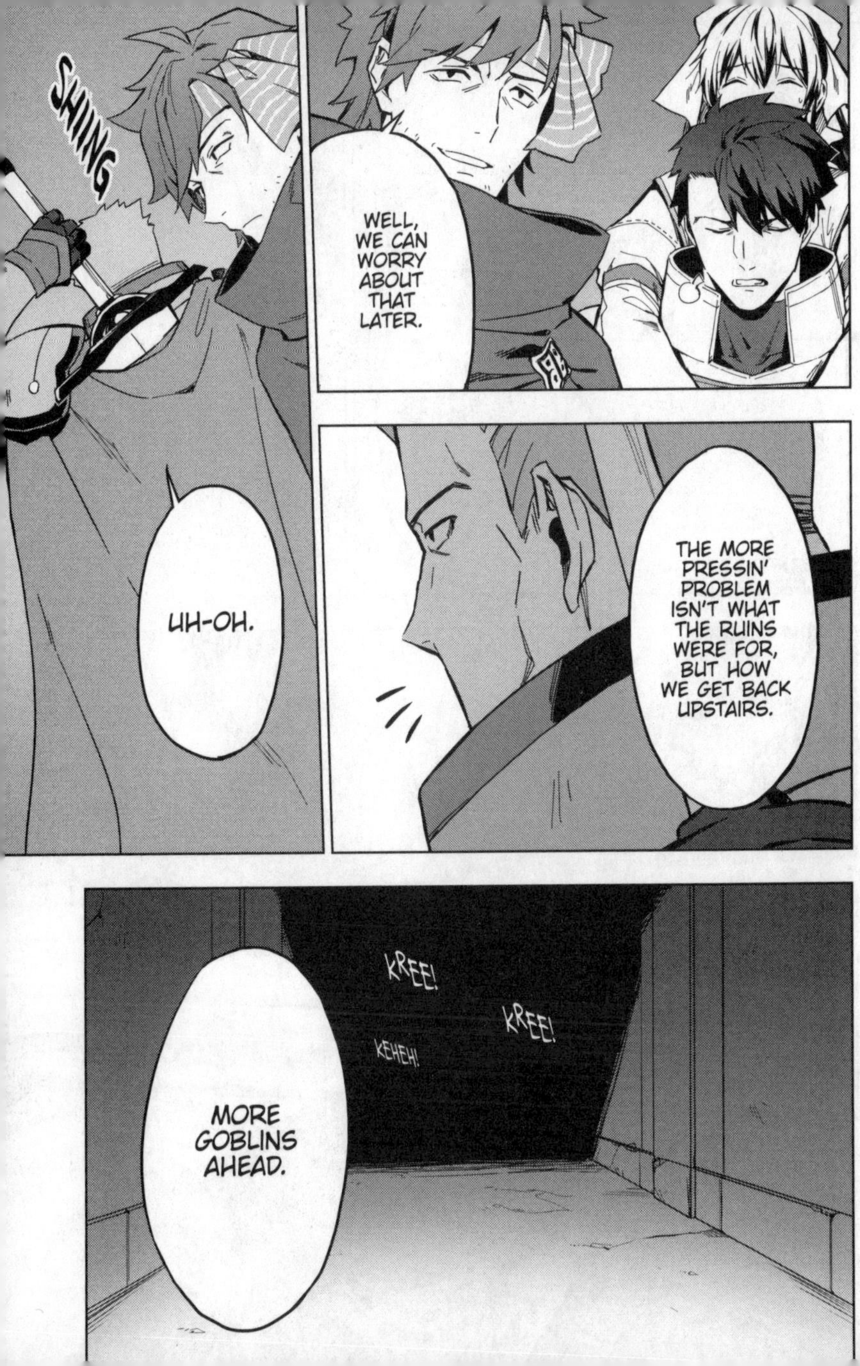
WELL, WE CAN WORRY ABOUT THAT LATER.
THE MORE PRESSIN' PROBLEM ISN'T WHAT THE RUINS WERE FOR, BUT HOW WE GET BACK UPSTAIRS.
SHING
UH-OH.
KREE!
KREE!
KEHEH!
MORE GOBLINS AHEAD.

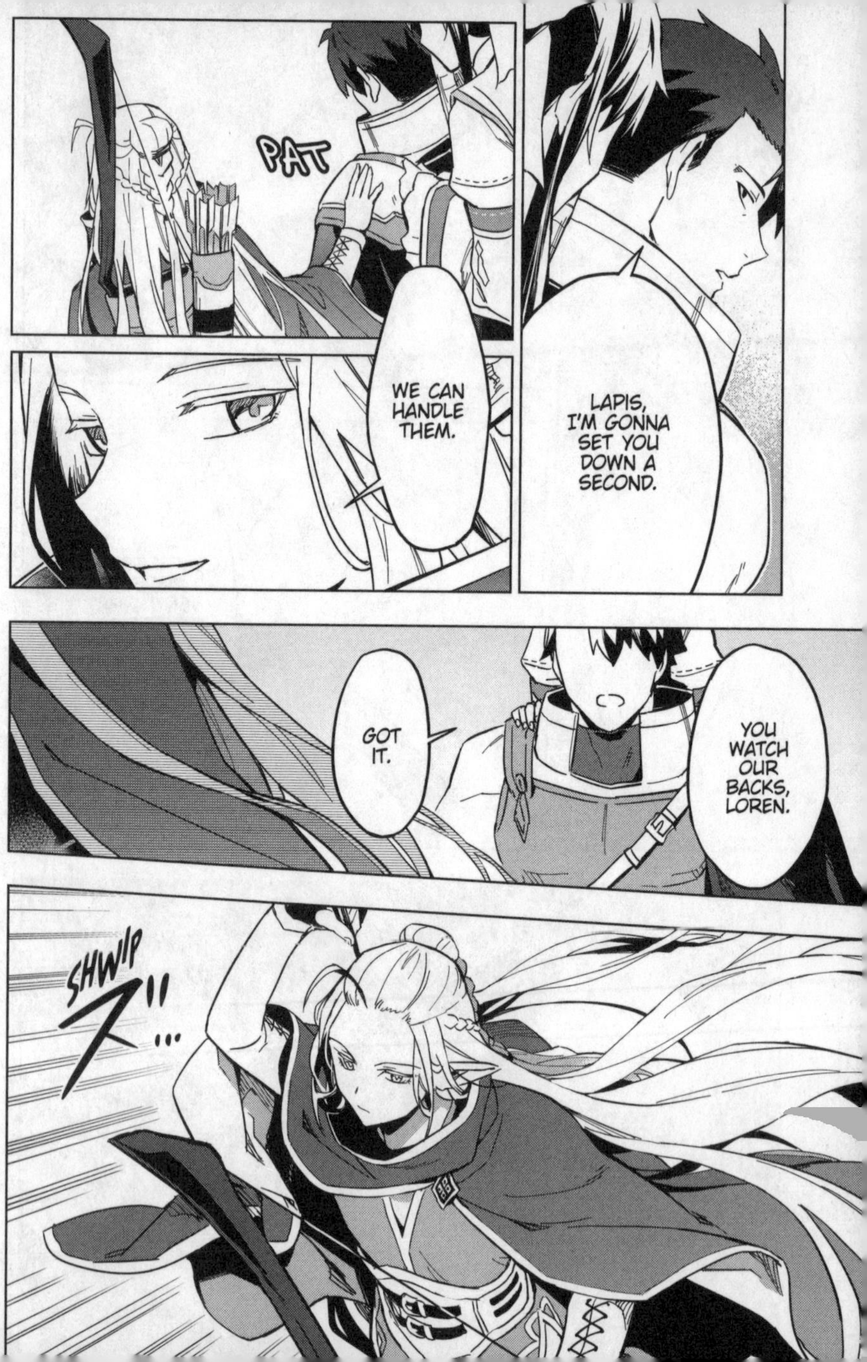

LAPIS, I'M GONNA SET YOU DOWN A SECOND.
PAT
WE CAN HANDLE THEM.
YOU WATCH OUR BACKS, LOREN.
GOT IT.
SHWIP

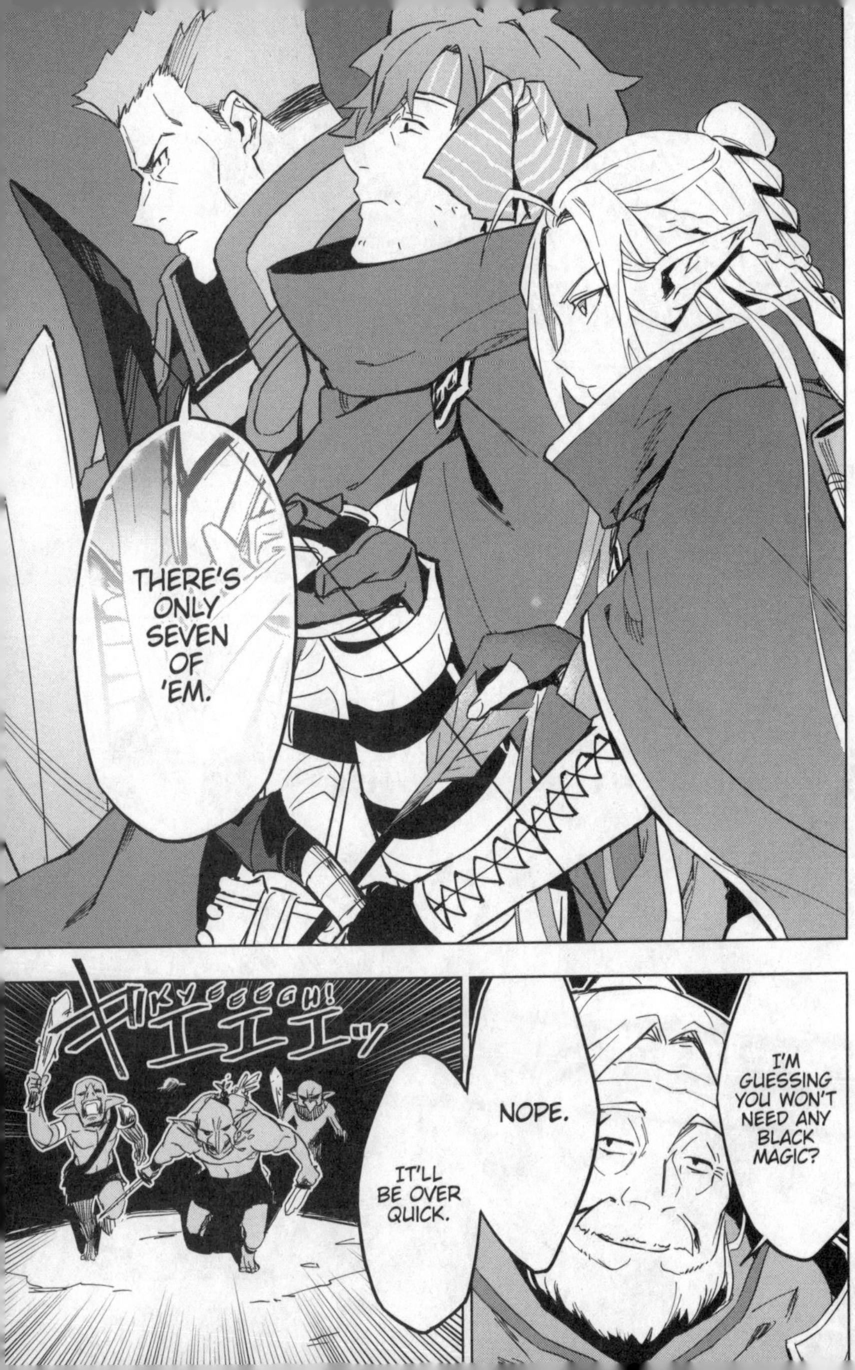
THERE'S ONLY SEVEN OF 'EM.
I'M GUESSING YOU WON'T NEED ANY BLACK MAGIC?
NOPE.
IT'LL BE OVER QUICK.
キエエエッ
IKYEEEGH!

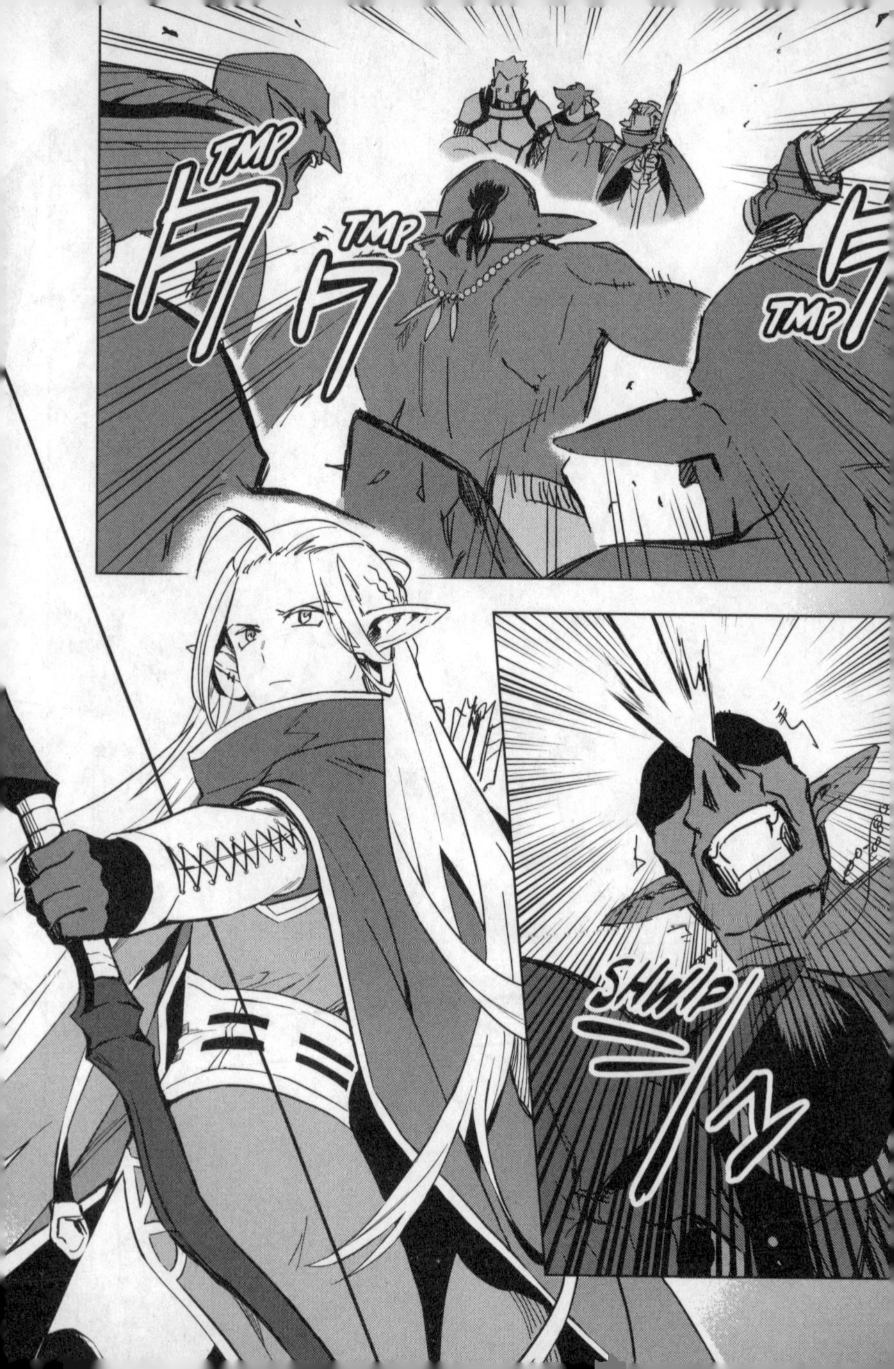
TMP
TMP
TMP
SHWIP

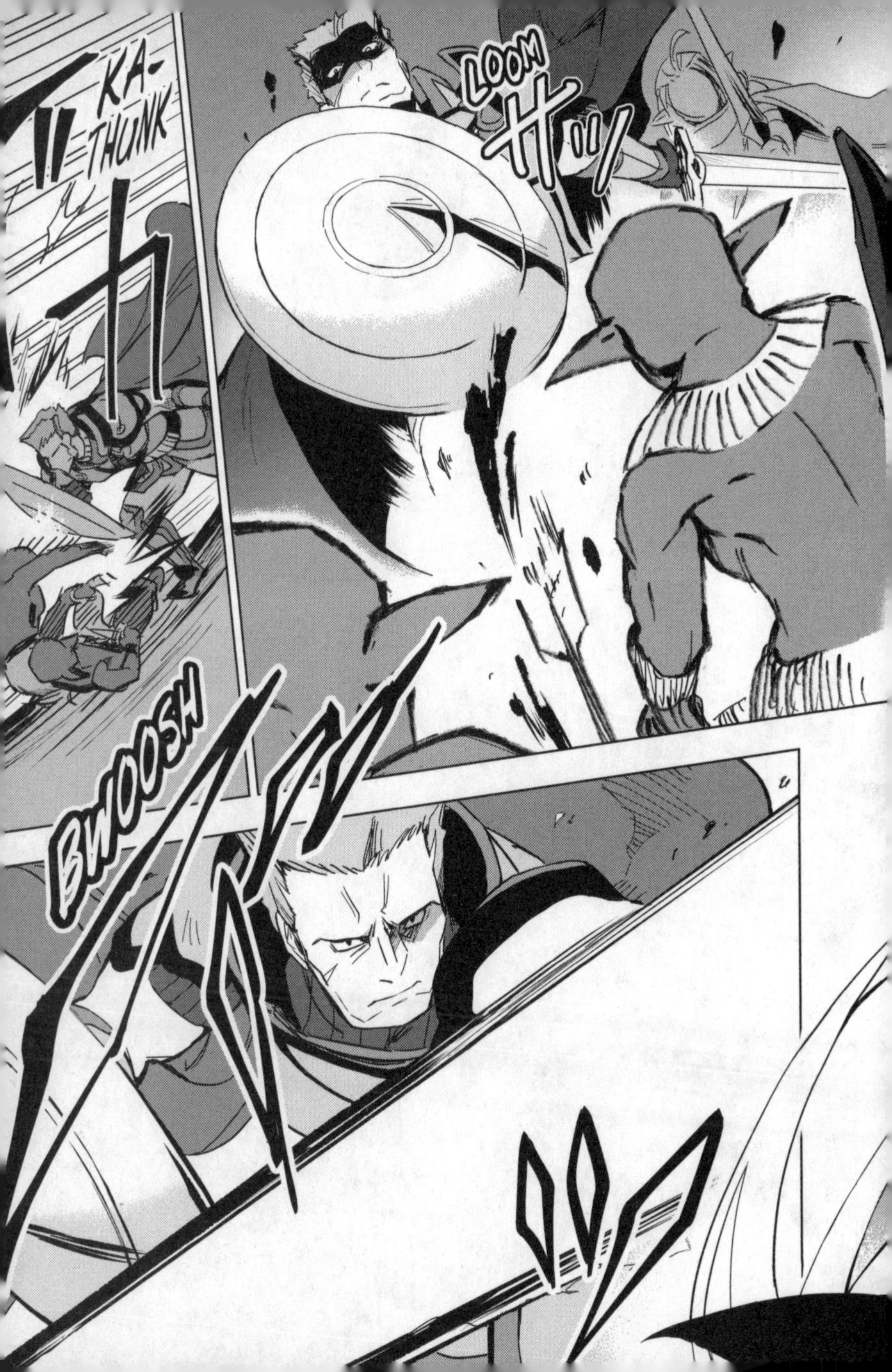
LOOM
KA-THUNK
BWOOSH

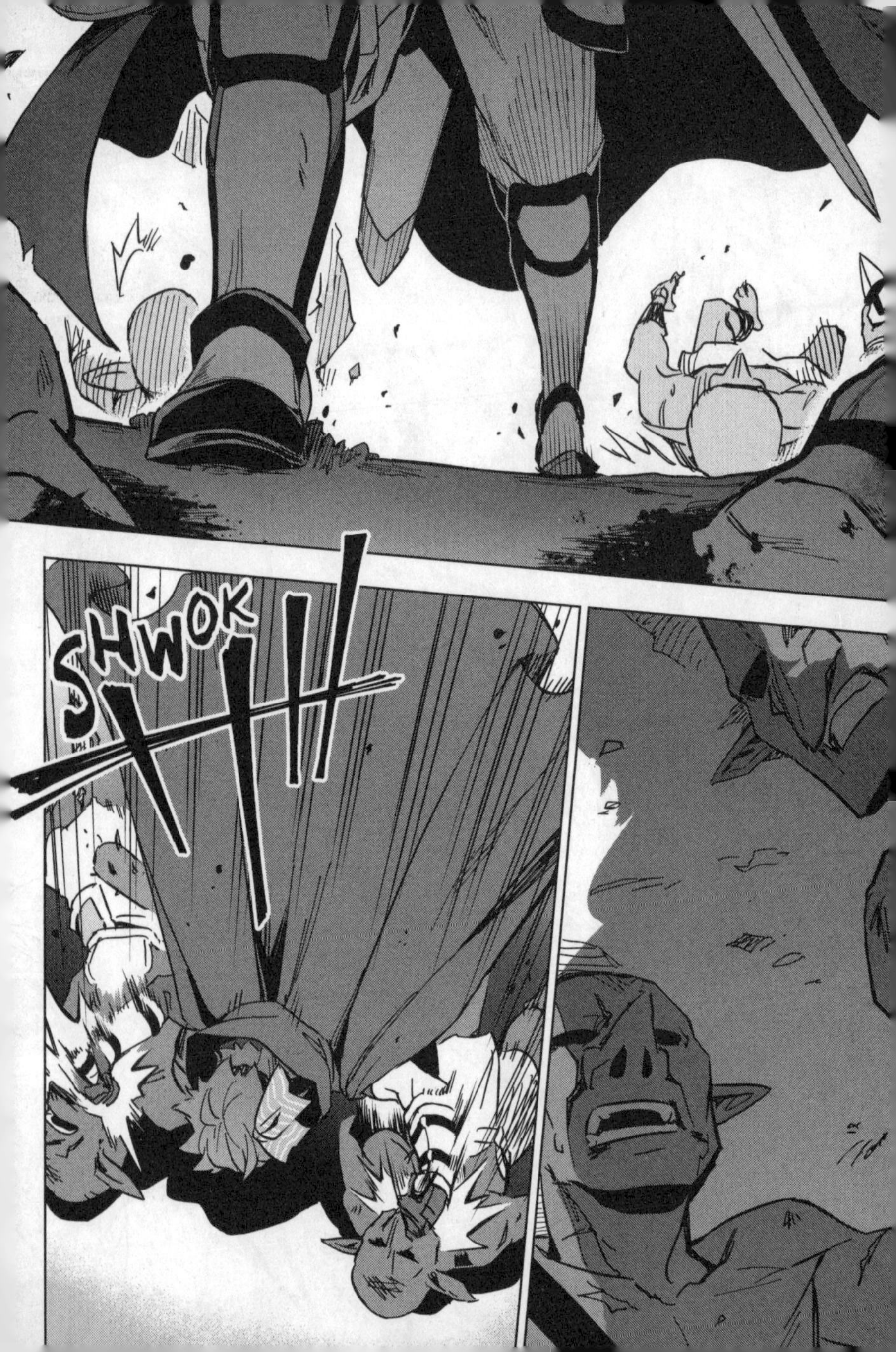
SHWOK

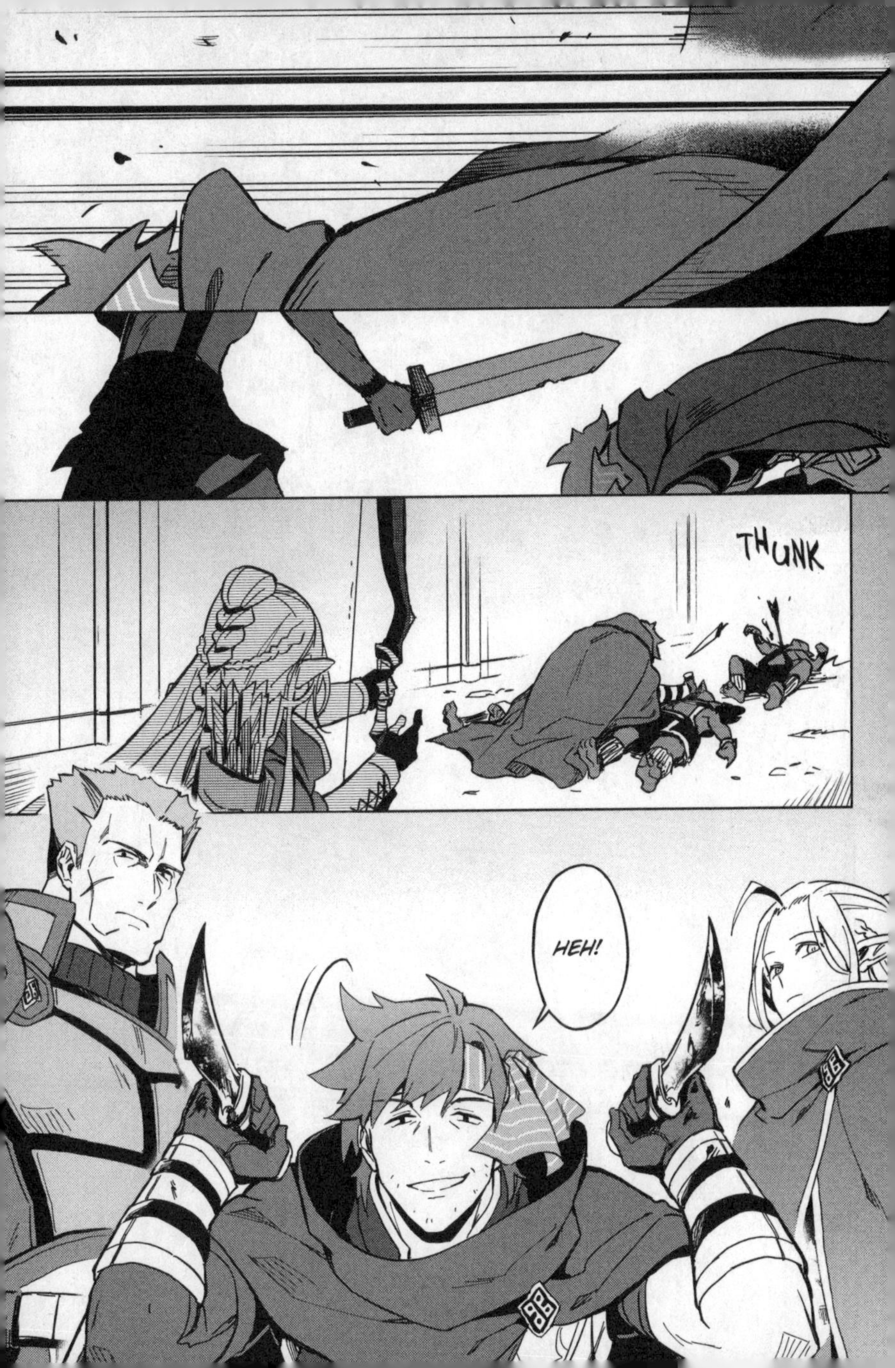
THUNK
HEH!

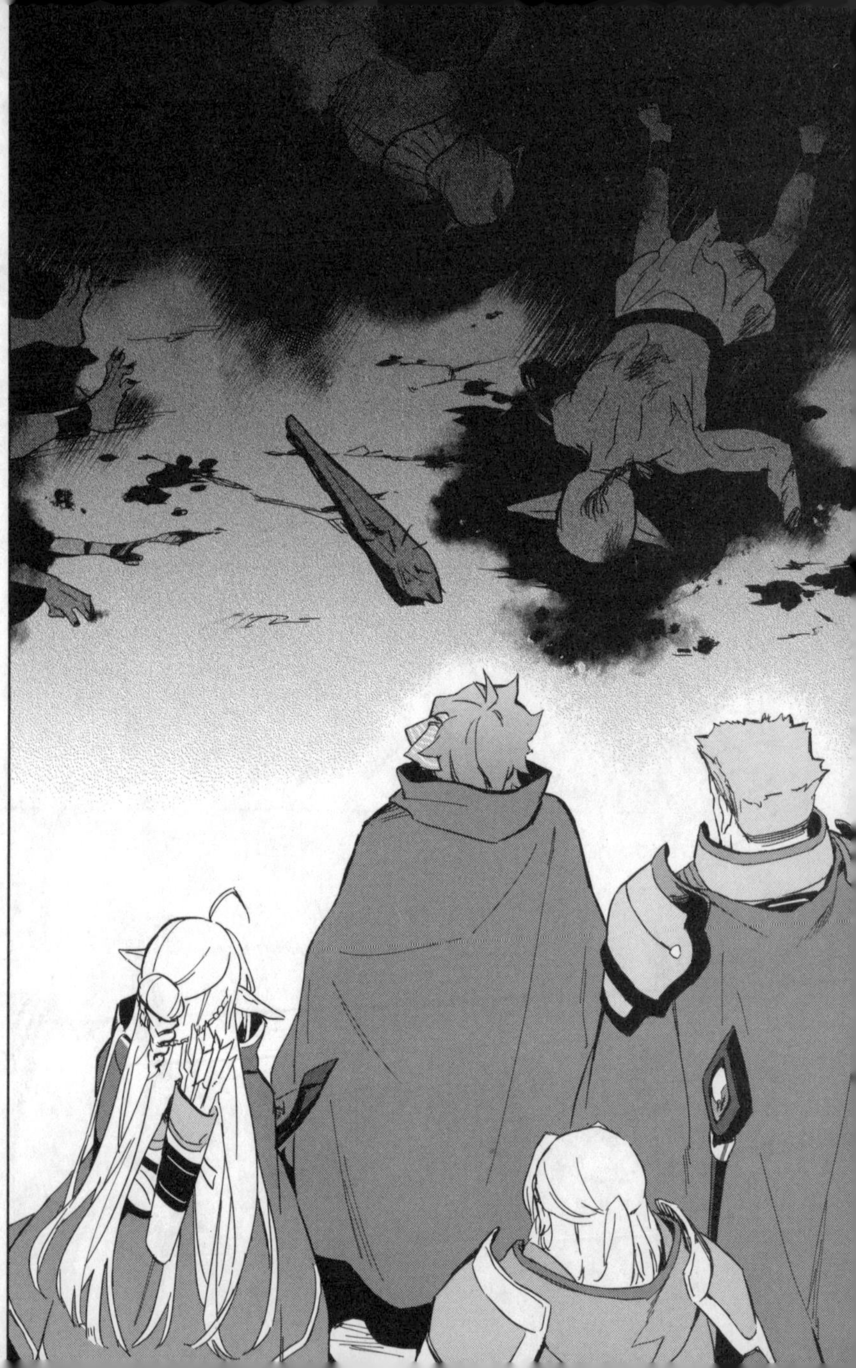

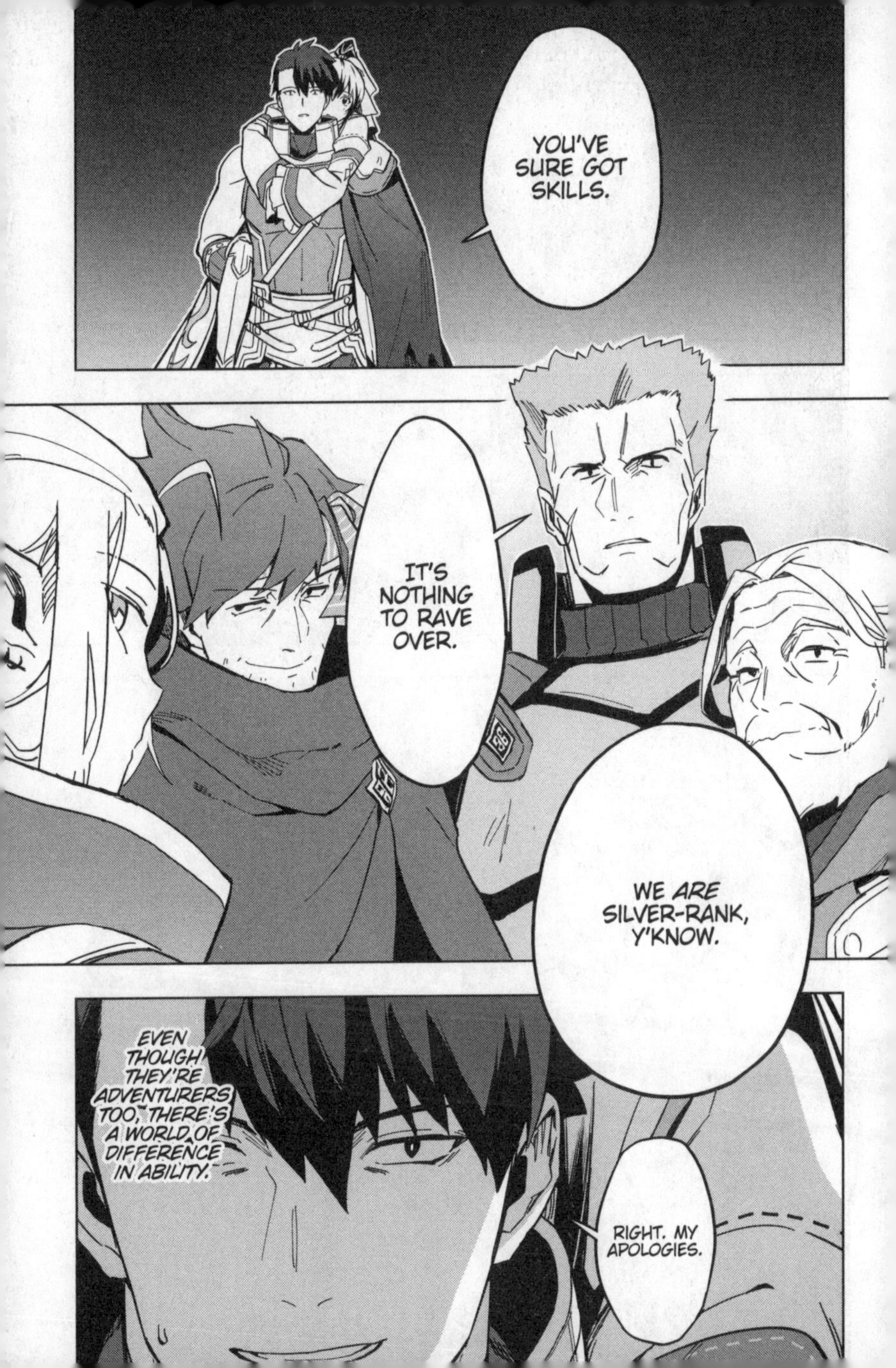
YOU'VE SURE GOT SKILLS.
IT'S NOTHING TO RAVE OVER.
WE ARE SILVER-RANK, Y'KNOW.
RIGHT. MY APOLOGIES.
EVEN THOUGH THEY'RE ADVENTURERS TOO, THERE'S A WORLD OF DIFFERENCE IN ABILITY.

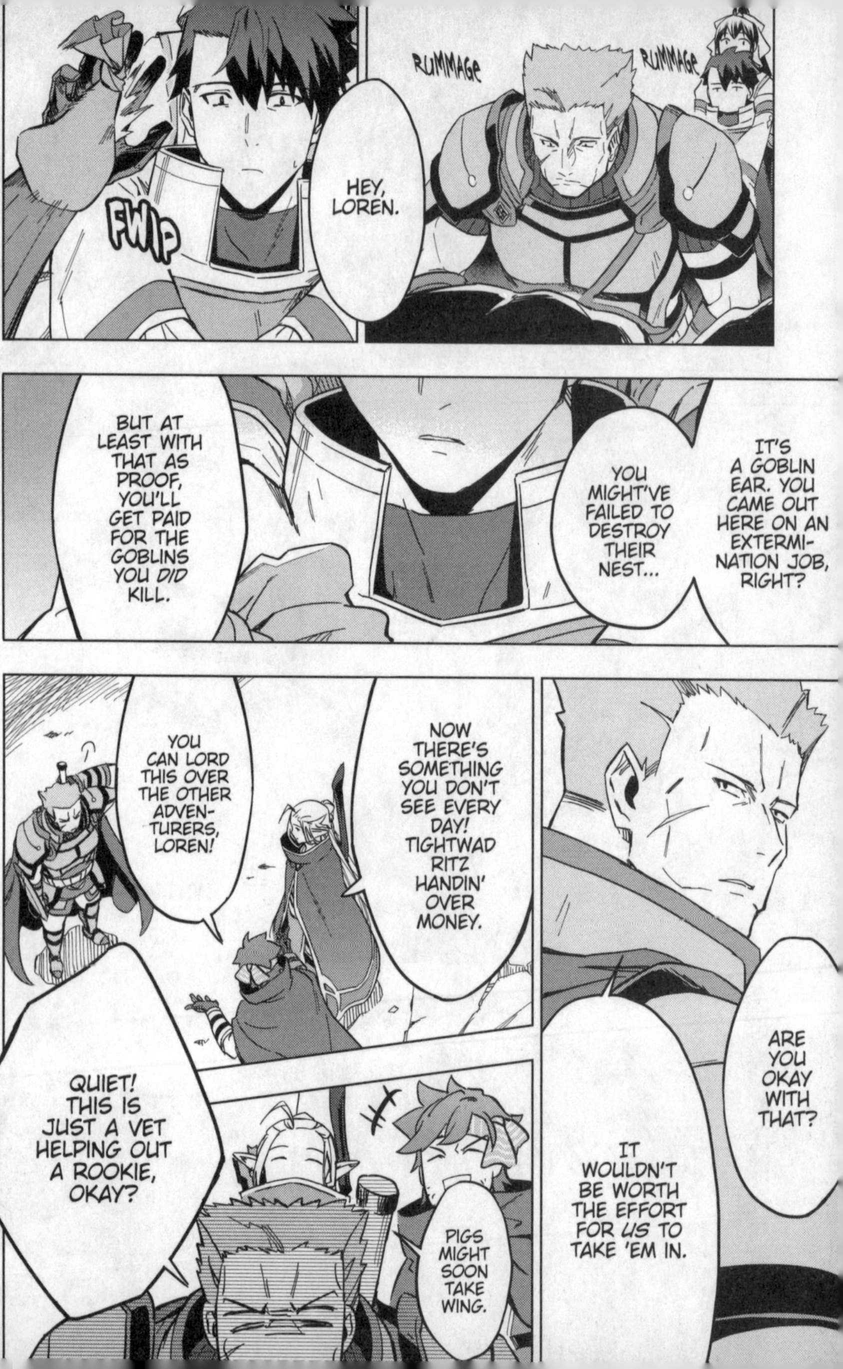
RUMMAGE
RUMMAGE
HEY, LOREN.
FWIP
IT'S A GOBLIN EAR. YOU CAME OUT HERE ON AN EXTERMINATION JOB, RIGHT?
YOU MIGHT'VE FAILED TO DESTROY THEIR NEST...
BUT AT LEAST WITH THAT AS PROOF, YOU'LL GET PAID FOR THE GOBLINS YOU DID KILL.
ARE YOU OKAY WITH THAT?
IT WOULDN'T BE WORTH THE EFFORT FOR US TO TAKE 'EM IN.
NOW THERE'S SOMETHING YOU DON'T SEE EVERY DAY! TIGHTWAD RITZ HANDIN' OVER MONEY.
YOU CAN LORD THIS OVER THE OTHER ADVENTURERS, LOREN!
QUIET! THIS IS JUST A VET HELPING OUT A ROOKIE, OKAY?
PIGS MIGHT SOON TAKE WING.

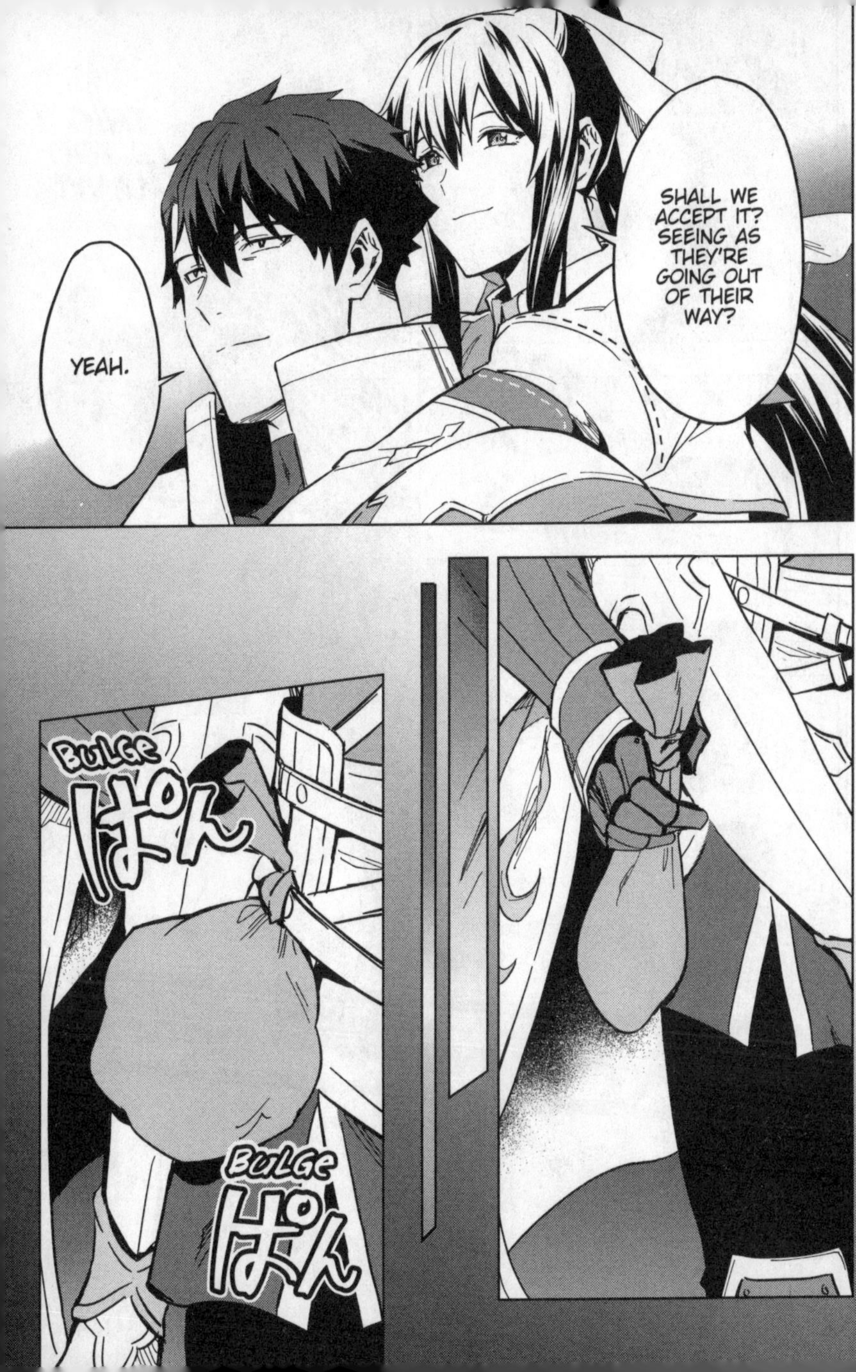
SHALL WE ACCEPT IT? SEEING AS THEY'RE GOING OUT OF THEIR WAY?
YEAH.
BULGE
ぱん
BULGE
ぱん

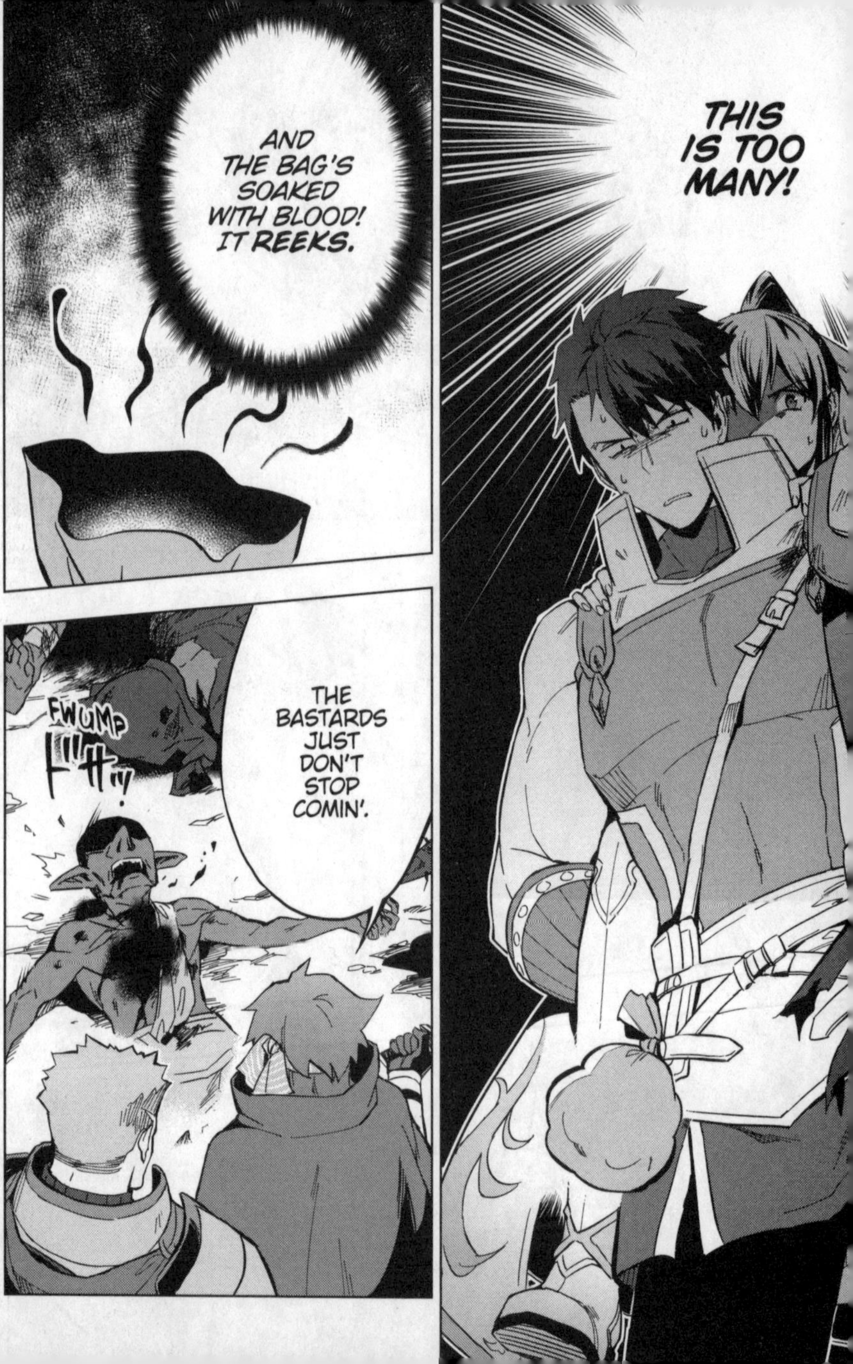
THIS IS TOO MANY!
AND THE BAG'S SOAKED WITH BLOOD! IT REEKS.
FWUMP
THE BASTARDS JUST DON'T STOP COMIN'.

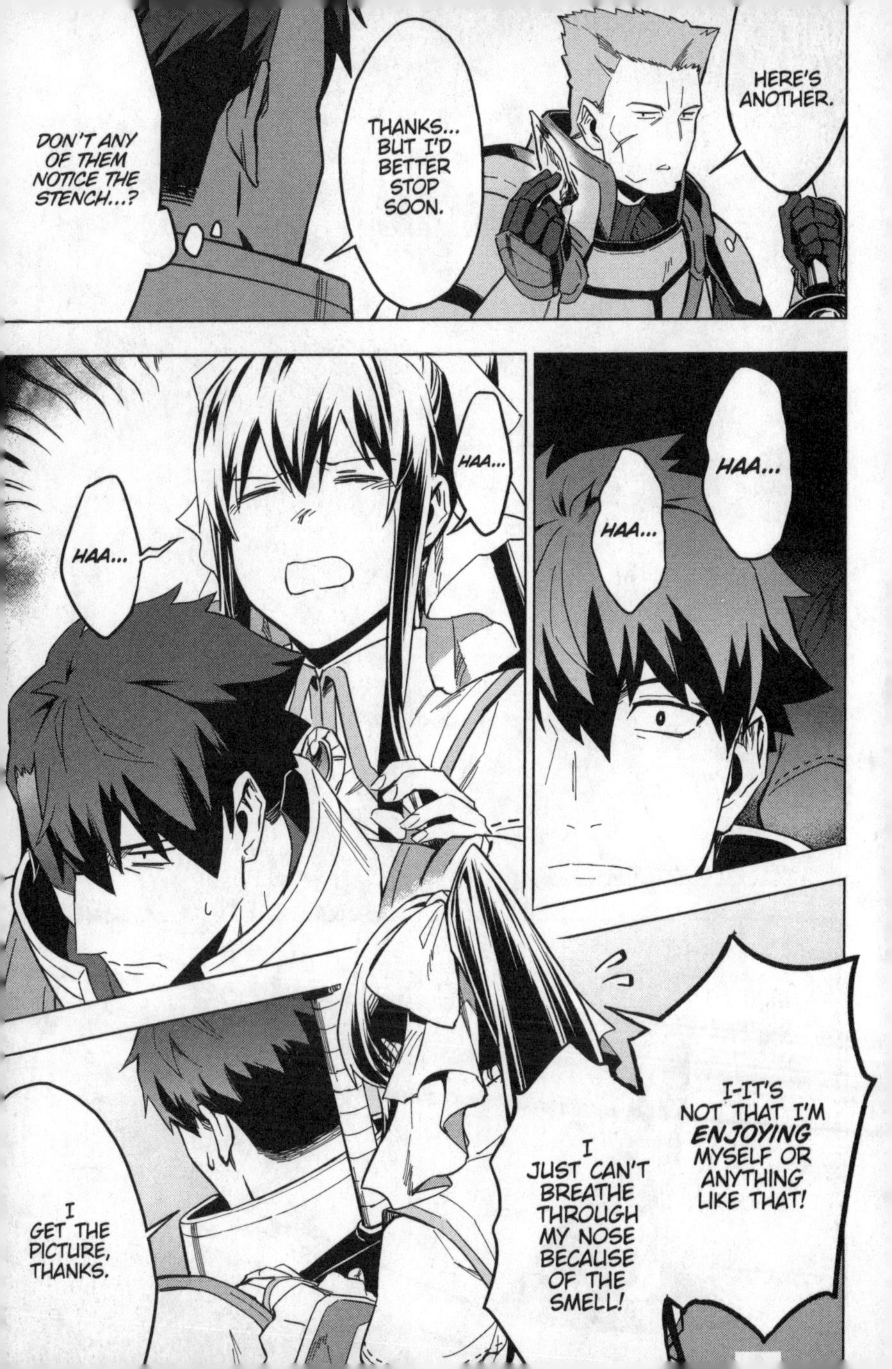
HERE'S ANOTHER.
THANKS... BUT I'D BETTER STOP SOON.
DON'T ANY OF THEM NOTICE THE STENCH...?
HAA...
HAA...
HAA...
HAA...
I-IT'S NOT THAT I'M ENJOYING MYSELF OR ANYTHING LIKE THAT!
I JUST CAN'T BREATHE THROUGH MY NOSE BECAUSE OF THE SMELL!
I GET THE PICTURE, THANKS.

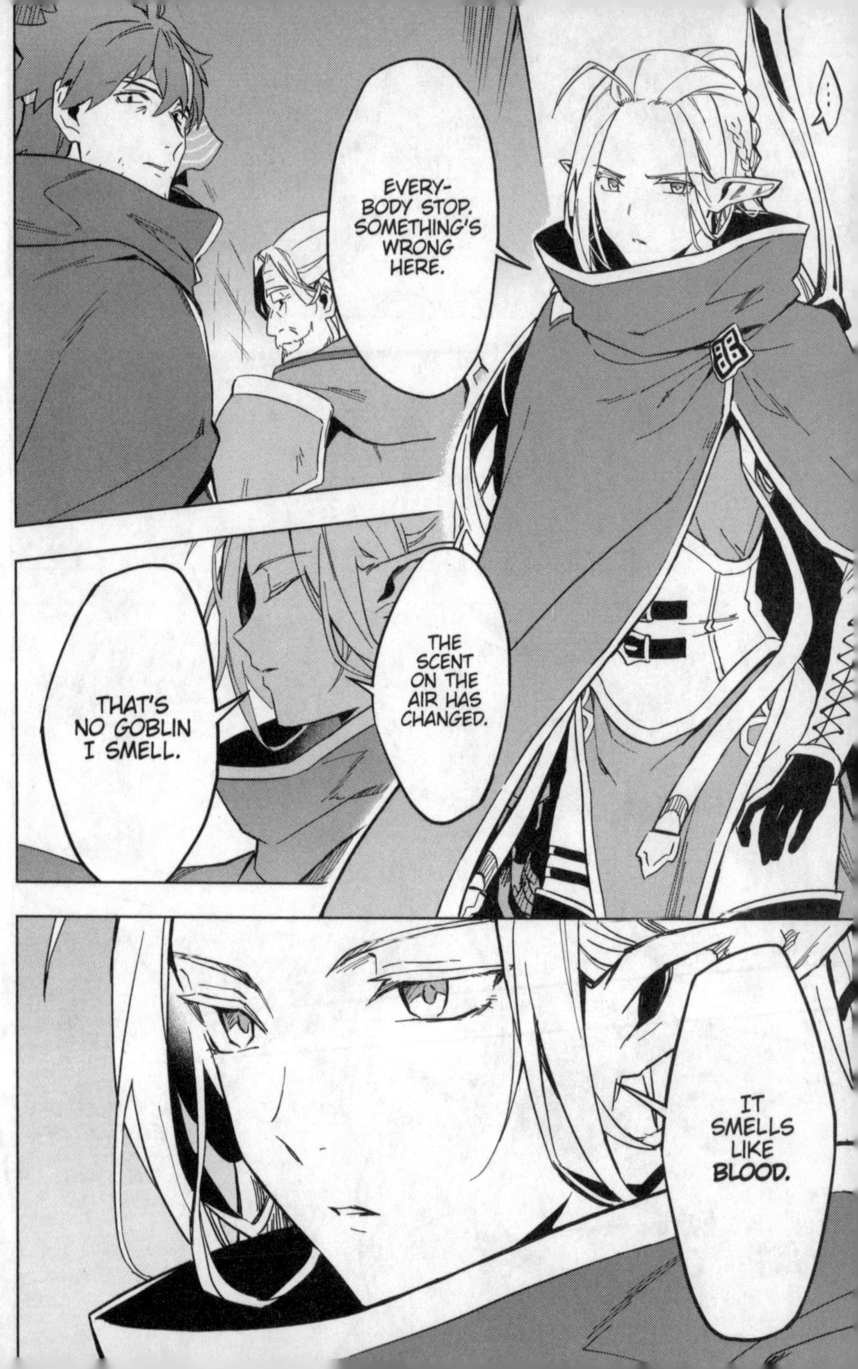
...
EVERY-BODY STOP. SOMETHING'S WRONG HERE.
THE SCENT ON THE AIR HAS CHANGED.
THAT'S NO GOBLIN I SMELL.
IT SMELLS LIKE BLOOD.

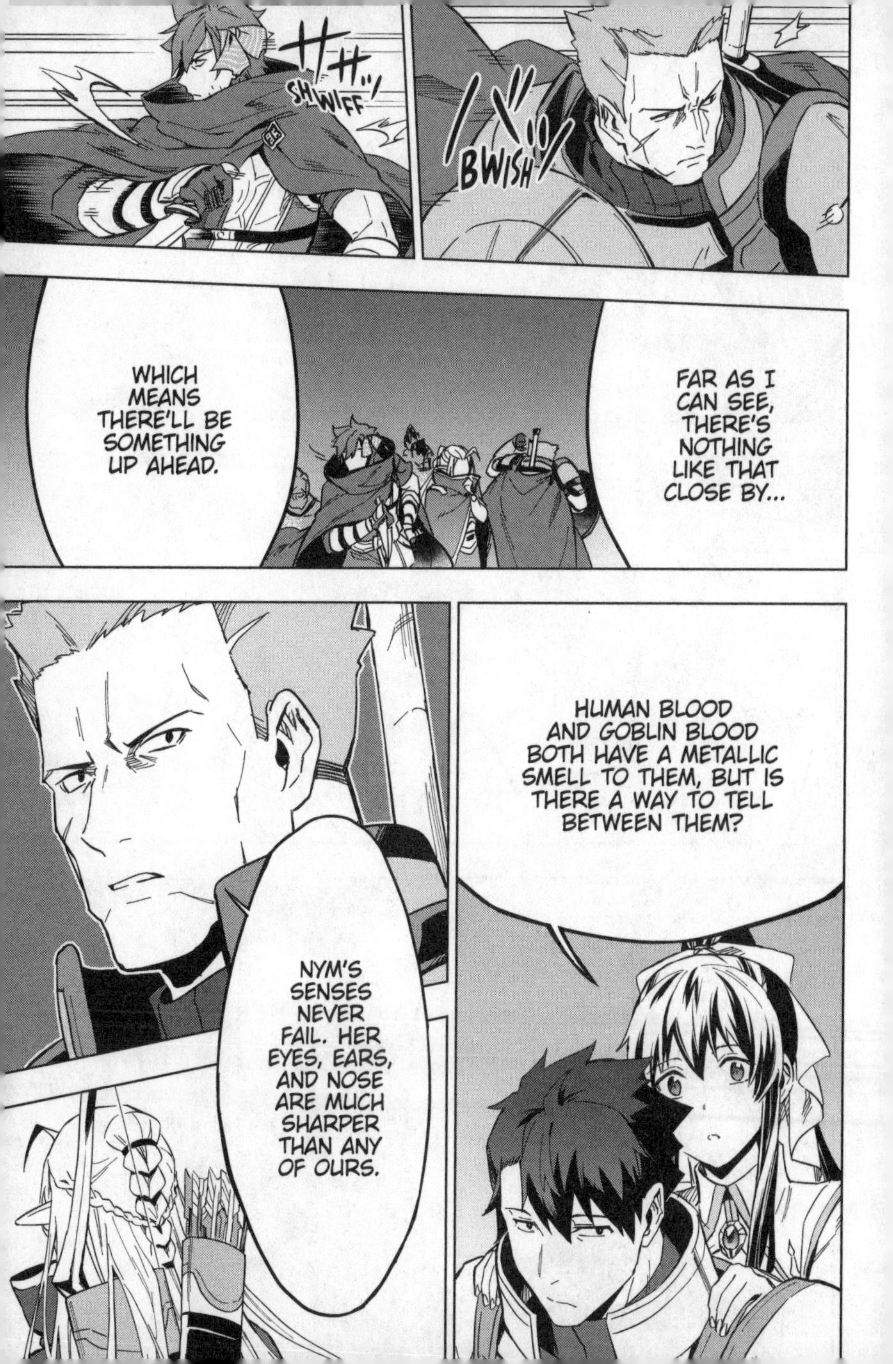
BWISH
SHWIFF
FAR AS I CAN SEE, THERE'S NOTHING LIKE THAT CLOSE BY...
WHICH MEANS THERE'LL BE SOMETHING UP AHEAD.
HUMAN BLOOD AND GOBLIN BLOOD BOTH HAVE A METALLIC SMELL TO THEM, BUT IS THERE A WAY TO TELL BETWEEN THEM?
NYM'S SENSES NEVER FAIL. HER EYES, EARS, AND NOSE ARE MUCH SHARPER THAN ANY OF OURS.

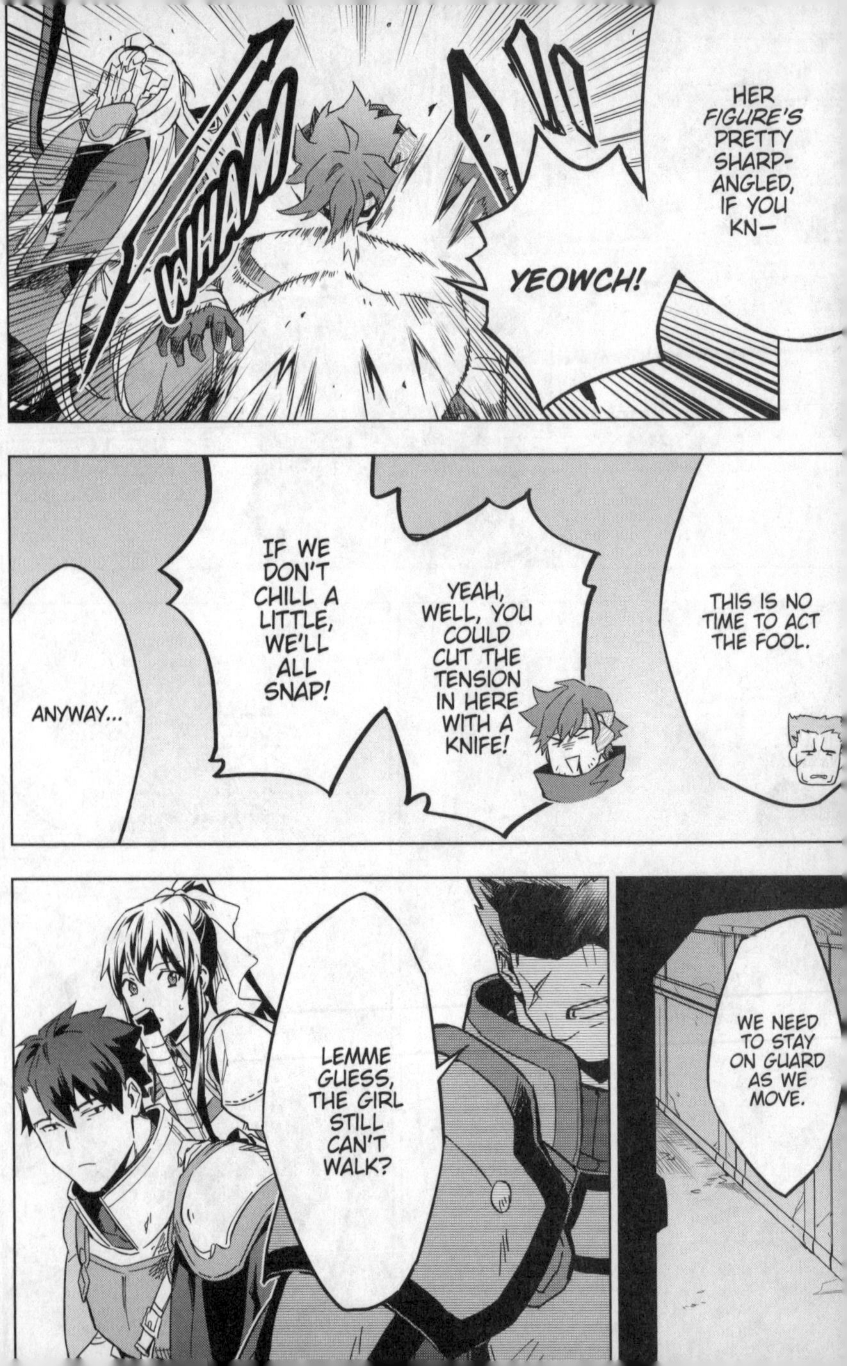
HER FIGURE'S PRETTY SHARP-ANGLED, IF YOU KN—
WHAM
YEOWCH!
THIS IS NO TIME TO ACT THE FOOL.
YEAH, WELL, YOU COULD CUT THE TENSION IN HERE WITH A KNIFE!
IF WE DON'T CHILL A LITTLE, WE'LL ALL SNAP!
ANYWAY...
WE NEED TO STAY ON GUARD AS WE MOVE.
LEMME GUESS, THE GIRL STILL CAN'T WALK?

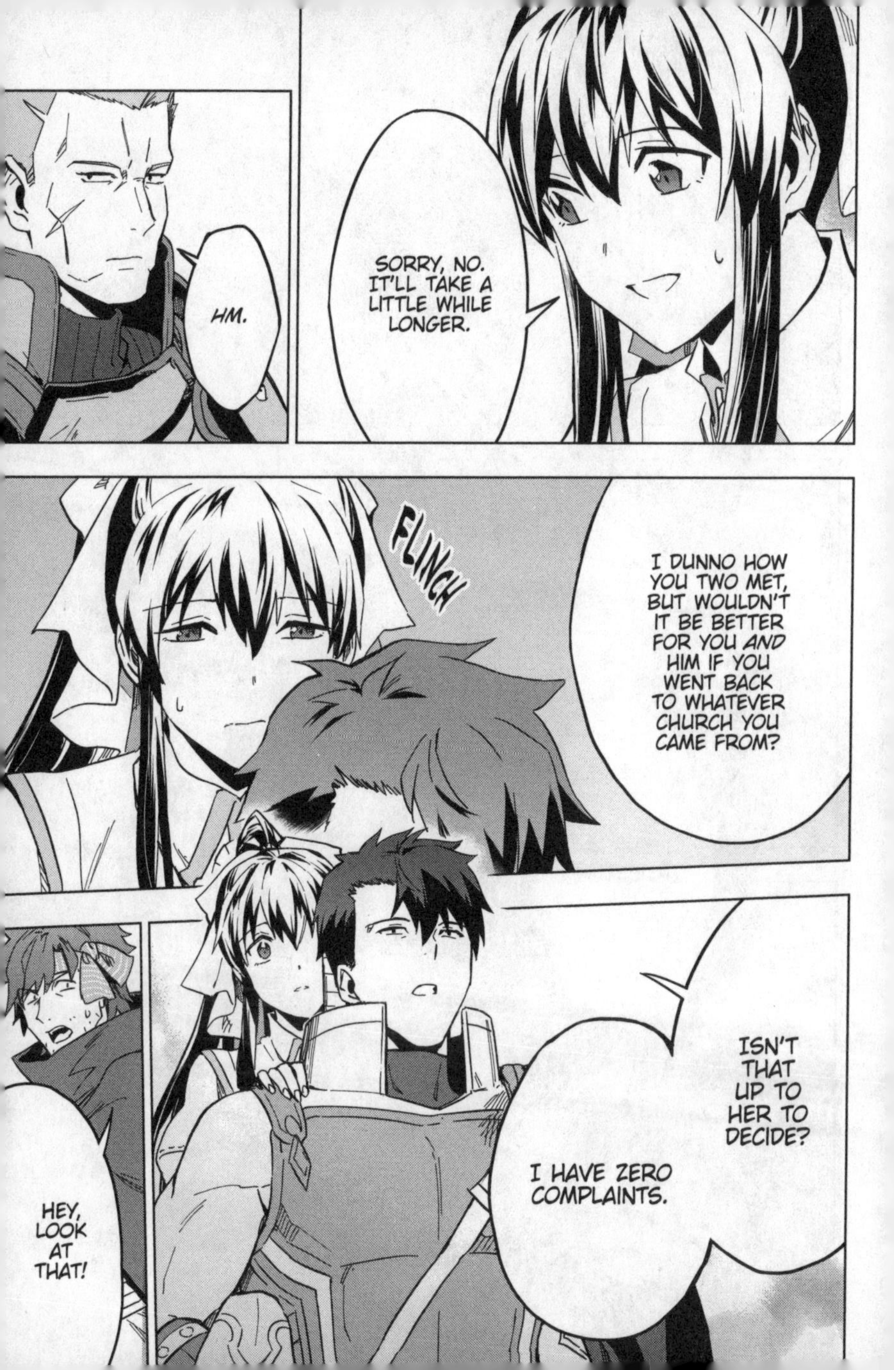
SORRY, NO. IT'LL TAKE A LITTLE WHILE LONGER.
HM.
I DUNNO HOW YOU TWO MET, BUT WOULDN'T IT BE BETTER FOR YOU *AND* HIM IF YOU WENT BACK TO WHATEVER CHURCH YOU CAME FROM?
FLINCH
ISN'T THAT UP TO HER TO DECIDE?
I HAVE ZERO COMPLAINTS.
HEY, LOOK AT THAT!

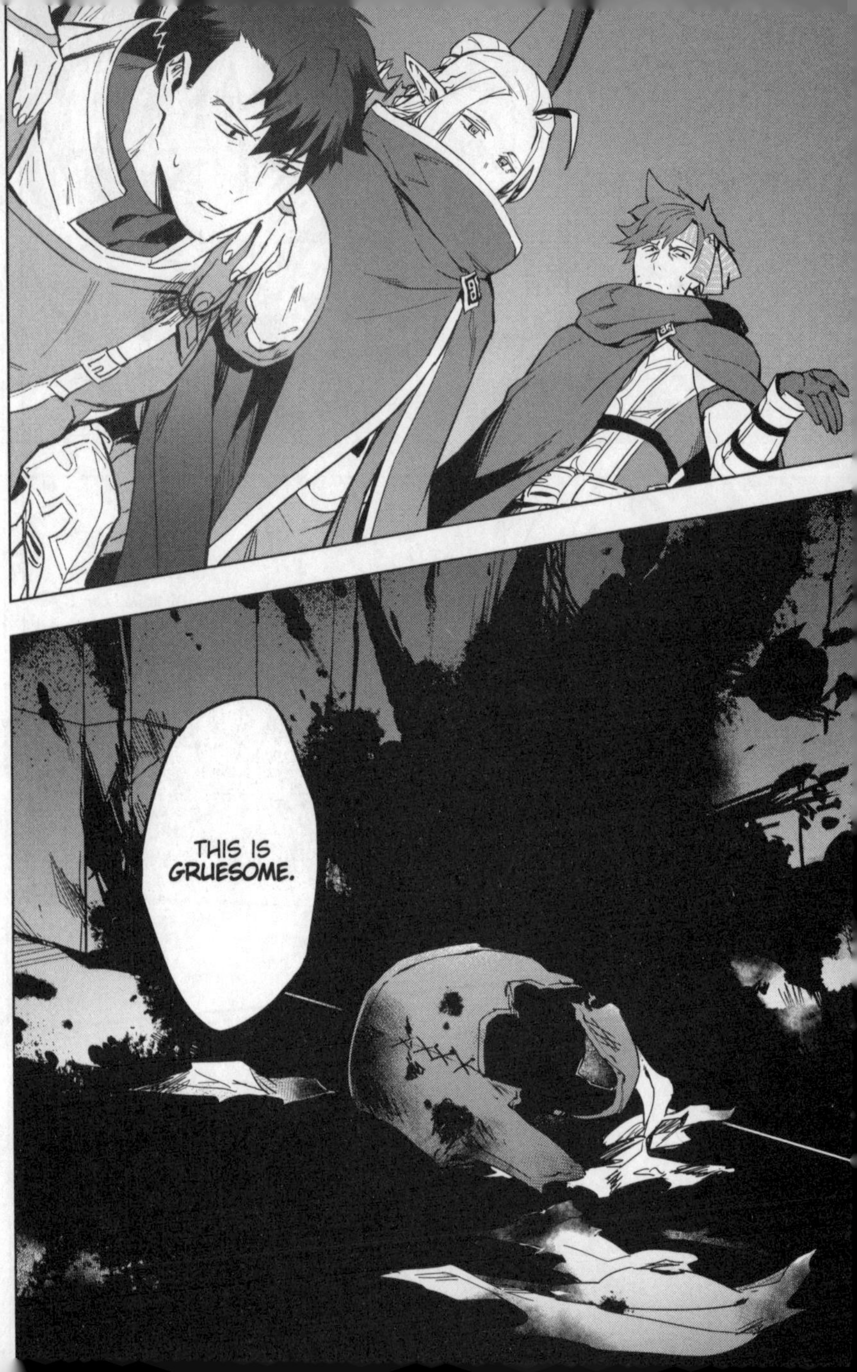
THIS IS GRUESOME.

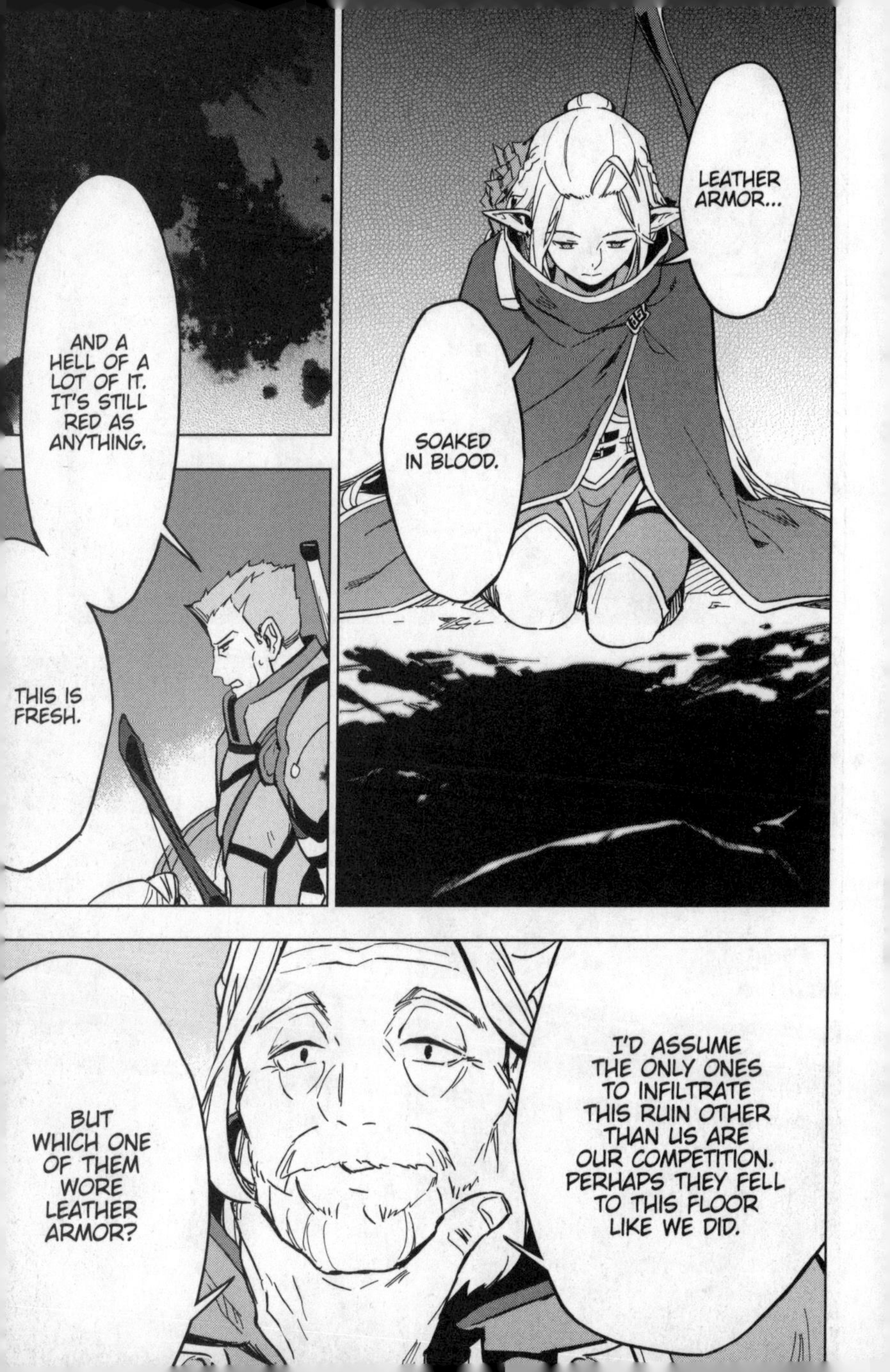
LEATHER ARMOR...
SOAKED IN BLOOD.
AND A HELL OF A LOT OF IT. IT'S STILL RED AS ANYTHING.
THIS IS FRESH.
I'D ASSUME THE ONLY ONES TO INFILTRATE THIS RUIN OTHER THAN US ARE OUR COMPETITION. PERHAPS THEY FELL TO THIS FLOOR LIKE WE DID.
BUT WHICH ONE OF THEM WORE LEATHER ARMOR?

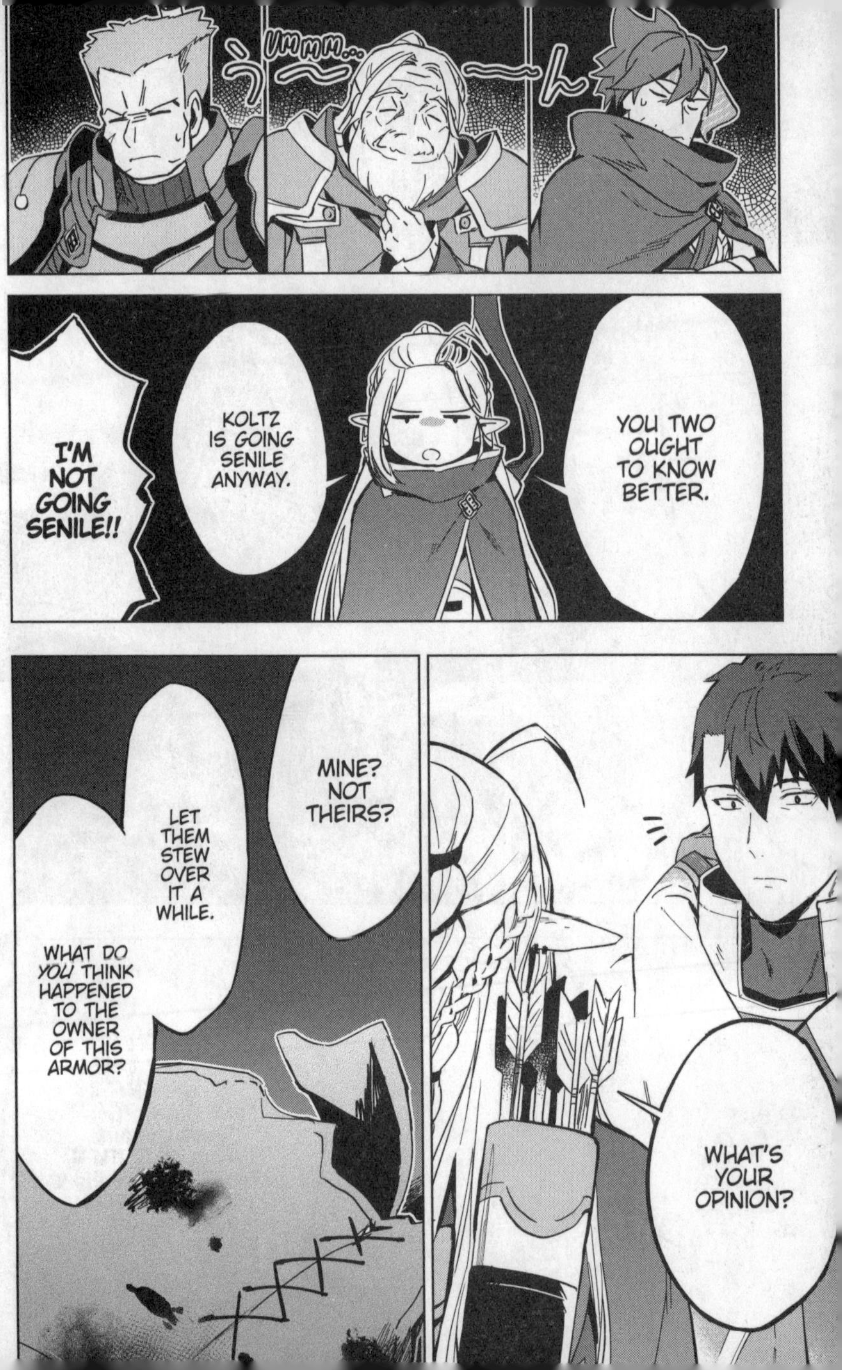
UMMM...
YOU TWO OUGHT TO KNOW BETTER.
KOLTZ IS GOING SENILE ANYWAY.
I'M NOT GOING SENILE!!
WHAT'S YOUR OPINION?
MINE? NOT THEIRS?
LET THEM STEW OVER IT A WHILE.
WHAT DO *YOU* THINK HAPPENED TO THE OWNER OF THIS ARMOR?

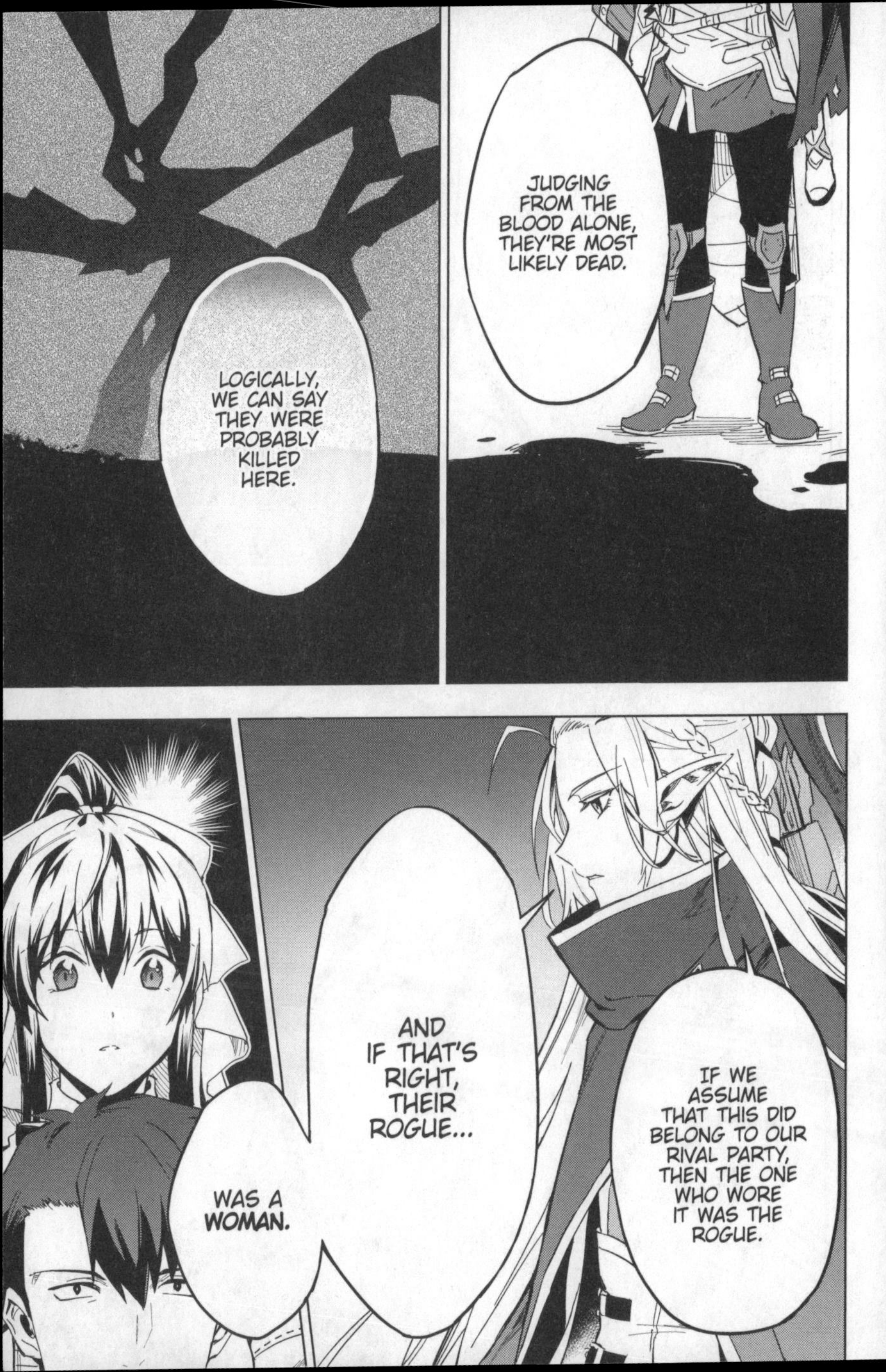
JUDGING FROM THE BLOOD ALONE, THEY'RE MOST LIKELY DEAD.
LOGICALLY, WE CAN SAY THEY WERE PROBABLY KILLED HERE.
IF WE ASSUME THAT THIS DID BELONG TO OUR RIVAL PARTY, THEN THE ONE WHO WORE IT WAS THE ROGUE.
AND IF THAT'S RIGHT, THEIR ROGUE...
WAS A WOMAN.

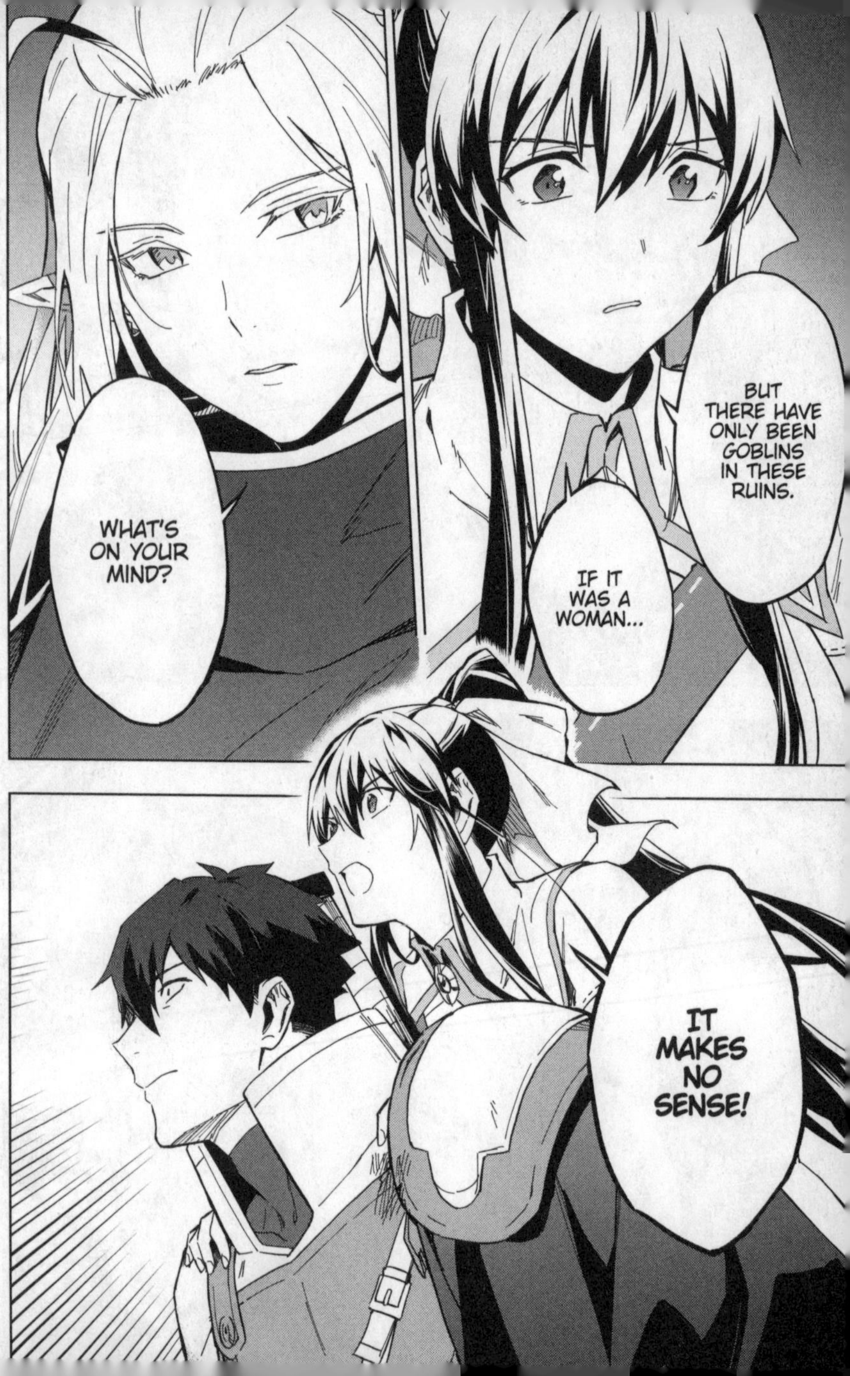
BUT THERE HAVE ONLY BEEN GOBLINS IN THESE RUINS.
IF IT WAS A WOMAN...
WHAT'S ON YOUR MIND?
IT MAKES NO SENSE!

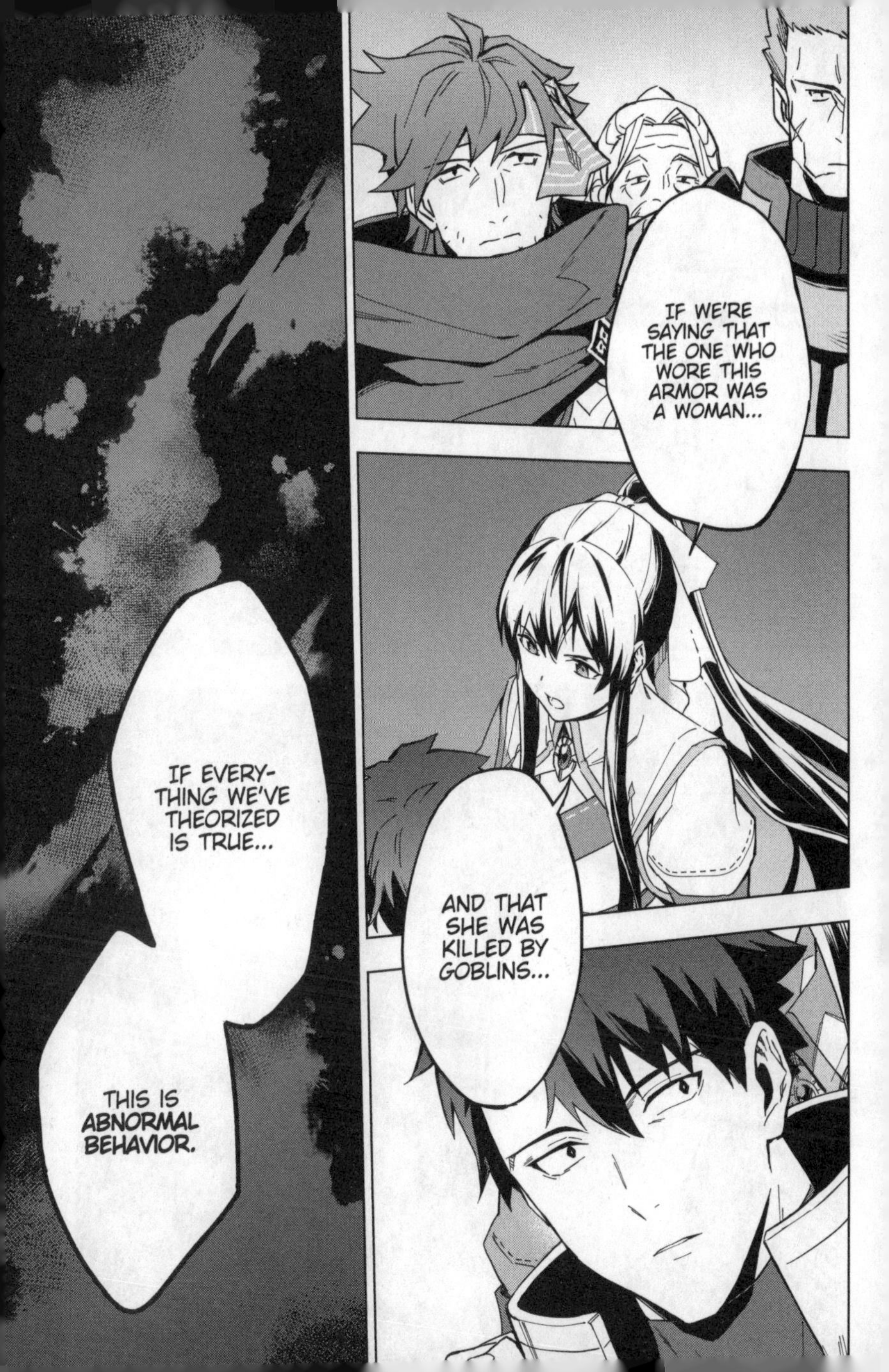
IF WE'RE SAYING THAT THE ONE WHO WORE THIS ARMOR WAS A WOMAN...
AND THAT SHE WAS KILLED BY GOBLINS...
IF EVERY-THING WE'VE THEORIZED IS TRUE...
THIS IS ABNORMAL BEHAVIOR.

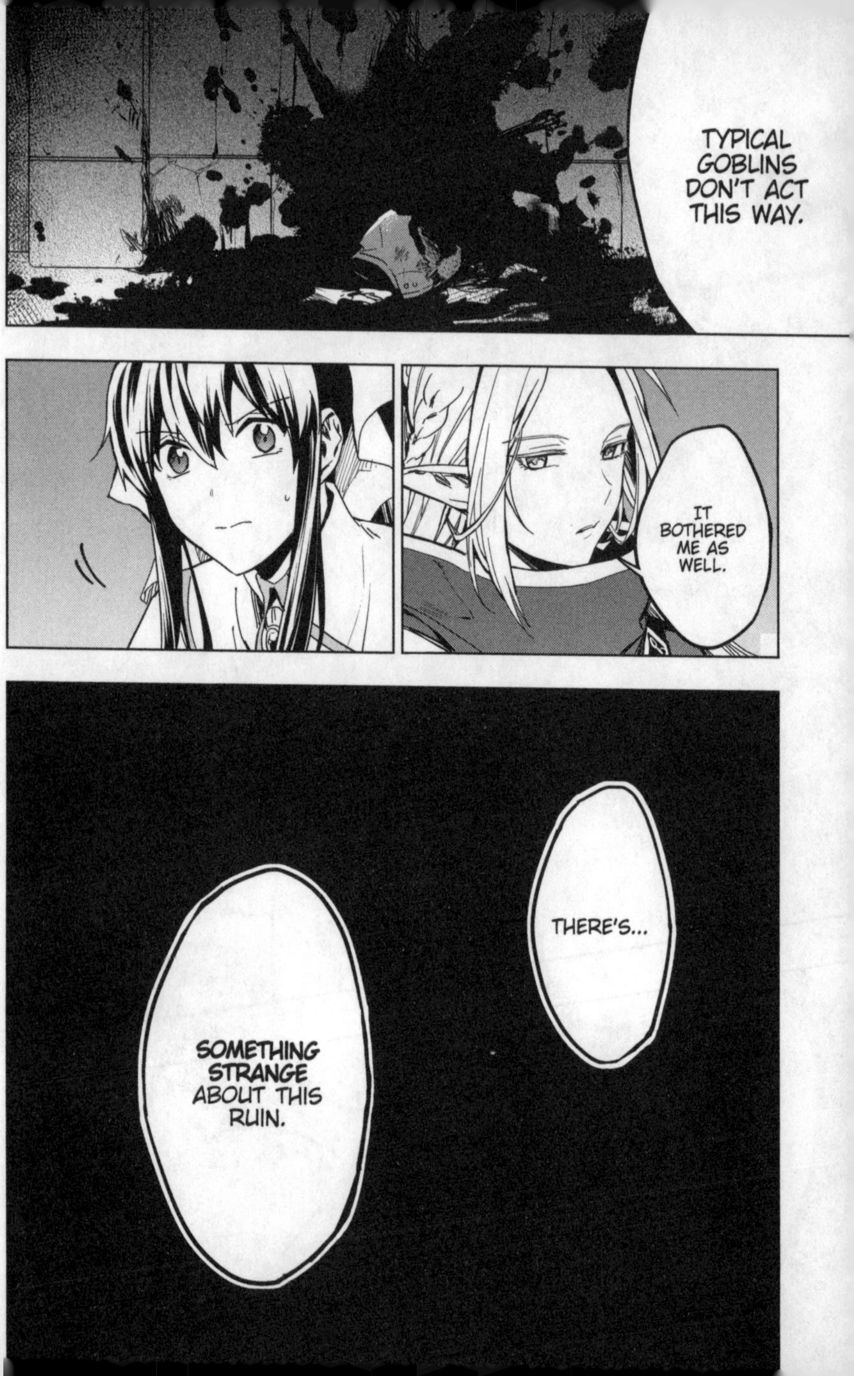
TYPICAL GOBLINS DON'T ACT THIS WAY.
IT BOTHERED ME AS WELL.
THERE'S...
SOMETHING STRANGE ABOUT THIS RUIN.

THE Strange Adventure OF A Broke MERCENARY

CHAPTER 8 CONJECTURE LEADS BACK TO THE START
SOMETHING STRANGE?
WEREN'T WE JUST SAYING THAT THE ONLY ENEMIES WE'VE COME ACROSS IN THIS RUIN HAVE BEEN GOBLINS?

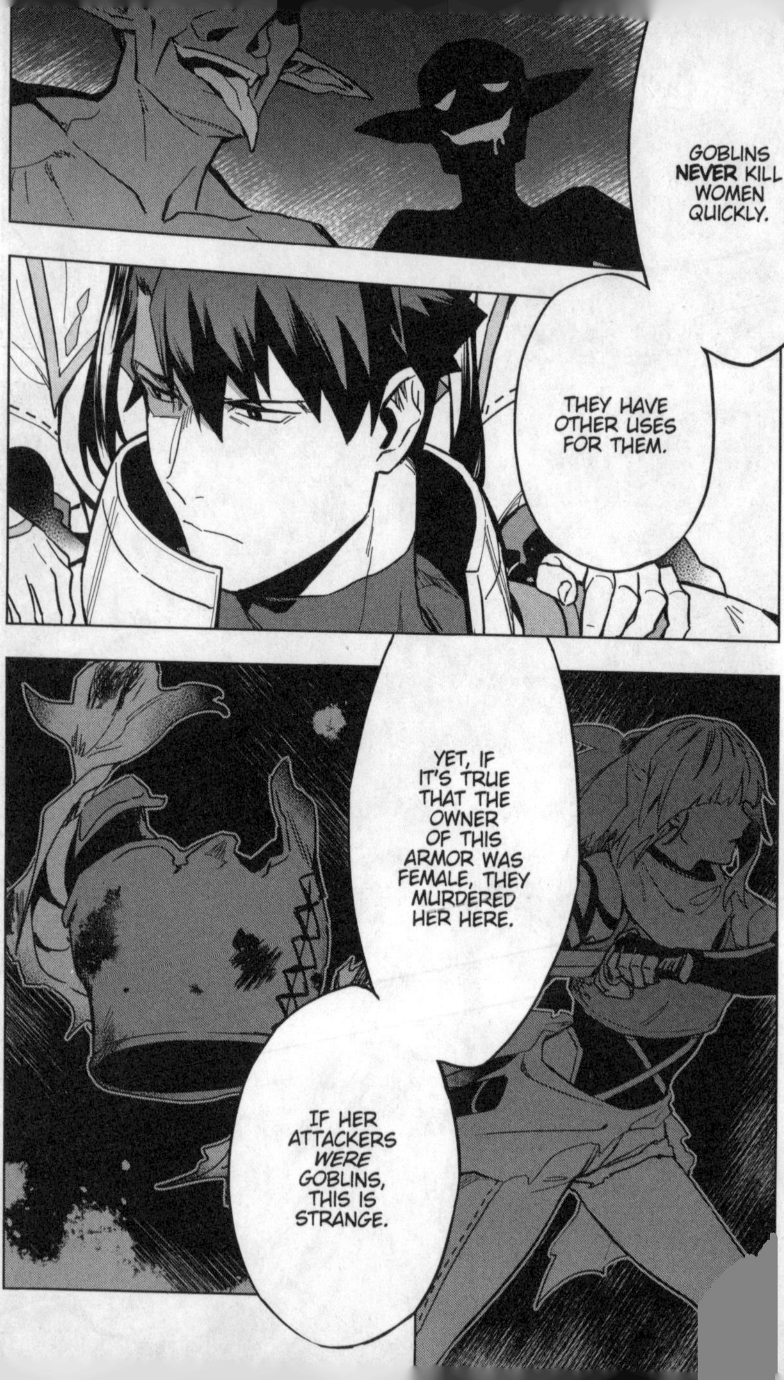
GOBLINS **NEVER** KILL WOMEN QUICKLY.
THEY HAVE OTHER USES FOR THEM.
YET, IF IT'S TRUE THAT THE OWNER OF THIS ARMOR WAS FEMALE, THEY MURDERED HER HERE.
IF HER ATTACKERS *WERE* GOBLINS, THIS IS STRANGE.

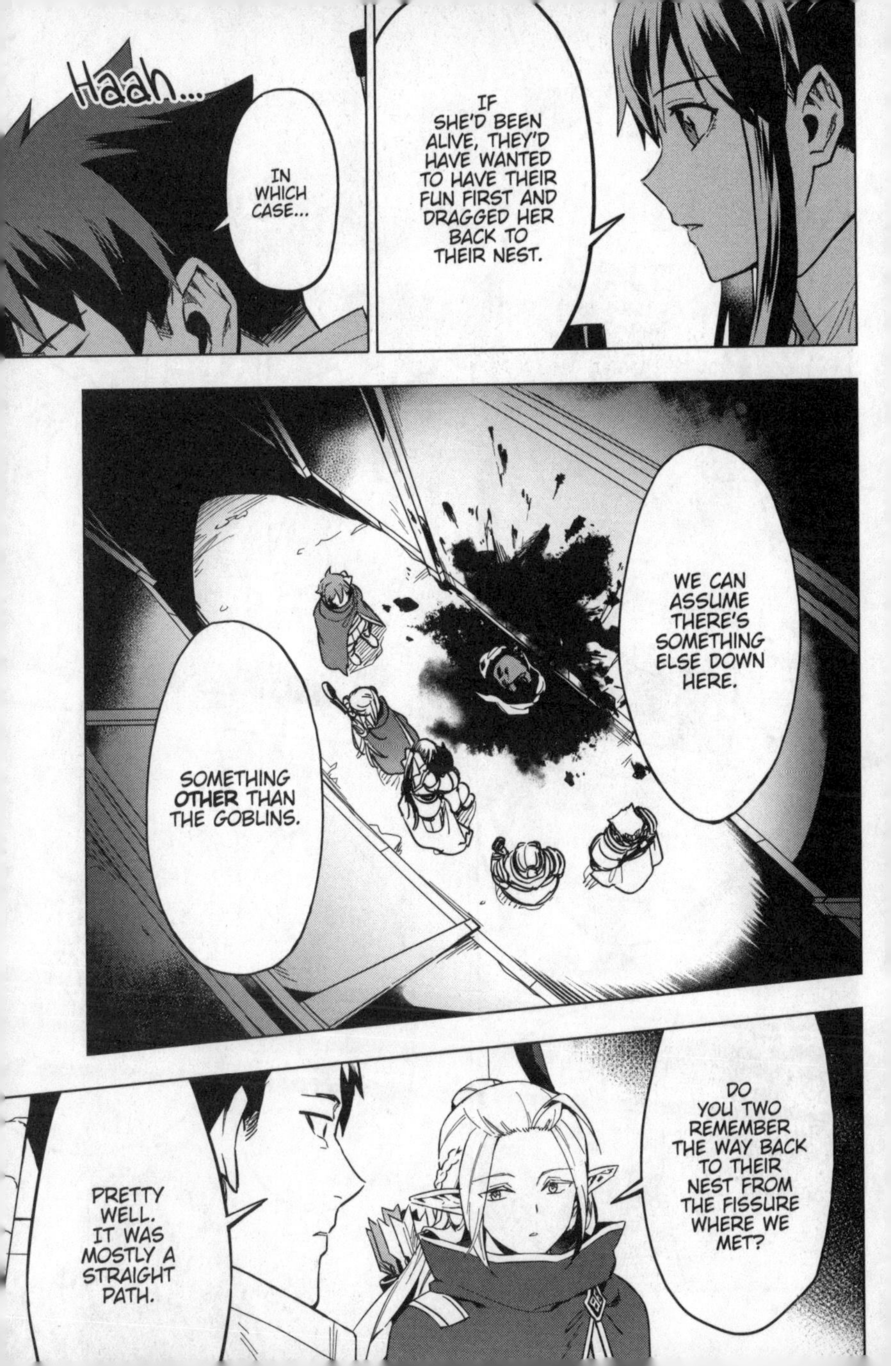
IF SHE'D BEEN ALIVE, THEY'D HAVE WANTED TO HAVE THEIR FUN FIRST AND DRAGGED HER BACK TO THEIR NEST.
Haaah...
IN WHICH CASE...
WE CAN ASSUME THERE'S SOMETHING ELSE DOWN HERE.
SOMETHING OTHER THAN THE GOBLINS.
DO YOU TWO REMEMBER THE WAY BACK TO THEIR NEST FROM THE FISSURE WHERE WE MET?
PRETTY WELL. IT WAS MOSTLY A STRAIGHT PATH.

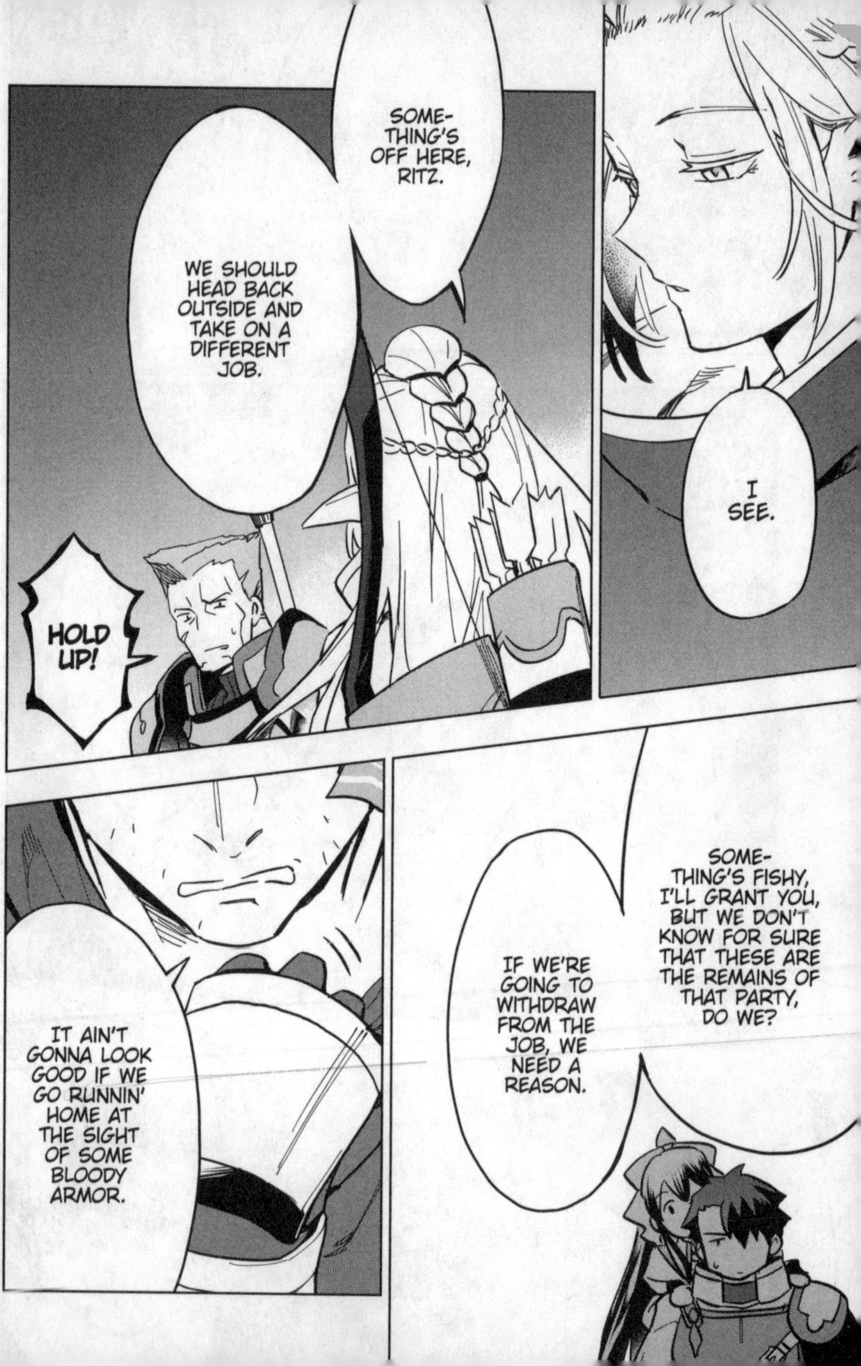
I SEE.
SOME-THING'S OFF HERE, RITZ.
WE SHOULD HEAD BACK OUTSIDE AND TAKE ON A DIFFERENT JOB.
HOLD UP!
SOME-THING'S FISHY, I'LL GRANT YOU, BUT WE DON'T KNOW FOR SURE THAT THESE ARE THE REMAINS OF THAT PARTY, DO WE?
IF WE'RE GOING TO WITHDRAW FROM THE JOB, WE NEED A REASON.
IT AIN'T GONNA LOOK GOOD IF WE GO RUNNIN' HOME AT THE SIGHT OF SOME BLOODY ARMOR.

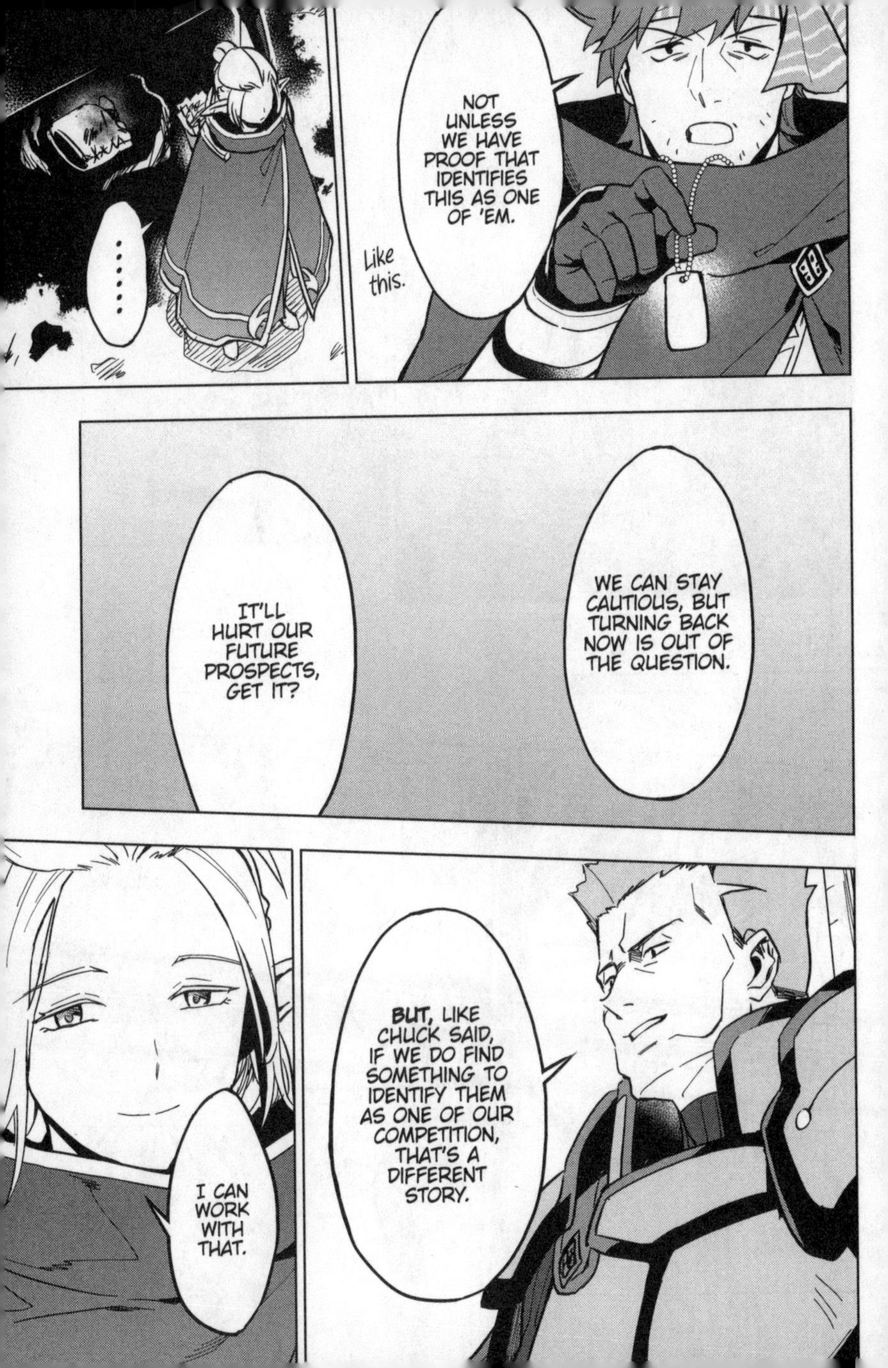
NOT UNLESS WE HAVE PROOF THAT IDENTIFIES THIS AS ONE OF 'EM.
Like this.
......
WE CAN STAY CAUTIOUS, BUT TURNING BACK NOW IS OUT OF THE QUESTION.
IT'LL HURT OUR FUTURE PROSPECTS, GET IT?
BUT, LIKE CHUCK SAID, IF WE DO FIND SOMETHING TO IDENTIFY THEM AS ONE OF OUR COMPETITION, THAT'S A DIFFERENT STORY.
I CAN WORK WITH THAT.

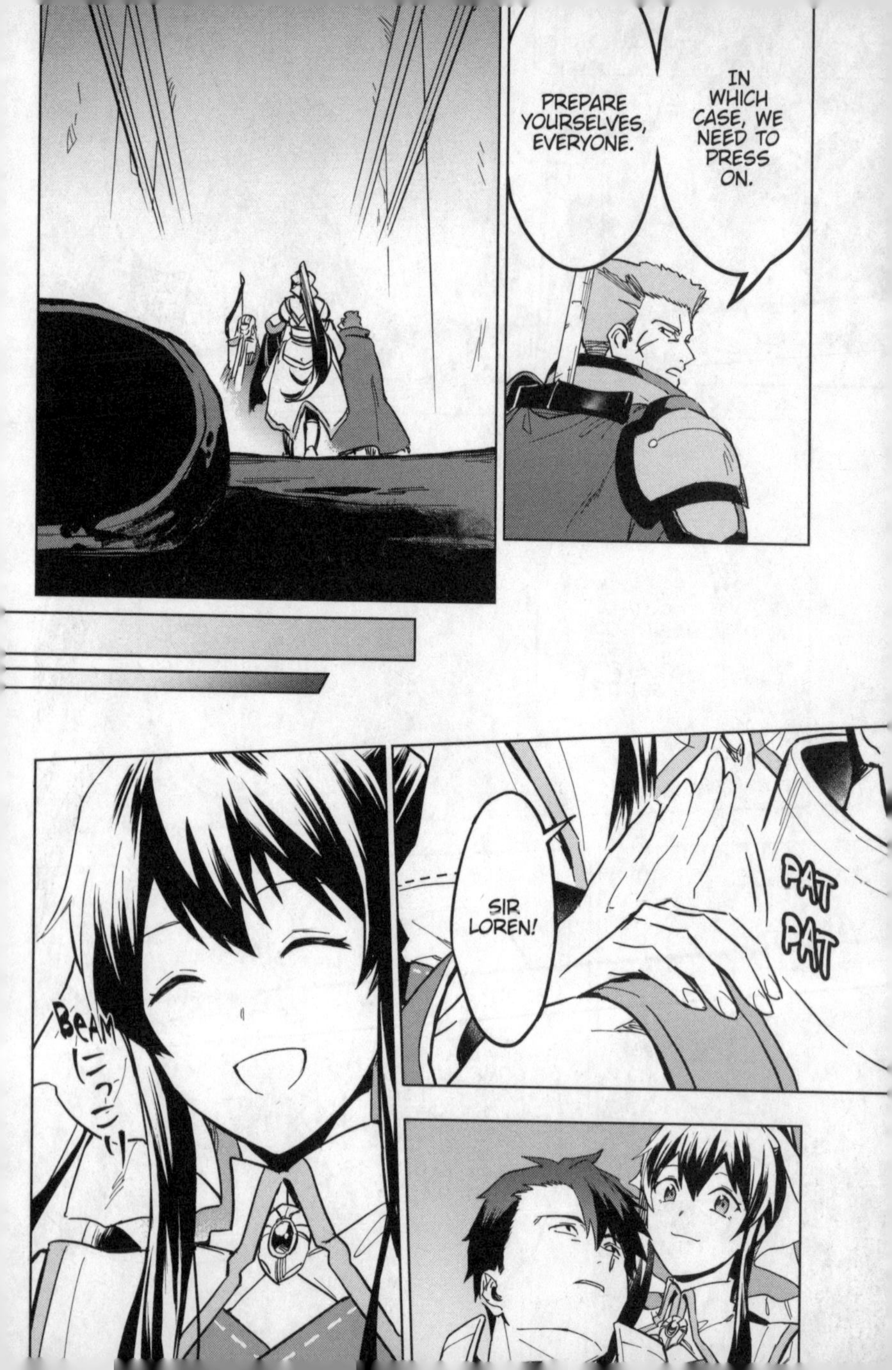
IN WHICH CASE, WE NEED TO PRESS ON.
PREPARE YOURSELVES, EVERYONE.
SIR LOREN!
PAT PAT
BEAM

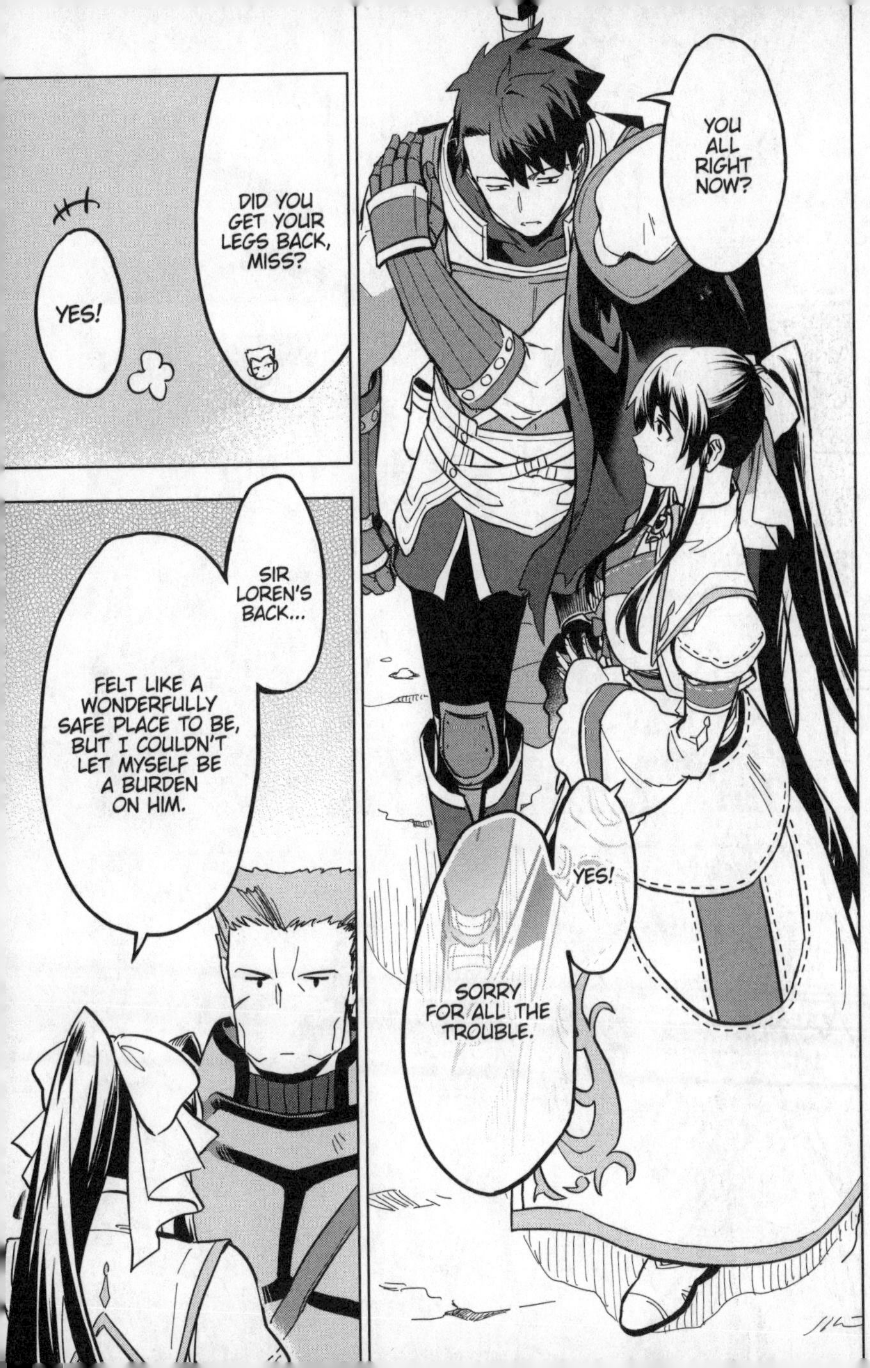
YOU ALL RIGHT NOW?
YES!
SORRY FOR ALL THE TROUBLE.
DID YOU GET YOUR LEGS BACK, MISS?
YES!
SIR LOREN'S BACK...
FELT LIKE A WONDERFULLY SAFE PLACE TO BE, BUT I COULDN'T LET MYSELF BE A BURDEN ON HIM.

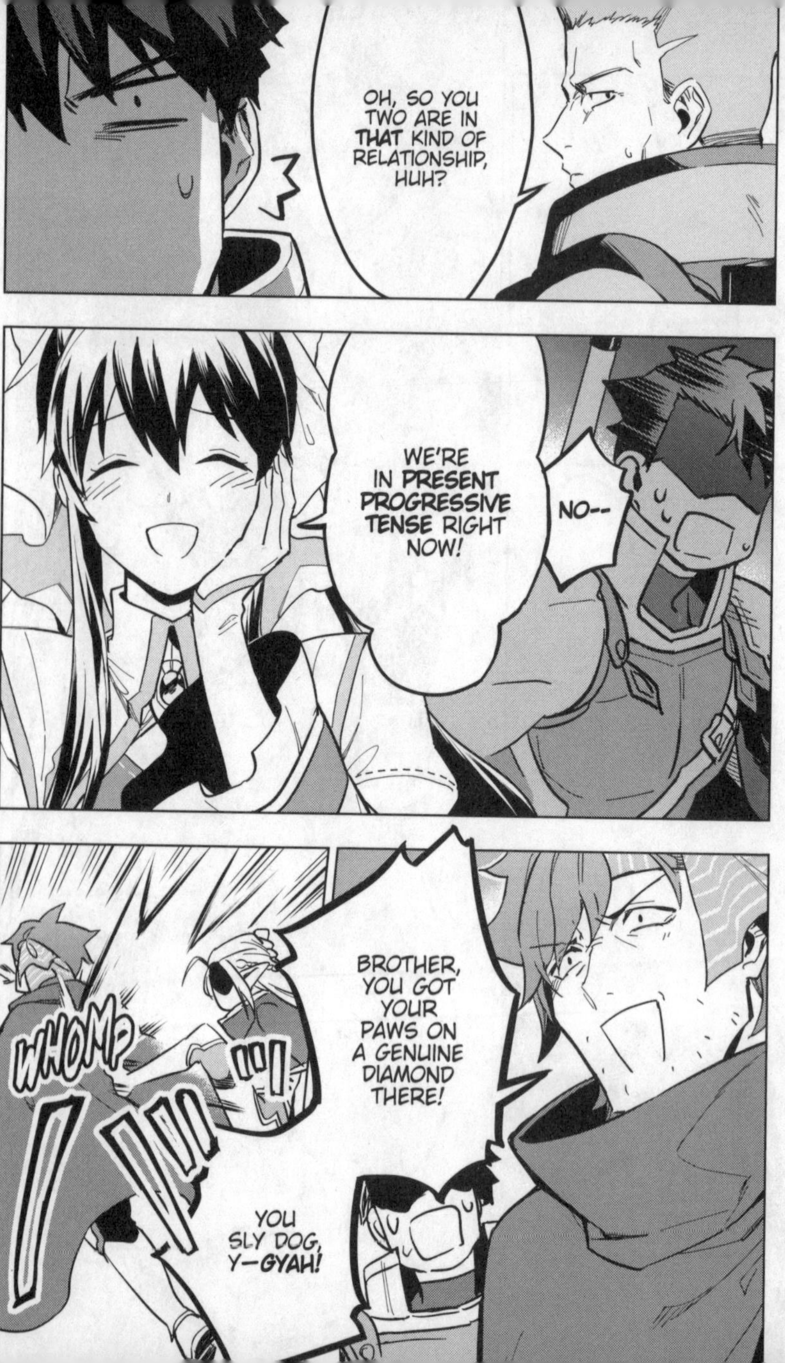
OH, SO YOU TWO ARE IN THAT KIND OF RELATIONSHIP, HUH?
NO--
WE'RE IN PRESENT PROGRESSIVE TENSE RIGHT NOW!
BROTHER, YOU GOT YOUR PAWS ON A GENUINE DIAMOND THERE!
WHOMP
YOU SLY DOG, Y—GYAH!

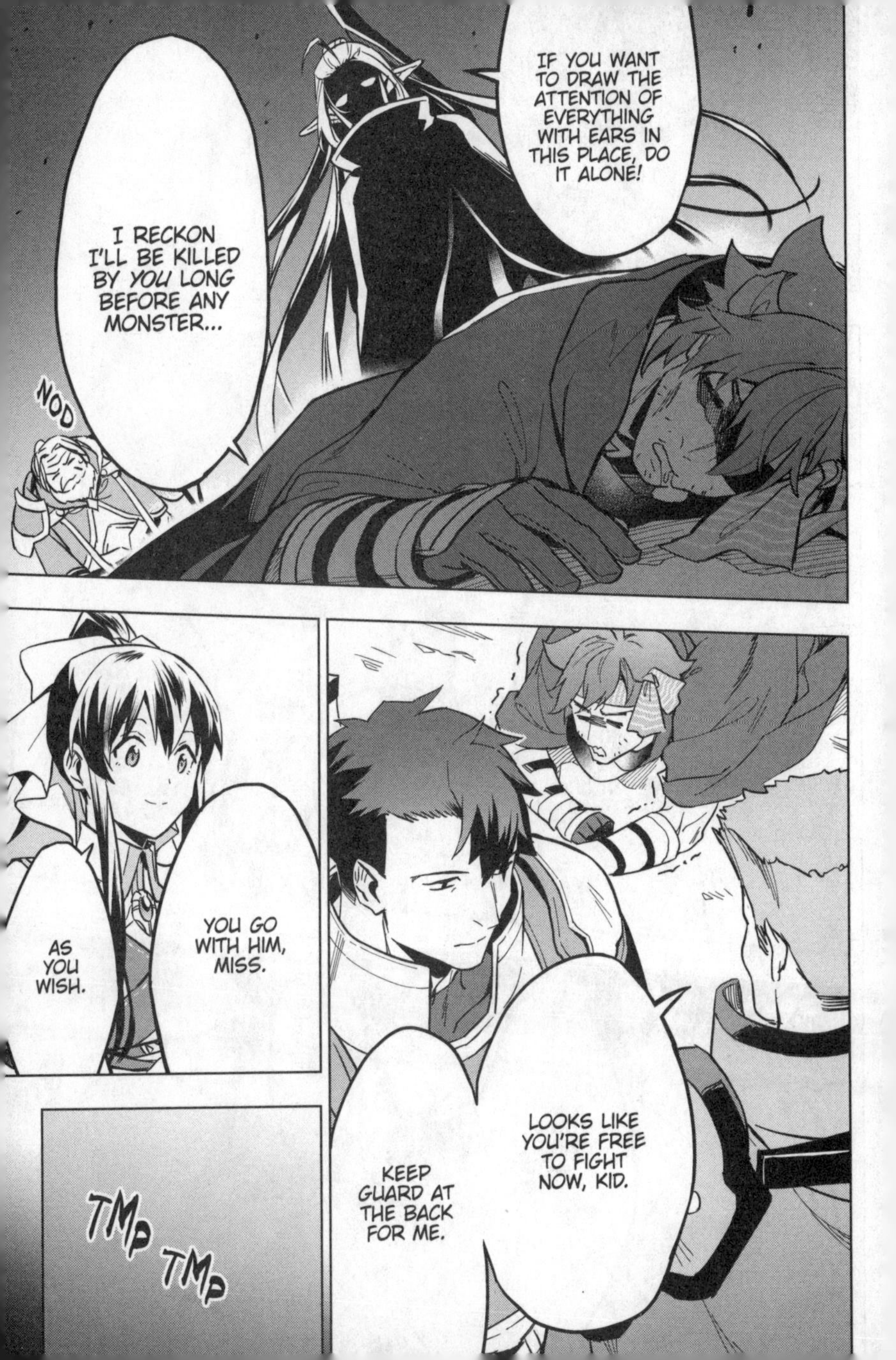
IF YOU WANT TO DRAW THE ATTENTION OF EVERYTHING WITH EARS IN THIS PLACE, DO IT ALONE!
I RECKON I'LL BE KILLED BY *YOU* LONG BEFORE ANY MONSTER...
NOD
LOOKS LIKE YOU'RE FREE TO FIGHT NOW, KID.
KEEP GUARD AT THE BACK FOR ME.
YOU GO WITH HIM, MISS.
AS YOU WISH.
TMP TMP

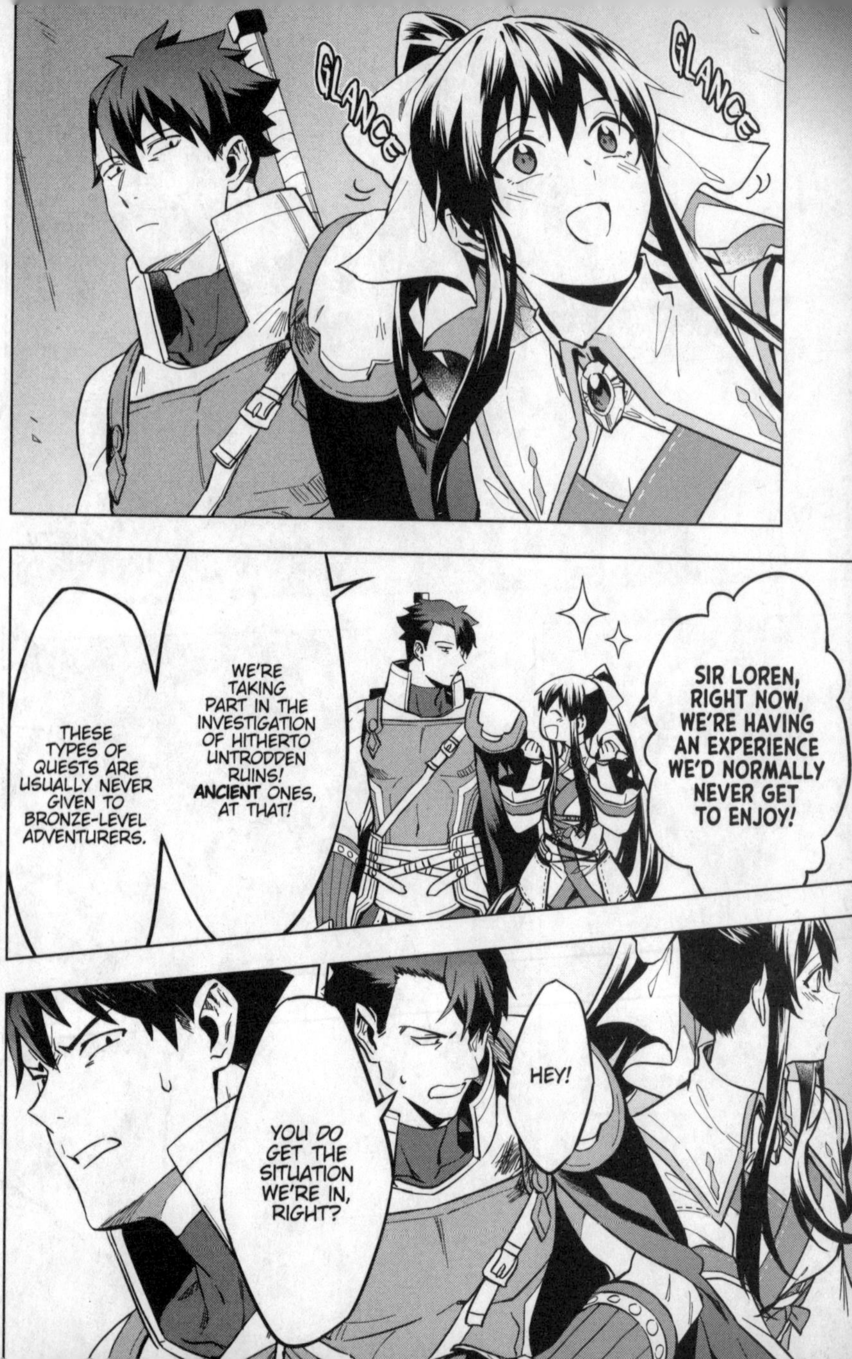
GLANCE
GLANCE
SIR LOREN, RIGHT NOW, WE'RE HAVING AN EXPERIENCE WE'D NORMALLY NEVER GET TO ENJOY!
WE'RE TAKING PART IN THE INVESTIGATION OF HITHERTO UNTRODDEN RUINS! ANCIENT ONES, AT THAT!
THESE TYPES OF QUESTS ARE USUALLY NEVER GIVEN TO BRONZE-LEVEL ADVENTURERS.
HEY!
YOU DO GET THE SITUATION WE'RE IN, RIGHT?

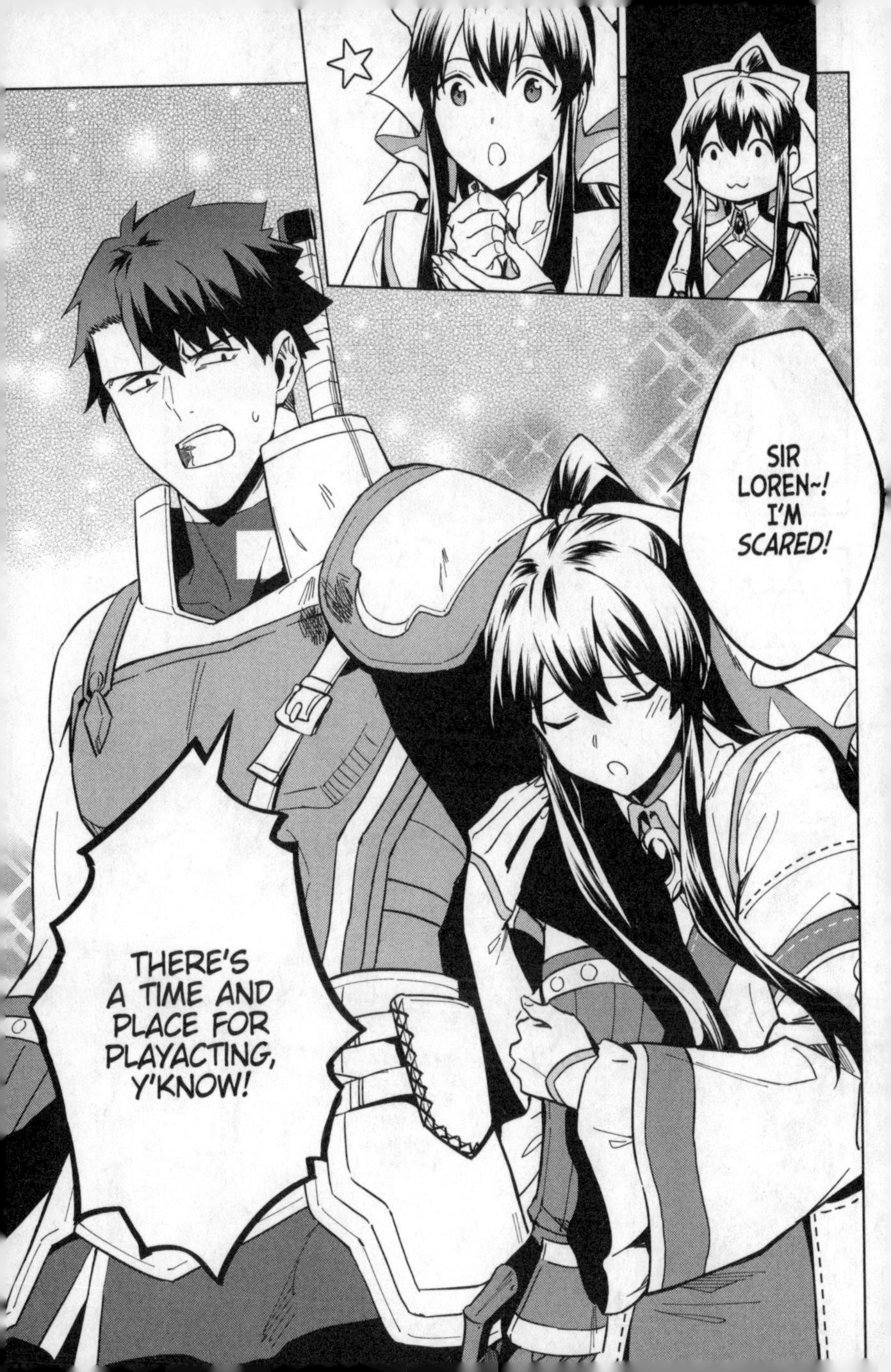
SIR LOREN~! I'M SCARED!
THERE'S A TIME AND PLACE FOR PLAYACTING, Y'KNOW!

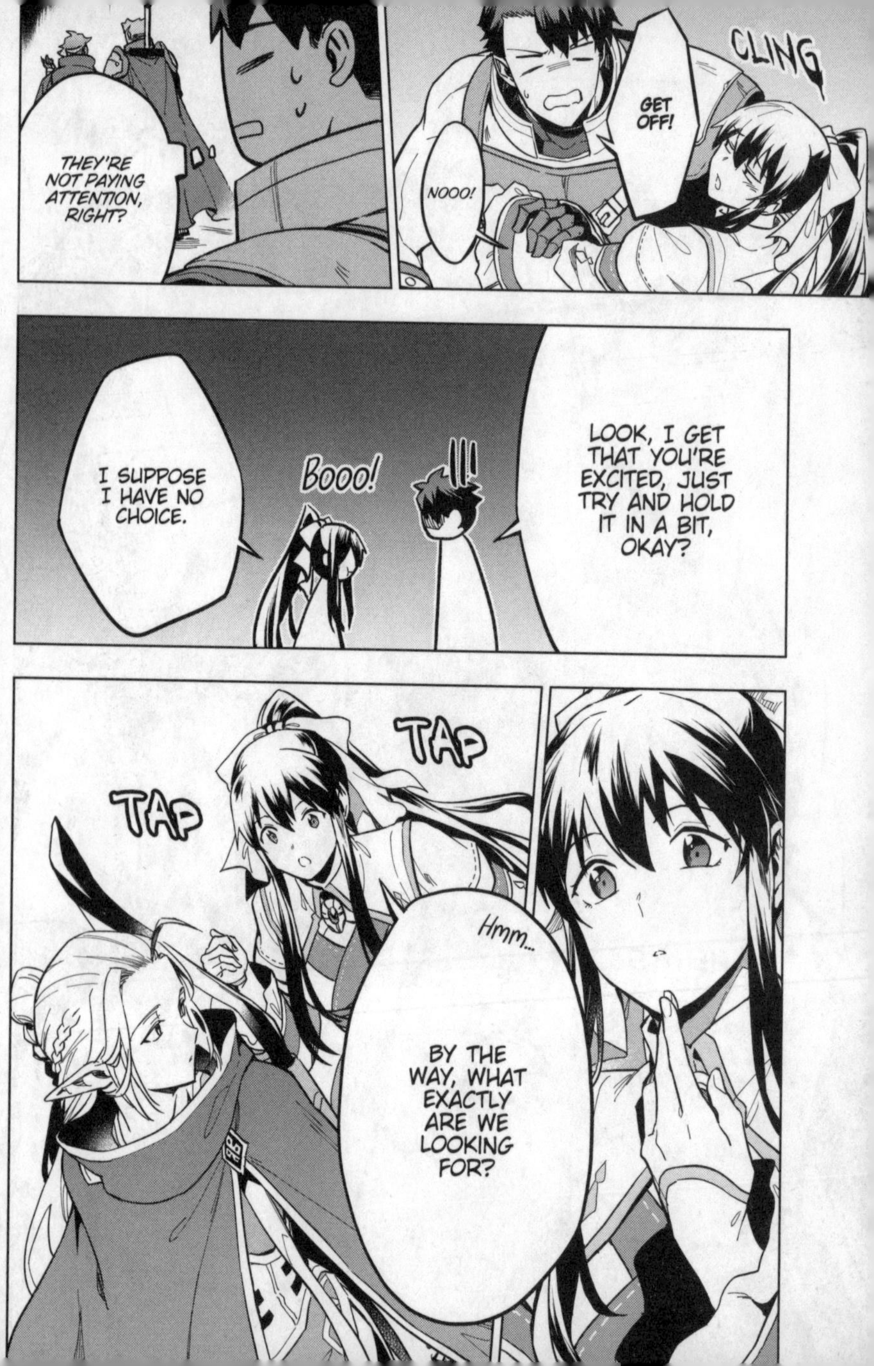
CLING
GET OFF!
NOOO!
THEY'RE NOT PAYING ATTENTION, RIGHT?
LOOK, I GET THAT YOU'RE EXCITED, JUST TRY AND HOLD IT IN A BIT, OKAY?
Booo!
I SUPPOSE I HAVE NO CHOICE.
Hmm...
BY THE WAY, WHAT EXACTLY ARE WE LOOKING FOR?
TAP
TAP

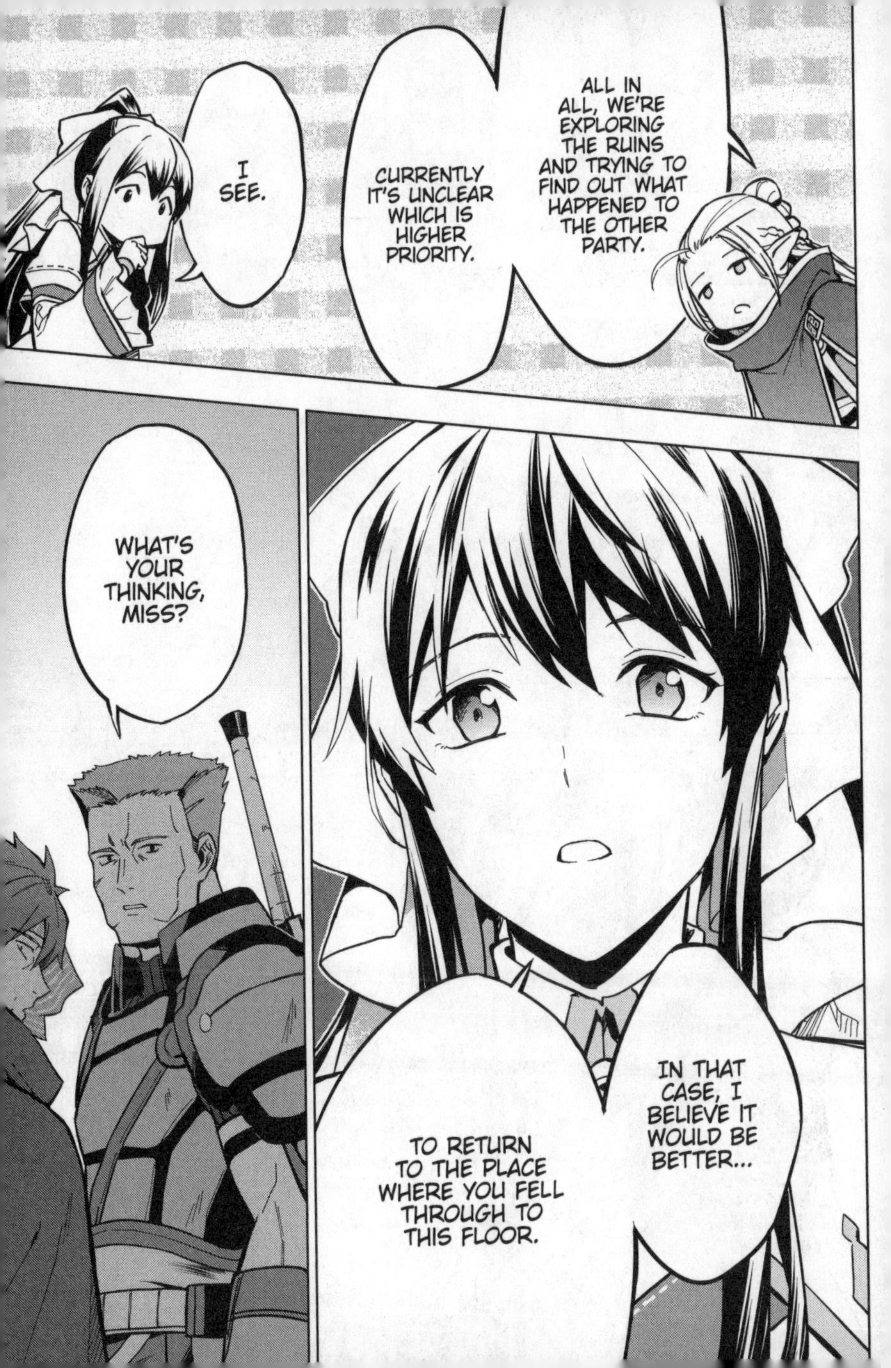
ALL IN ALL, WE'RE EXPLORING THE RUINS AND TRYING TO FIND OUT WHAT HAPPENED TO THE OTHER PARTY.
CURRENTLY IT'S UNCLEAR WHICH IS HIGHER PRIORITY.
I SEE.
IN THAT CASE, I BELIEVE IT WOULD BE BETTER...
TO RETURN TO THE PLACE WHERE YOU FELL THROUGH TO THIS FLOOR.
WHAT'S YOUR THINKING, MISS?

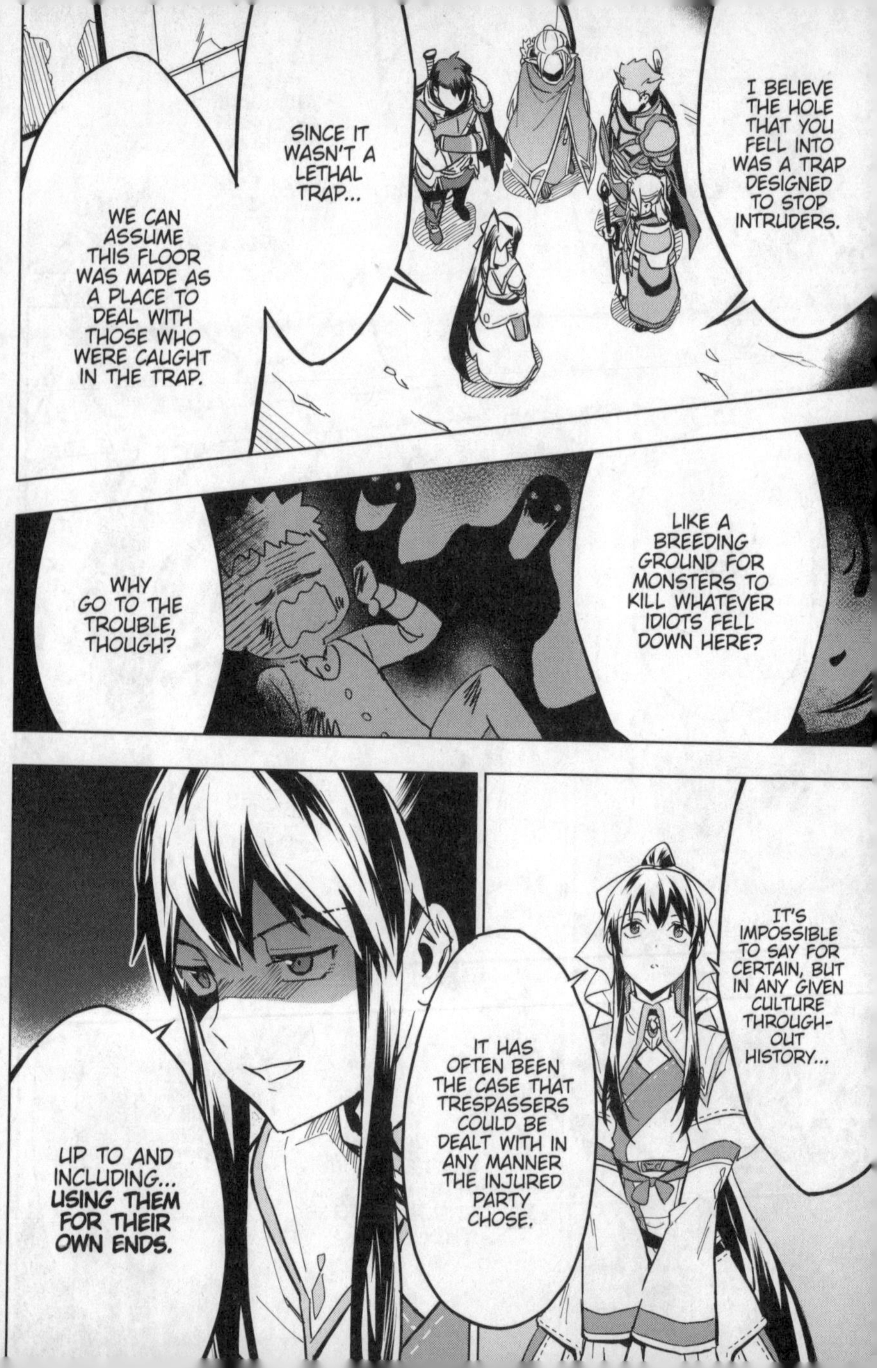
I BELIEVE THE HOLE THAT YOU FELL INTO WAS A TRAP DESIGNED TO STOP INTRUDERS.
SINCE IT WASN'T A LETHAL TRAP...
WE CAN ASSUME THIS FLOOR WAS MADE AS A PLACE TO DEAL WITH THOSE WHO WERE CAUGHT IN THE TRAP.
LIKE A BREEDING GROUND FOR MONSTERS TO KILL WHATEVER IDIOTS FELL DOWN HERE?
WHY GO TO THE TROUBLE, THOUGH?
IT'S IMPOSSIBLE TO SAY FOR CERTAIN, BUT IN ANY GIVEN CULTURE THROUGH-OUT HISTORY...
IT HAS OFTEN BEEN THE CASE THAT TRESPASSERS COULD BE DEALT WITH IN ANY MANNER THE INJURED PARTY CHOSE.
UP TO AND INCLUDING... **USING THEM FOR THEIR OWN ENDS.**

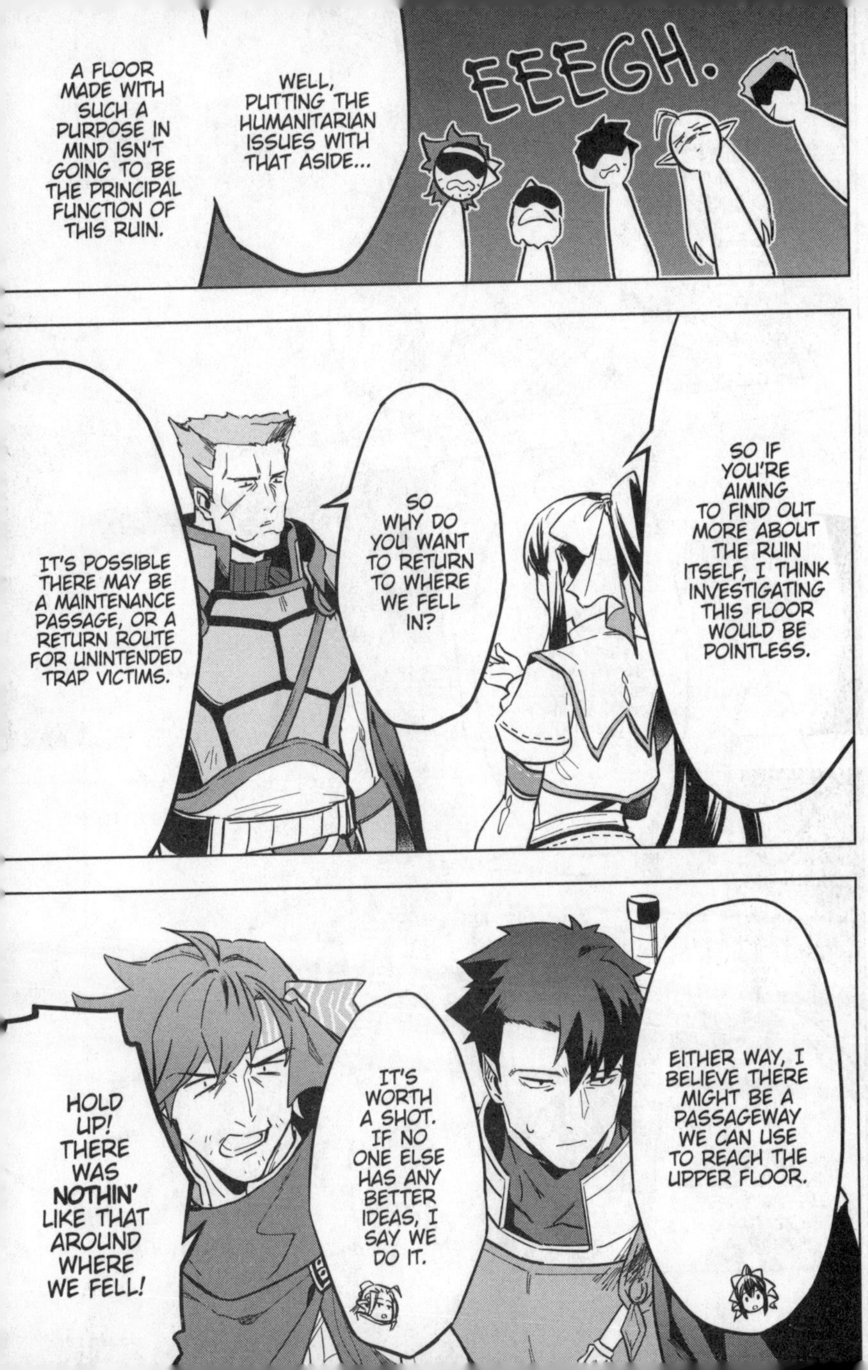
EEEGH.
WELL, PUTTING THE HUMANITARIAN ISSUES WITH THAT ASIDE...
A FLOOR MADE WITH SUCH A PURPOSE IN MIND ISN'T GOING TO BE THE PRINCIPAL FUNCTION OF THIS RUIN.
SO IF YOU'RE AIMING TO FIND OUT MORE ABOUT THE RUIN ITSELF, I THINK INVESTIGATING THIS FLOOR WOULD BE POINTLESS.
SO WHY DO YOU WANT TO RETURN TO WHERE WE FELL IN?
IT'S POSSIBLE THERE MAY BE A MAINTENANCE PASSAGE, OR A RETURN ROUTE FOR UNINTENDED TRAP VICTIMS.
EITHER WAY, I BELIEVE THERE MIGHT BE A PASSAGEWAY WE CAN USE TO REACH THE UPPER FLOOR.
IT'S WORTH A SHOT. IF NO ONE ELSE HAS ANY BETTER IDEAS, I SAY WE DO IT.
HOLD UP! THERE WAS **NOTHIN'** LIKE THAT AROUND WHERE WE FELL!

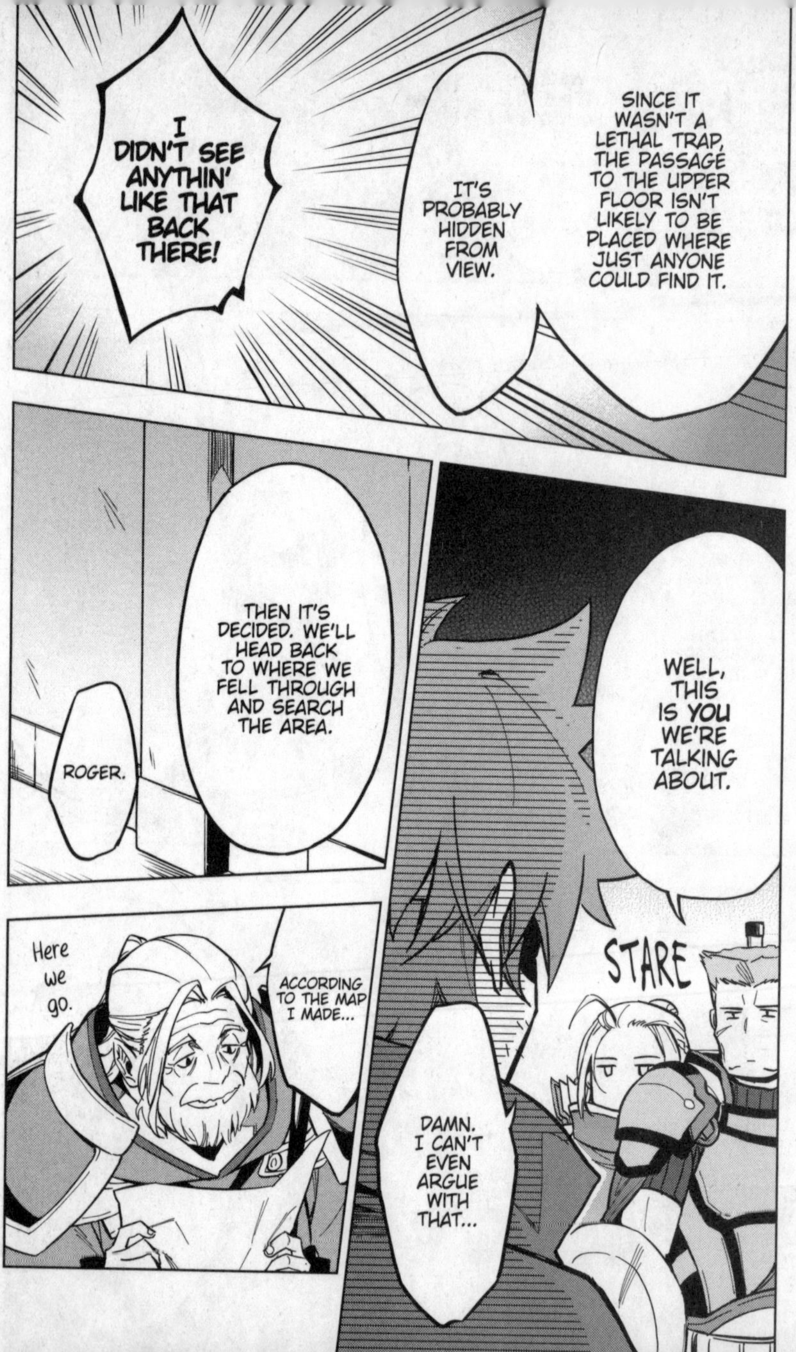
SINCE IT WASN'T A LETHAL TRAP, THE PASSAGE TO THE UPPER FLOOR ISN'T LIKELY TO BE PLACED WHERE JUST ANYONE COULD FIND IT.
IT'S PROBABLY HIDDEN FROM VIEW.
I DIDN'T SEE ANYTHIN' LIKE THAT BACK THERE!
WELL, THIS IS YOU WE'RE TALKING ABOUT.
STARE
DAMN. I CAN'T EVEN ARGUE WITH THAT...
THEN IT'S DECIDED. WE'LL HEAD BACK TO WHERE WE FELL THROUGH AND SEARCH THE AREA.
ROGER.
ACCORDING TO THE MAP I MADE...
Here we go.

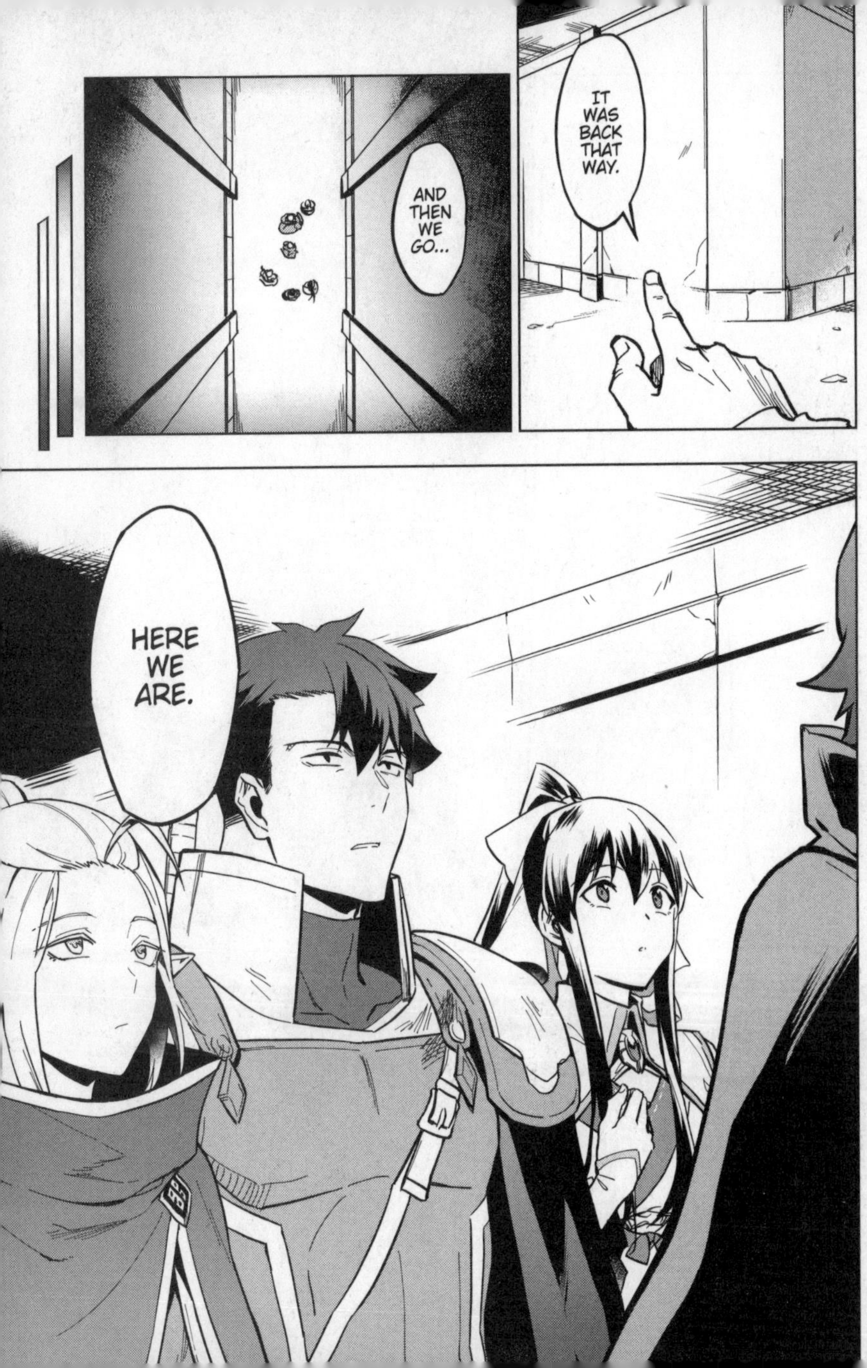
IT WAS BACK THAT WAY.
AND THEN WE GO...
HERE WE ARE.

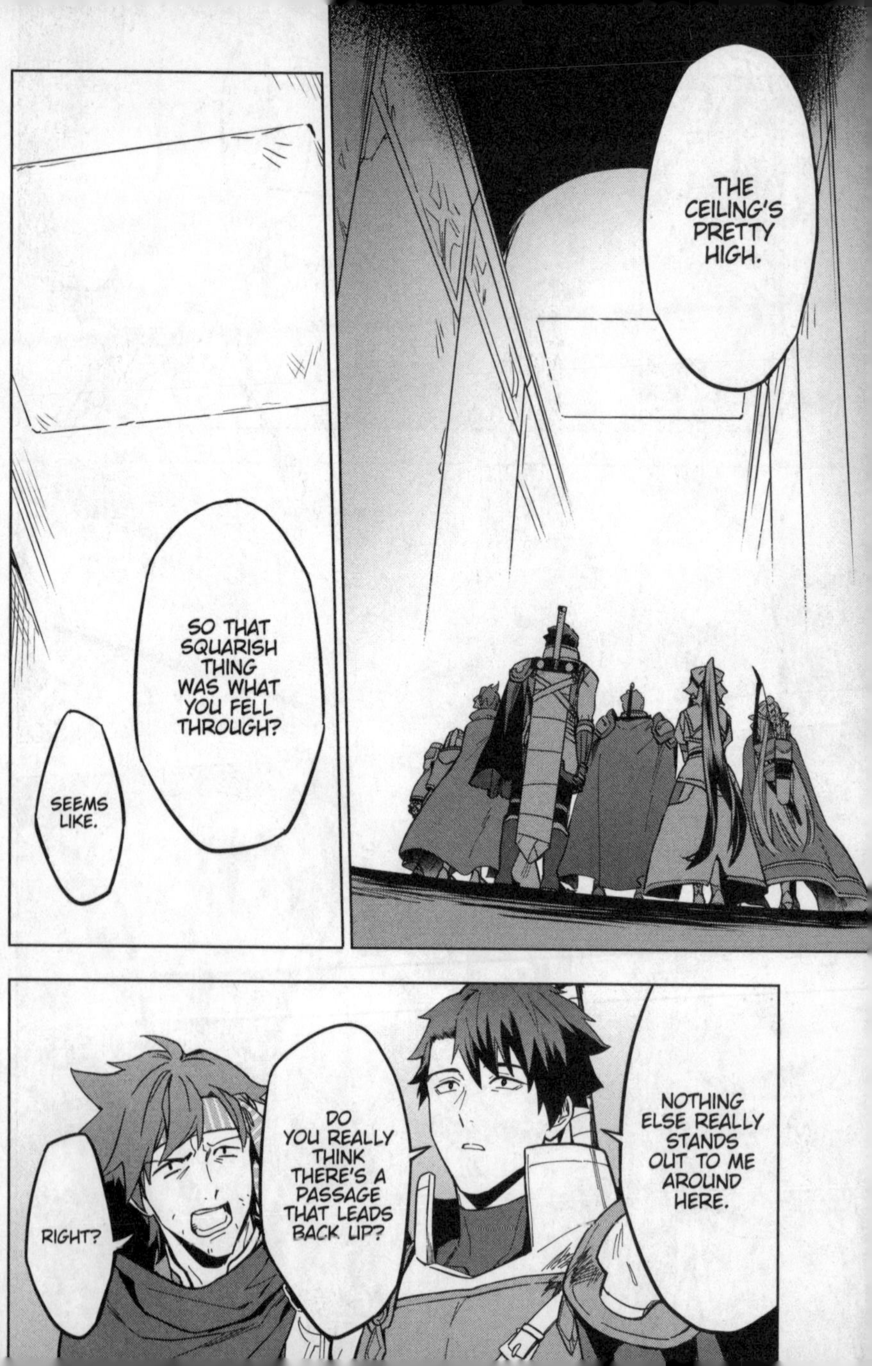
THE CEILING'S PRETTY HIGH.
SO THAT SQUARISH THING WAS WHAT YOU FELL THROUGH?
SEEMS LIKE.
NOTHING ELSE REALLY STANDS OUT TO ME AROUND HERE.
DO YOU REALLY THINK THERE'S A PASSAGE THAT LEADS BACK UP?
RIGHT?

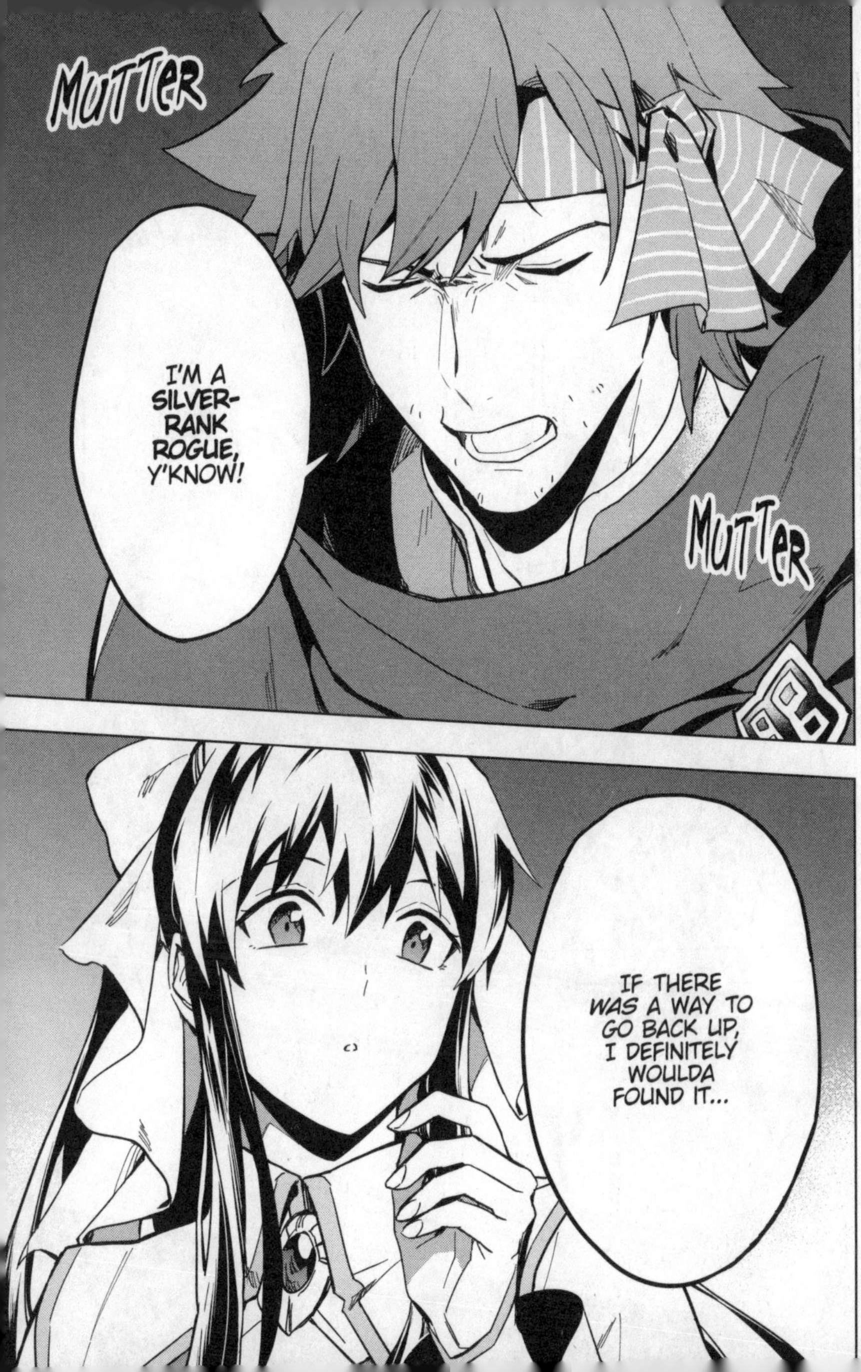
MUTTER
I'M A SILVER-RANK ROGUE, Y'KNOW!
MUTTER
IF THERE WAS A WAY TO GO BACK UP, I DEFINITELY WOULDA FOUND IT...

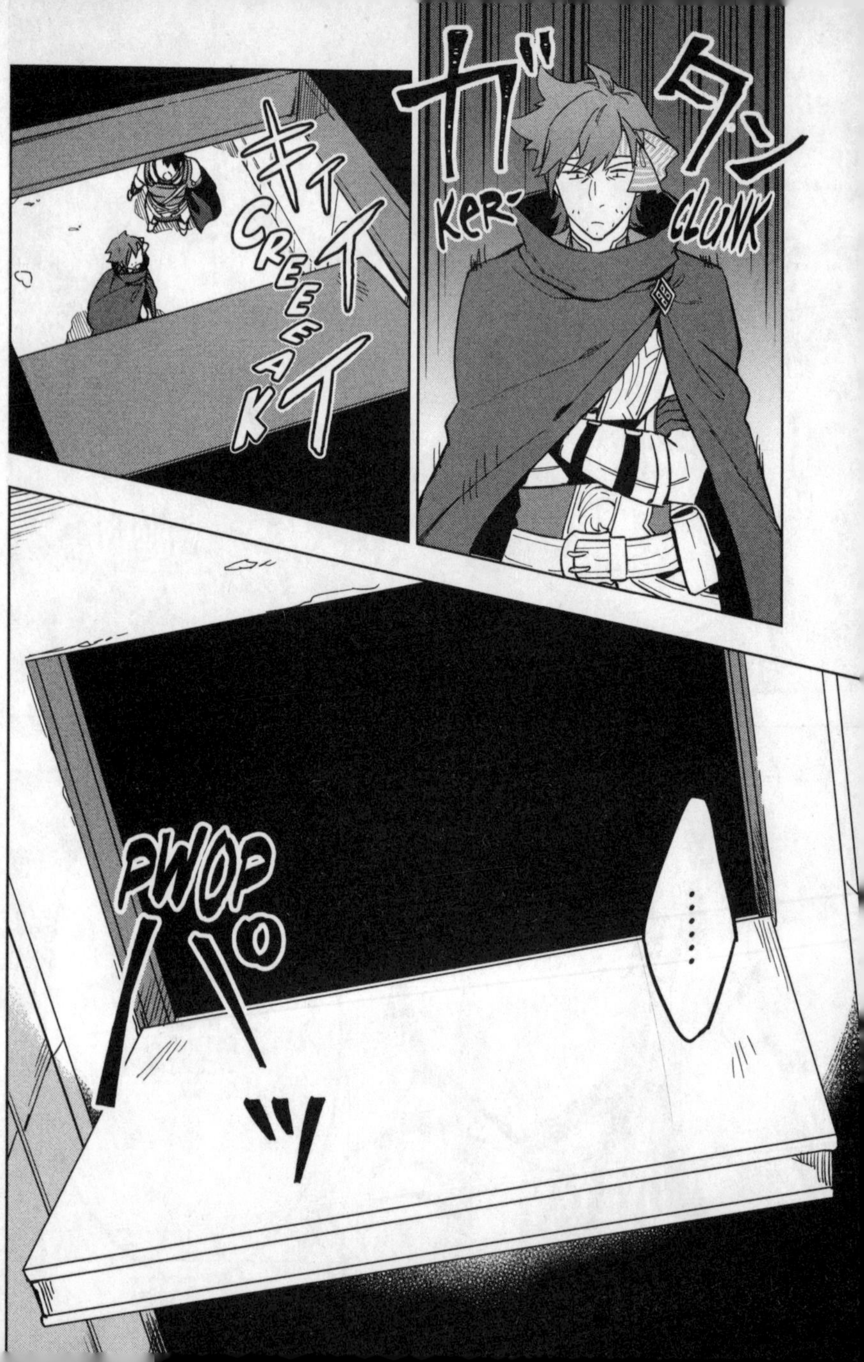
ガタン
KER-CLUNK
キイイ
CREEEAK
......
パッ
PWOP

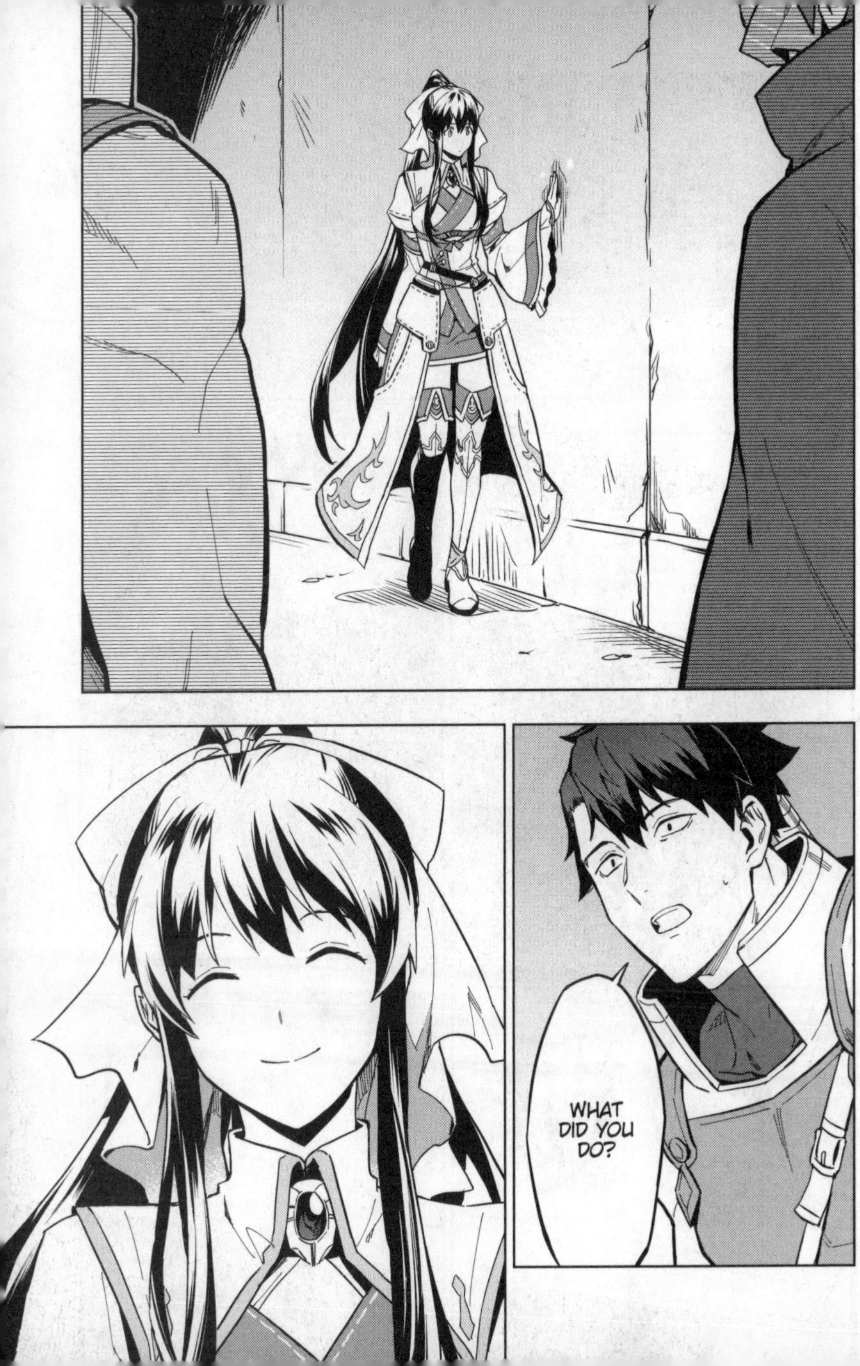
WHAT DID YOU DO?

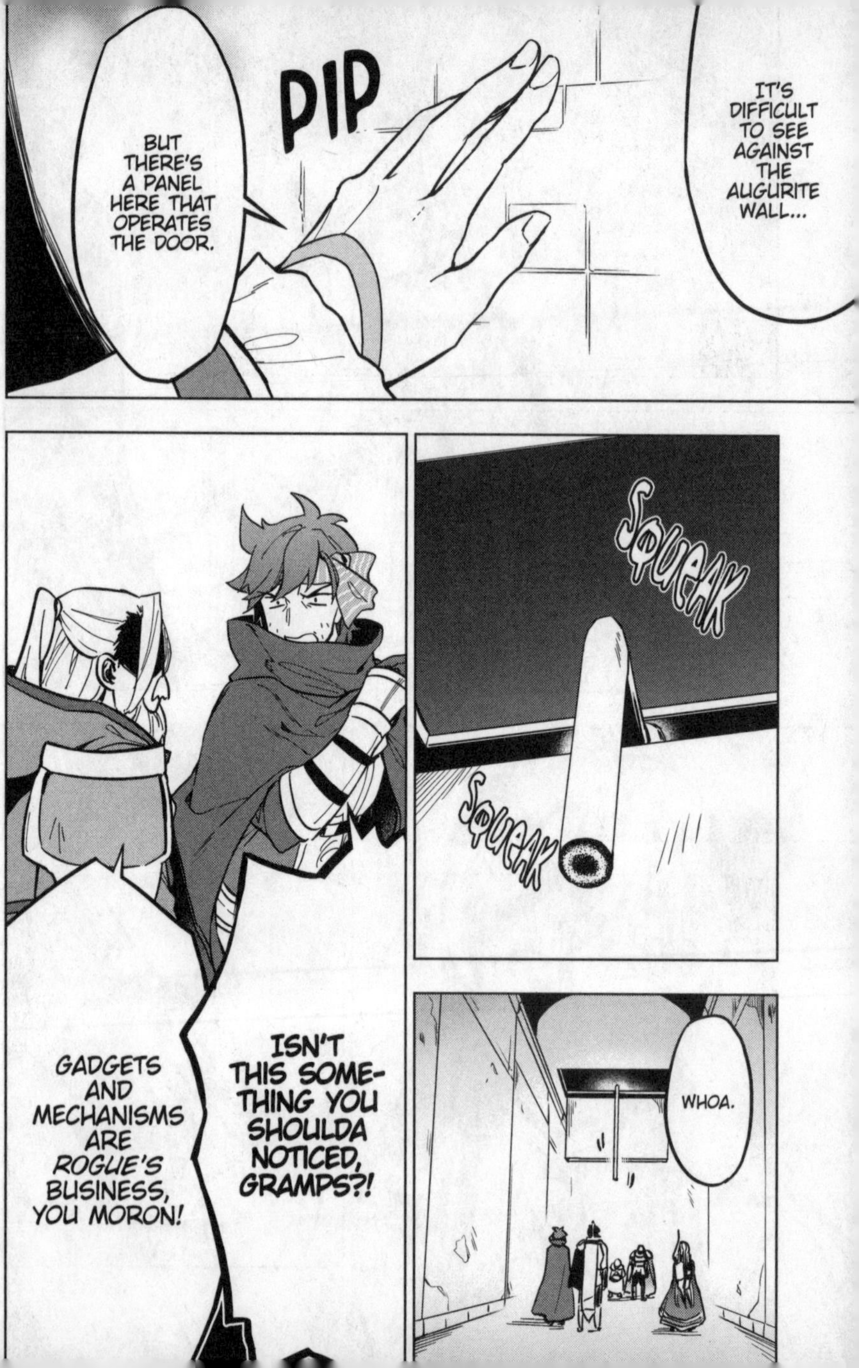
IT'S DIFFICULT TO SEE AGAINST THE AUGURITE WALL...
PIP
BUT THERE'S A PANEL HERE THAT OPERATES THE DOOR.
SQUEAK
SQUEAK
WHOA.
ISN'T THIS SOME-THING YOU SHOULDA NOTICED, GRAMPS?!
GADGETS AND MECHANISMS ARE *ROGUE'S* BUSINESS, YOU MORON!

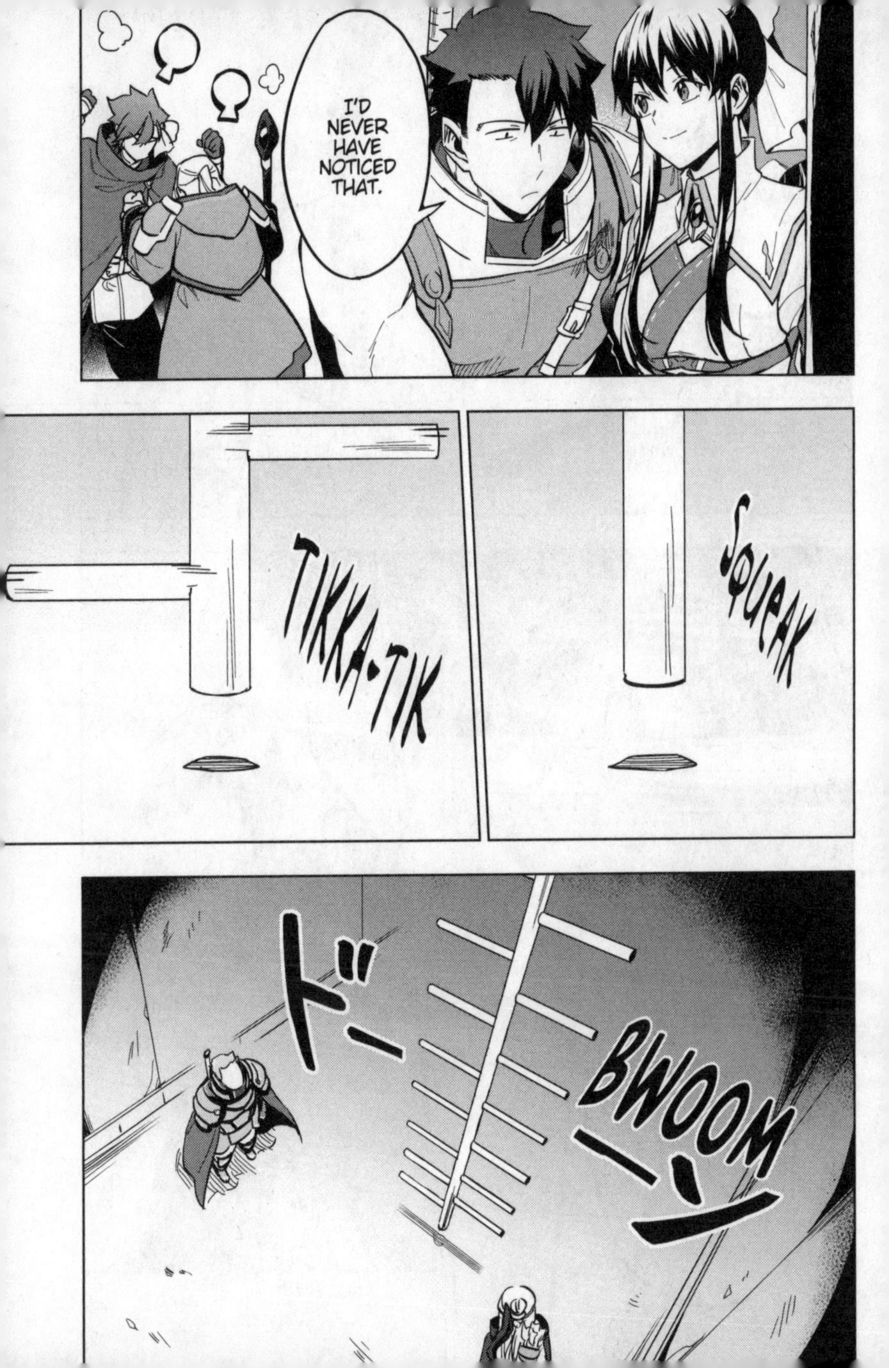
I'D NEVER HAVE NOTICED THAT.
SQUEAK
TIKKA-TIK
ドーン
BWOOM

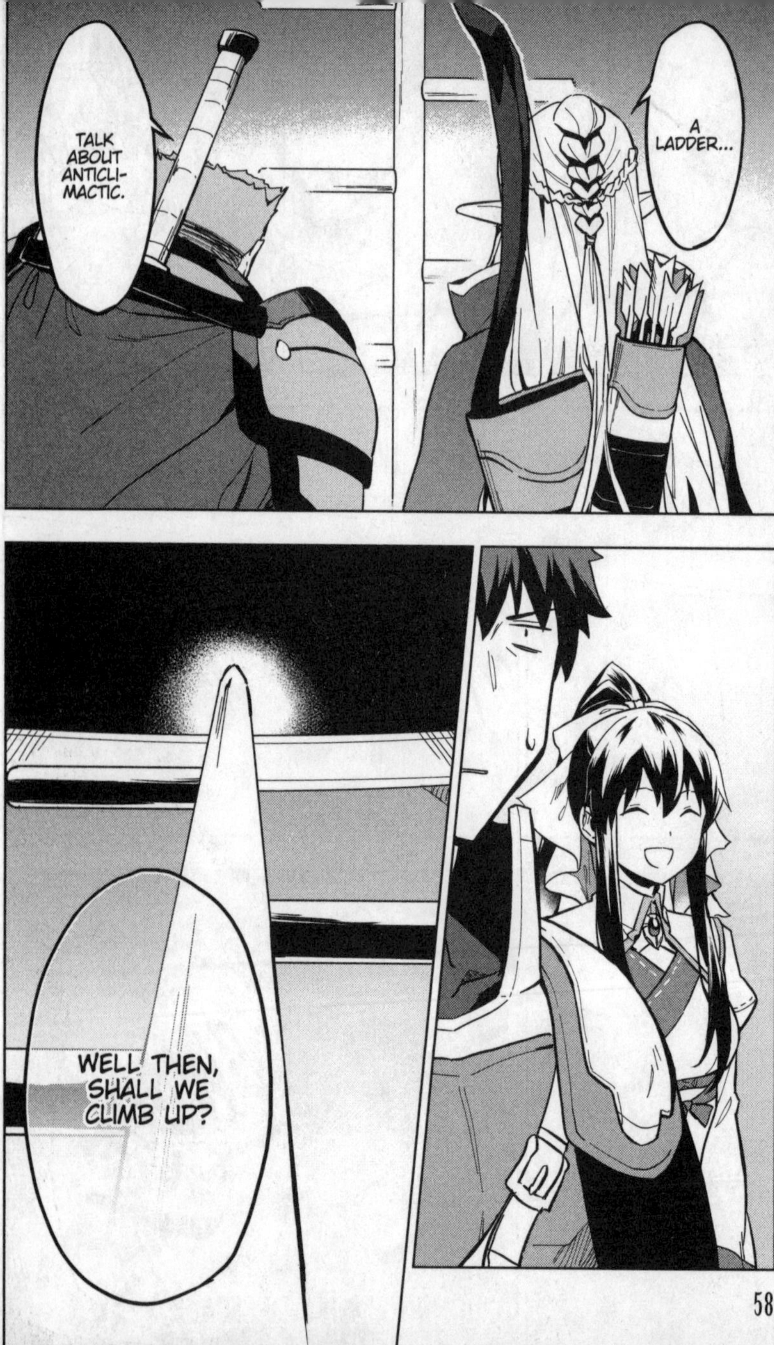
A LADDER...
TALK ABOUT ANTICLI-MACTIC.
WELL THEN, SHALL WE CLIMB UP?

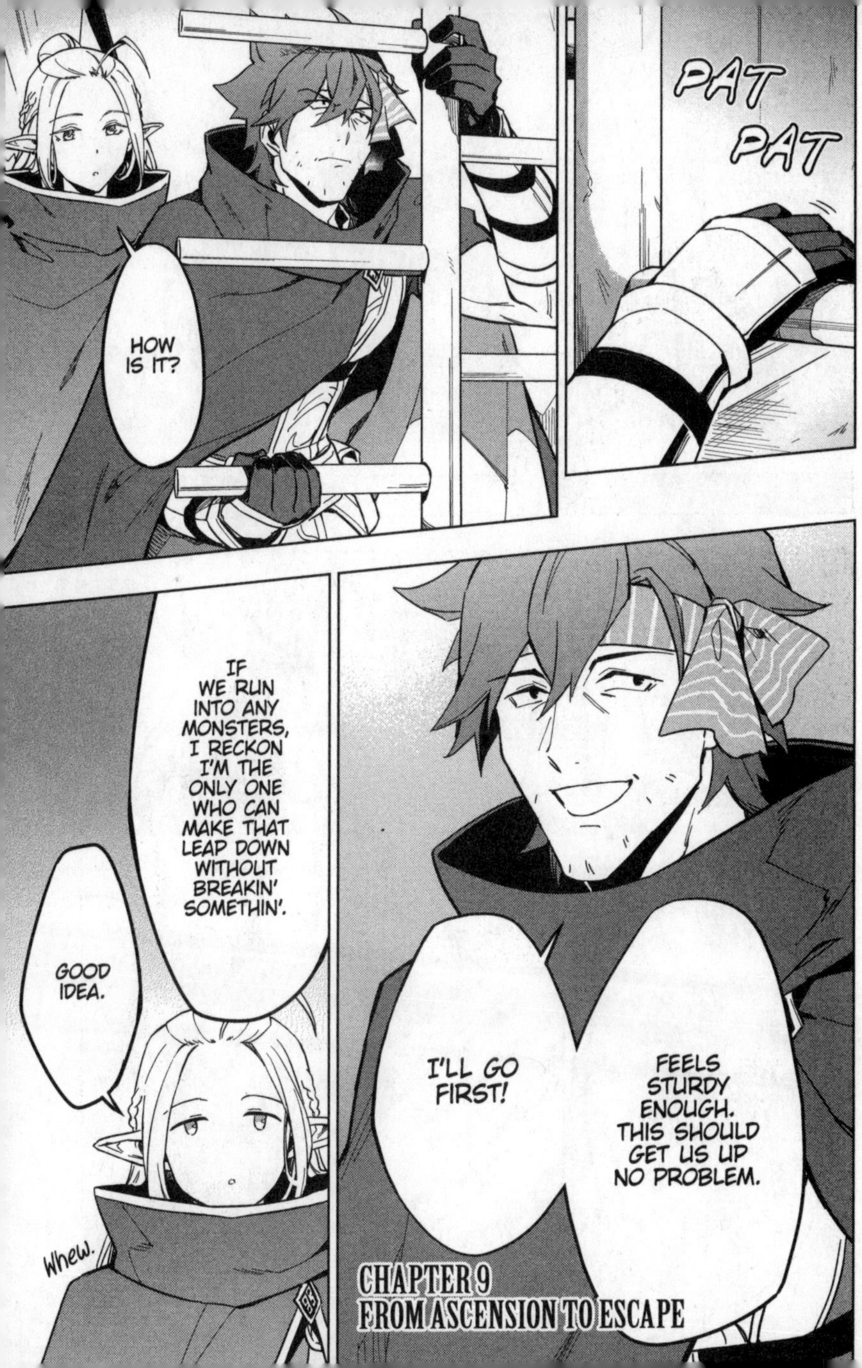
PAT PAT
HOW IS IT?
FEELS STURDY ENOUGH. THIS SHOULD GET US UP NO PROBLEM.
I'LL GO FIRST!
CHAPTER 9
FROM ASCENSION TO ESCAPE
IF WE RUN INTO ANY MONSTERS, I RECKON I'M THE ONLY ONE WHO CAN MAKE THAT LEAP DOWN WITHOUT BREAKIN' SOMETHIN'.
GOOD IDEA.
Whew.

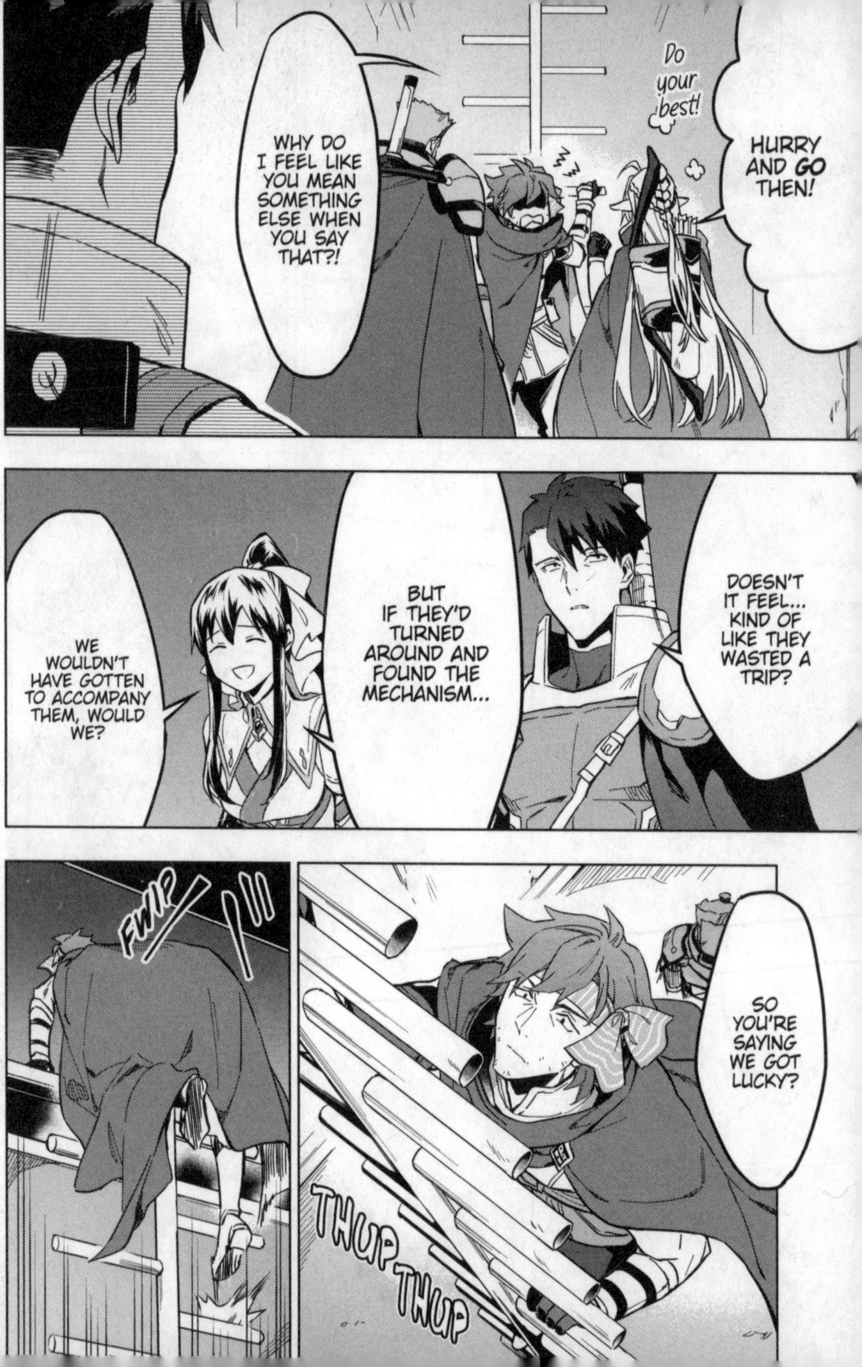
HURRY AND GO THEN!
Do your best!
WHY DO I FEEL LIKE YOU MEAN SOMETHING ELSE WHEN YOU SAY THAT?!
DOESN'T IT FEEL... KIND OF LIKE THEY WASTED A TRIP?
BUT IF THEY'D TURNED AROUND AND FOUND THE MECHANISM...
WE WOULDN'T HAVE GOTTEN TO ACCOMPANY THEM, WOULD WE?
SO YOU'RE SAYING WE GOT LUCKY?
THUP THUP
FWIP
!!

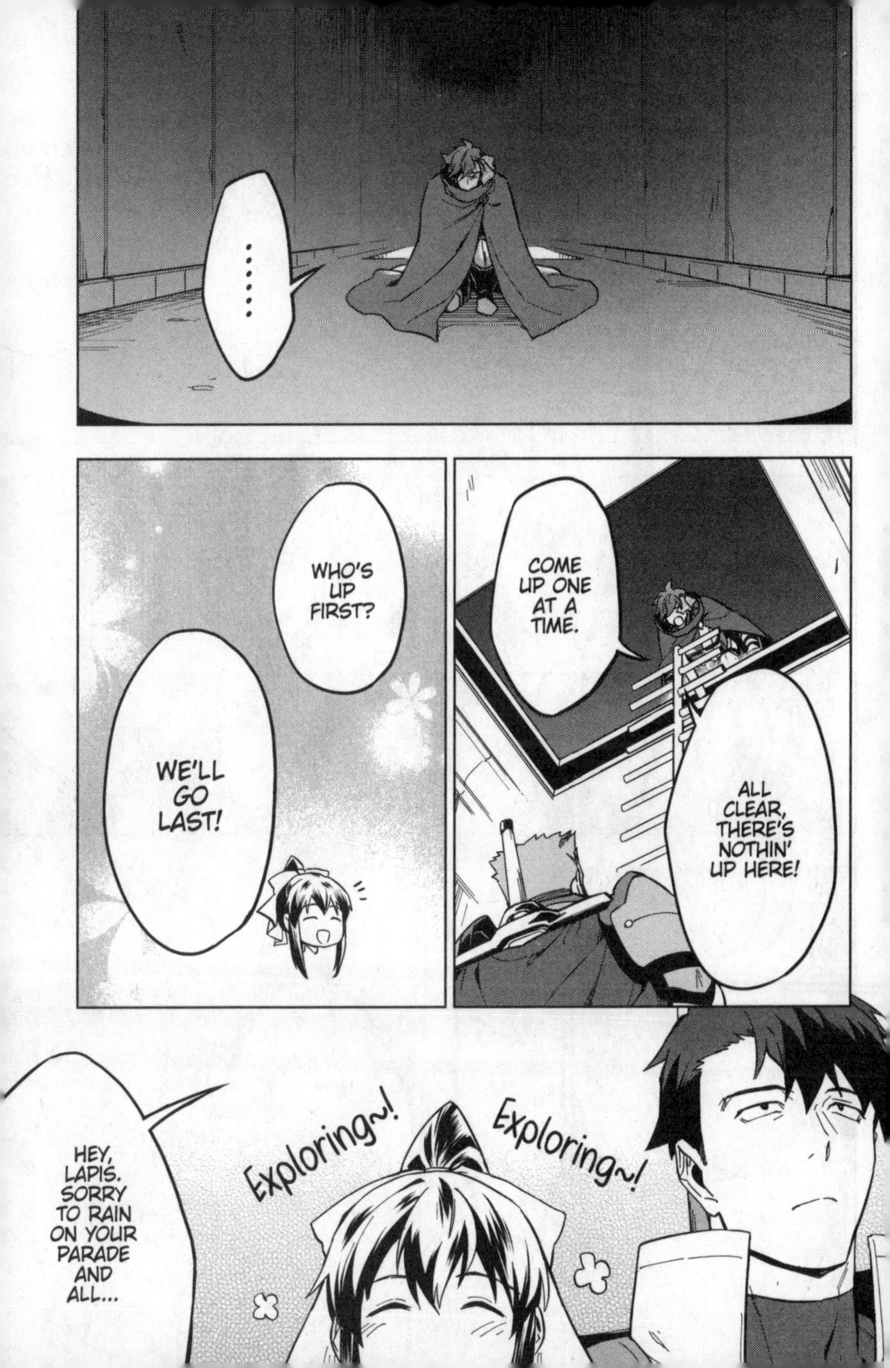
……
ALL CLEAR, THERE'S NOTHIN' UP HERE!
COME UP ONE AT A TIME.
WHO'S UP FIRST?
WE'LL GO LAST!
Exploring~!
Exploring~!
HEY, LAPIS. SORRY TO RAIN ON YOUR PARADE AND ALL...

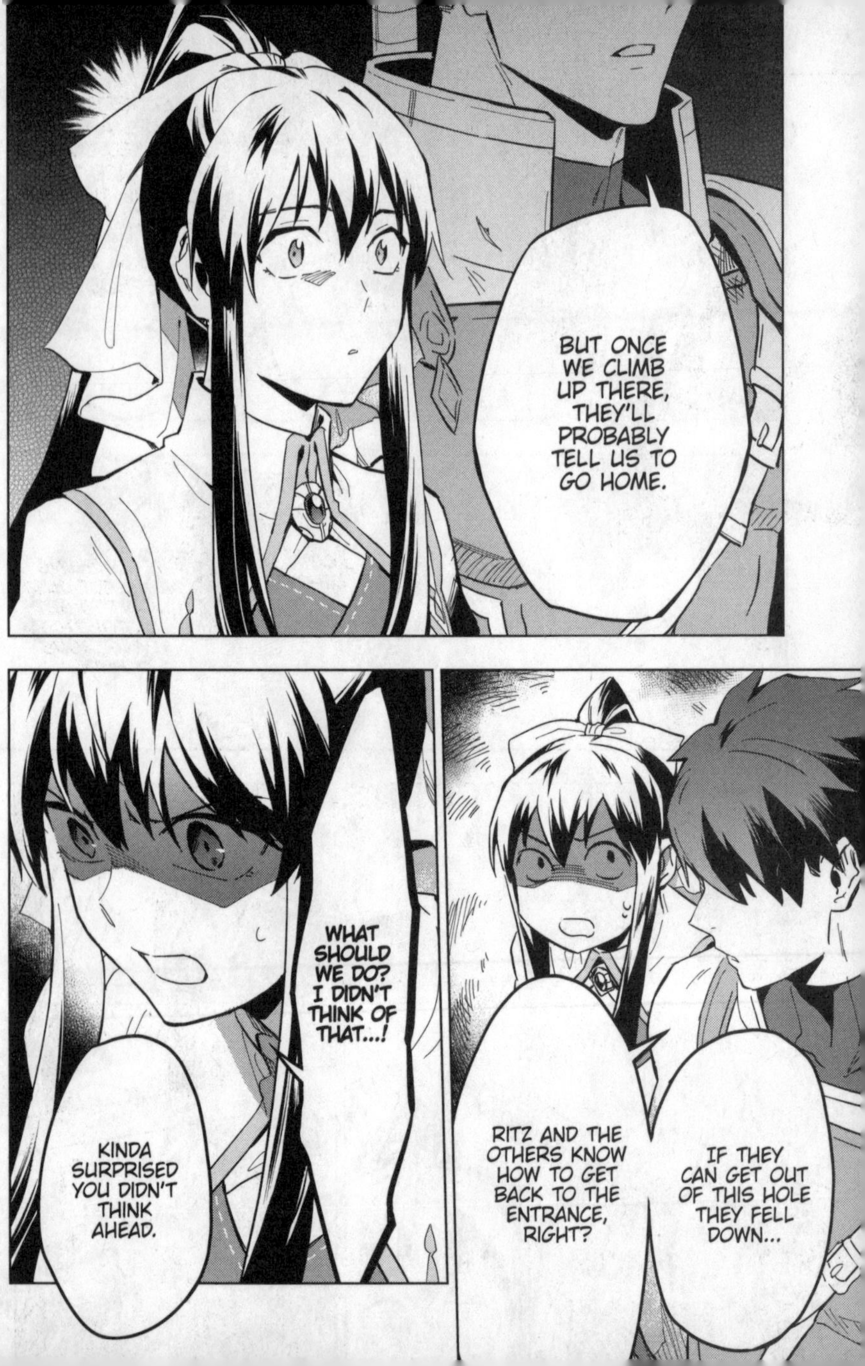
BUT ONCE WE CLIMB UP THERE, THEY'LL PROBABLY TELL US TO GO HOME.
IF THEY CAN GET OUT OF THIS HOLE THEY FELL DOWN...
RITZ AND THE OTHERS KNOW HOW TO GET BACK TO THE ENTRANCE, RIGHT?
WHAT SHOULD WE DO? I DIDN'T THINK OF THAT...!
KINDA SURPRISED YOU DIDN'T THINK AHEAD.

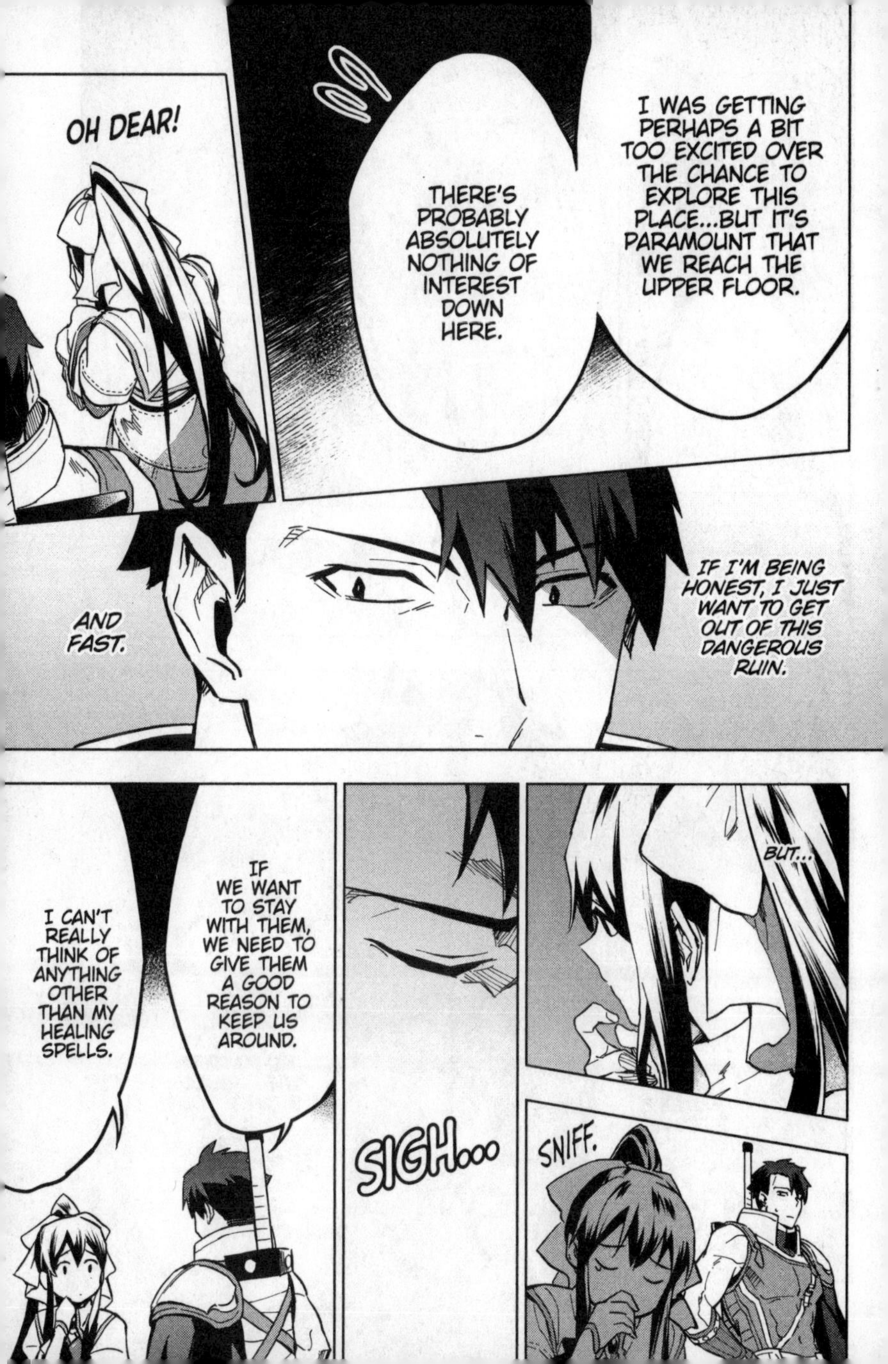
I WAS GETTING PERHAPS A BIT TOO EXCITED OVER THE CHANCE TO EXPLORE THIS PLACE...BUT IT'S PARAMOUNT THAT WE REACH THE UPPER FLOOR.
THERE'S PROBABLY ABSOLUTELY NOTHING OF INTEREST DOWN HERE.
OH DEAR!
IF I'M BEING HONEST, I JUST WANT TO GET OUT OF THIS DANGEROUS RUIN.
AND FAST.
BUT...
SNIFF.
SIGH...
IF WE WANT TO STAY WITH THEM, WE NEED TO GIVE THEM A GOOD REASON TO KEEP US AROUND.
I CAN'T REALLY THINK OF ANYTHING OTHER THAN MY HEALING SPELLS.

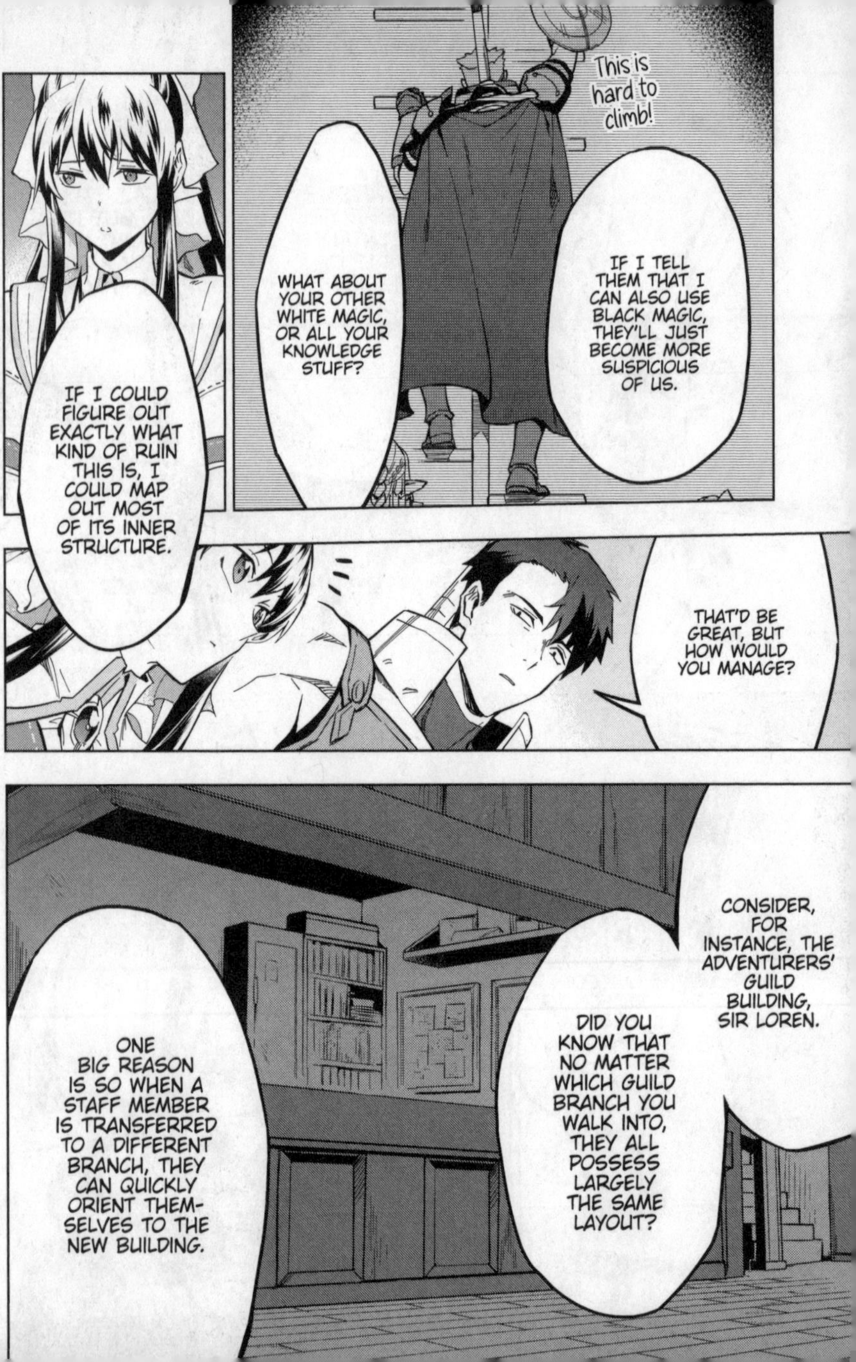
This is hard to climb!
IF I TELL THEM THAT I CAN ALSO USE BLACK MAGIC, THEY'LL JUST BECOME MORE SUSPICIOUS OF US.
WHAT ABOUT YOUR OTHER WHITE MAGIC, OR ALL YOUR KNOWLEDGE STUFF?
IF I COULD FIGURE OUT EXACTLY WHAT KIND OF RUIN THIS IS, I COULD MAP OUT MOST OF ITS INNER STRUCTURE.
THAT'D BE GREAT, BUT HOW WOULD YOU MANAGE?
CONSIDER, FOR INSTANCE, THE ADVENTURERS' GUILD BUILDING, SIR LOREN.
DID YOU KNOW THAT NO MATTER WHICH GUILD BRANCH YOU WALK INTO, THEY ALL POSSESS LARGELY THE SAME LAYOUT?
ONE BIG REASON IS SO WHEN A STAFF MEMBER IS TRANSFERRED TO A DIFFERENT BRANCH, THEY CAN QUICKLY ORIENT THEM-SELVES TO THE NEW BUILDING.

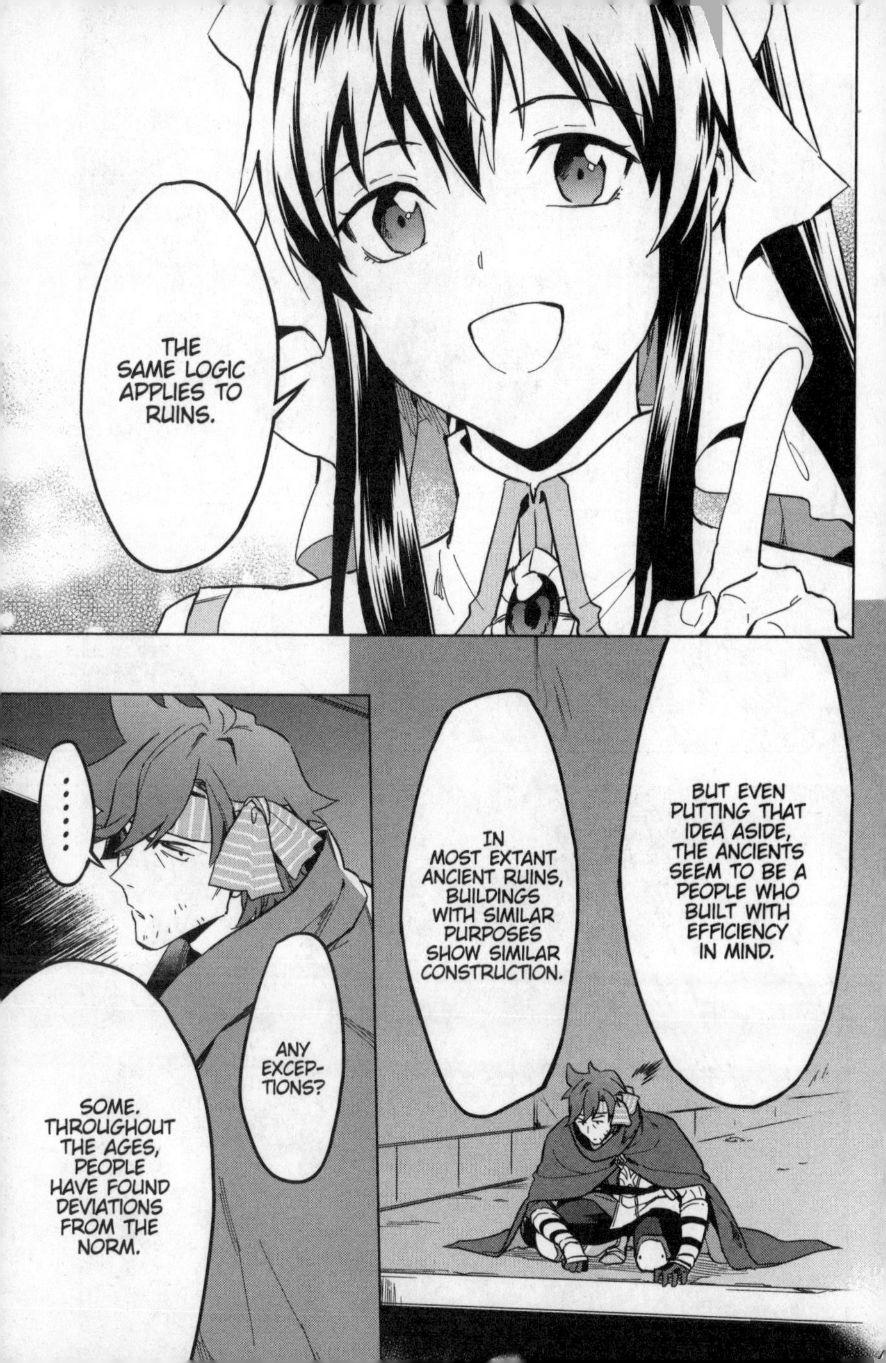
THE SAME LOGIC APPLIES TO RUINS.
BUT EVEN PUTTING THAT IDEA ASIDE, THE ANCIENTS SEEM TO BE A PEOPLE WHO BUILT WITH EFFICIENCY IN MIND.
IN MOST EXTANT ANCIENT RUINS, BUILDINGS WITH SIMILAR PURPOSES SHOW SIMILAR CONSTRUCTION.
......
ANY EXCEP-TIONS?
SOME. THROUGHOUT THE AGES, PEOPLE HAVE FOUND DEVIATIONS FROM THE NORM.

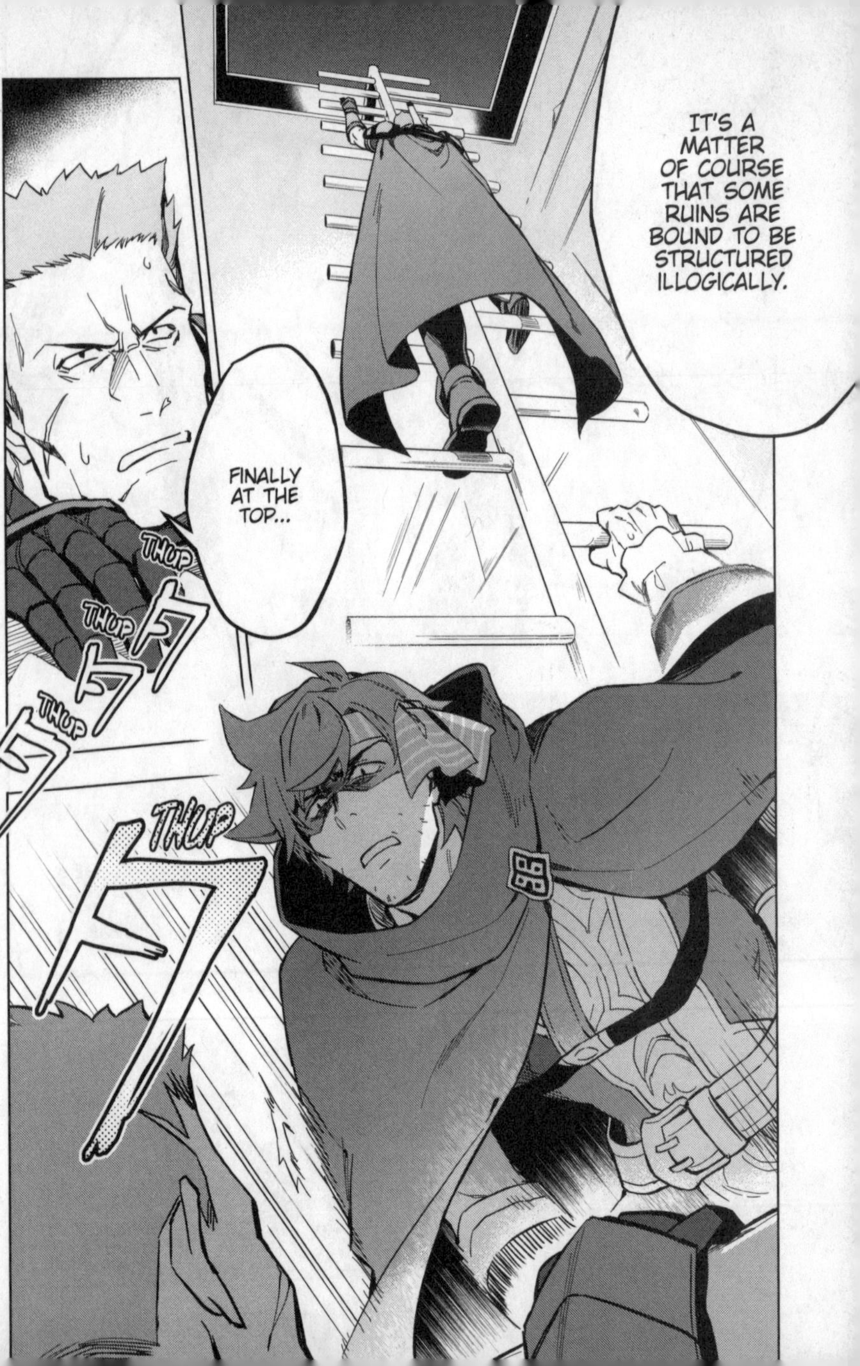
IT'S A MATTER OF COURSE THAT SOME RUINS ARE BOUND TO BE STRUCTURED ILLOGICALLY.
FINALLY AT THE TOP...
THUP
THUP
THUP
THUP

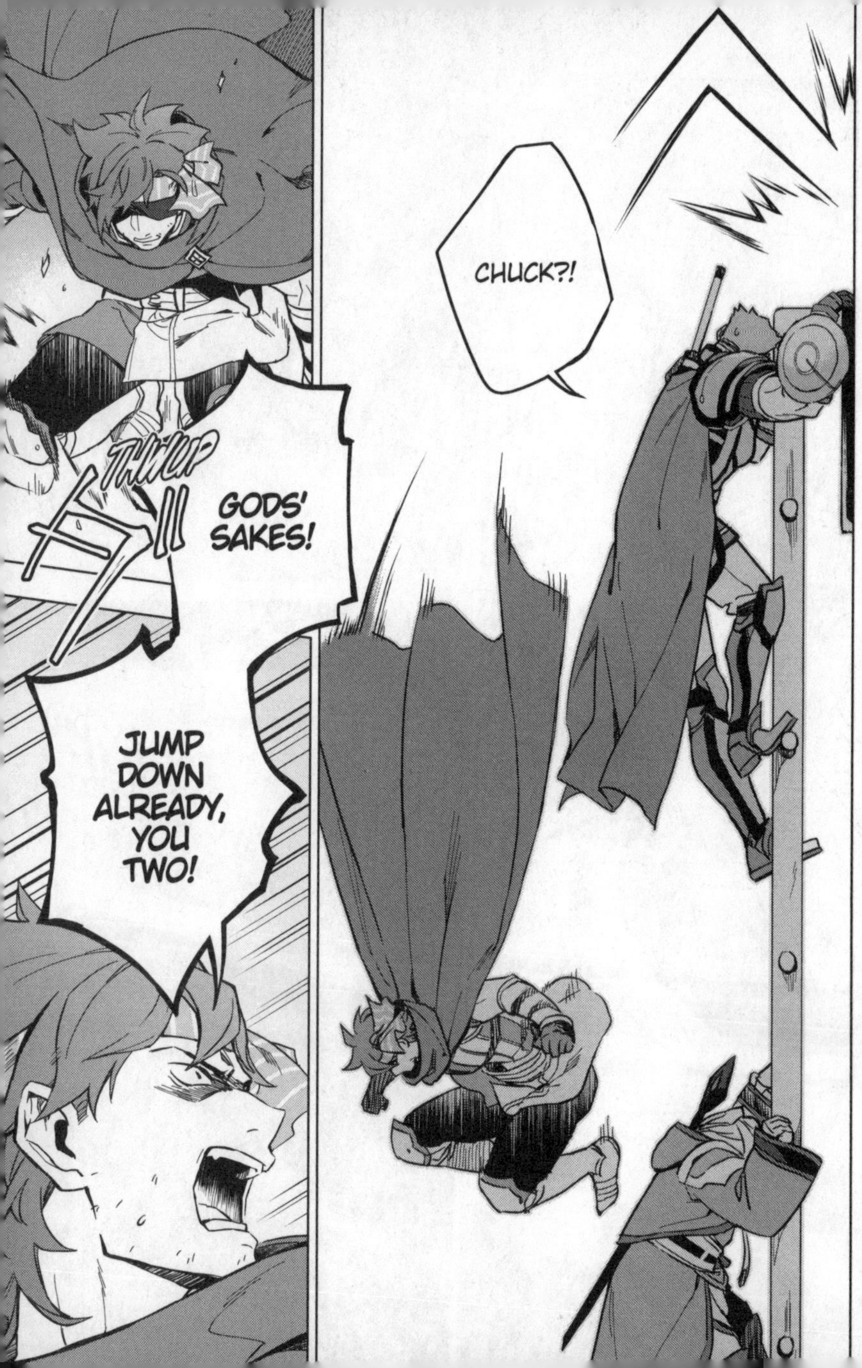
CHUCK?!
THWUP
GODS' SAKES!
JUMP DOWN ALREADY, YOU TWO!

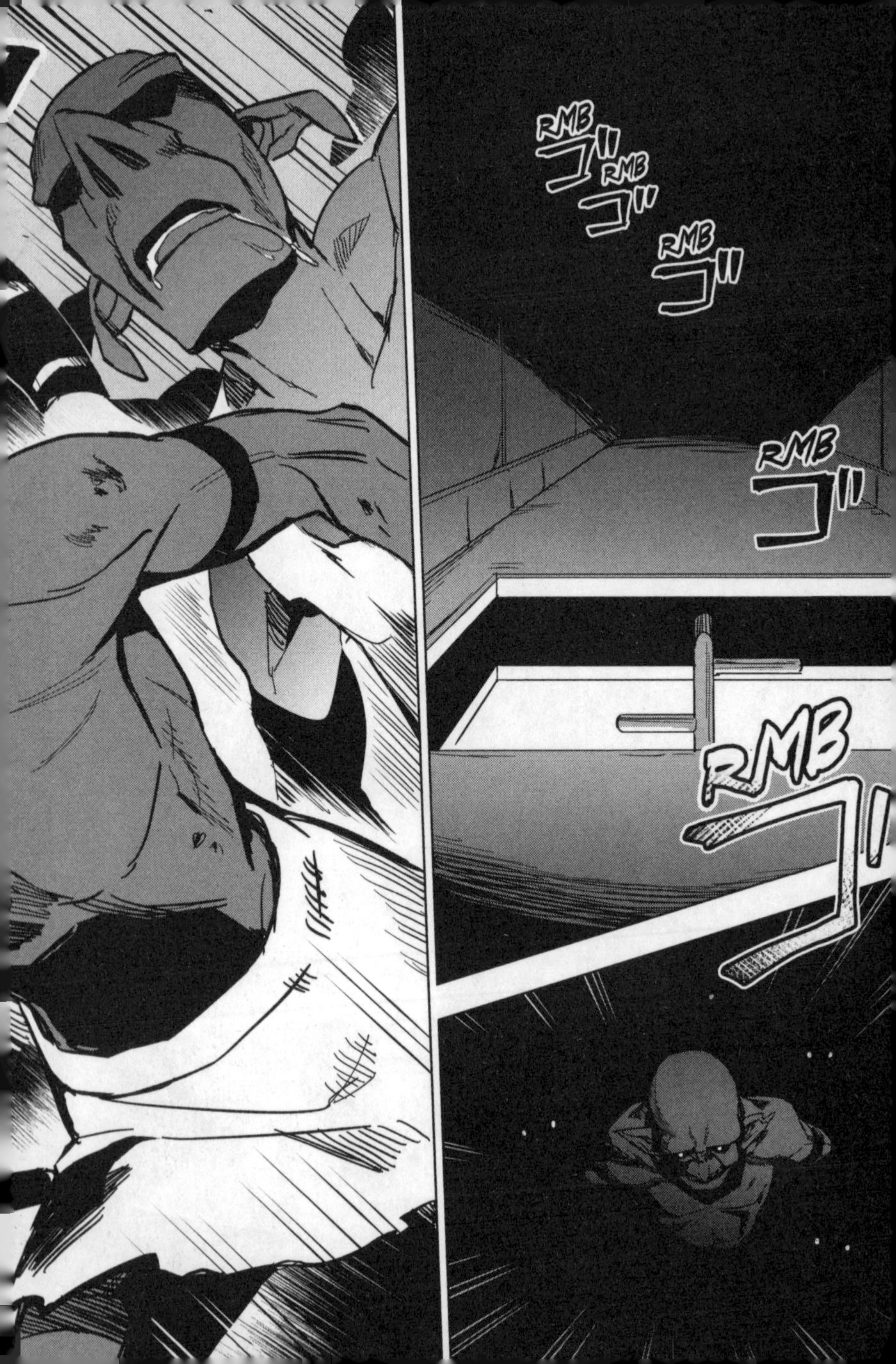
RMB
ゴ
RMB
ゴ
RMB
ゴ
RMB
ゴ
RMB
ゴ

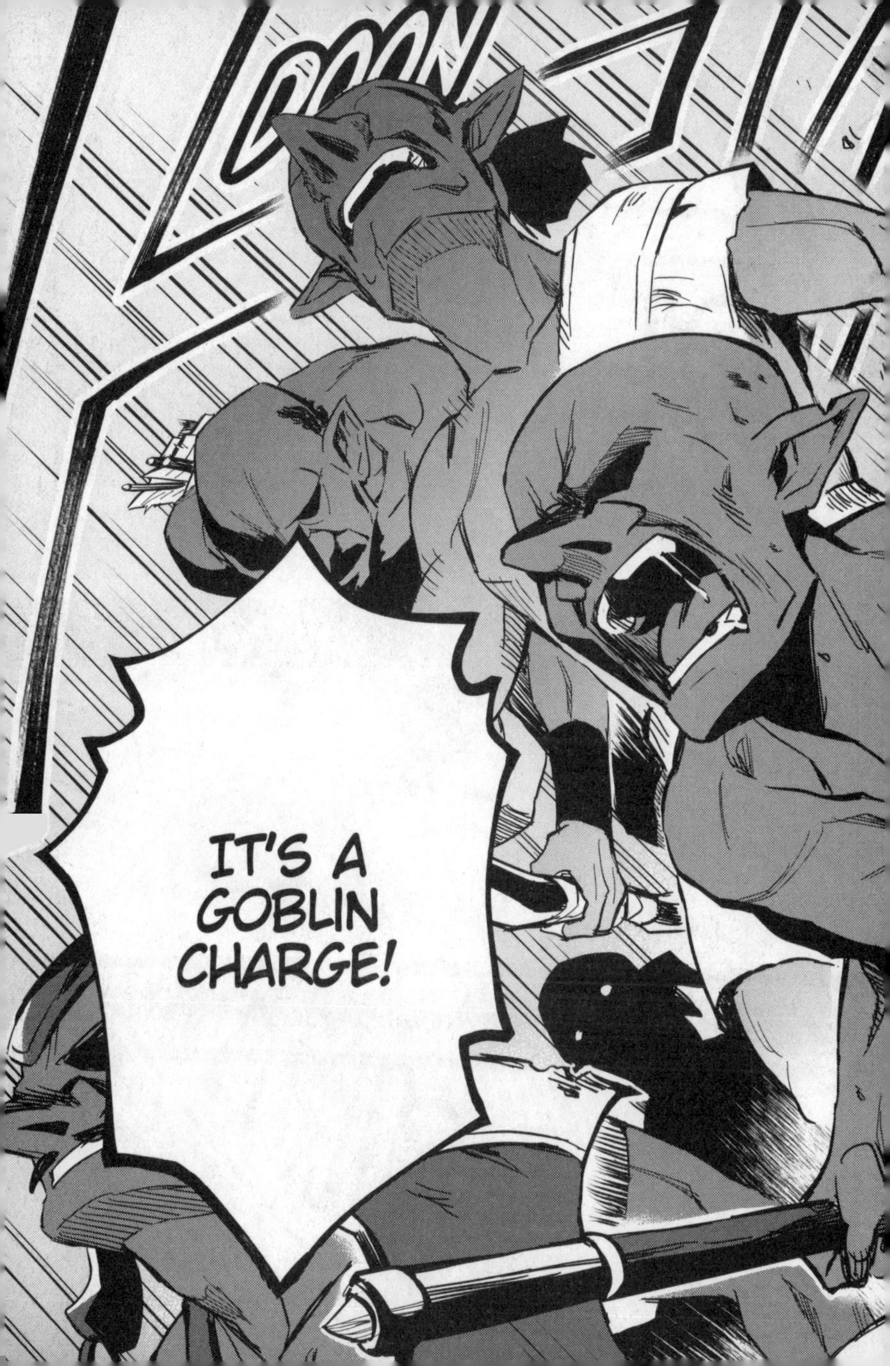
DOON
IT'S A GOBLIN CHARGE!

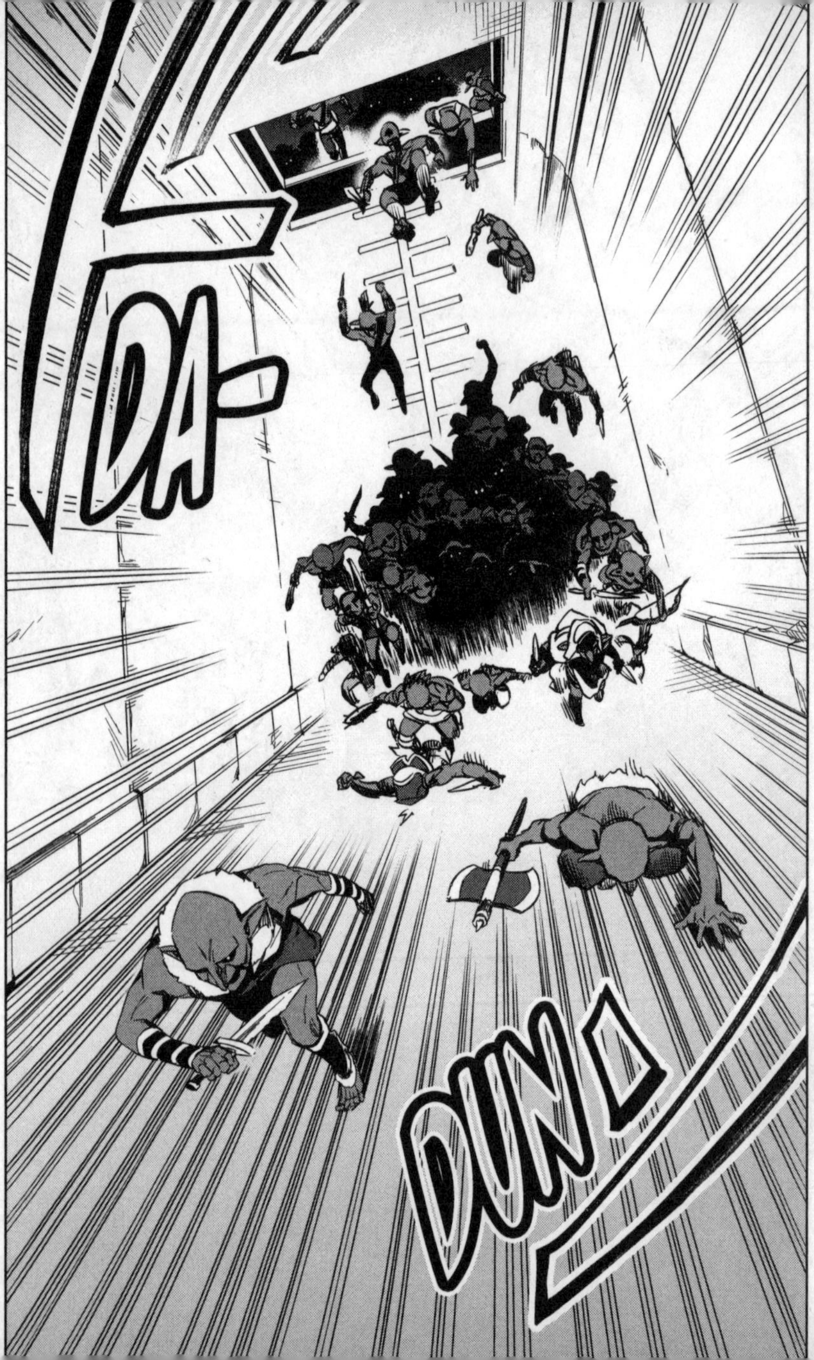
DA-
DUN

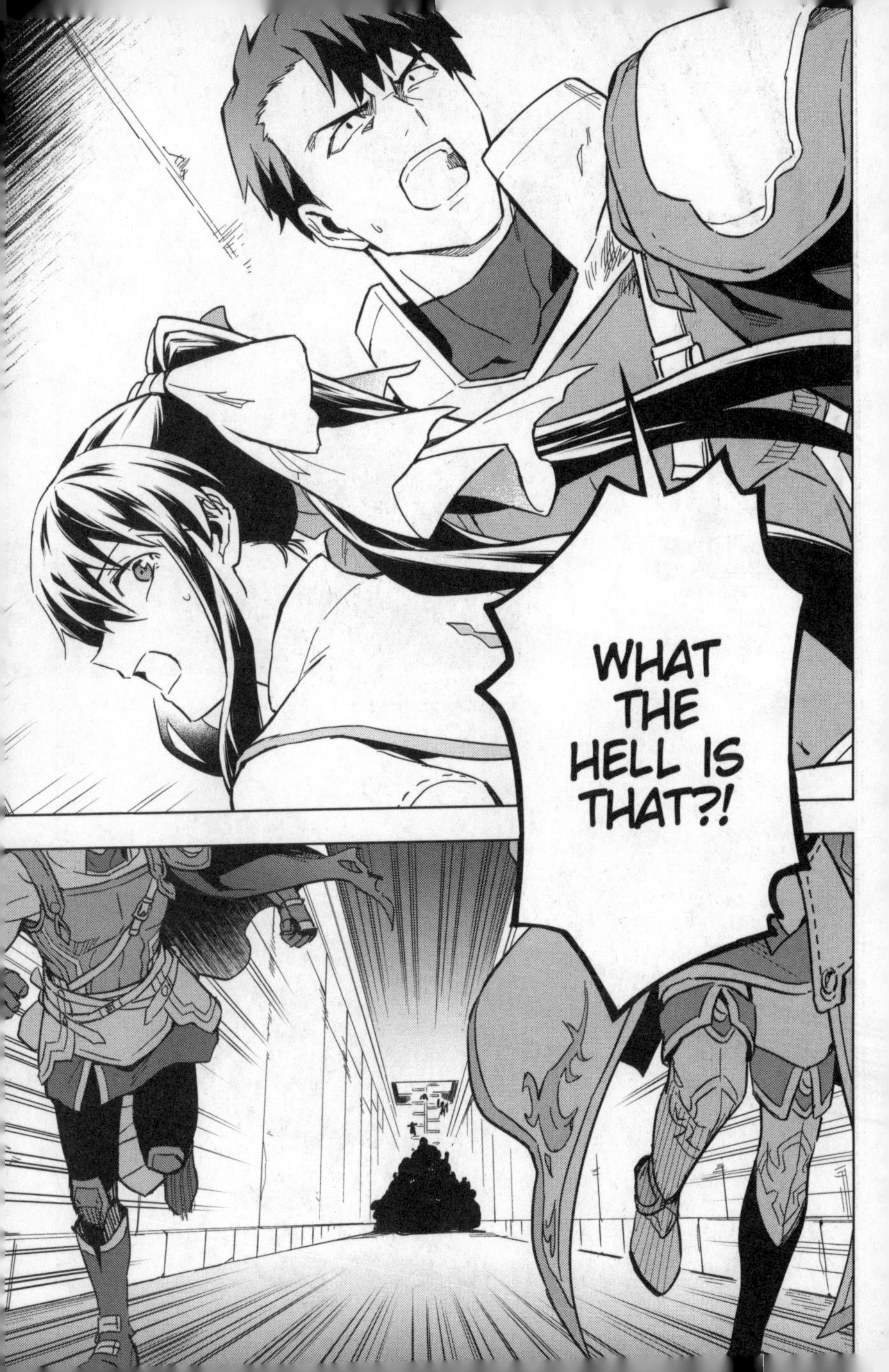
WHAT THE HELL IS THAT?!

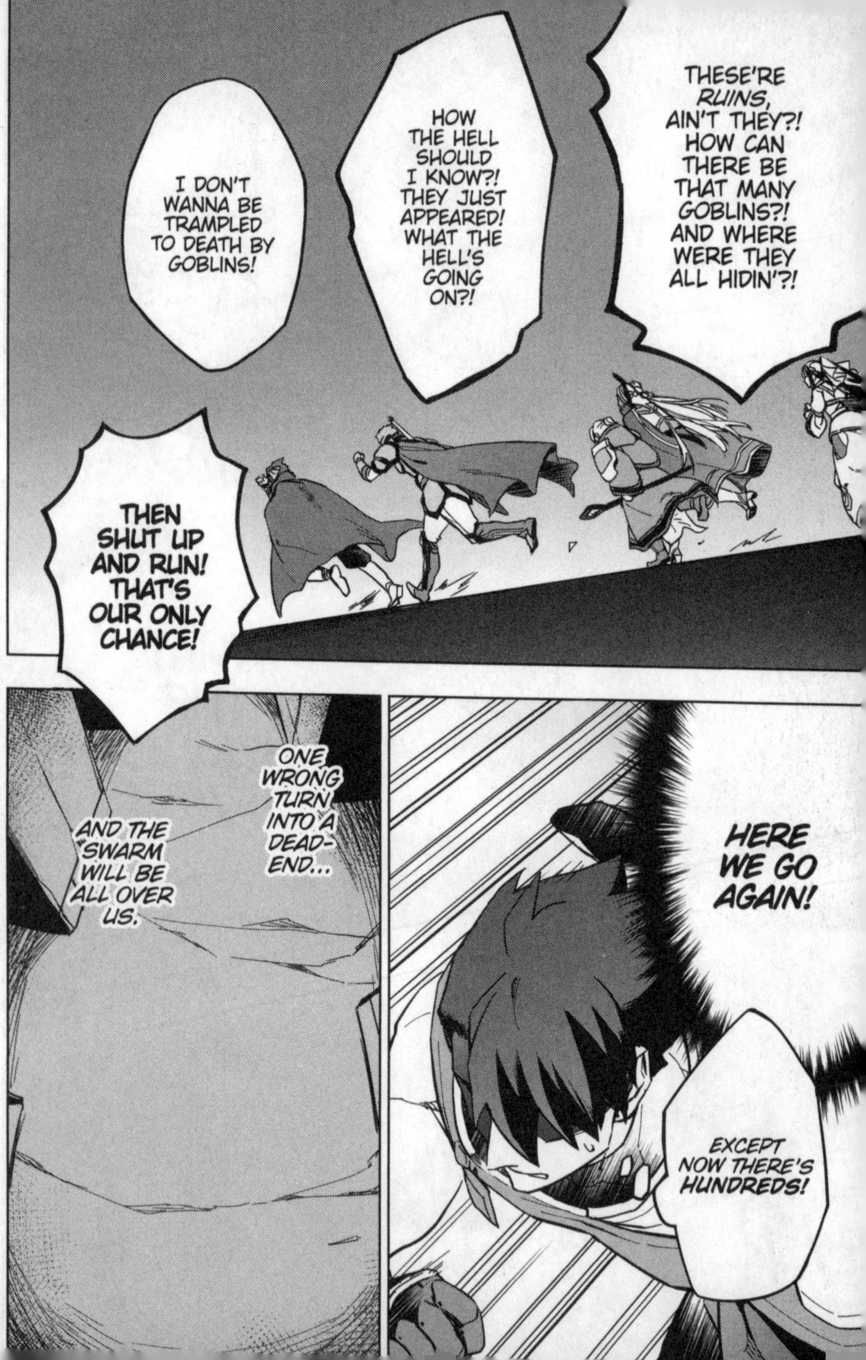
THESE'RE RUINS, AIN'T THEY?! HOW CAN THERE BE THAT MANY GOBLINS?! AND WHERE WERE THEY ALL HIDIN'?!
HOW THE HELL SHOULD I KNOW?! THEY JUST APPEARED! WHAT THE HELL'S GOING ON?!
I DON'T WANNA BE TRAMPLED TO DEATH BY GOBLINS!
THEN SHUT UP AND RUN! THAT'S OUR ONLY CHANCE!
HERE WE GO AGAIN!
EXCEPT NOW THERE'S HUNDREDS!
ONE WRONG TURN INTO A DEAD-END...
AND THE SWARM WILL BE ALL OVER US.

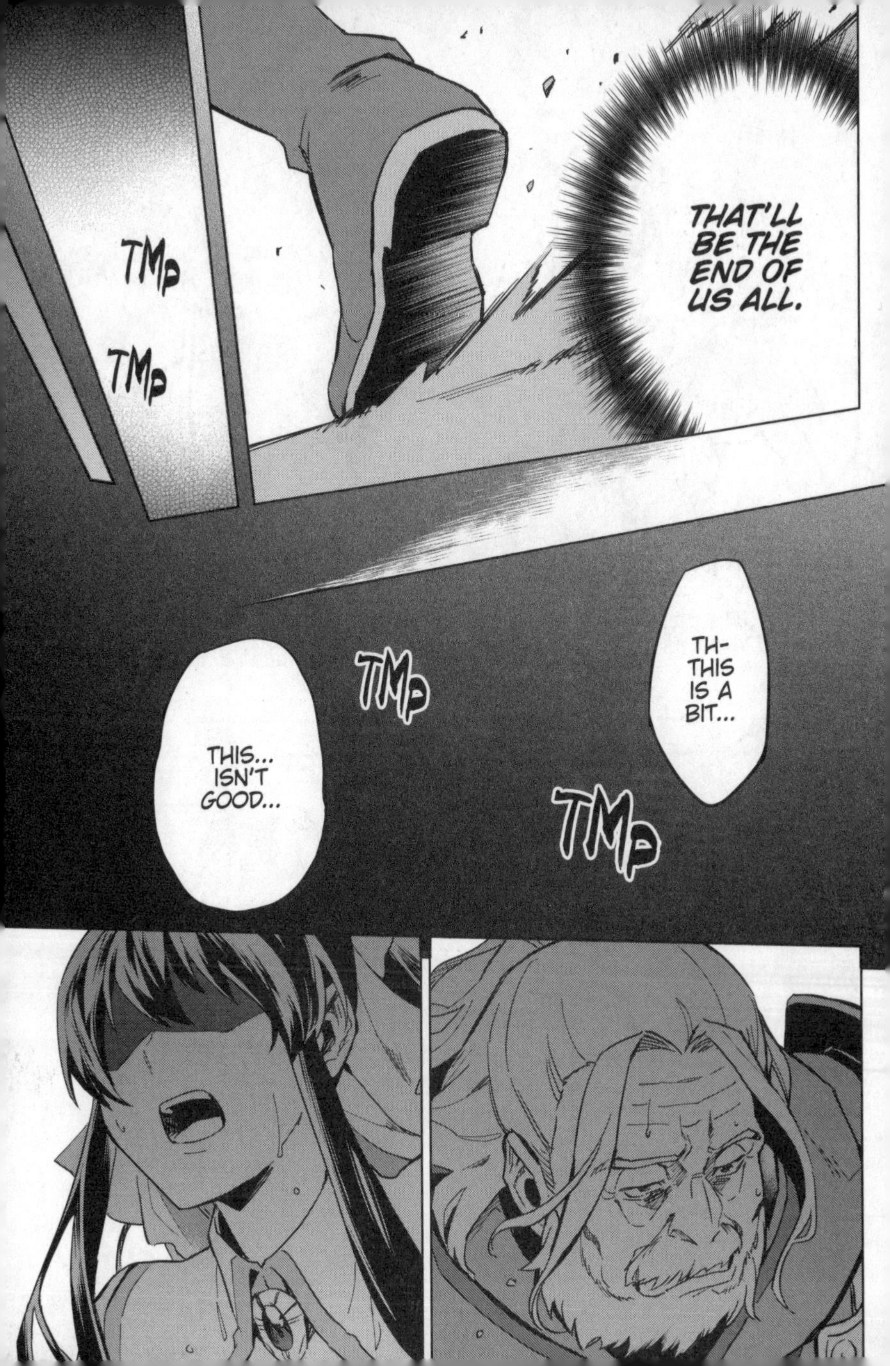
THAT'LL BE THE END OF US ALL.
TMP
TMP
TH- THIS IS A BIT...
TMP
TMP
THIS... ISN'T GOOD...

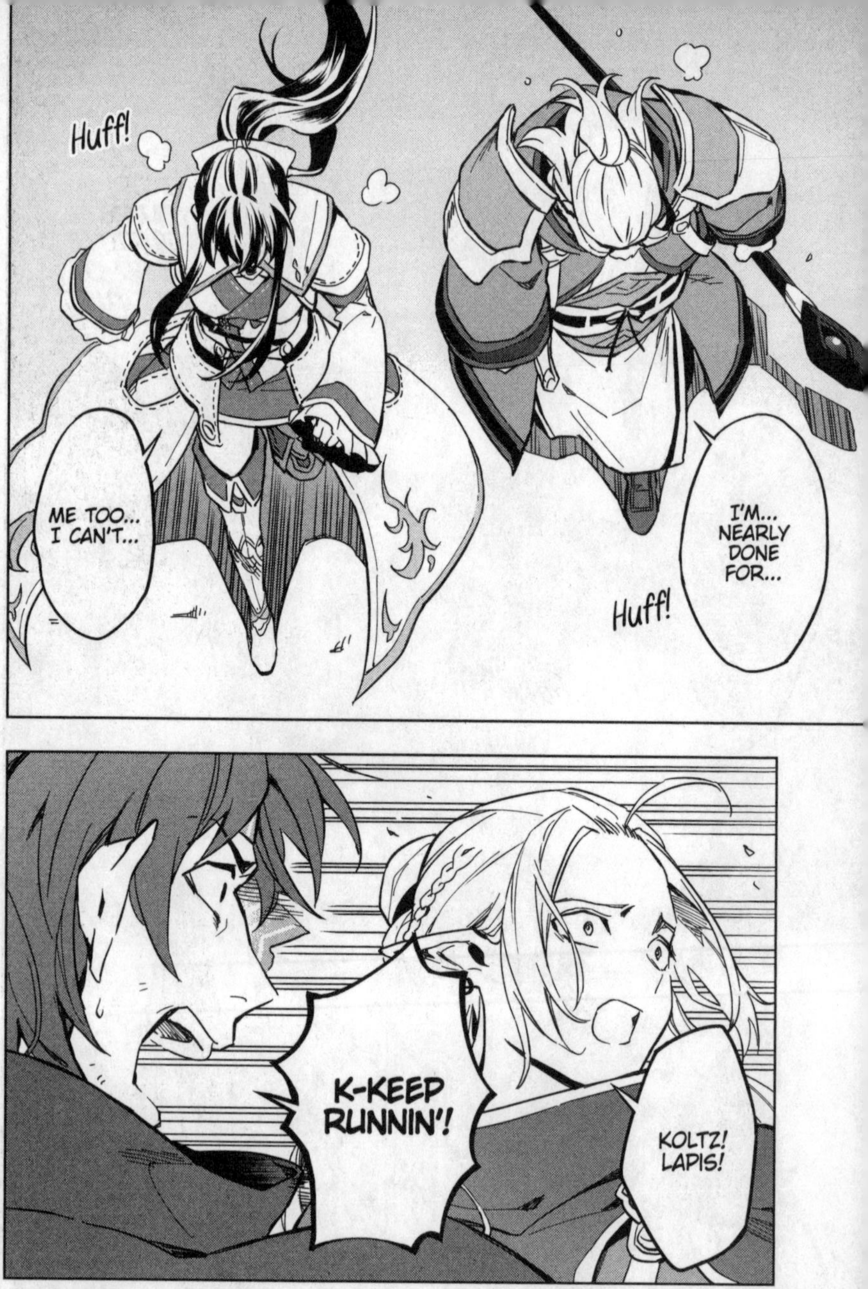
I'M... NEARLY DONE FOR...
Huff!
Huff!
ME TOO... I CAN'T...
KOLTZ! LAPIS!
K-KEEP RUNNIN'!

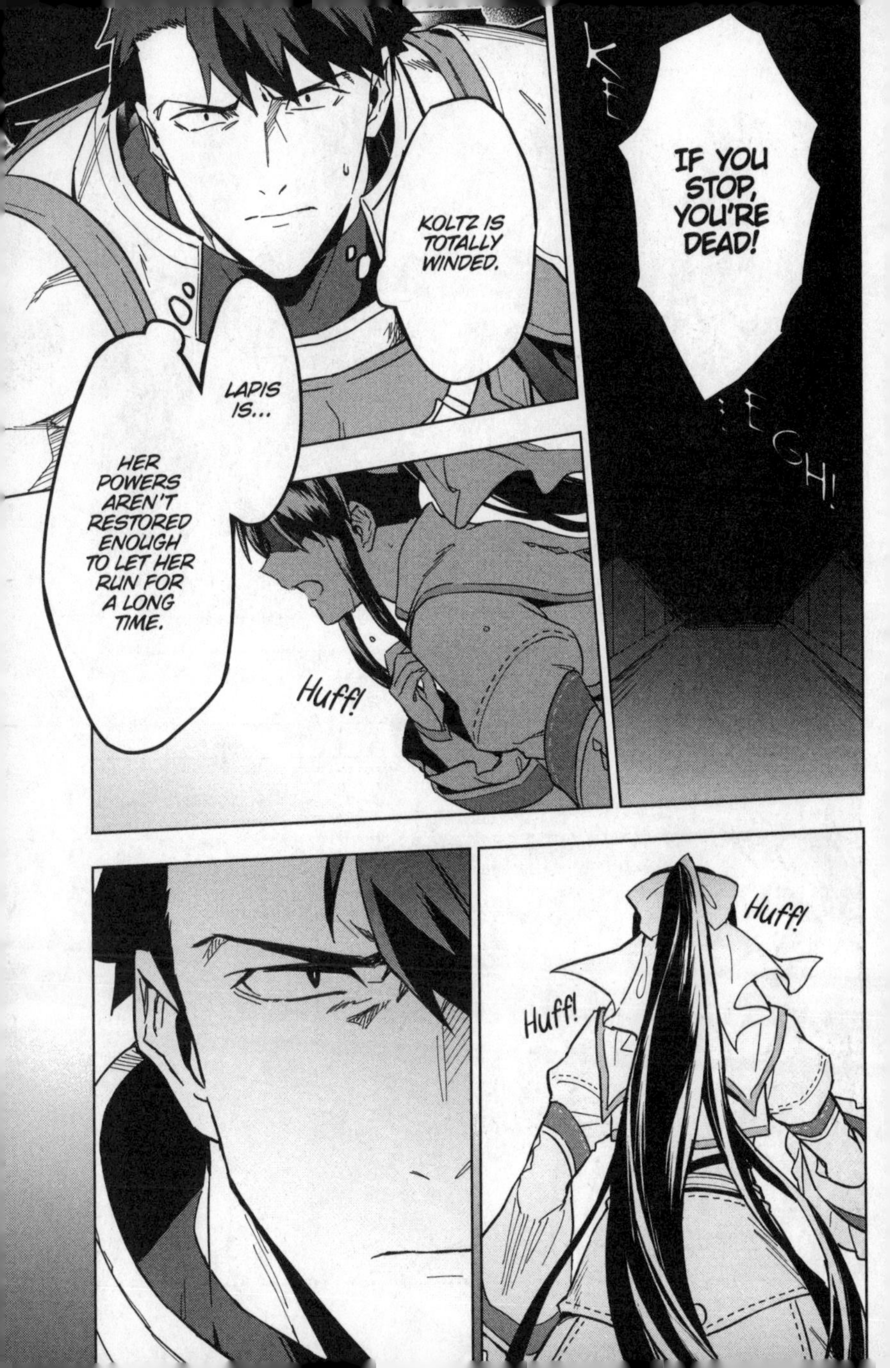
IF YOU STOP, YOU'RE DEAD!
KOLTZ IS TOTALLY WINDED.
LAPIS IS...
HER POWERS AREN'T RESTORED ENOUGH TO LET HER RUN FOR A LONG TIME.
Huff!
Huff!
Huff!

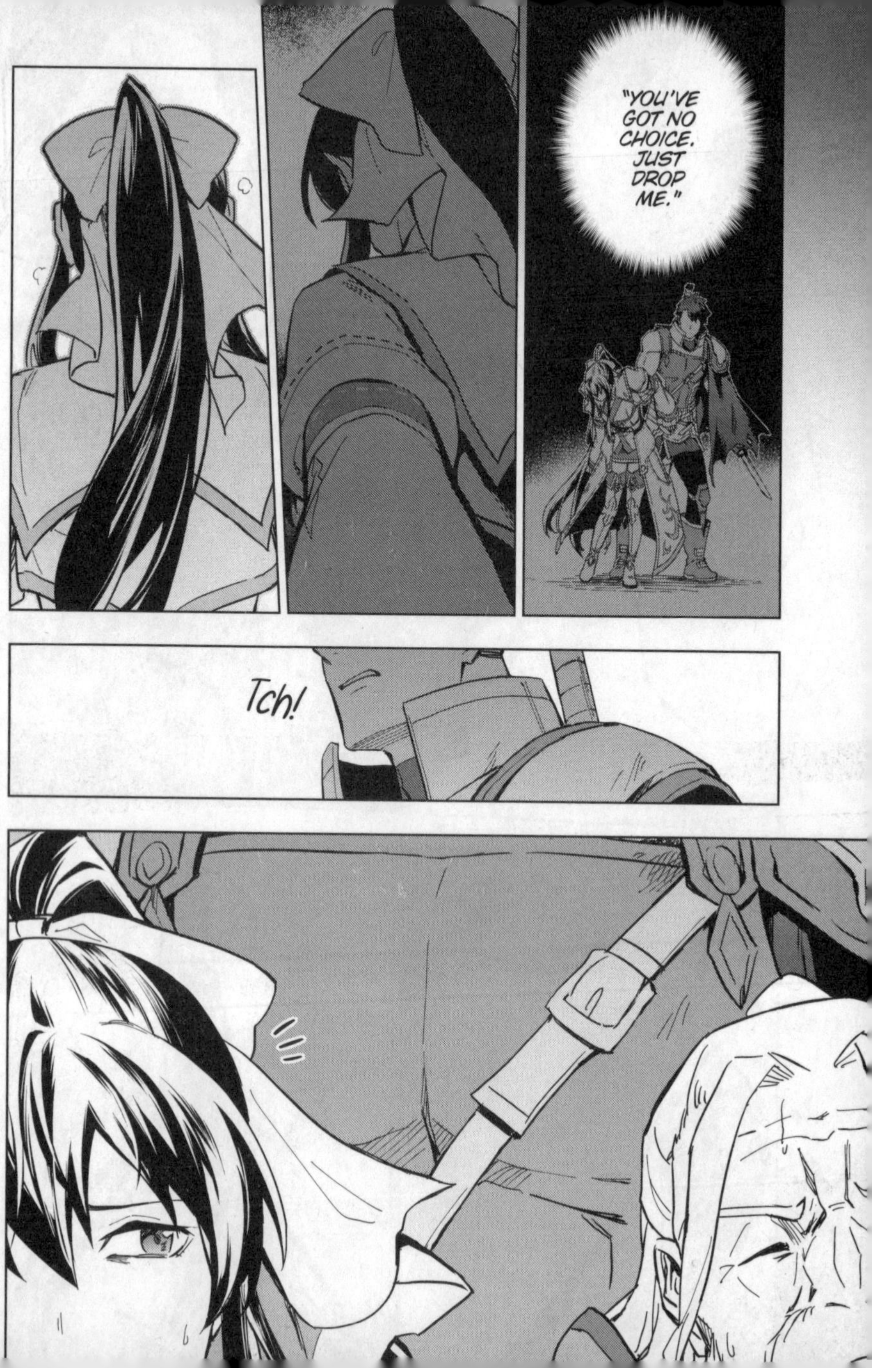
"YOU'VE GOT NO CHOICE. JUST DROP ME."
Tch!

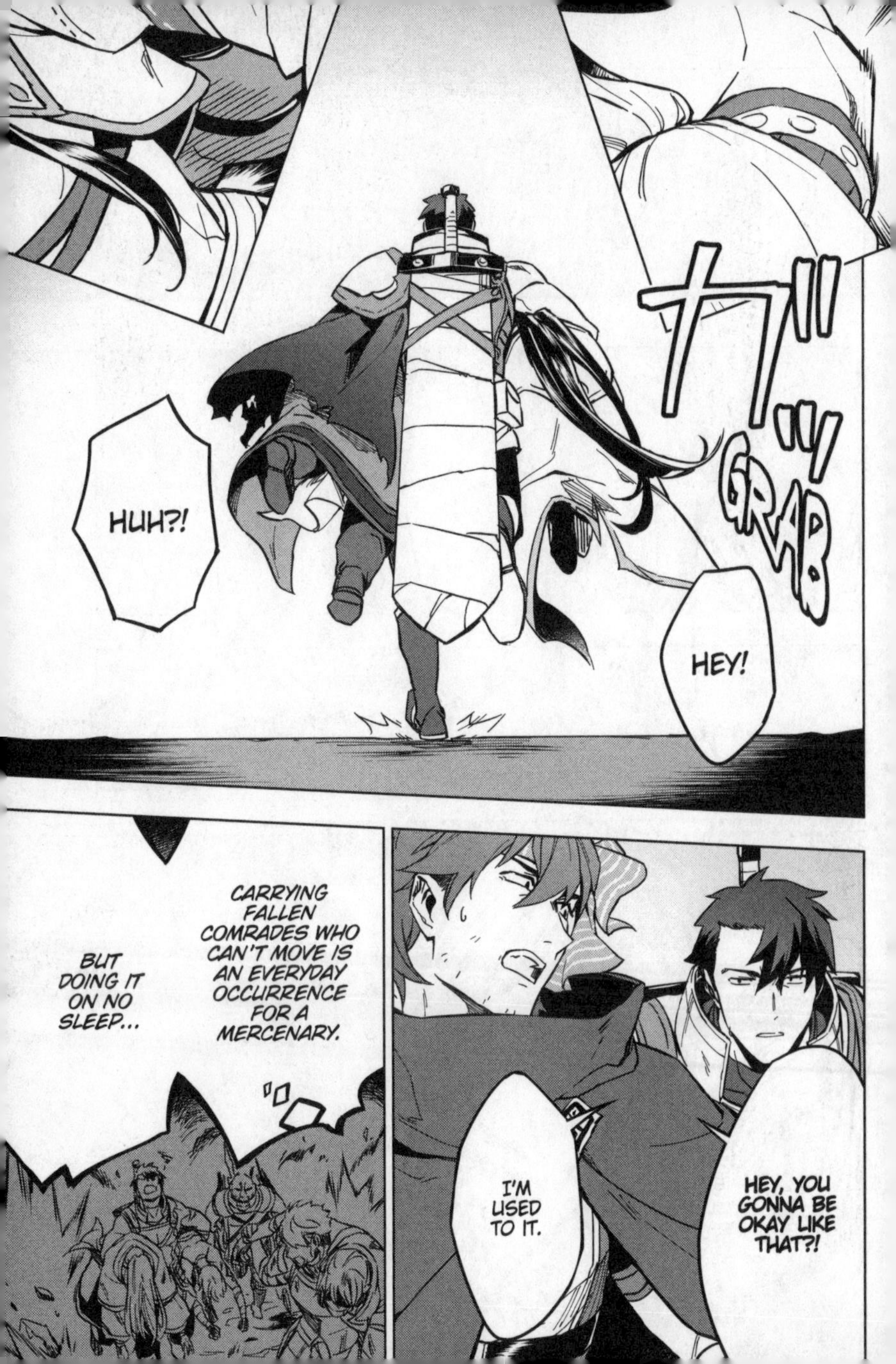
ガッ
GRAB!
HEY!
HUH?!
HEY, YOU GONNA BE OKAY LIKE THAT?!
I'M USED TO IT.
CARRYING FALLEN COMRADES WHO CAN'T MOVE IS AN EVERYDAY OCCURRENCE FOR A MERCENARY.
BUT DOING IT ON NO SLEEP...

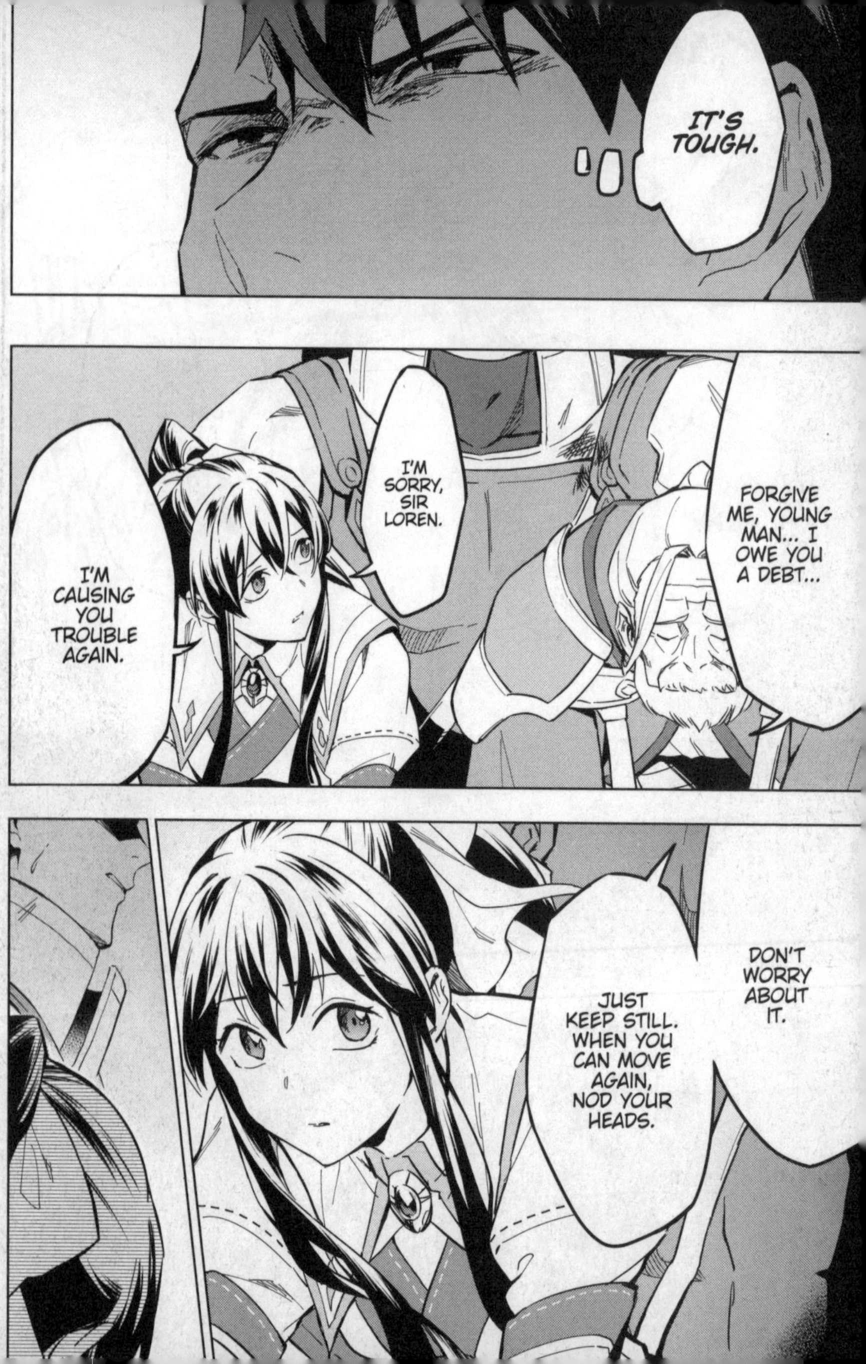
IT'S TOUGH.
FORGIVE ME, YOUNG MAN... I OWE YOU A DEBT...
I'M SORRY, SIR LOREN.
I'M CAUSING YOU TROUBLE AGAIN.
DON'T WORRY ABOUT IT.
JUST KEEP STILL. WHEN YOU CAN MOVE AGAIN, NOD YOUR HEADS.

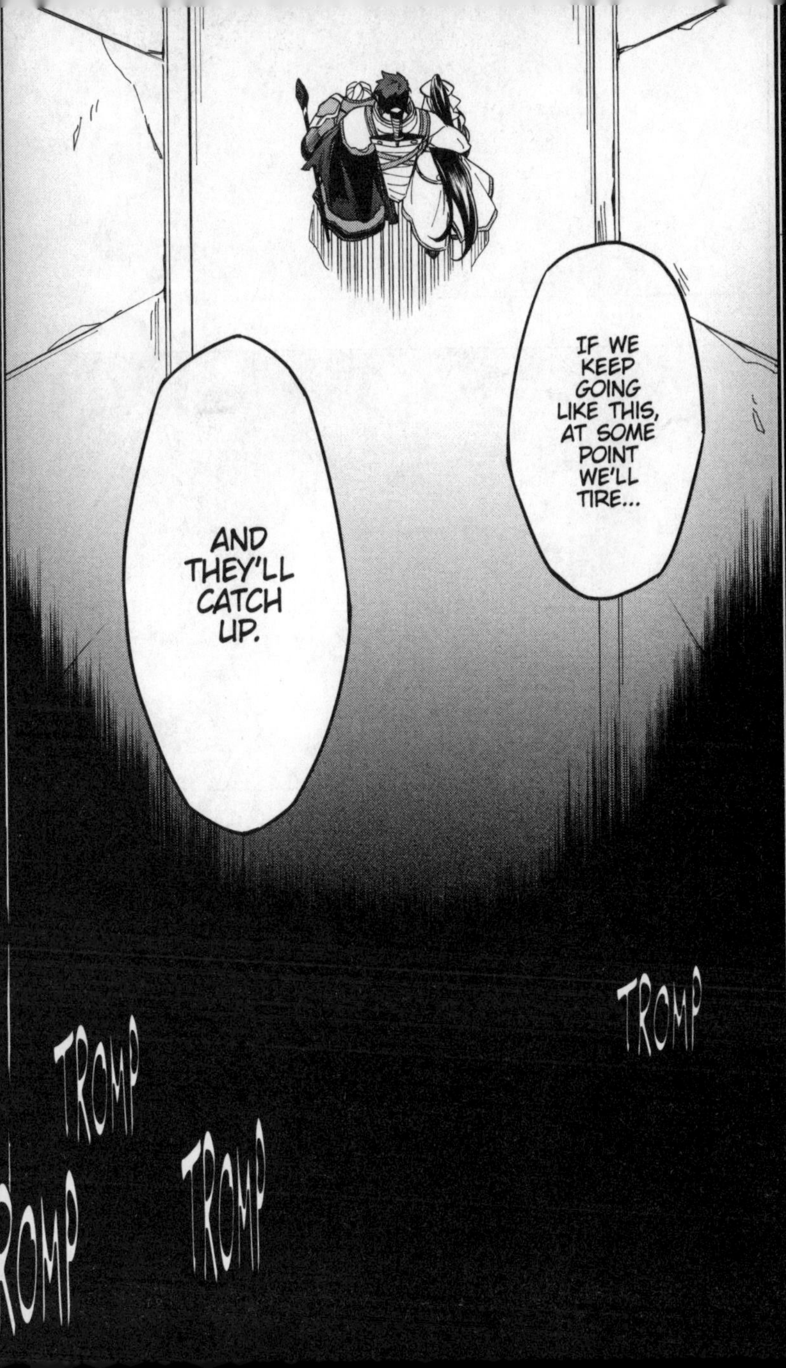
IF WE KEEP GOING LIKE THIS, AT SOME POINT WE'LL TIRE...
AND THEY'LL CATCH UP.
TROMP
TROMP
TROMP
TROMP

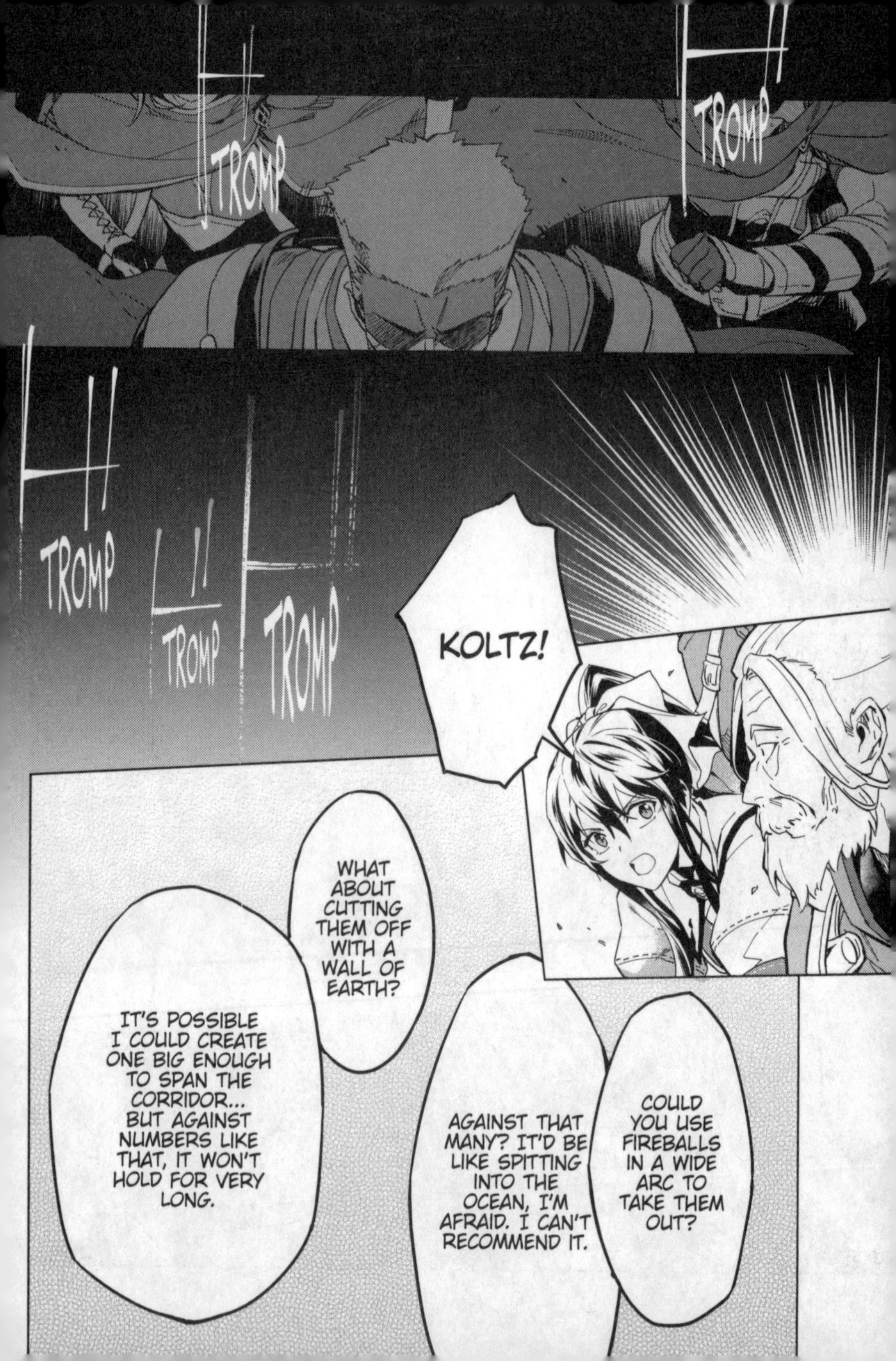
TROMP
TROMP
TROMP
TROMP
TROMP
KOLTZ!
COULD YOU USE FIREBALLS IN A WIDE ARC TO TAKE THEM OUT?
AGAINST THAT MANY? IT'D BE LIKE SPITTING INTO THE OCEAN, I'M AFRAID. I CAN'T RECOMMEND IT.
WHAT ABOUT CUTTING THEM OFF WITH A WALL OF EARTH?
IT'S POSSIBLE I COULD CREATE ONE BIG ENOUGH TO SPAN THE CORRIDOR... BUT AGAINST NUMBERS LIKE THAT, IT WON'T HOLD FOR VERY LONG.

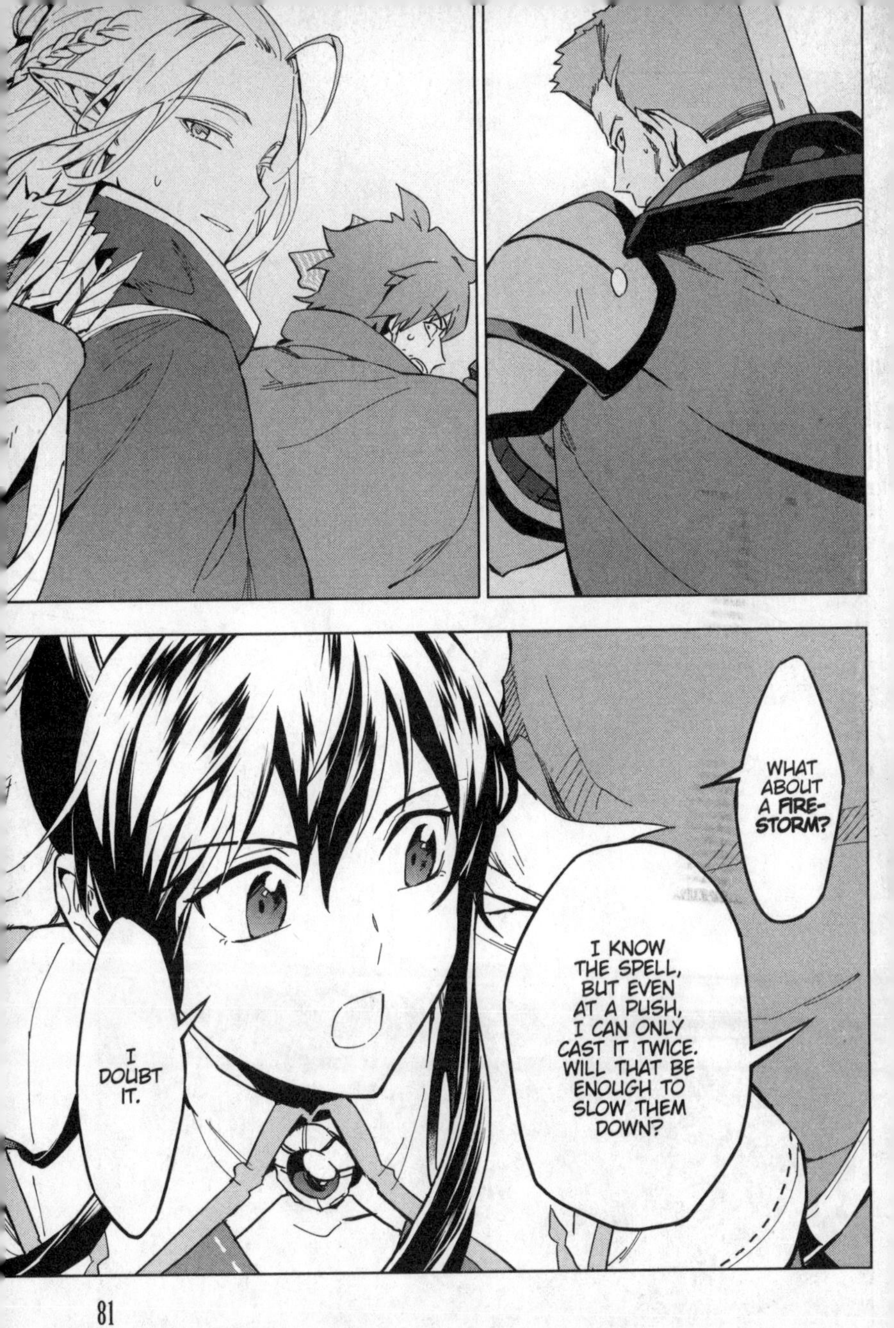
WHAT ABOUT A FIRE-STORM?
I KNOW THE SPELL, BUT EVEN AT A PUSH, I CAN ONLY CAST IT TWICE. WILL THAT BE ENOUGH TO SLOW THEM DOWN?
I DOUBT IT.

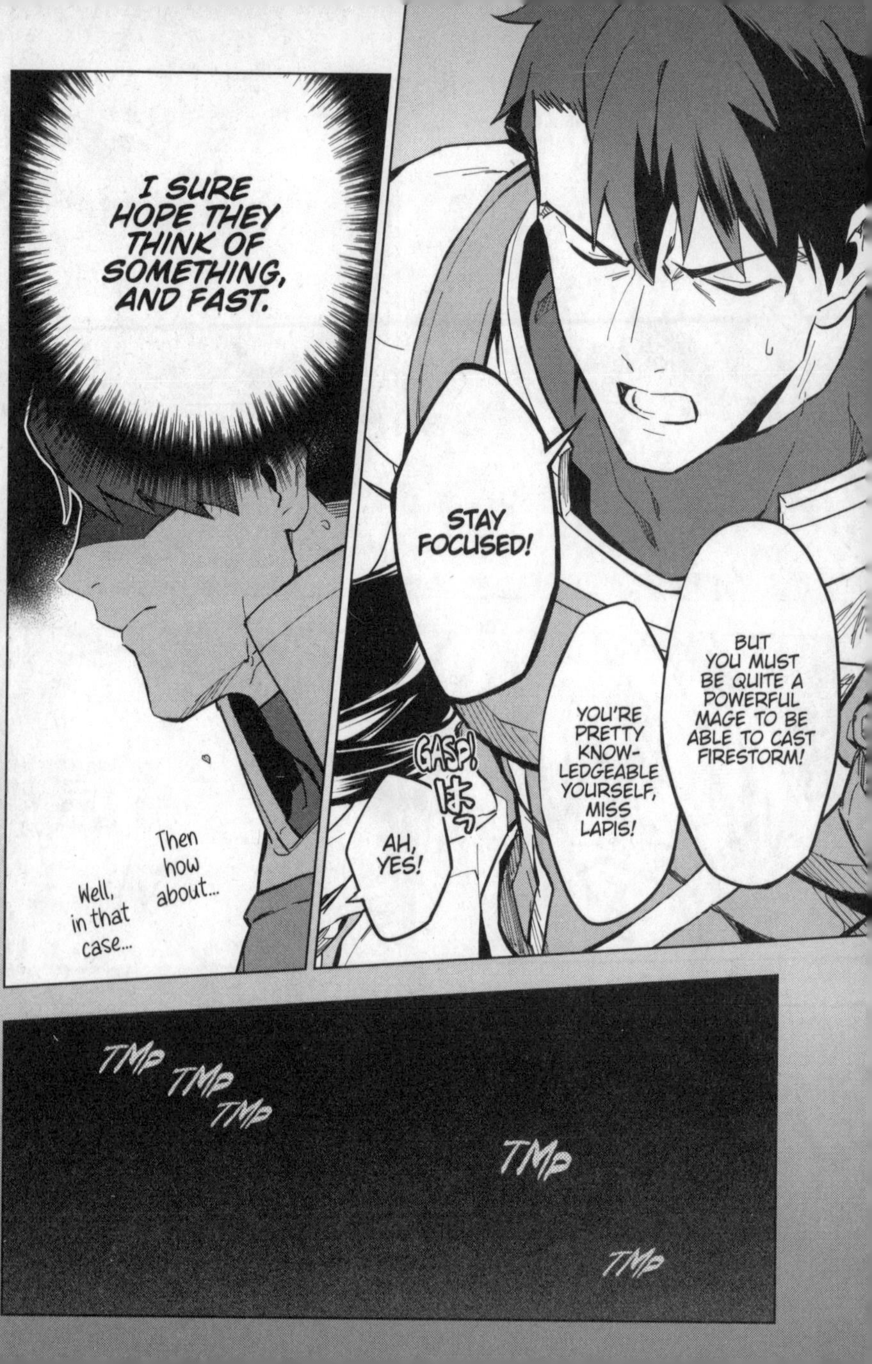
BUT YOU MUST BE QUITE A POWERFUL MAGE TO BE ABLE TO CAST FIRESTORM!
YOU'RE PRETTY KNOW-LEDGEABLE YOURSELF, MISS LAPIS!
STAY FOCUSED!
GASP! はっ
AH, YES!
I SURE HOPE THEY THINK OF SOMETHING, AND FAST.
Then how about...
Well, in that case...
TMP TMP TMP
TMP
TMP

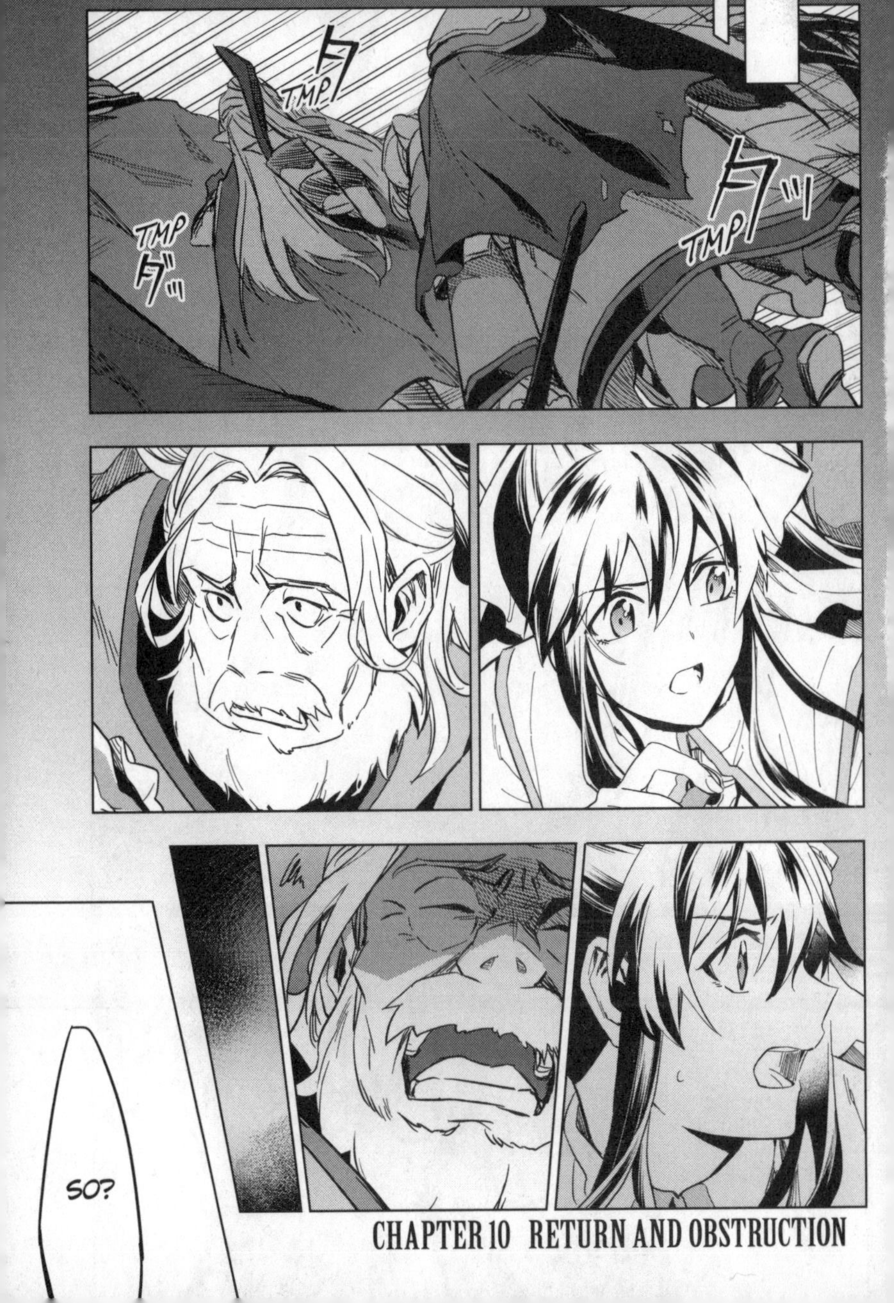
TMP
TMP
TMP
SO?

CHAPTER 10 RETURN AND OBSTRUCTION

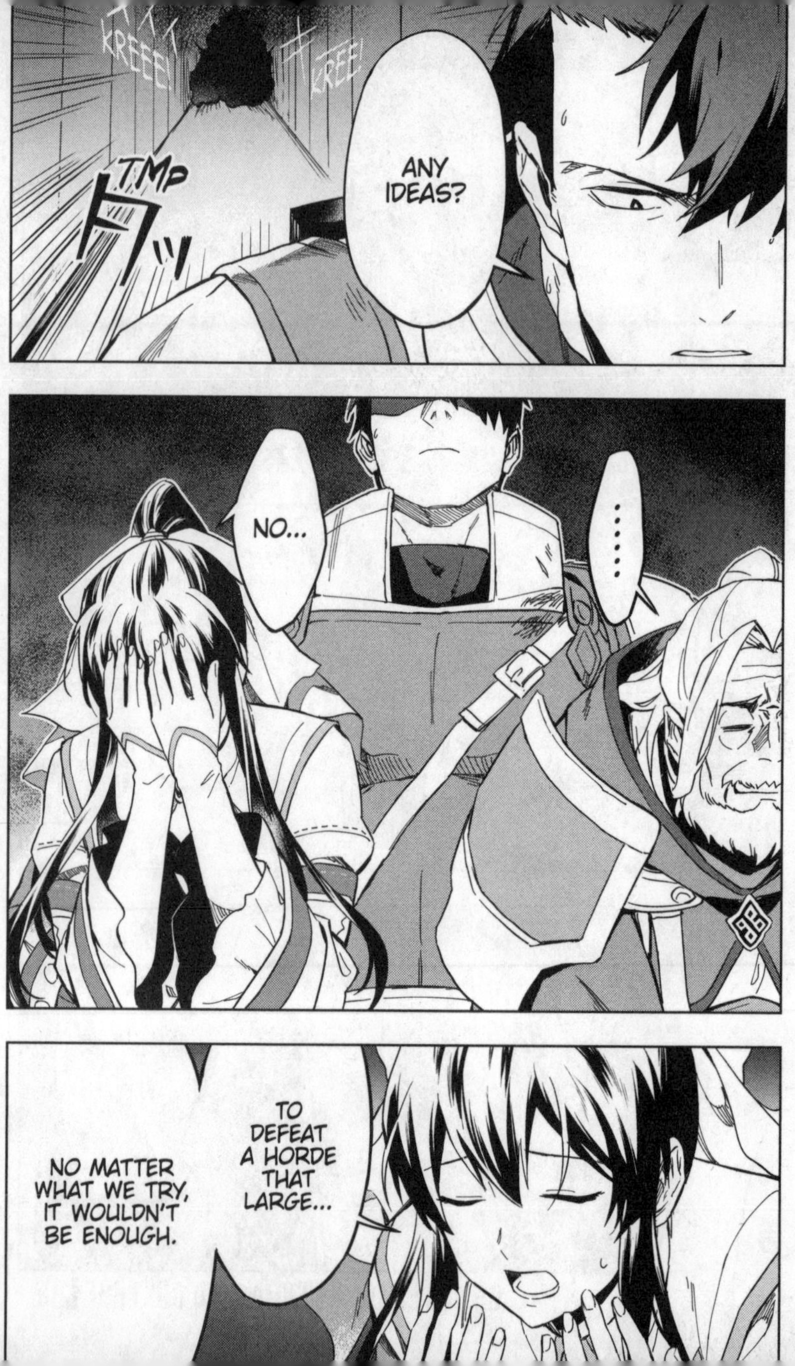
KREE!
KREEE!
ANY IDEAS?
TMP
......
NO...
TO DEFEAT A HORDE THAT LARGE...
NO MATTER WHAT WE TRY, IT WOULDN'T BE ENOUGH.

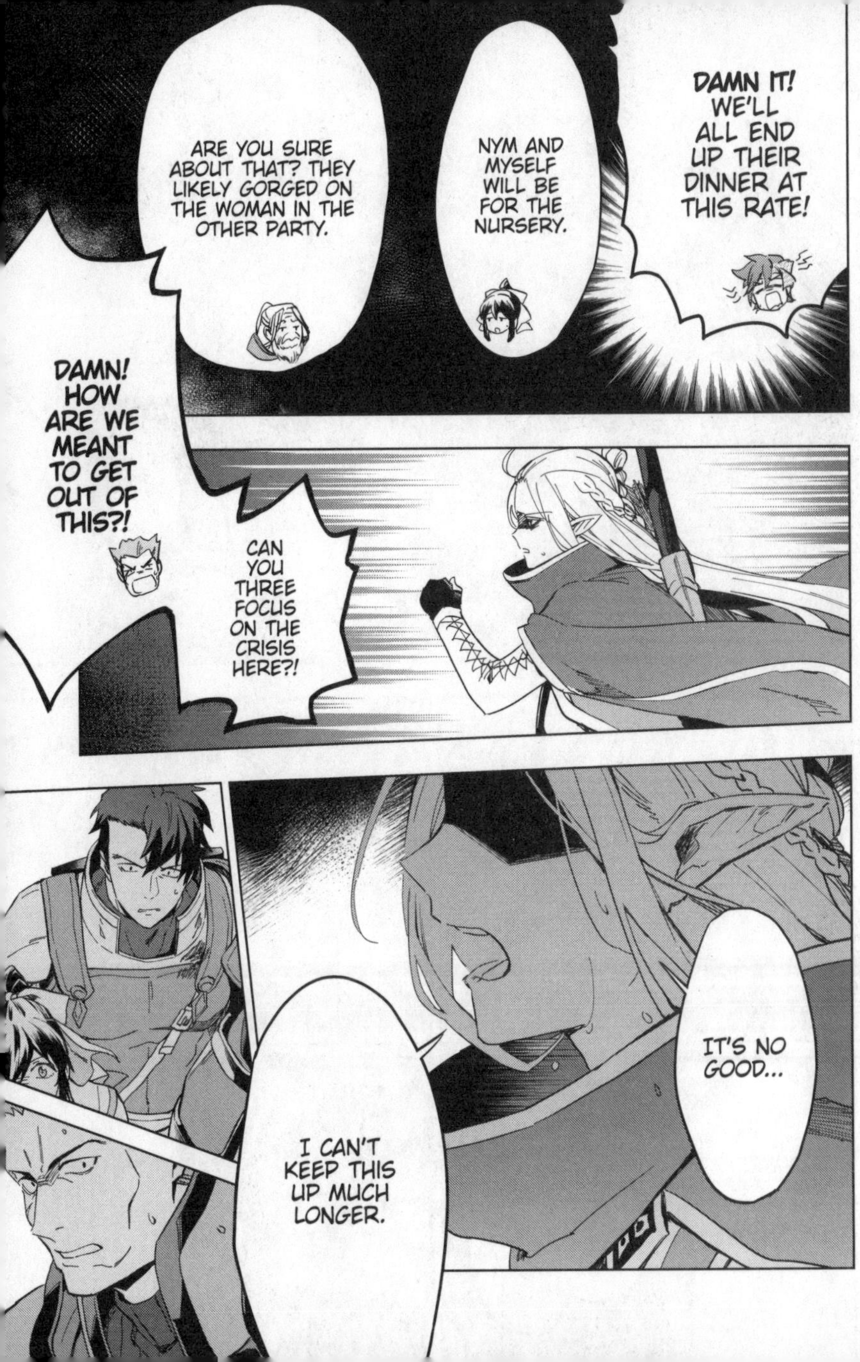
DAMN IT! WE'LL ALL END UP THEIR DINNER AT THIS RATE!
NYM AND MYSELF WILL BE FOR THE NURSERY.
ARE YOU SURE ABOUT THAT? THEY LIKELY GORGED ON THE WOMAN IN THE OTHER PARTY.
DAMN! HOW ARE WE MEANT TO GET OUT OF THIS?!
CAN YOU THREE FOCUS ON THE CRISIS HERE?!
IT'S NO GOOD...
I CAN'T KEEP THIS UP MUCH LONGER.

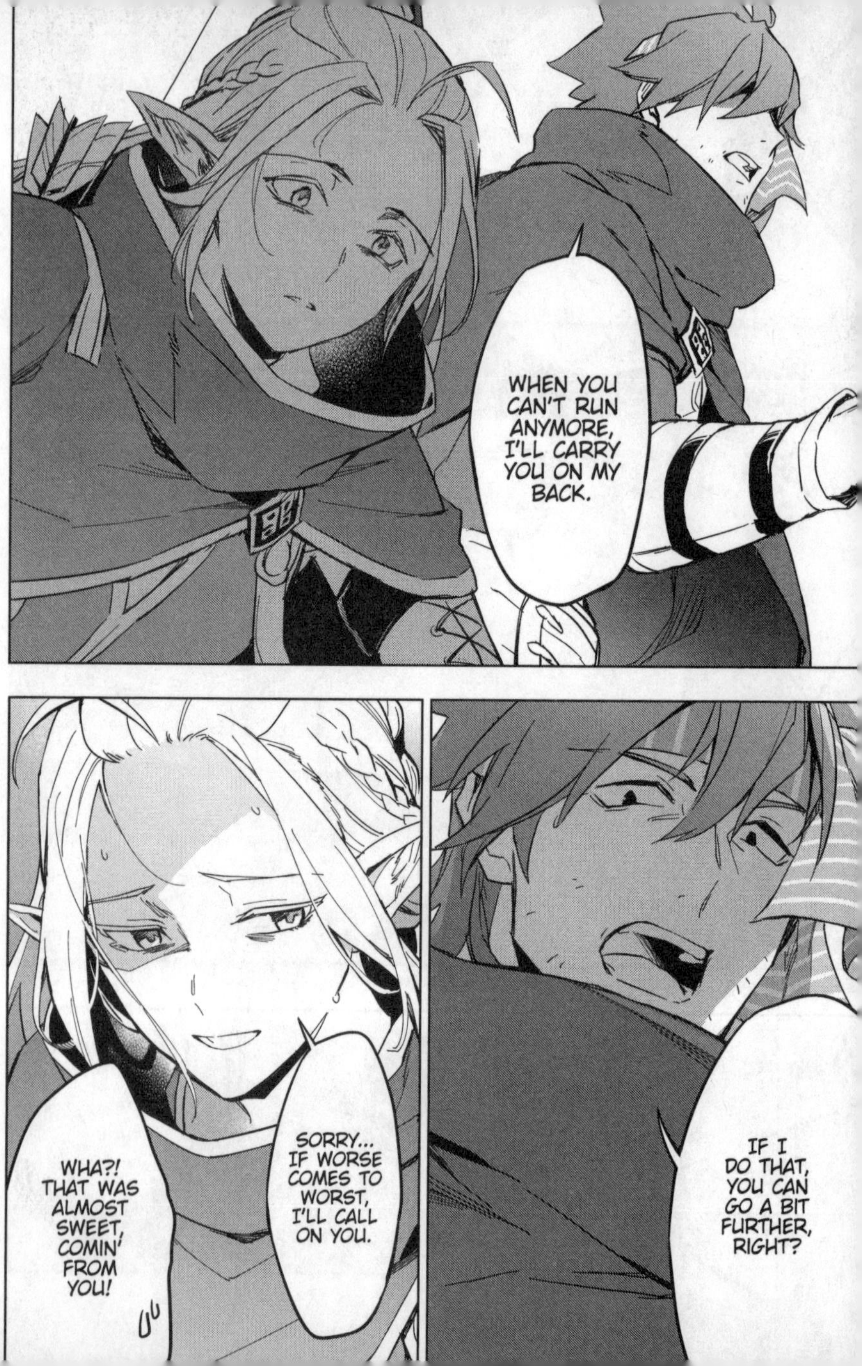
WHEN YOU CAN'T RUN ANYMORE, I'LL CARRY YOU ON MY BACK.
IF I DO THAT, YOU CAN GO A BIT FURTHER, RIGHT?
SORRY... IF WORSE COMES TO WORST, I'LL CALL ON YOU.
WHA?! THAT WAS ALMOST SWEET, COMIN' FROM YOU!

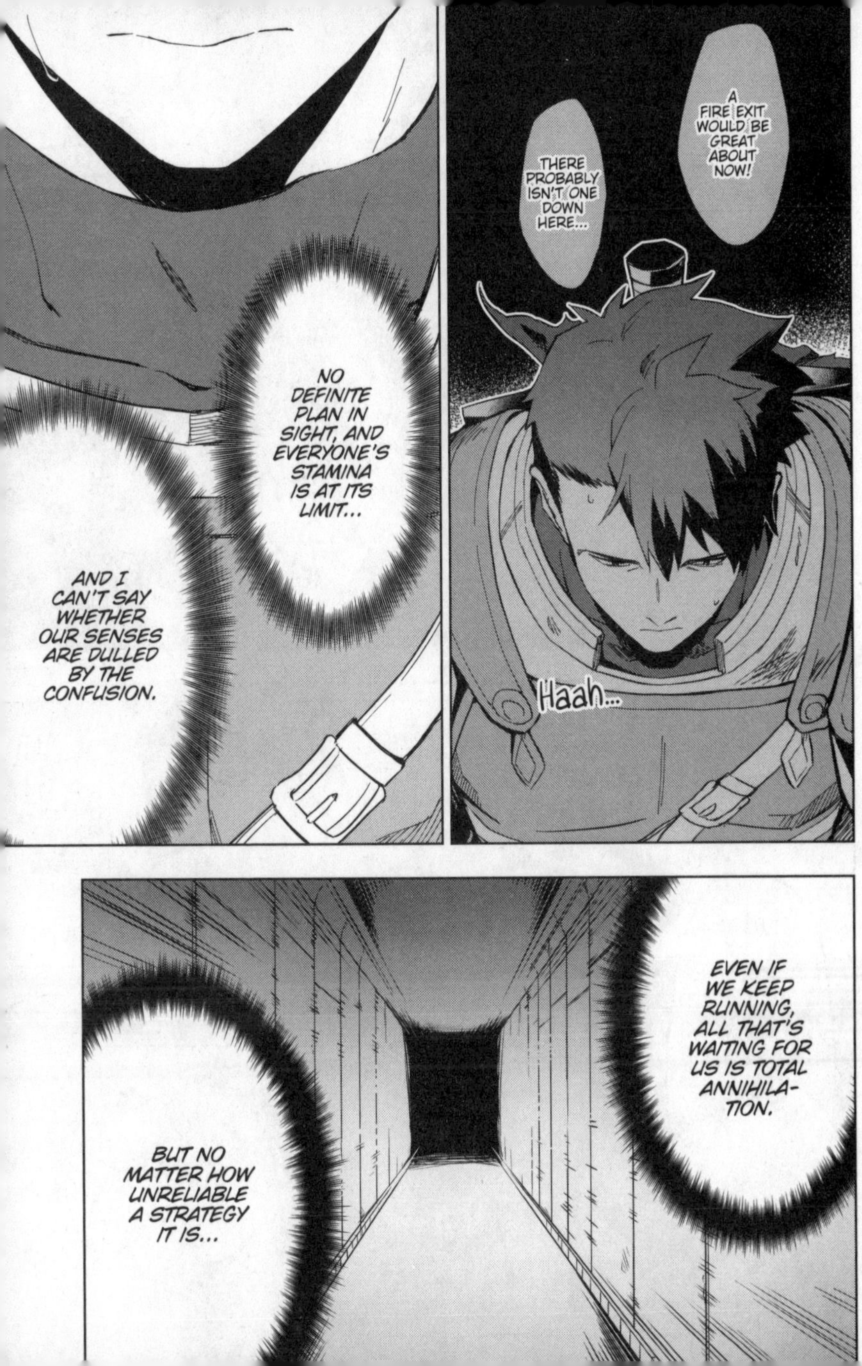
A FIRE EXIT WOULD BE GREAT ABOUT NOW!
THERE PROBABLY ISN'T ONE DOWN HERE...
Haah...
NO DEFINITE PLAN IN SIGHT, AND EVERYONE'S STAMINA IS AT ITS LIMIT...
AND I CAN'T SAY WHETHER OUR SENSES ARE DULLED BY THE CONFUSION.
EVEN IF WE KEEP RUNNING, ALL THAT'S WAITING FOR US IS TOTAL ANNIHILA-TION.
BUT NO MATTER HOW UNRELIABLE A STRATEGY IT IS...

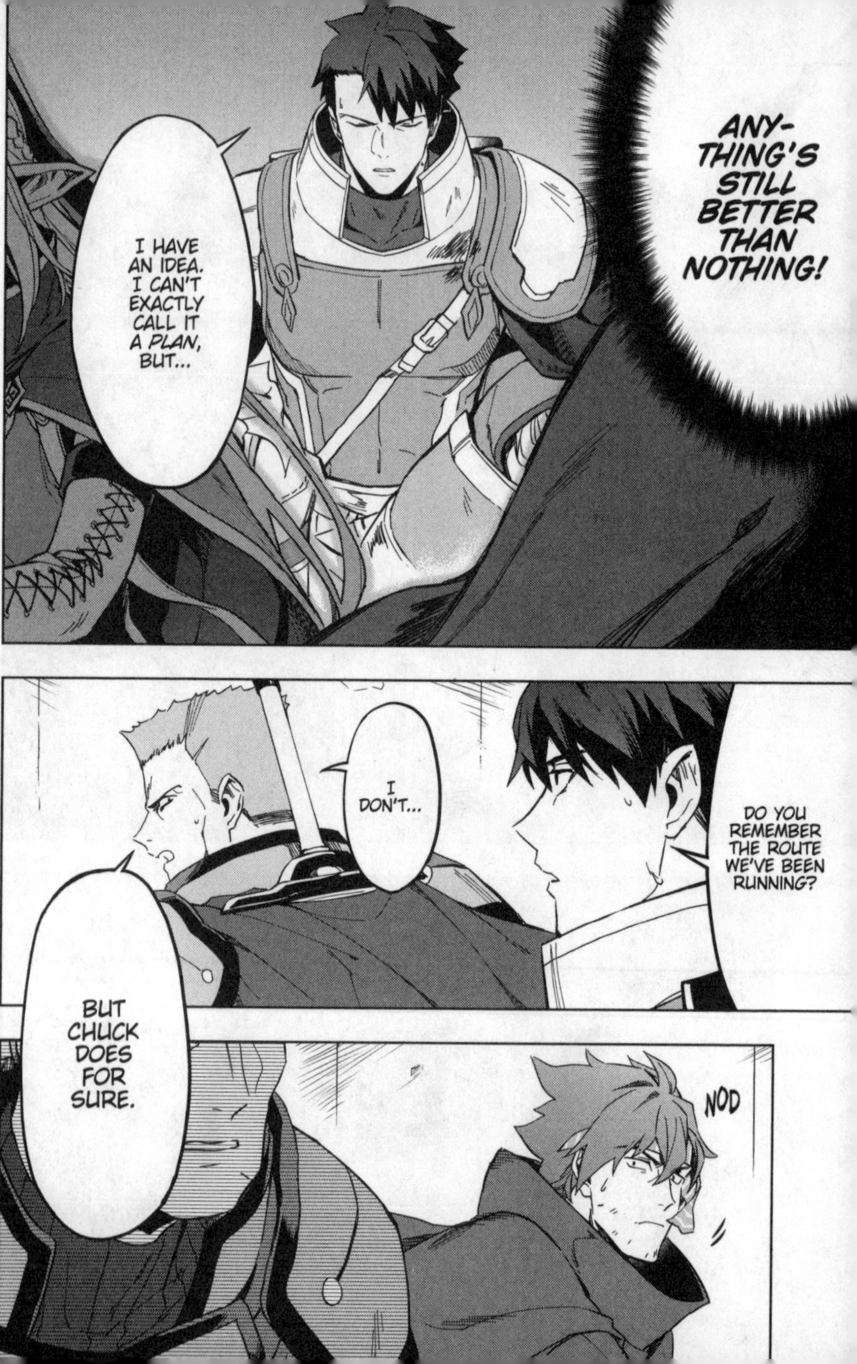
ANY-THING'S STILL BETTER THAN NOTHING!
I HAVE AN IDEA. I CAN'T EXACTLY CALL IT A *PLAN*, BUT...
DO YOU REMEMBER THE ROUTE WE'VE BEEN RUNNING?
I DON'T...
BUT CHUCK DOES FOR SURE.
NOD

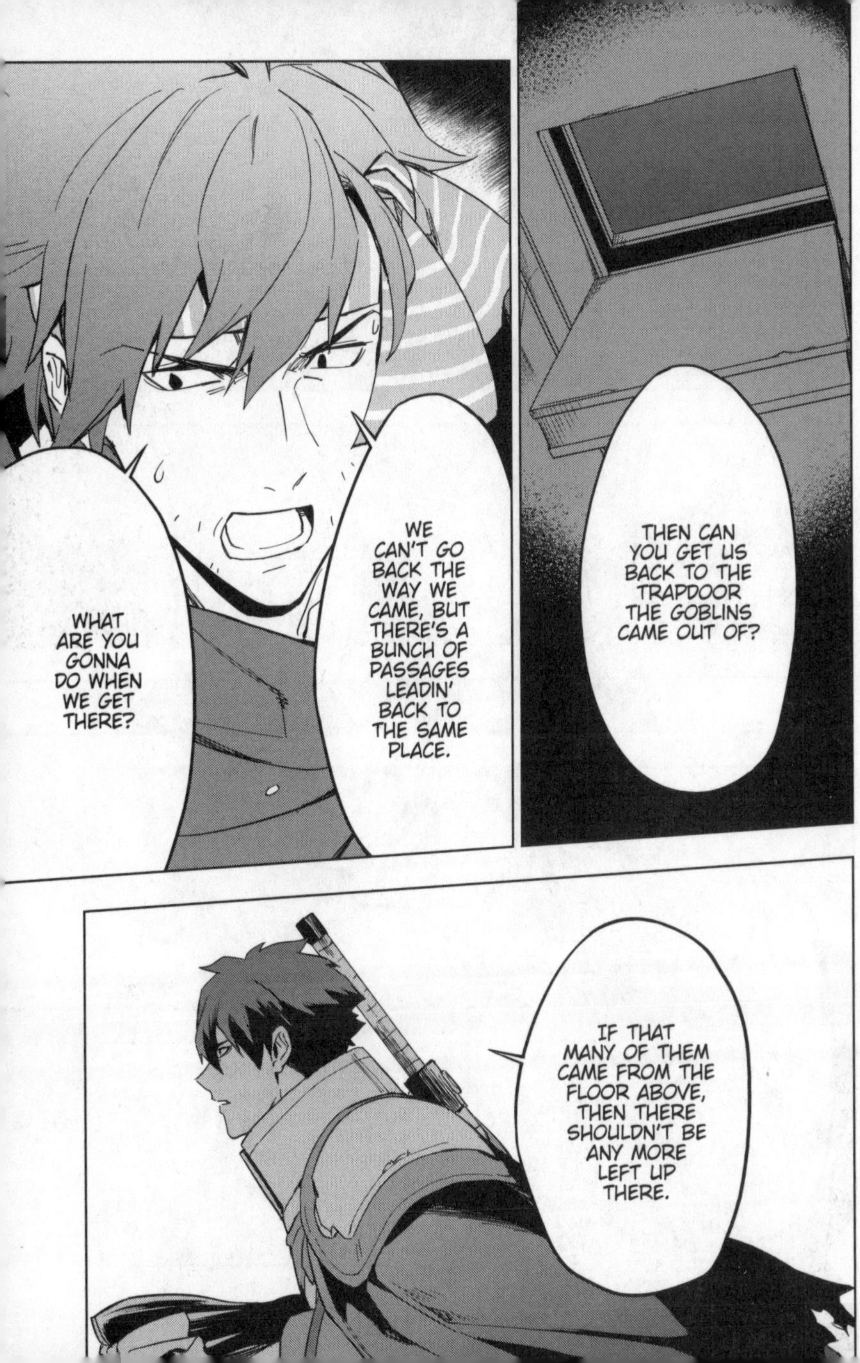
THEN CAN YOU GET US BACK TO THE TRAPDOOR THE GOBLINS CAME OUT OF?
WE CAN'T GO BACK THE WAY WE CAME, BUT THERE'S A BUNCH OF PASSAGES LEADIN' BACK TO THE SAME PLACE.
WHAT ARE YOU GONNA DO WHEN WE GET THERE?
IF THAT MANY OF THEM CAME FROM THE FLOOR ABOVE, THEN THERE SHOULDN'T BE ANY MORE LEFT UP THERE.

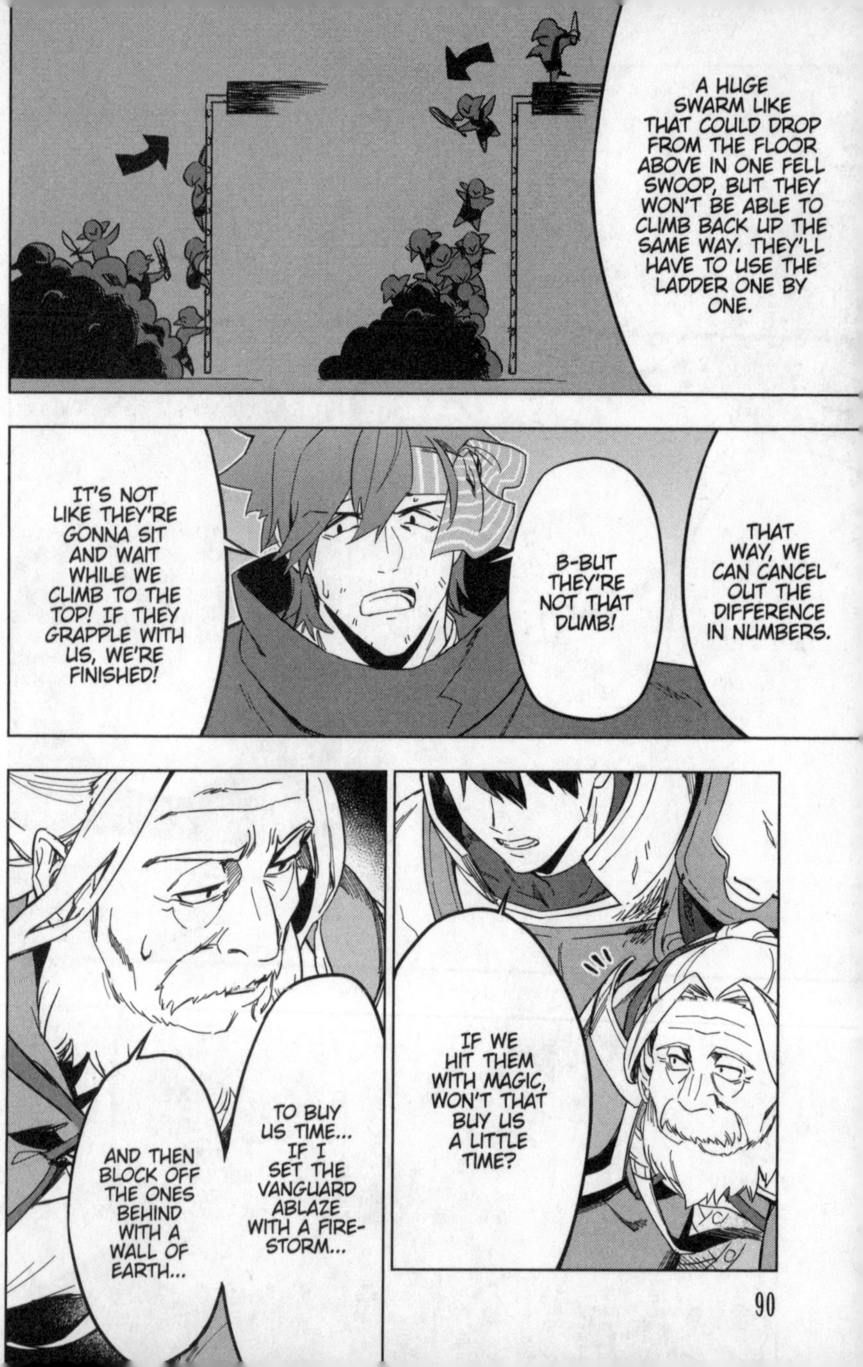
A HUGE SWARM LIKE THAT COULD DROP FROM THE FLOOR ABOVE IN ONE FELL SWOOP, BUT THEY WON'T BE ABLE TO CLIMB BACK UP THE SAME WAY. THEY'LL HAVE TO USE THE LADDER ONE BY ONE.
THAT WAY, WE CAN CANCEL OUT THE DIFFERENCE IN NUMBERS.
B-BUT THEY'RE NOT THAT DUMB!
IT'S NOT LIKE THEY'RE GONNA SIT AND WAIT WHILE WE CLIMB TO THE TOP! IF THEY GRAPPLE WITH US, WE'RE FINISHED!
IF WE HIT THEM WITH MAGIC, WON'T THAT BUY US A LITTLE TIME?
TO BUY US TIME... IF I SET THE VANGUARD ABLAZE WITH A FIRE-STORM...
AND THEN BLOCK OFF THE ONES BEHIND WITH A WALL OF EARTH...

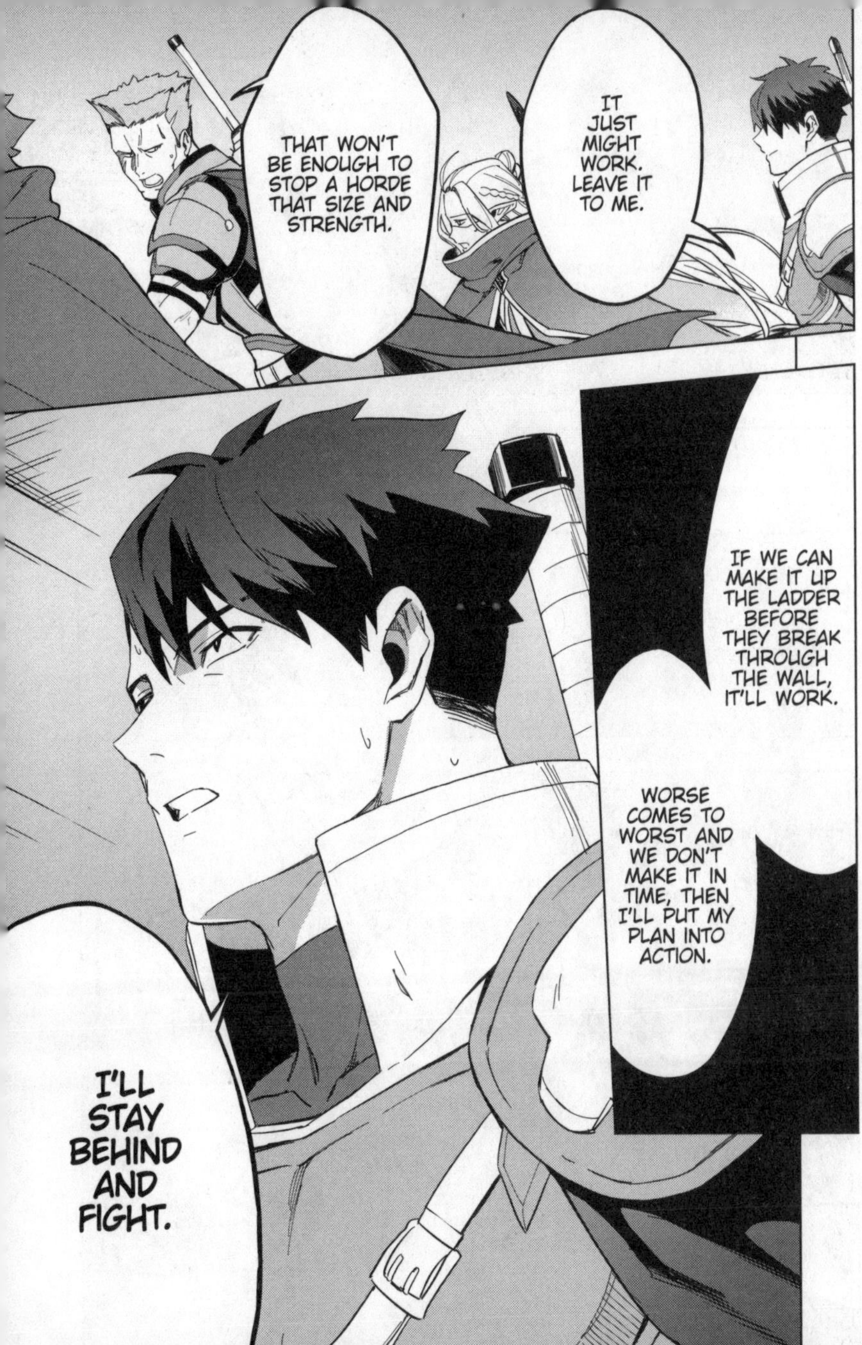
IT JUST MIGHT WORK. LEAVE IT TO ME.
THAT WON'T BE ENOUGH TO STOP A HORDE THAT SIZE AND STRENGTH.
IF WE CAN MAKE IT UP THE LADDER BEFORE THEY BREAK THROUGH THE WALL, IT'LL WORK.
WORSE COMES TO WORST AND WE DON'T MAKE IT IN TIME, THEN I'LL PUT MY PLAN INTO ACTION.
I'LL STAY BEHIND AND FIGHT.

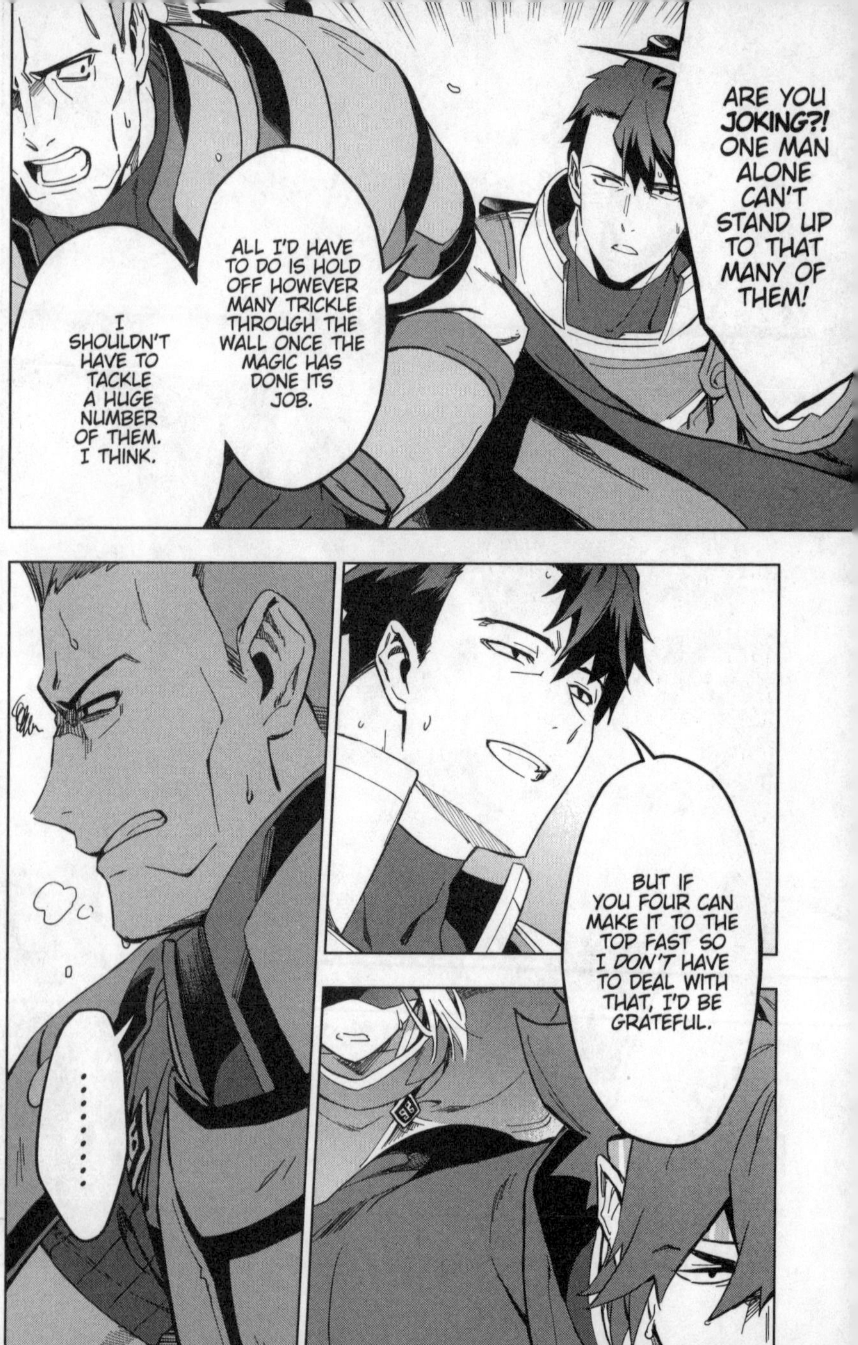
ARE YOU JOKING?! ONE MAN ALONE CAN'T STAND UP TO THAT MANY OF THEM!
ALL I'D HAVE TO DO IS HOLD OFF HOWEVER MANY TRICKLE THROUGH THE WALL ONCE THE MAGIC HAS DONE ITS JOB.
I SHOULDN'T HAVE TO TACKLE A HUGE NUMBER OF THEM. I THINK.
BUT IF YOU FOUR CAN MAKE IT TO THE TOP FAST SO I *DON'T* HAVE TO DEAL WITH THAT, I'D BE GRATEFUL.
....

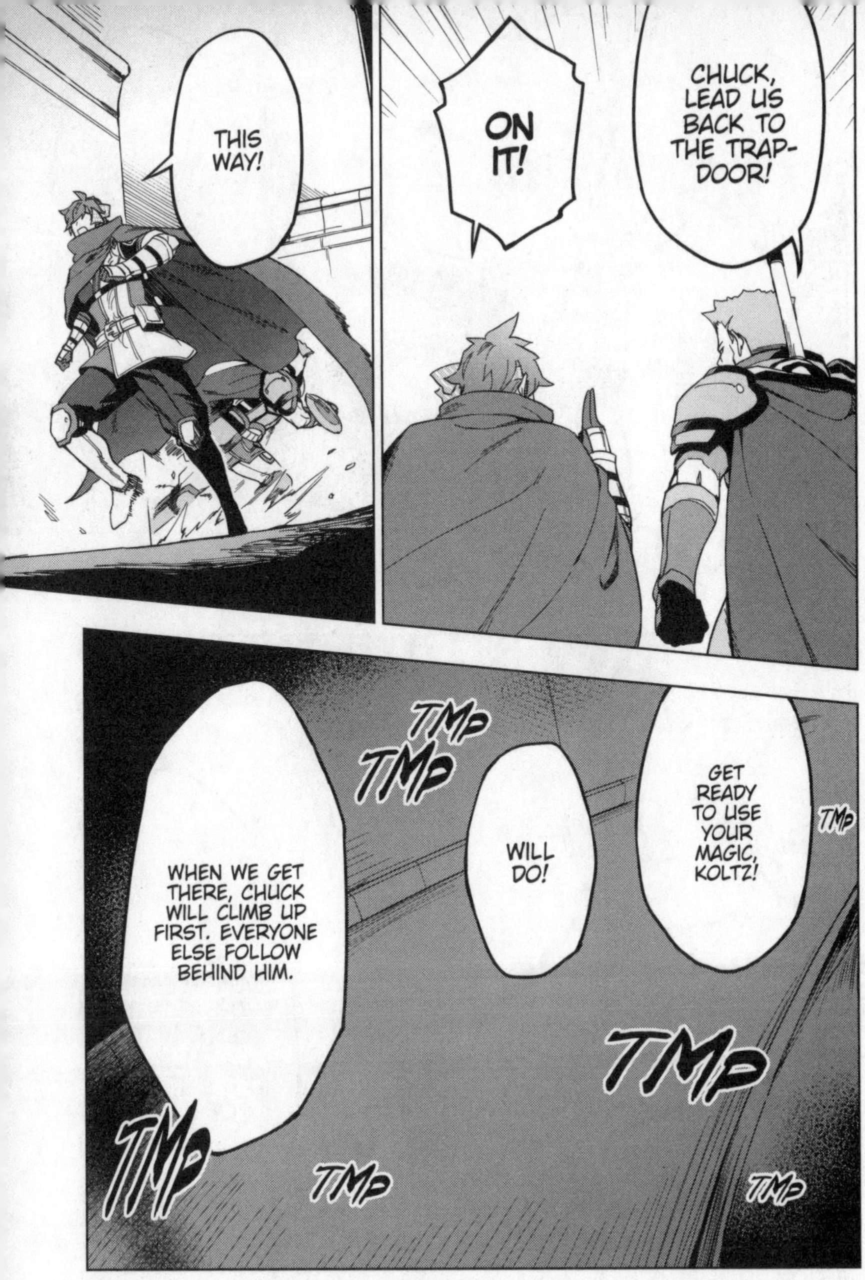
CHUCK, LEAD US BACK TO THE TRAP-DOOR!
ON IT!
THIS WAY!
GET READY TO USE YOUR MAGIC, KOLTZ!
TMP
WILL DO!
TMP
TMP
WHEN WE GET THERE, CHUCK WILL CLIMB UP FIRST. EVERYONE ELSE FOLLOW BEHIND HIM.
TMP
TMP
TMP
TMP

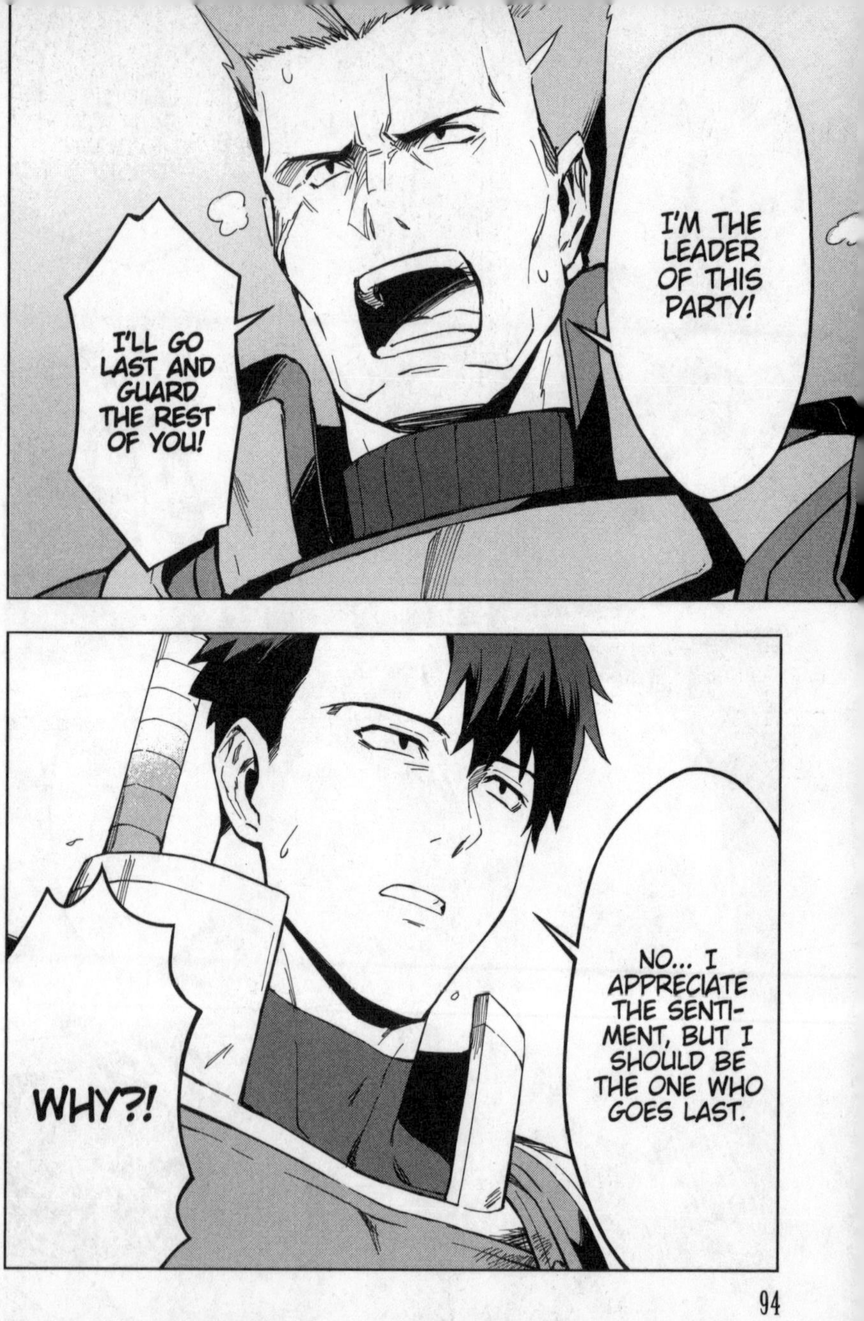
I'M THE LEADER OF THIS PARTY!
I'LL GO LAST AND GUARD THE REST OF YOU!
NO... I APPRECIATE THE SENTI-MENT, BUT I SHOULD BE THE ONE WHO GOES LAST.
WHY?!

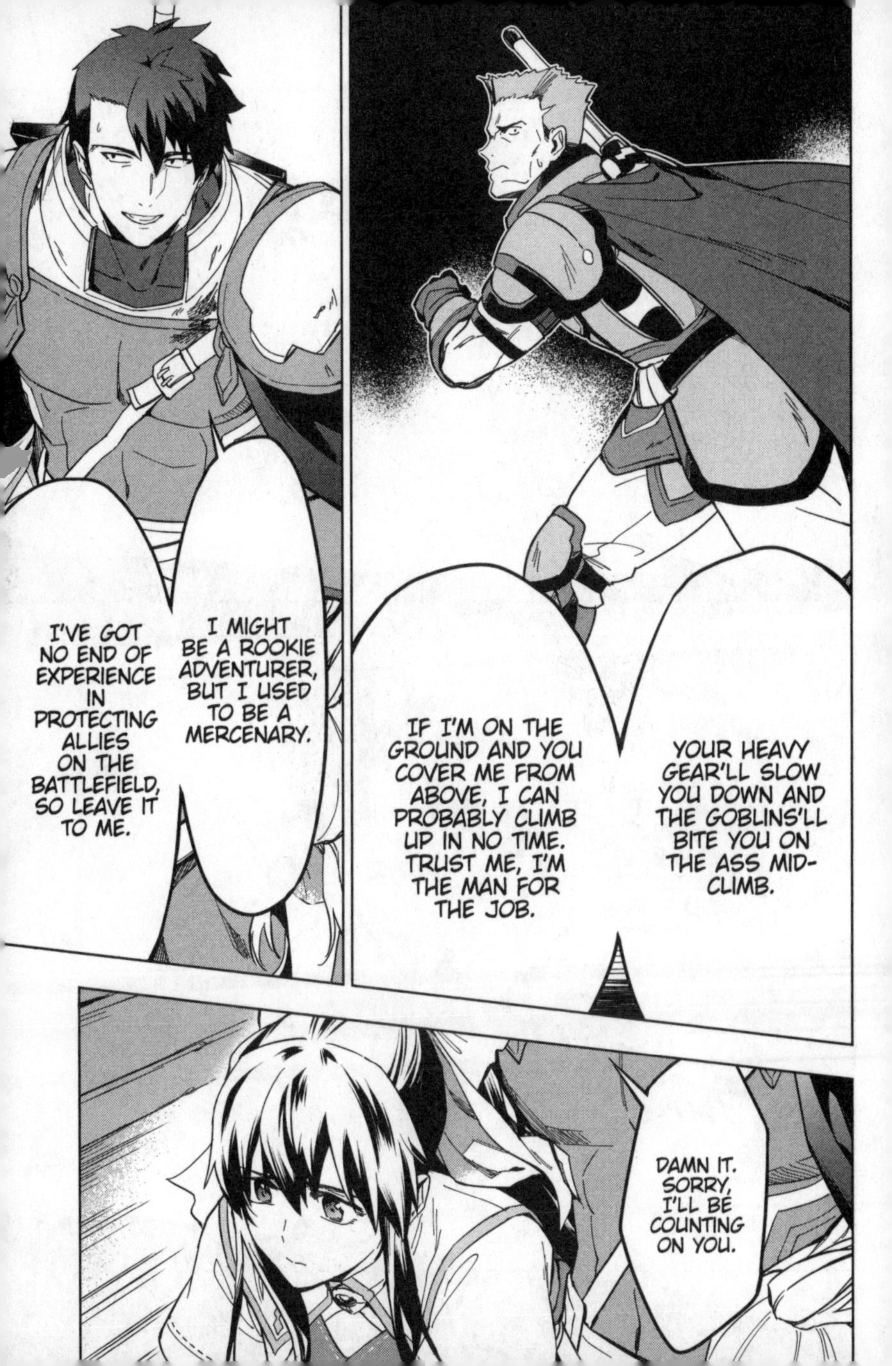
YOUR HEAVY GEAR'LL SLOW YOU DOWN AND THE GOBLINS'LL BITE YOU ON THE ASS MID-CLIMB.
IF I'M ON THE GROUND AND YOU COVER ME FROM ABOVE, I CAN PROBABLY CLIMB UP IN NO TIME. TRUST ME, I'M THE MAN FOR THE JOB.
I MIGHT BE A ROOKIE ADVENTURER, BUT I USED TO BE A MERCENARY.
I'VE GOT NO END OF EXPERIENCE IN PROTECTING ALLIES ON THE BATTLEFIELD, SO LEAVE IT TO ME.
DAMN IT. SORRY, I'LL BE COUNTING ON YOU.

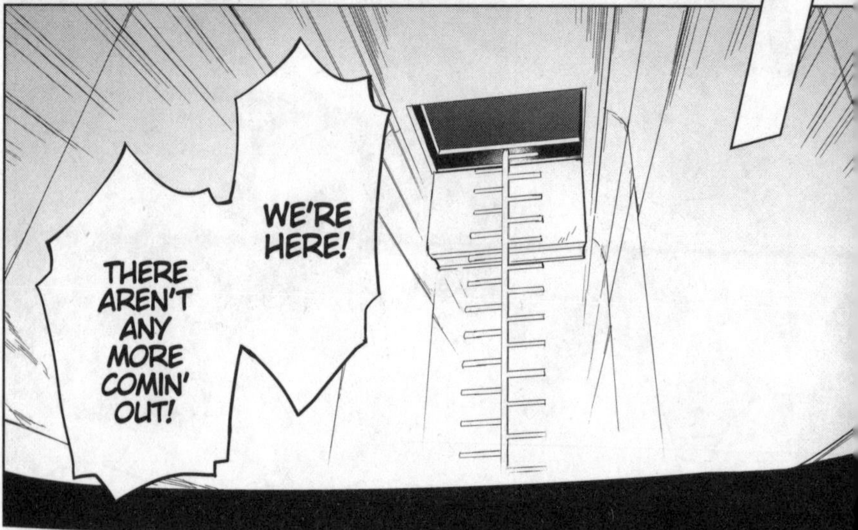
WE'RE HERE!
THERE AREN'T ANY MORE COMIN' OUT!
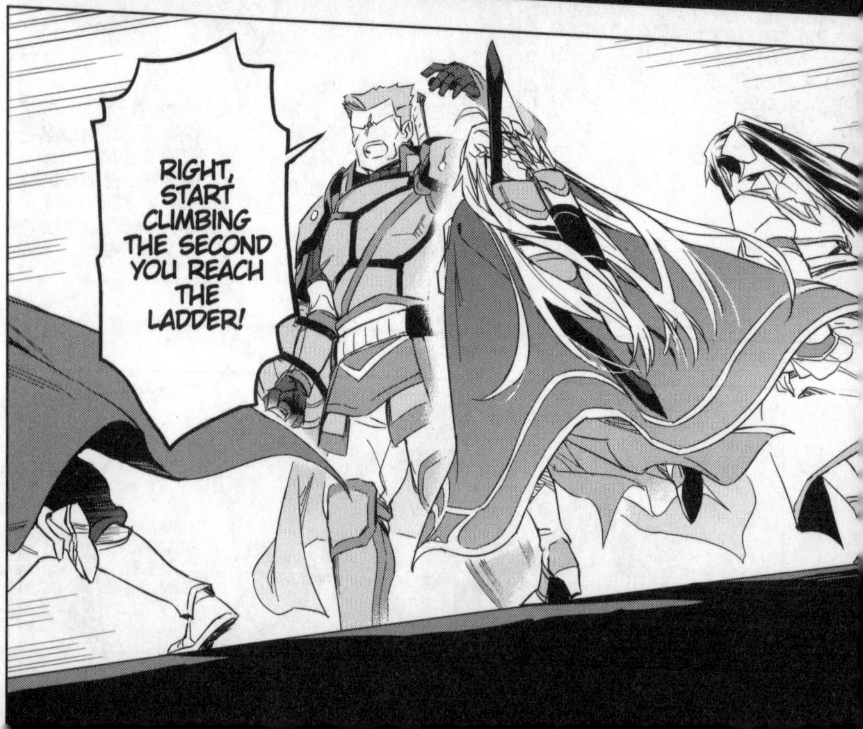
RIGHT, START CLIMBING THE SECOND YOU REACH THE LADDER!

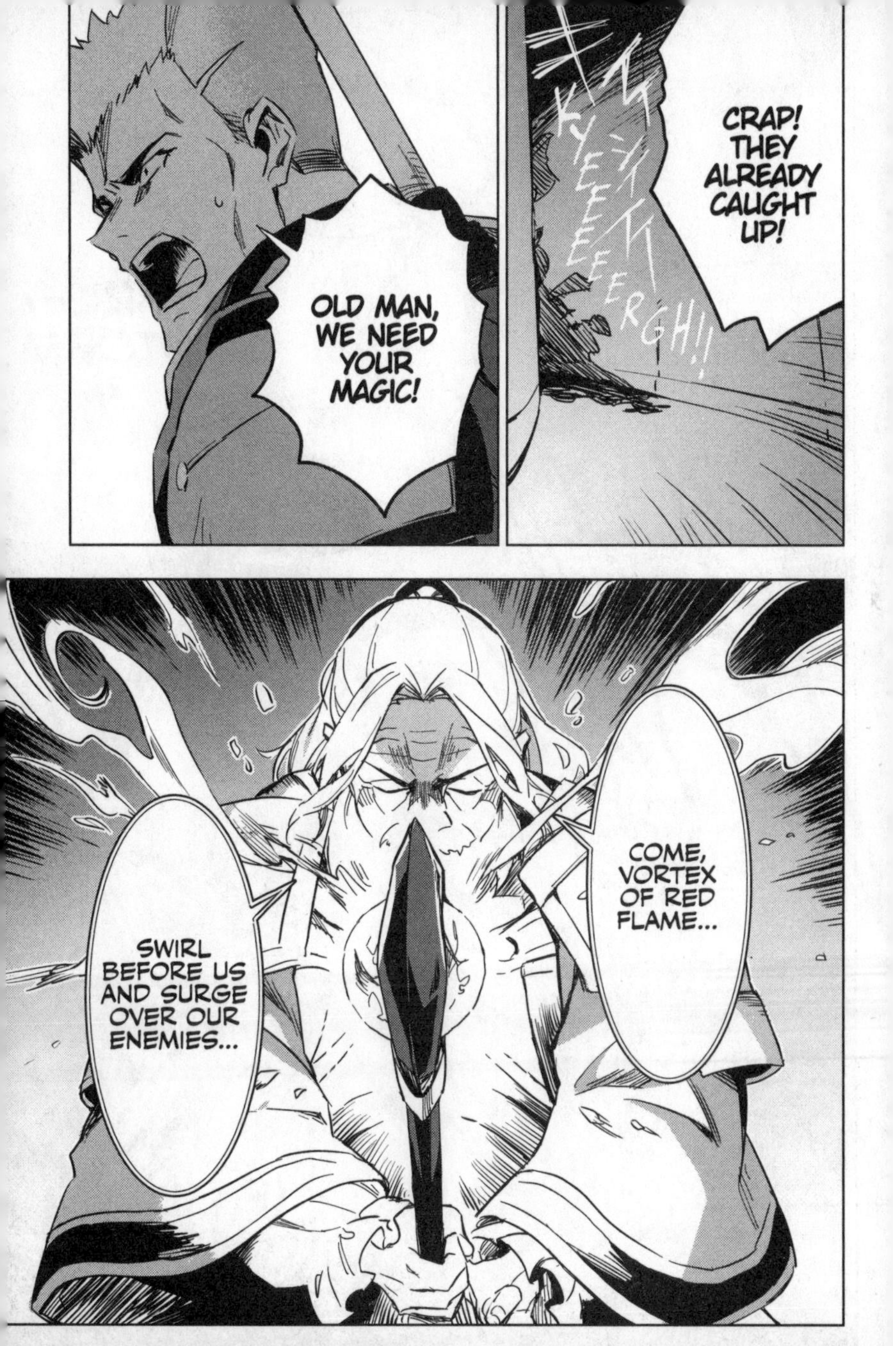
KYEEEEEERGH!!
CRAP! THEY ALREADY CAUGHT UP!
OLD MAN, WE NEED YOUR MAGIC!
COME, VORTEX OF RED FLAME...
SWIRL BEFORE US AND SURGE OVER OUR ENEMIES...

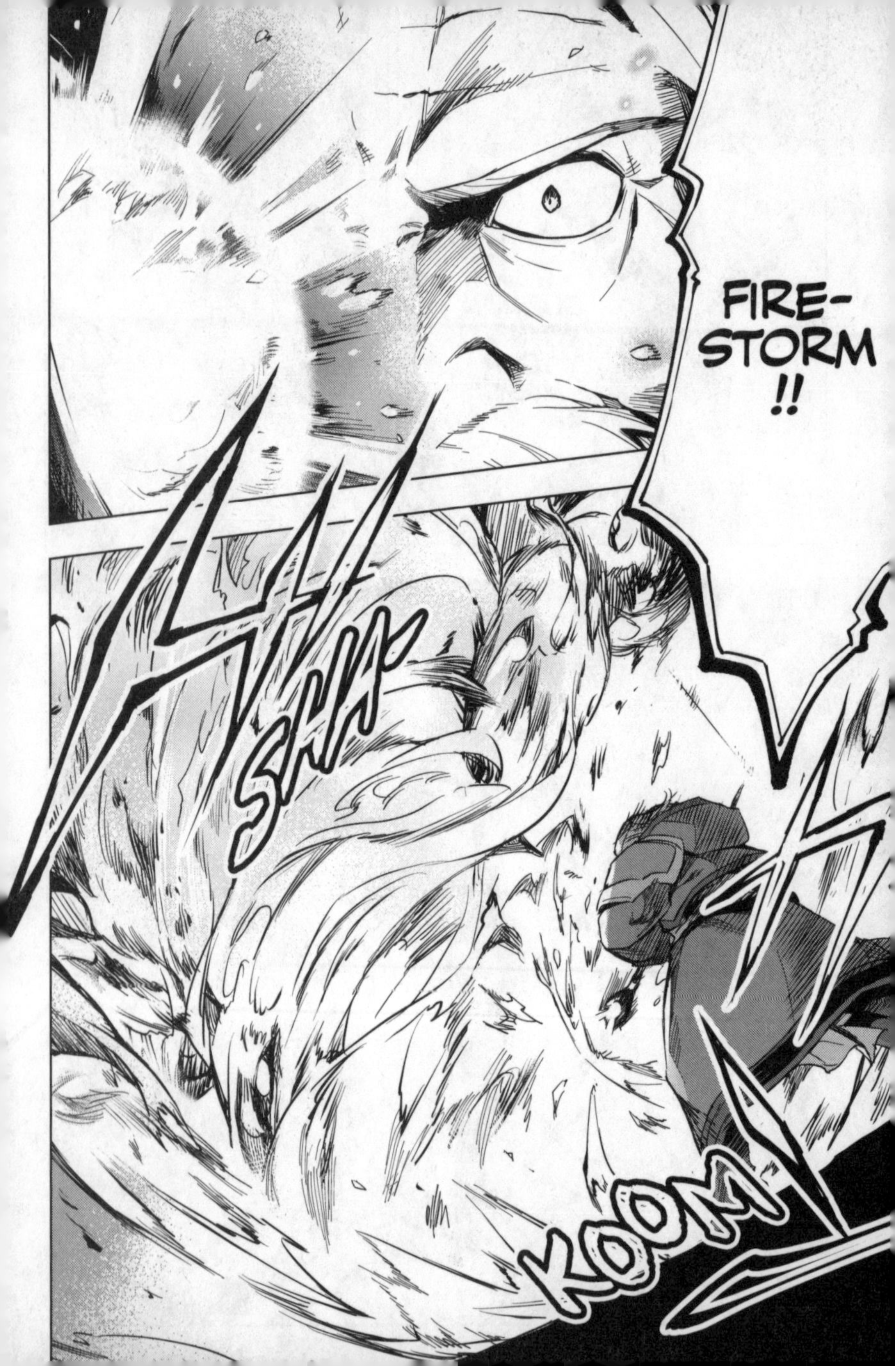
FIRE-STORM!!
KOOM

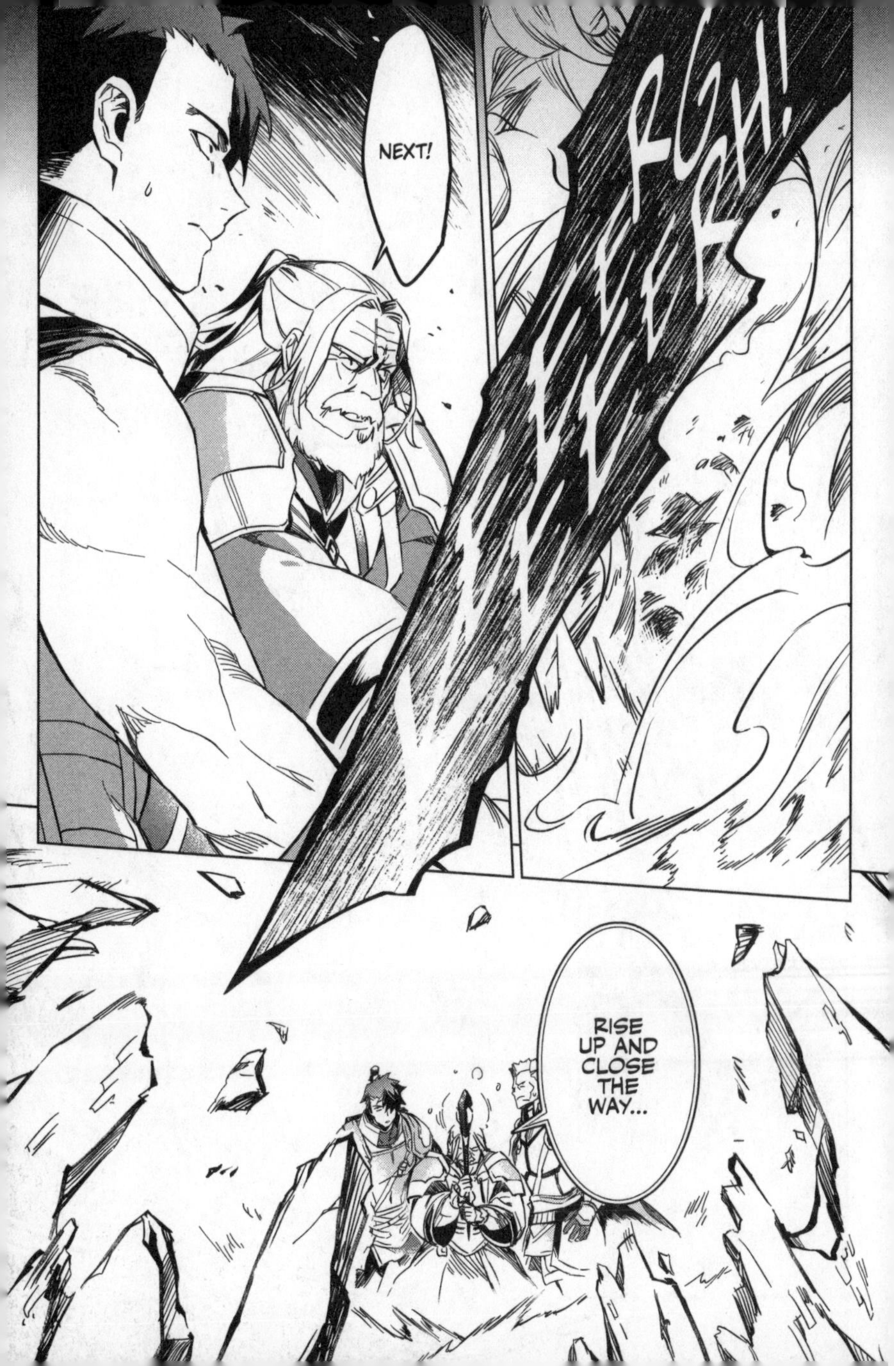
NEXT!
RISE UP AND CLOSE THE WAY...

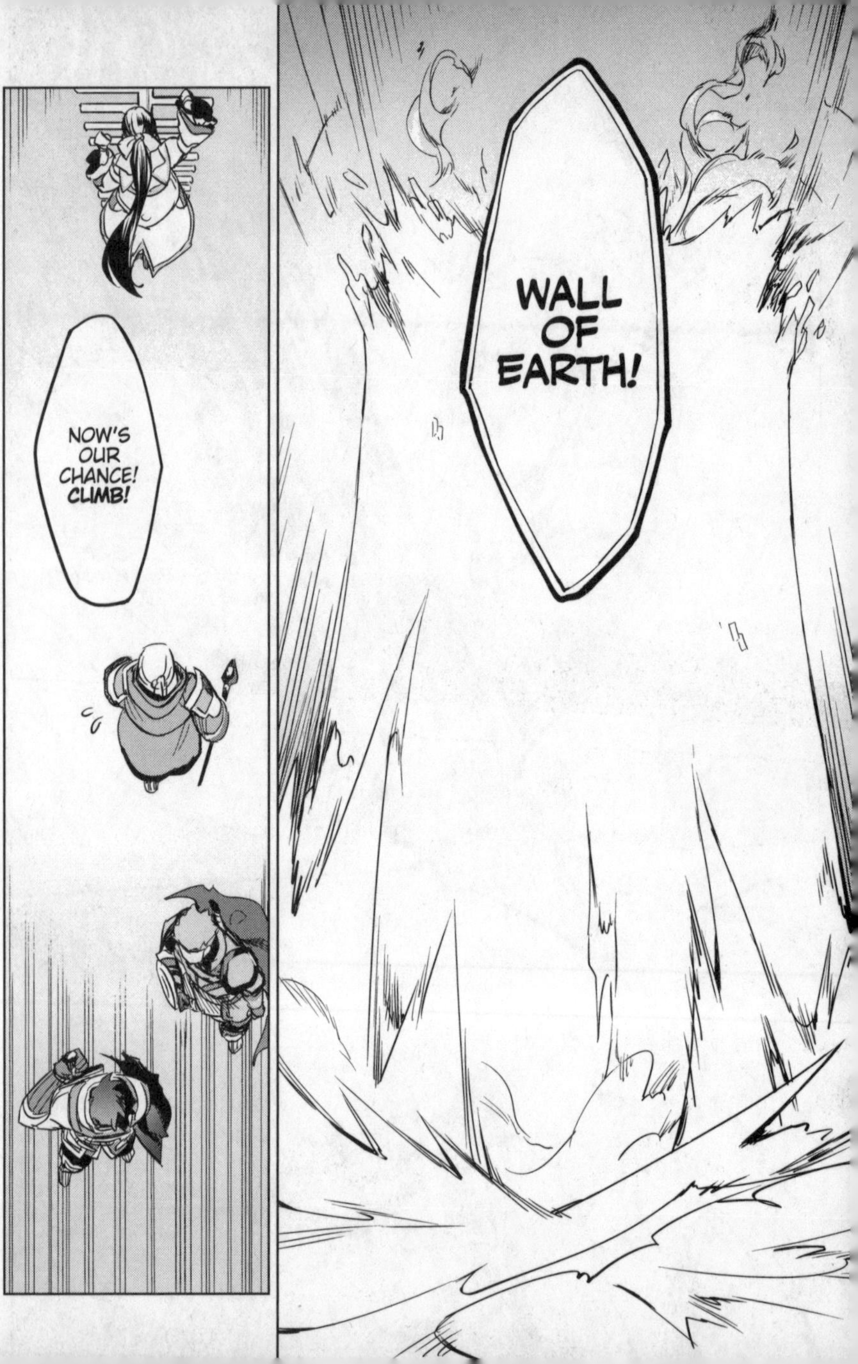
WALL OF EARTH!
NOW'S OUR CHANCE! CLIMB!

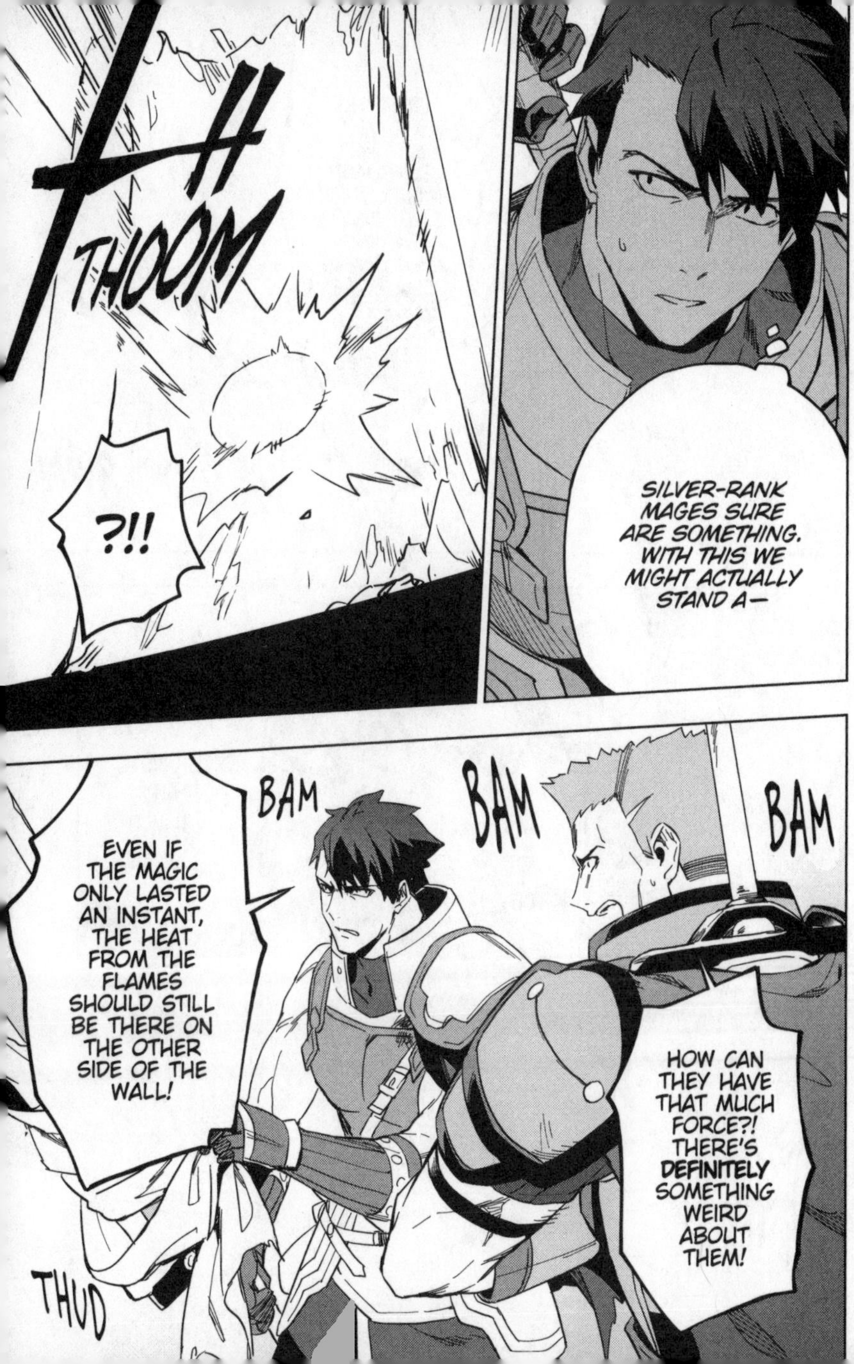
SILVER-RANK MAGES SURE ARE SOMETHING. WITH THIS WE MIGHT ACTUALLY STAND A—
THOOM
?!!
BAM
BAM
BAM
EVEN IF THE MAGIC ONLY LASTED AN INSTANT, THE HEAT FROM THE FLAMES SHOULD STILL BE THERE ON THE OTHER SIDE OF THE WALL!
HOW CAN THEY HAVE THAT MUCH FORCE?! THERE'S **DEFINITELY** SOMETHING WEIRD ABOUT THEM!
THUD

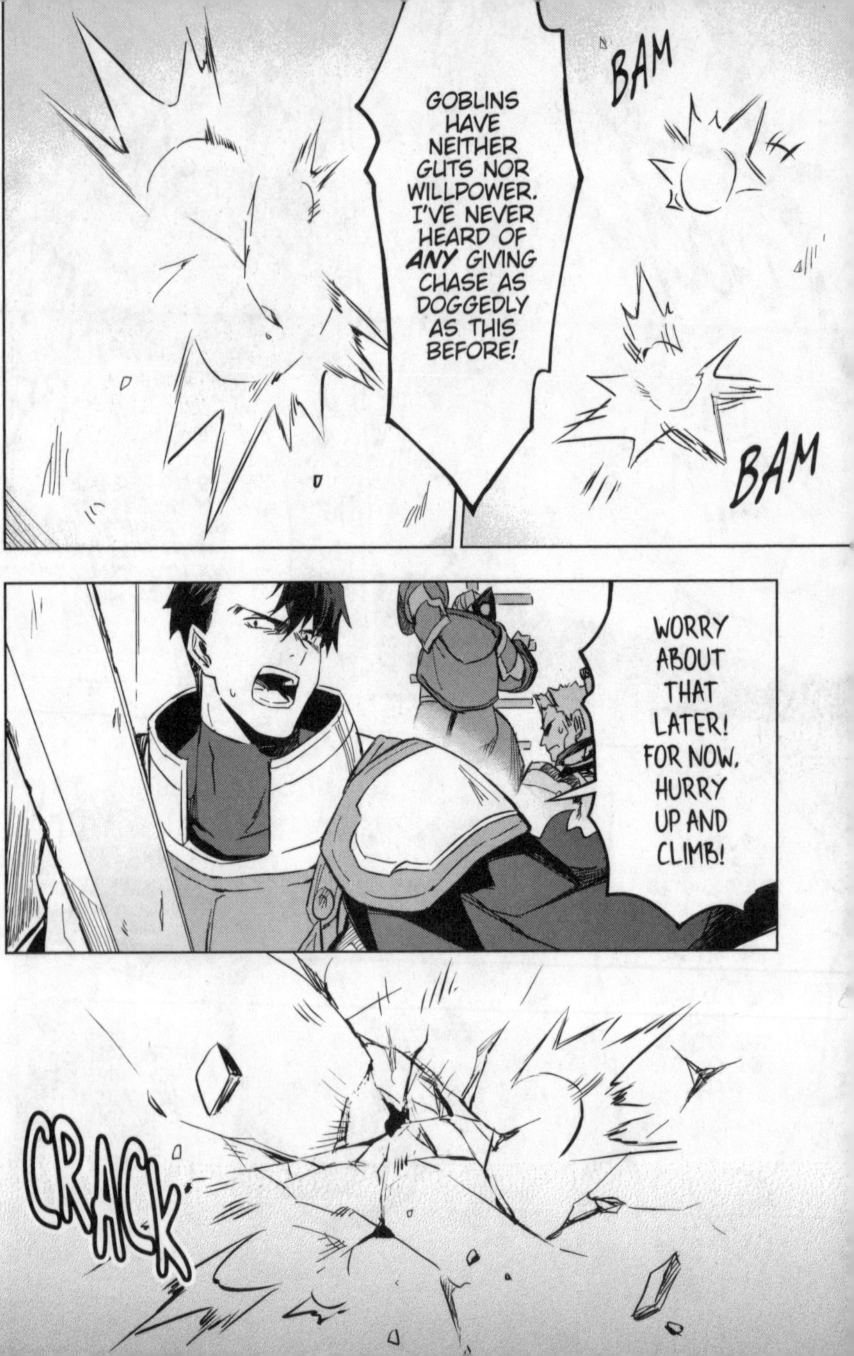
BAM
GOBLINS HAVE NEITHER GUTS NOR WILLPOWER. I'VE NEVER HEARD OF ANY GIVING CHASE AS DOGGEDLY AS THIS BEFORE!
BAM
WORRY ABOUT THAT LATER! FOR NOW, HURRY UP AND CLIMB!
CRACK

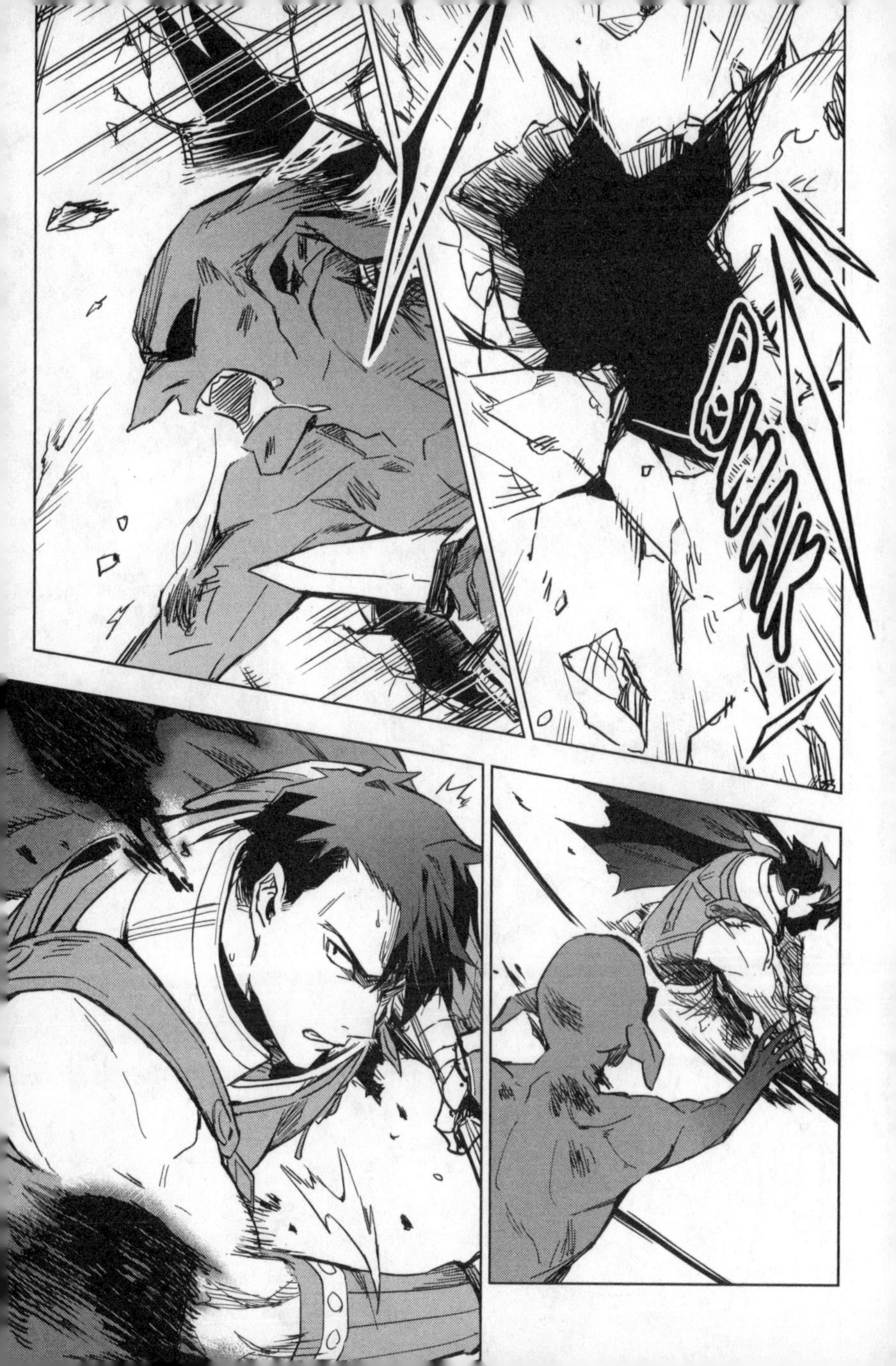
BWAK

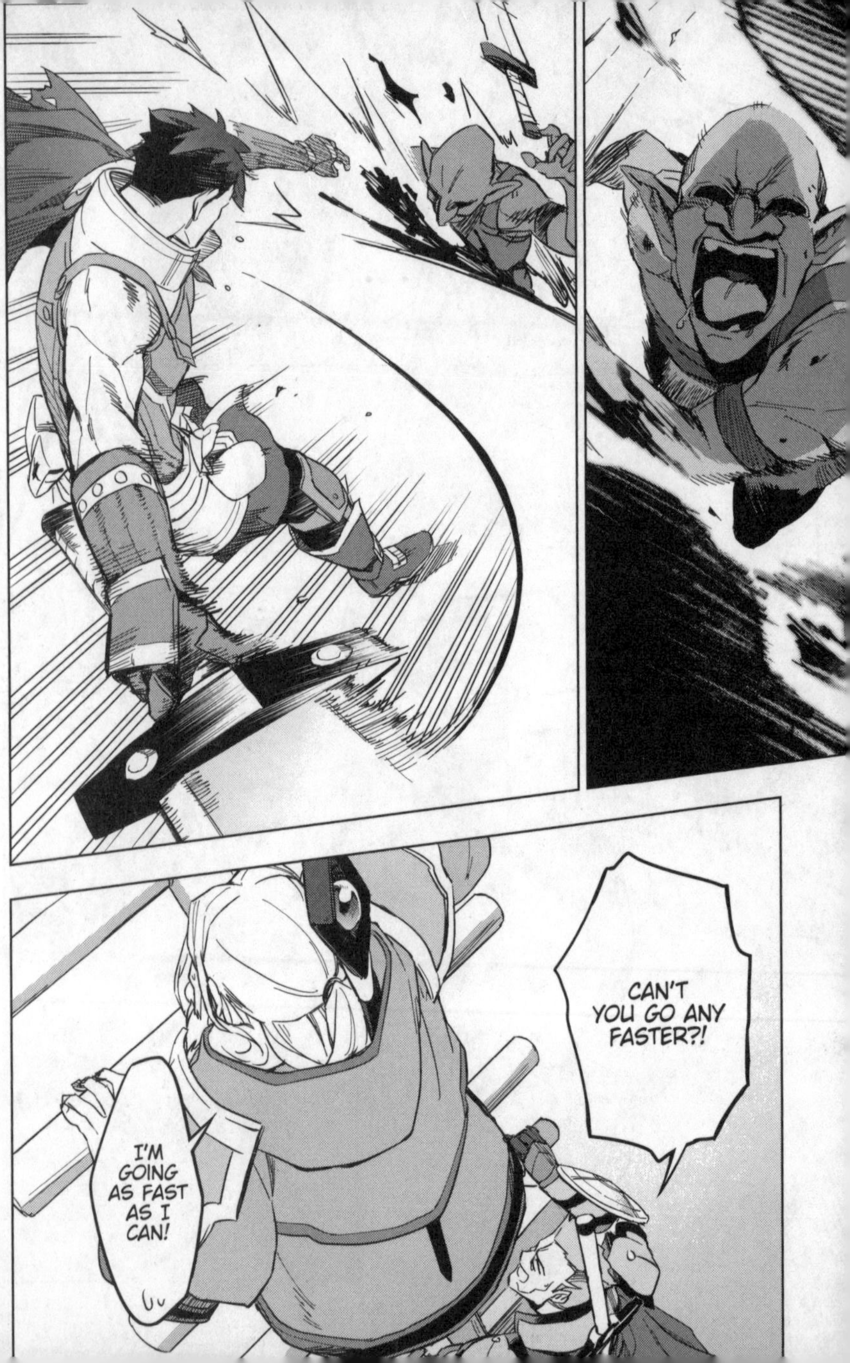
CAN'T YOU GO ANY FASTER?!
I'M GOING AS FAST AS I CAN!

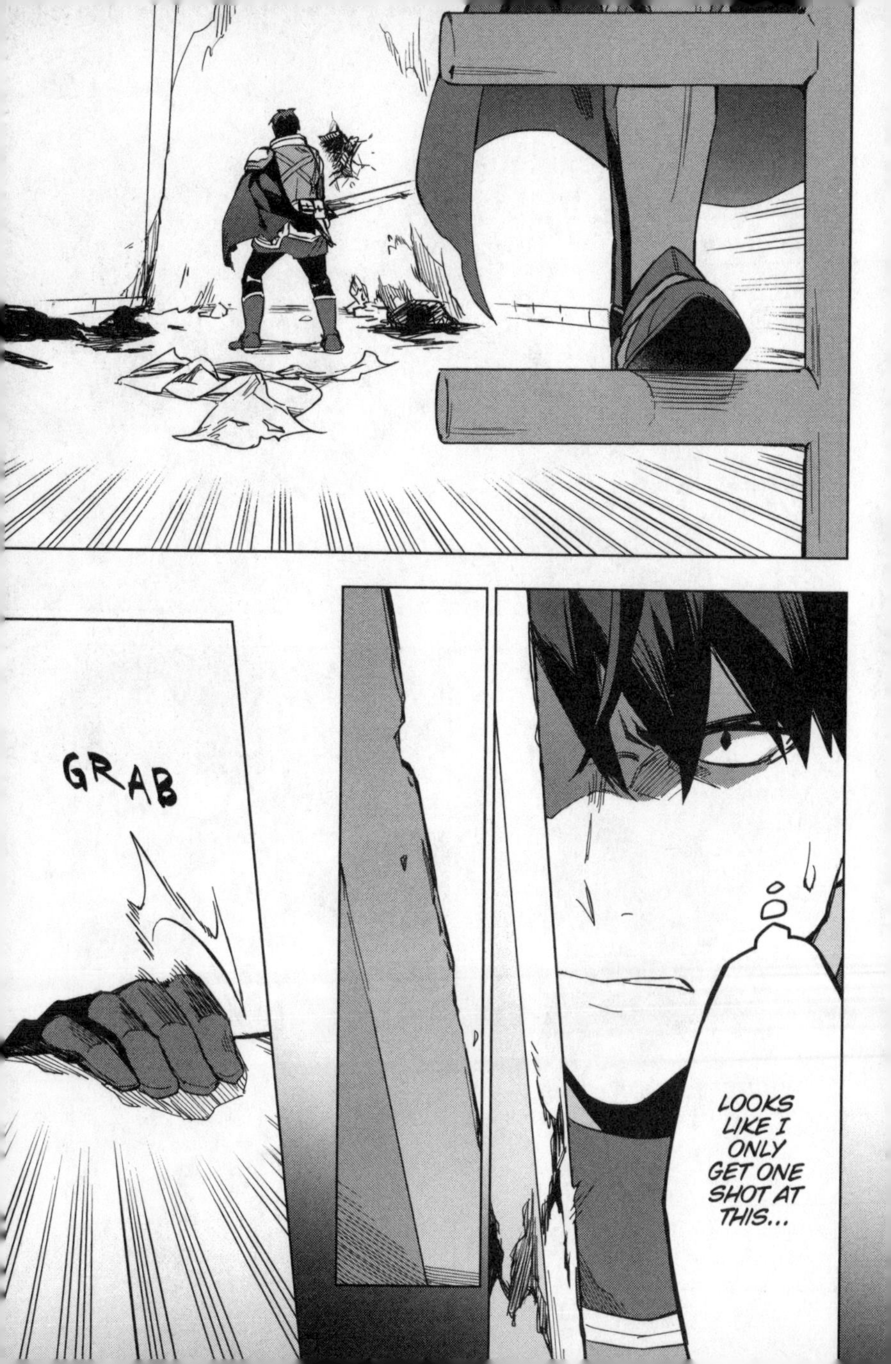

LOOKS LIKE I ONLY GET ONE SHOT AT THIS...
GRAB

GOOD...NO ENEMIES UP HERE.

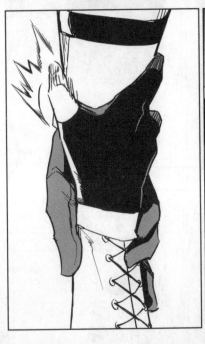

NYM!

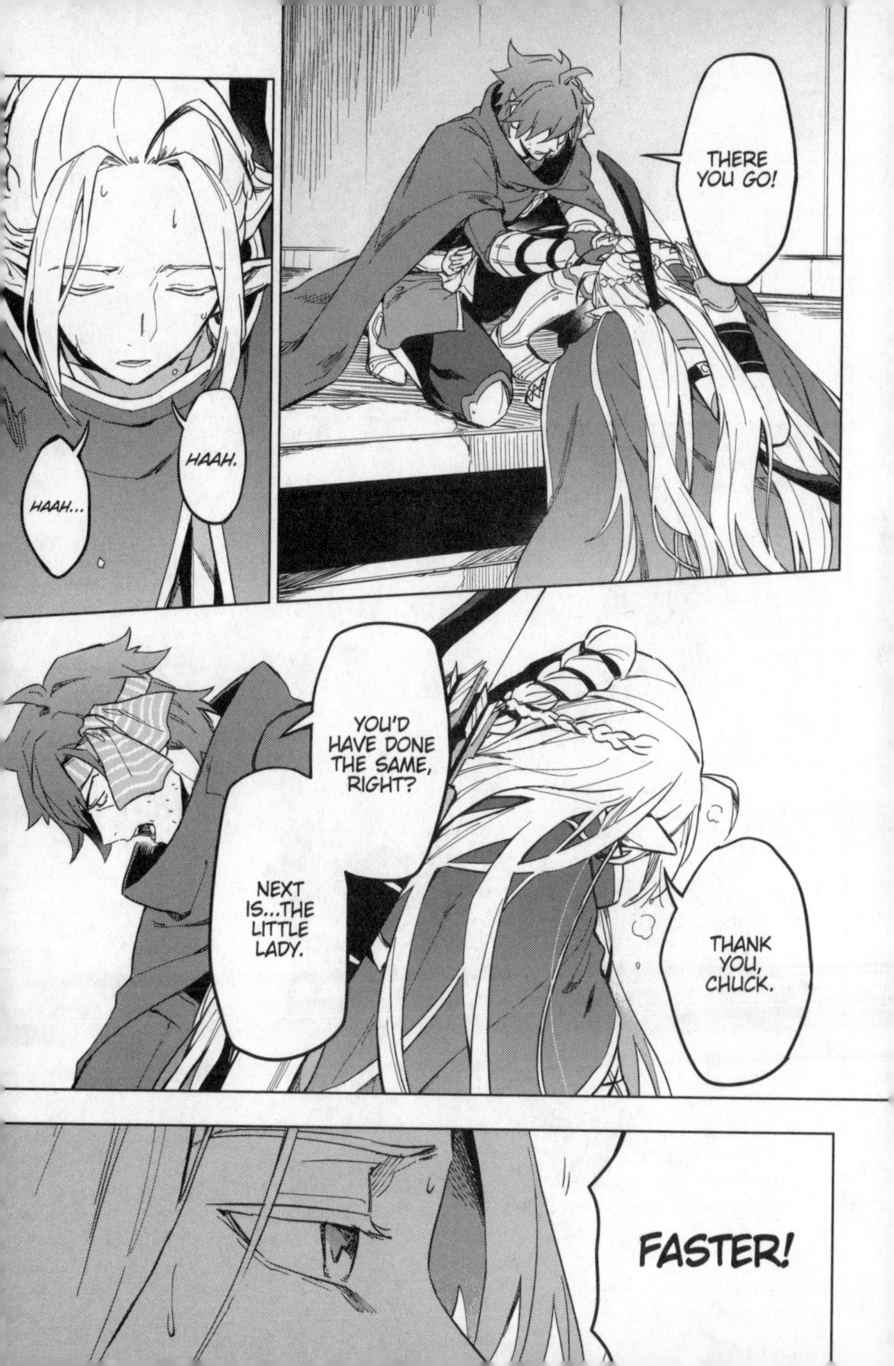
THERE YOU GO!
HAAH.
HAAH...
THANK YOU, CHUCK.
YOU'D HAVE DONE THE SAME, RIGHT?
NEXT IS...THE LITTLE LADY.
FASTER!

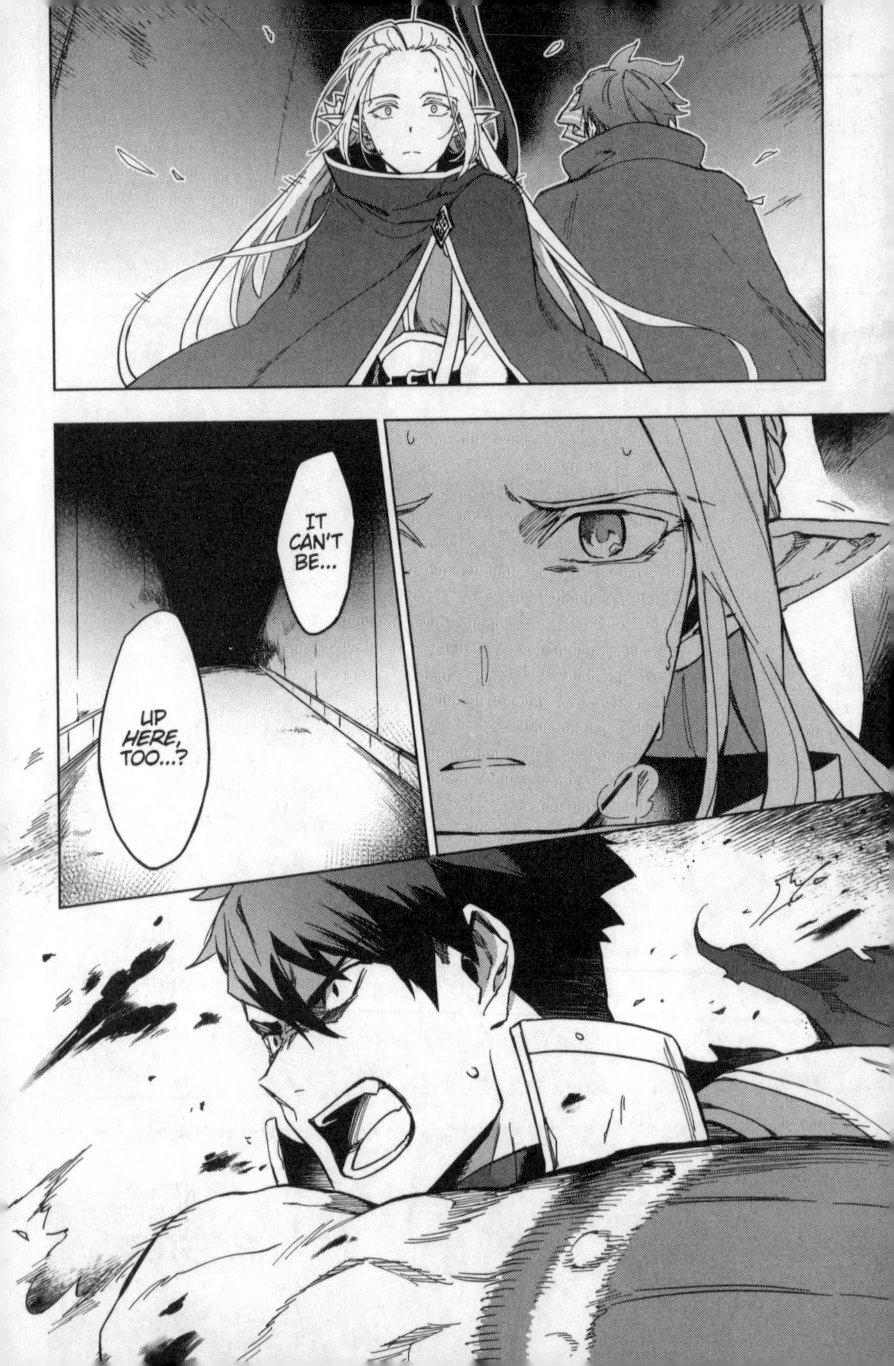
IT CAN'T BE...
UP HERE, TOO...?

CHAPTER 11 OBSTRUCTION TO EXPLANATION

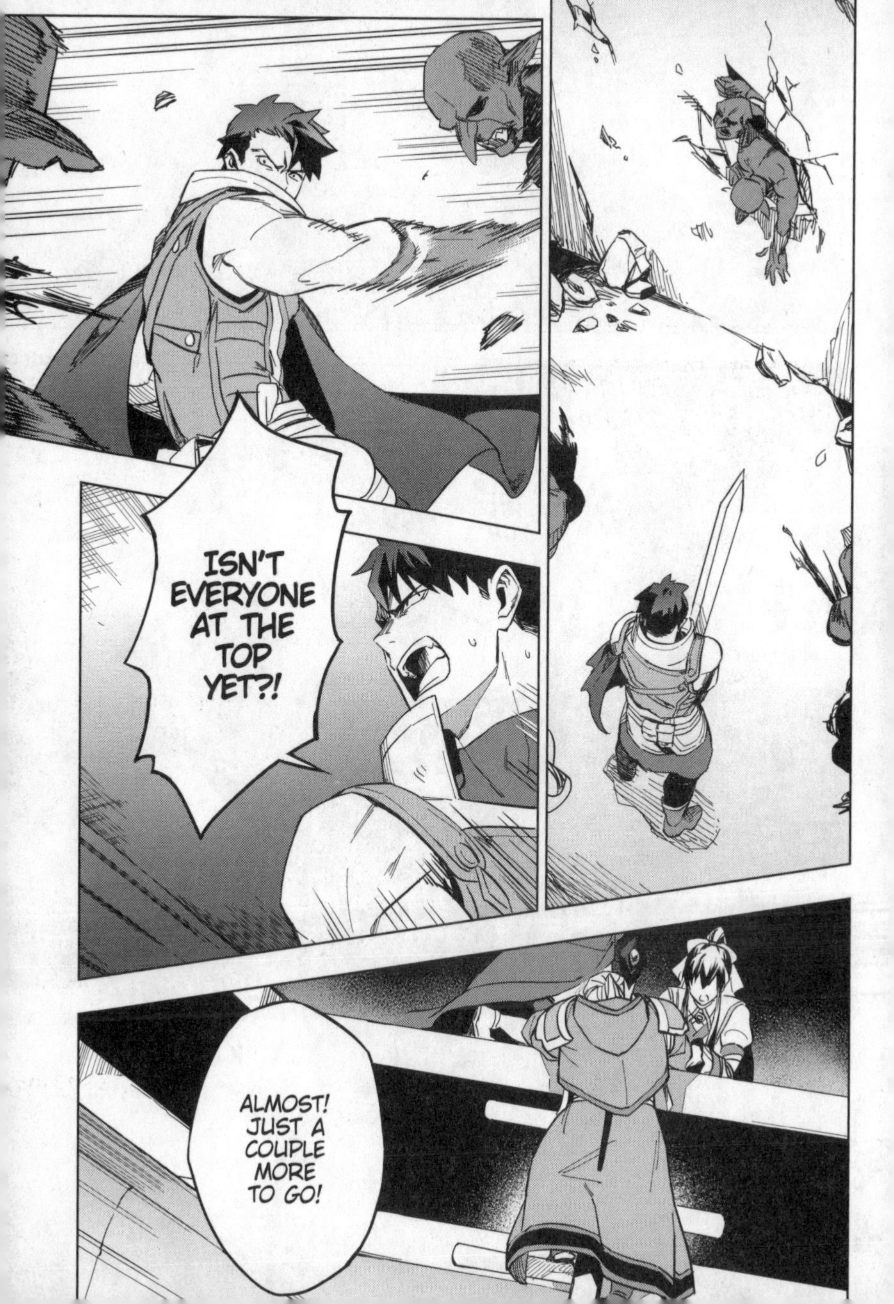
ISN'T EVERYONE AT THE TOP YET?!
ALMOST! JUST A COUPLE MORE TO GO!

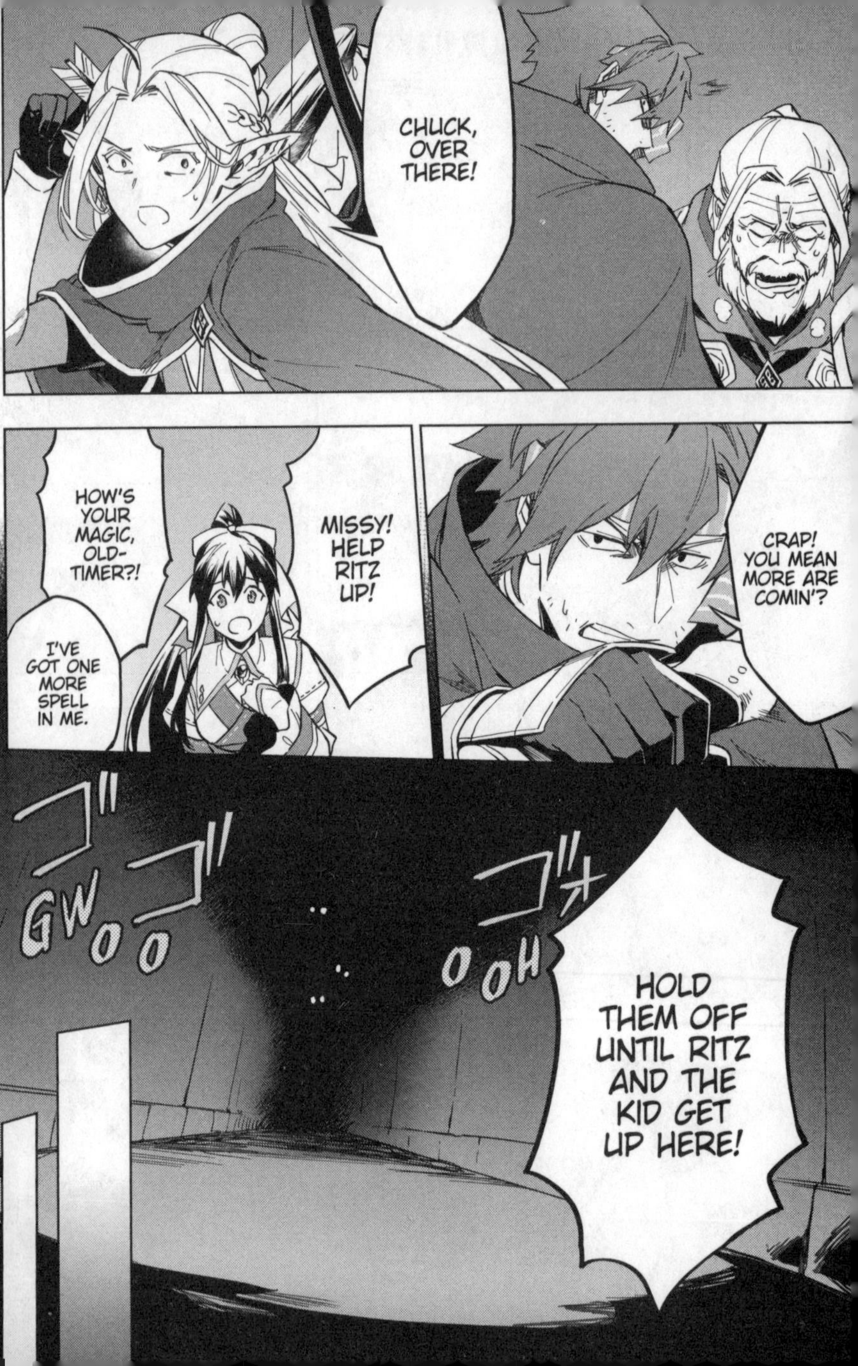
CHUCK, OVER THERE!
CRAP! YOU MEAN MORE ARE COMIN'?
MISSY! HELP RITZ UP!
HOW'S YOUR MAGIC, OLD-TIMER?!
I'VE GOT ONE MORE SPELL IN ME.
HOLD THEM OFF UNTIL RITZ AND THE KID GET UP HERE!
ゴゴゴォ
GWOOOOH

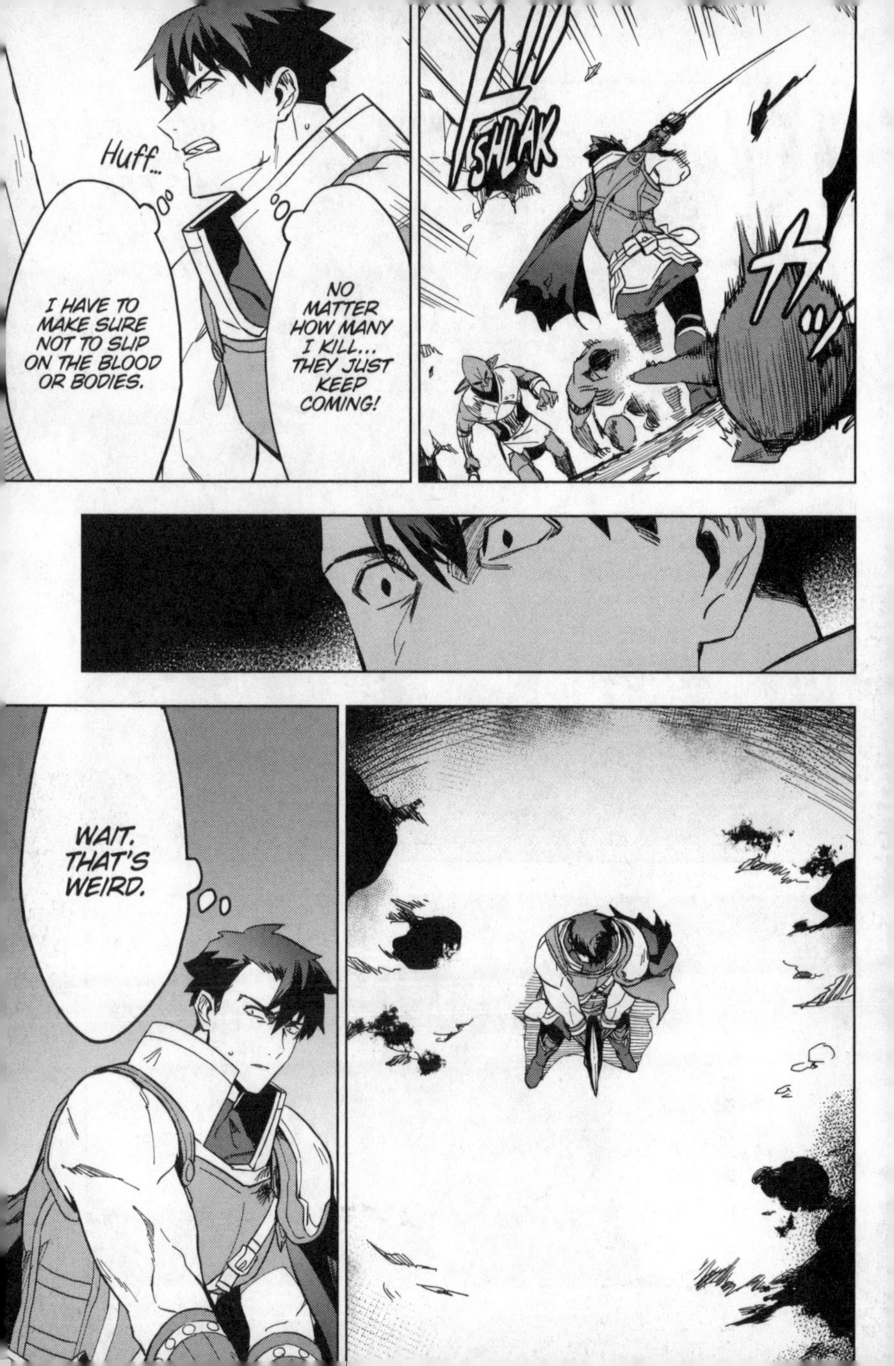
SHLAK
Huff...
NO MATTER HOW MANY I KILL... THEY JUST KEEP COMING!
I HAVE TO MAKE SURE NOT TO SLIP ON THE BLOOD OR BODIES.
WAIT. THAT'S WEIRD.

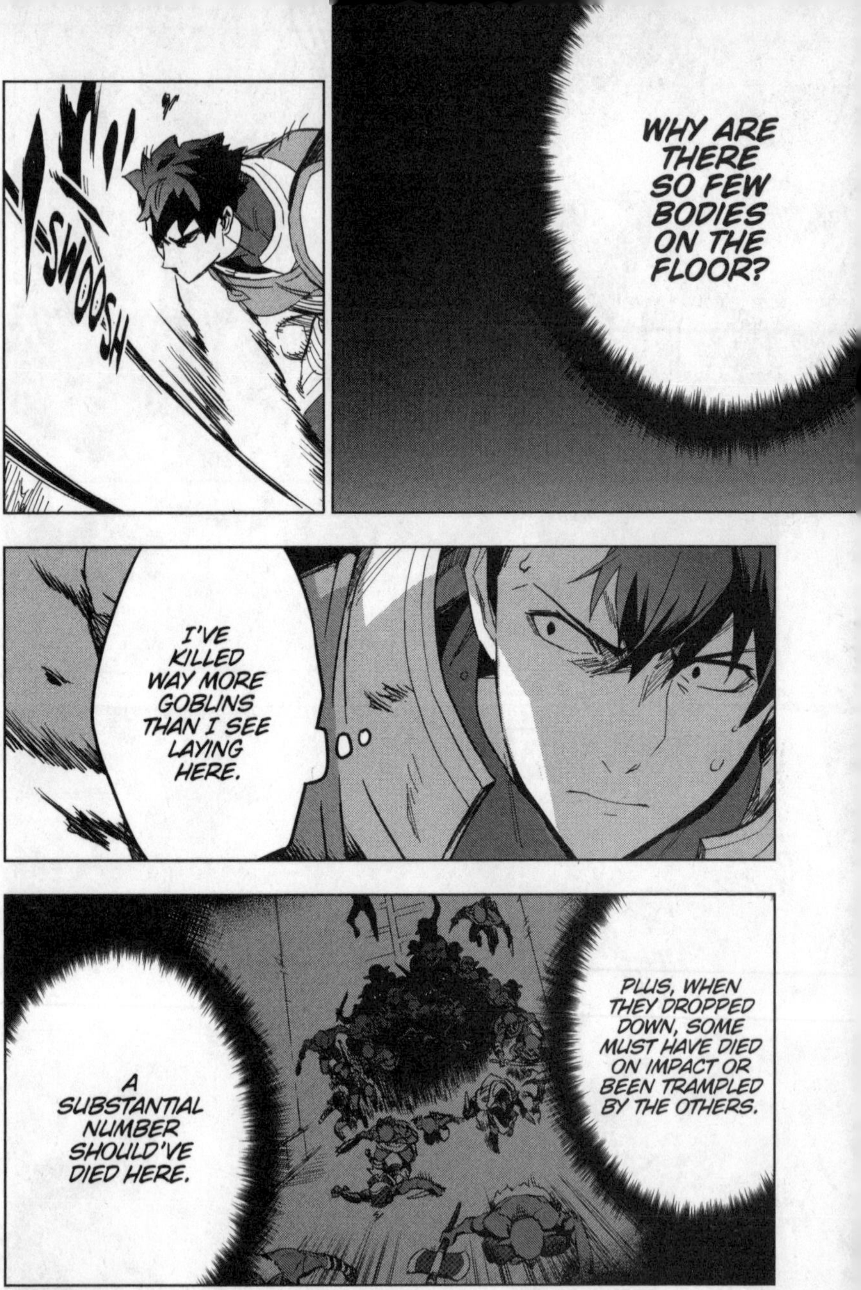
WHY ARE THERE SO FEW BODIES ON THE FLOOR?
SWOOSH
I'VE KILLED WAY MORE GOBLINS THAN I SEE LAYING HERE.
PLUS, WHEN THEY DROPPED DOWN, SOME MUST HAVE DIED ON IMPACT OR BEEN TRAMPLED BY THE OTHERS.
A SUBSTANTIAL NUMBER SHOULD'VE DIED HERE.

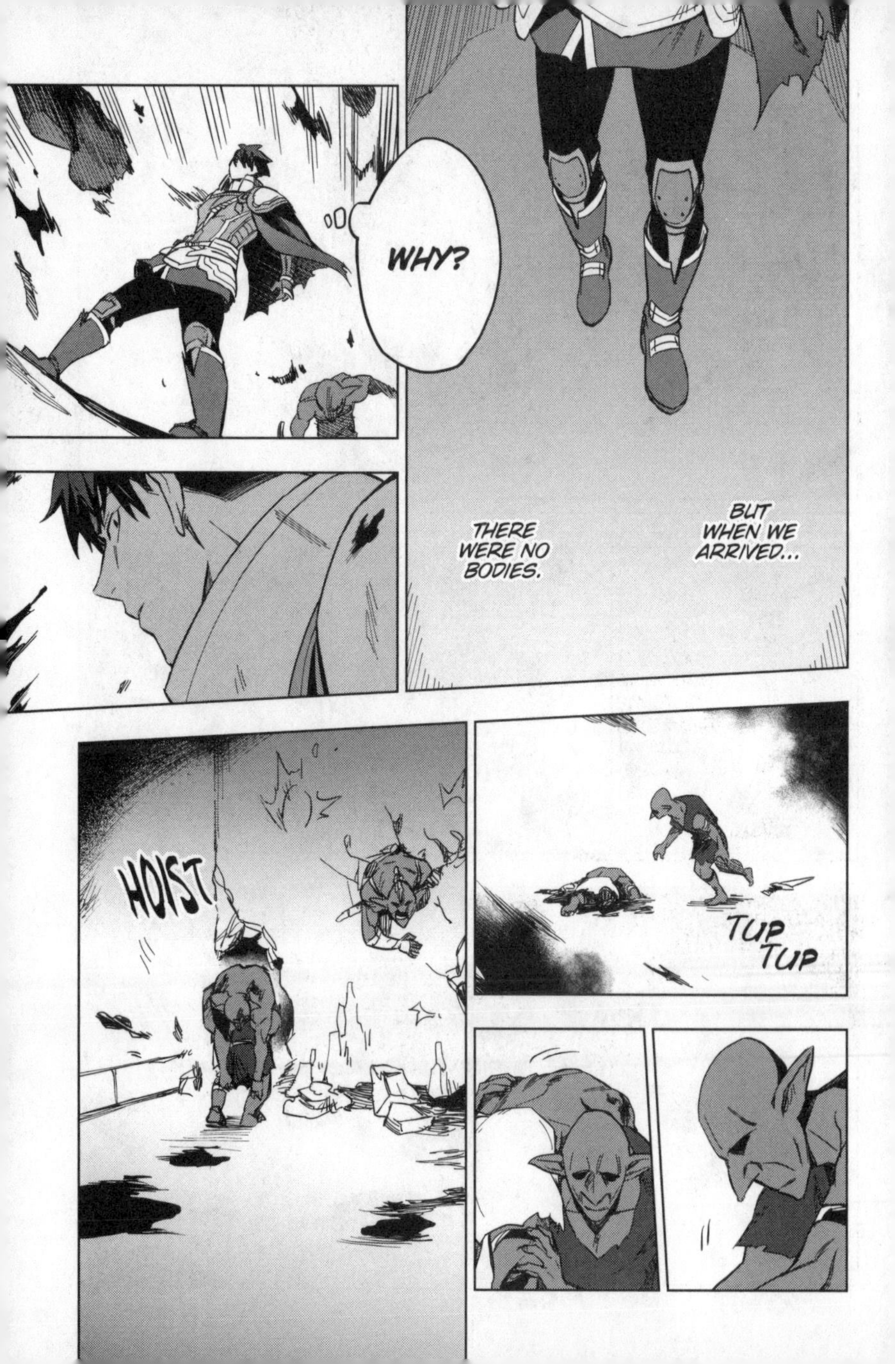
BUT WHEN WE ARRIVED...
THERE WERE NO BODIES.
WHY?
TUP TUP
HOIST

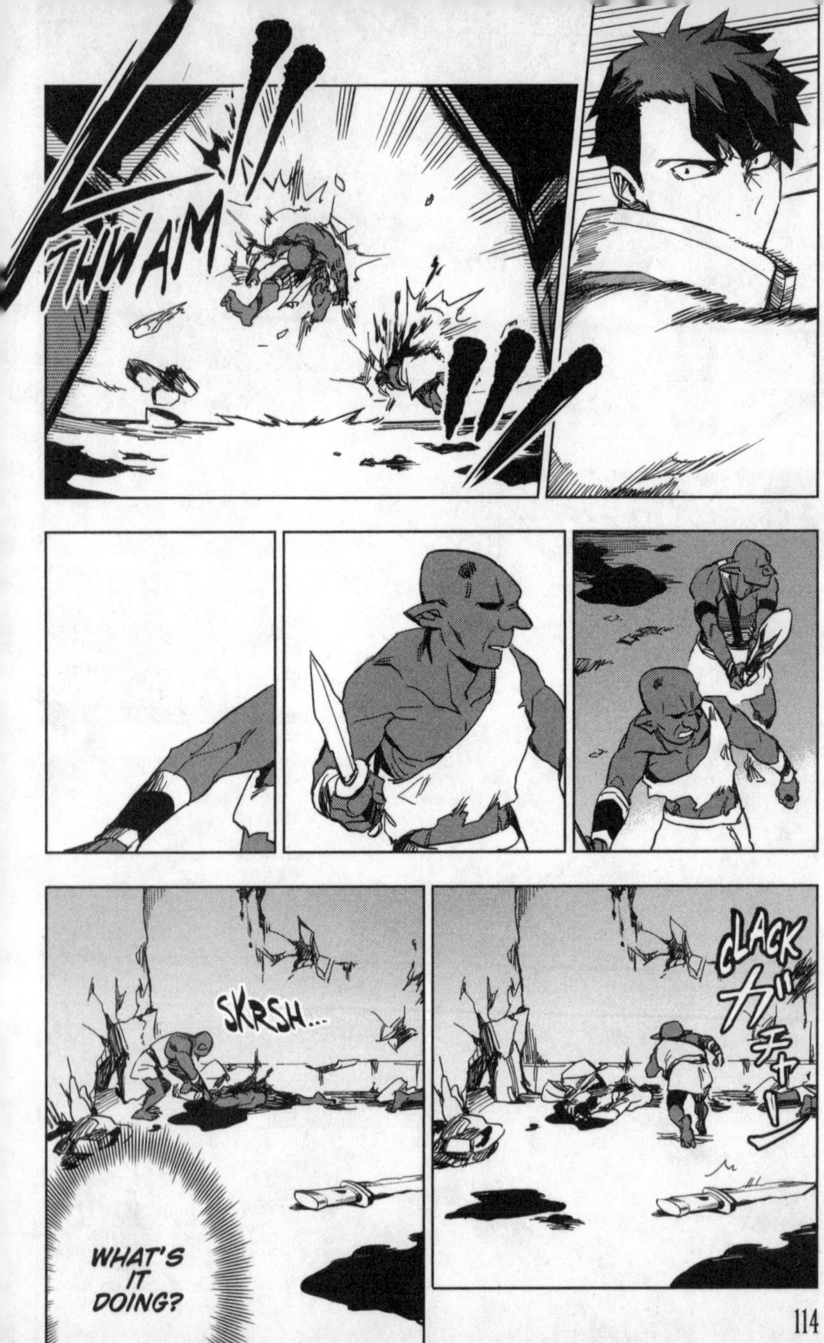
THWAM
CLACK
ガチャ
SKRSH...
WHAT'S IT DOING?

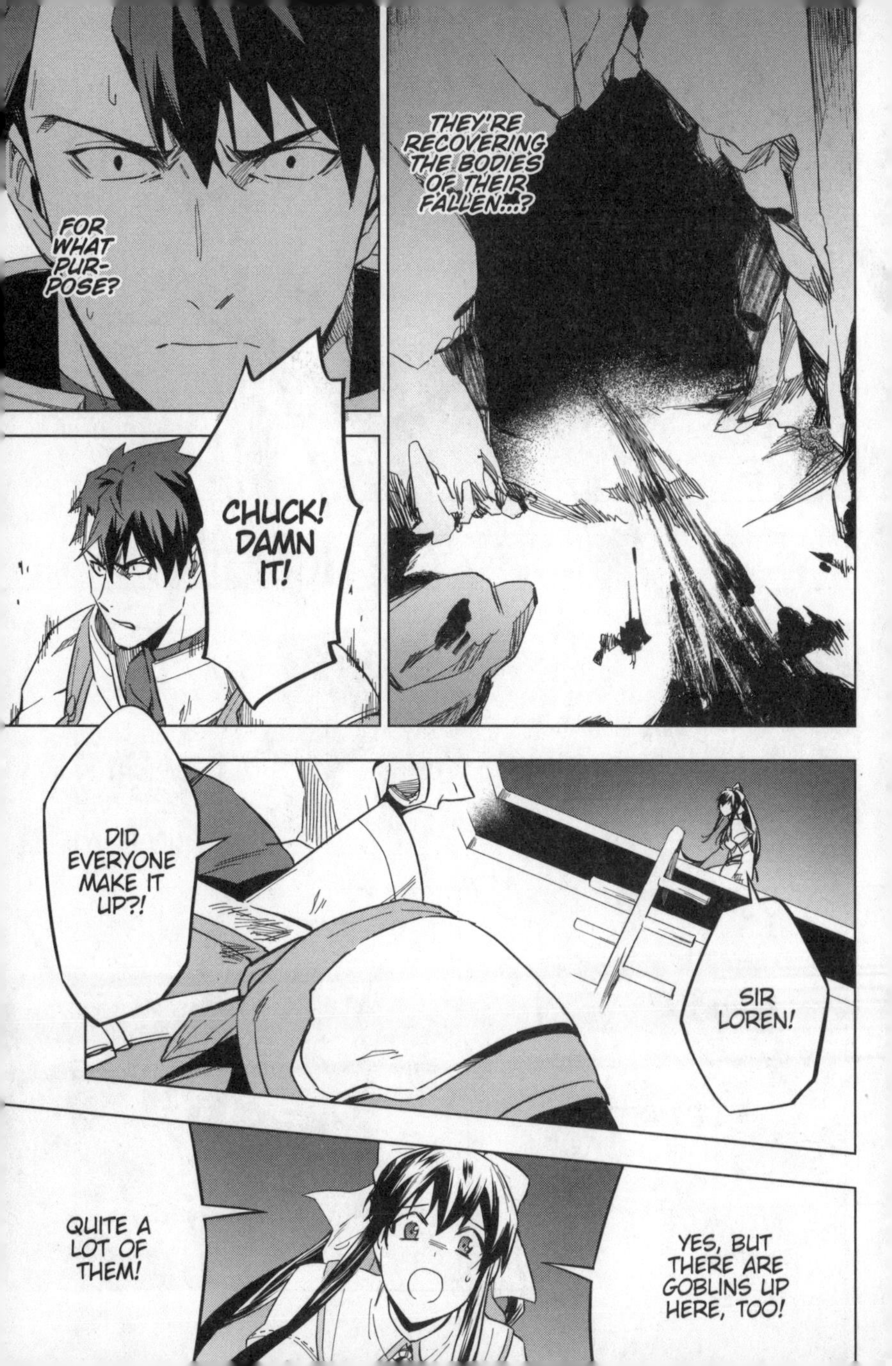
THEY'RE RECOVERING THE BODIES OF THEIR FALLEN...?
FOR WHAT PURPOSE?
CHUCK! DAMN IT!
SIR LOREN!
DID EVERYONE MAKE IT UP?!
YES, BUT THERE ARE GOBLINS UP HERE, TOO!
QUITE A LOT OF THEM!

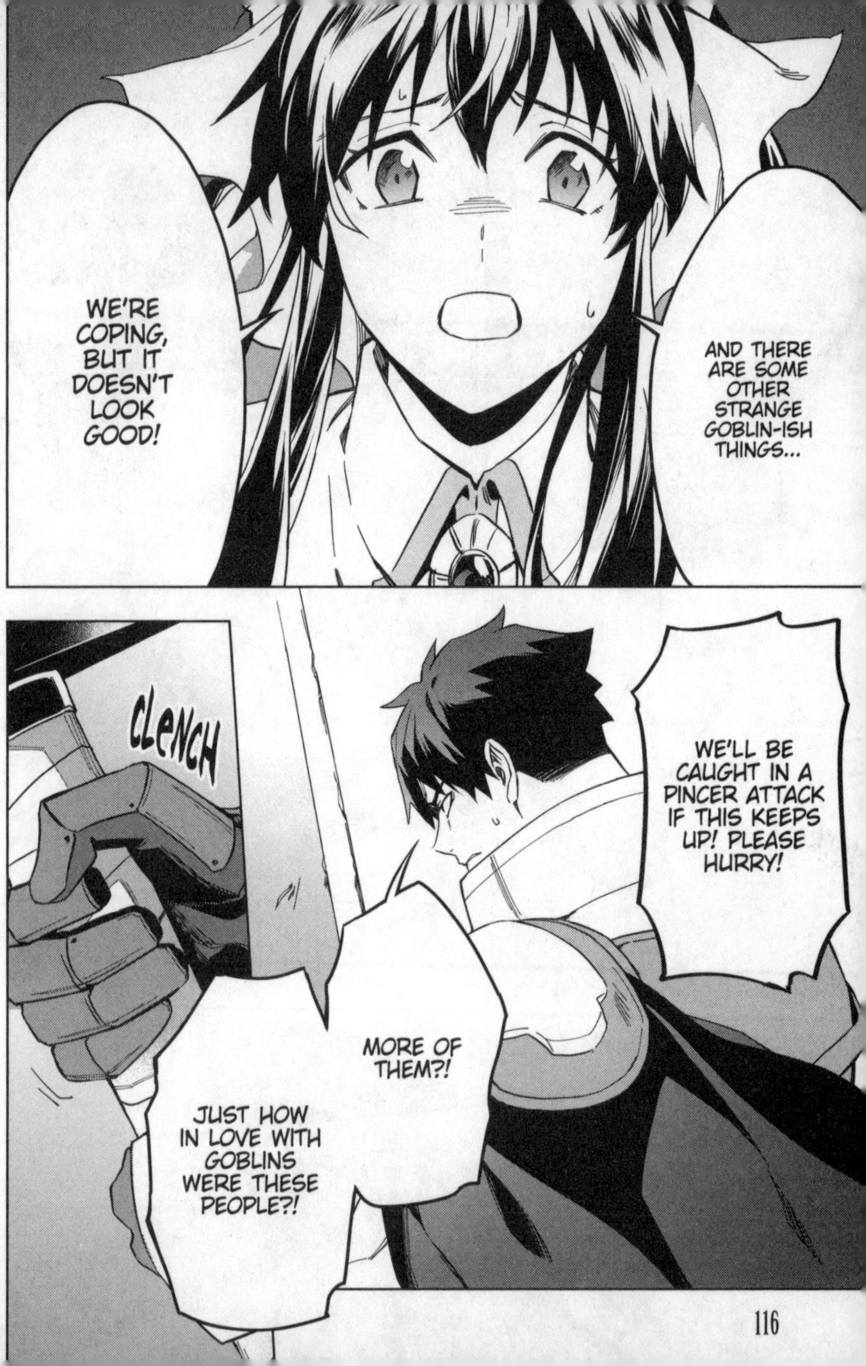
AND THERE ARE SOME OTHER STRANGE GOBLIN-ISH THINGS...
WE'RE COPING, BUT IT DOESN'T LOOK GOOD!
WE'LL BE CAUGHT IN A PINCER ATTACK IF THIS KEEPS UP! PLEASE HURRY!
CLENCH
MORE OF THEM?!
JUST HOW IN LOVE WITH GOBLINS WERE THESE PEOPLE?!

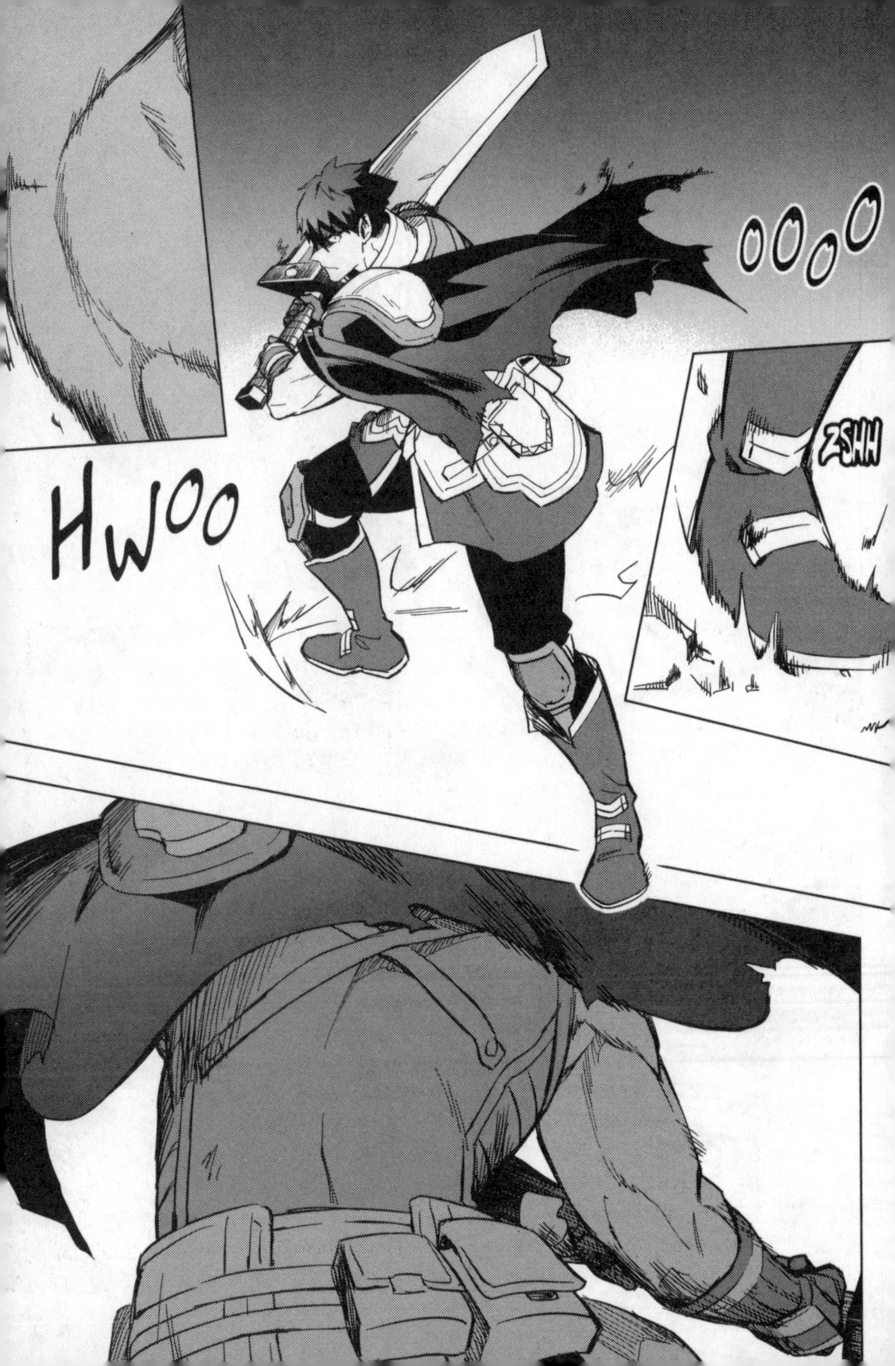
OOOO
ZSHH
HWOO

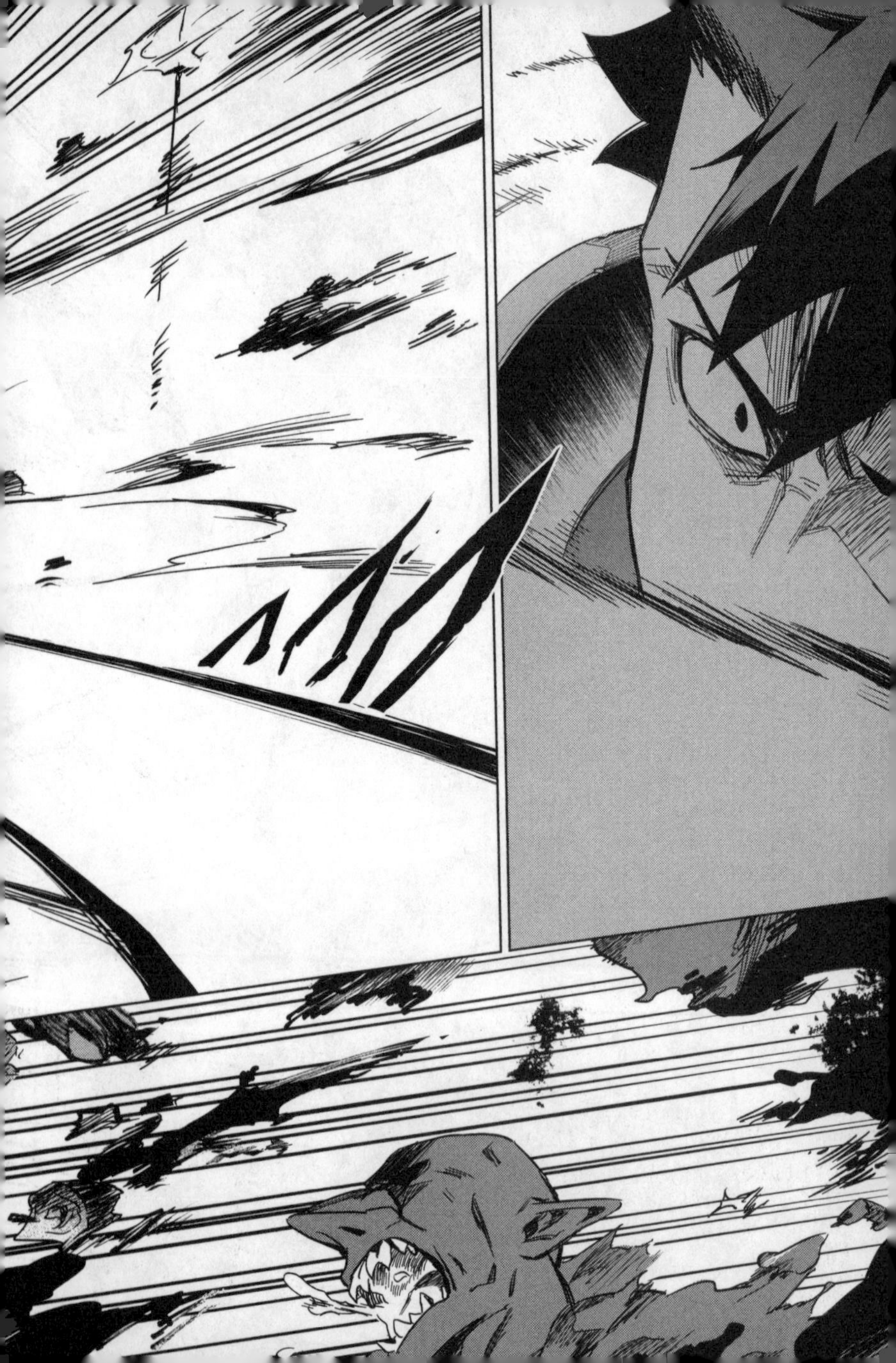

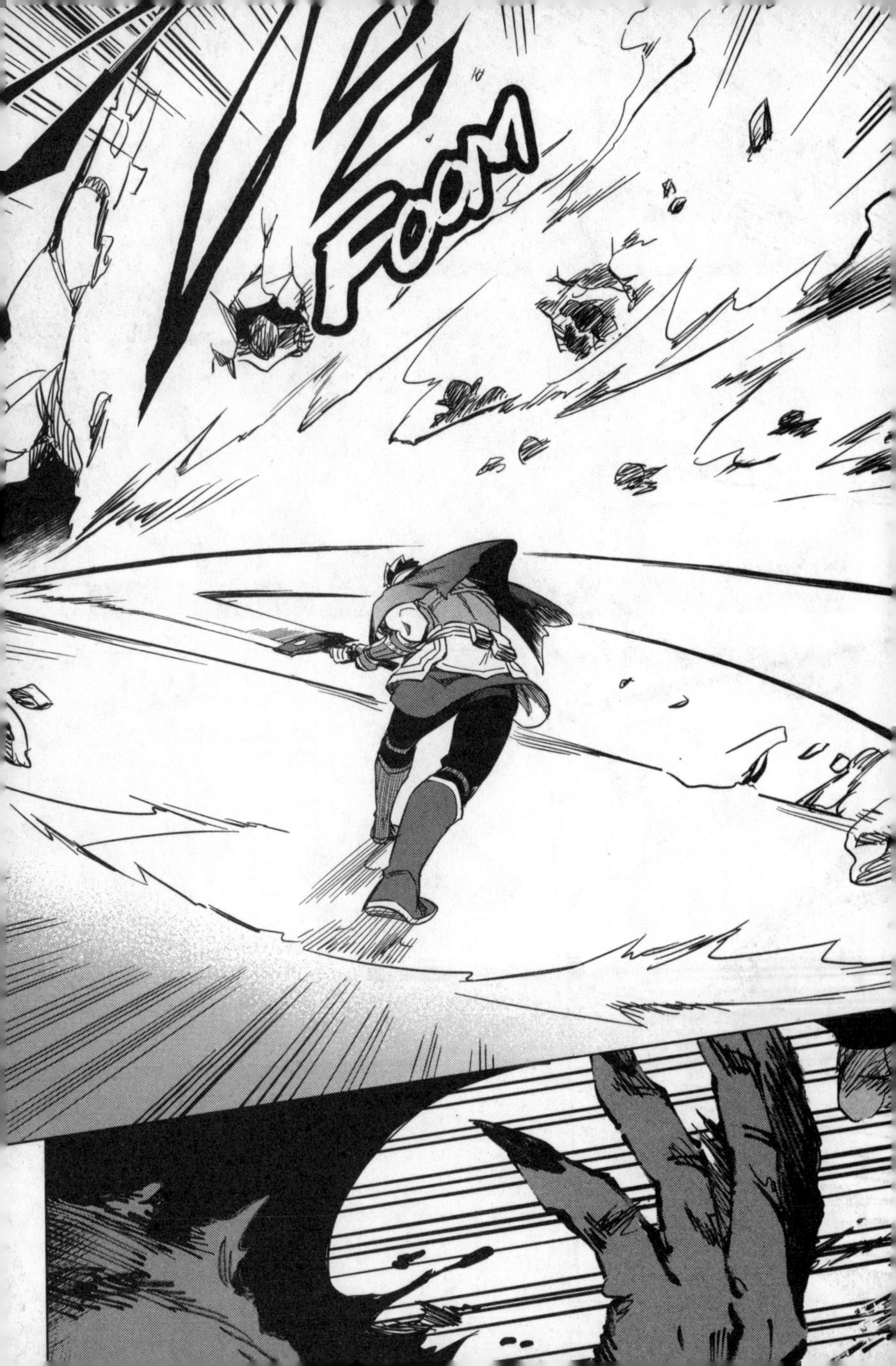
FOOM

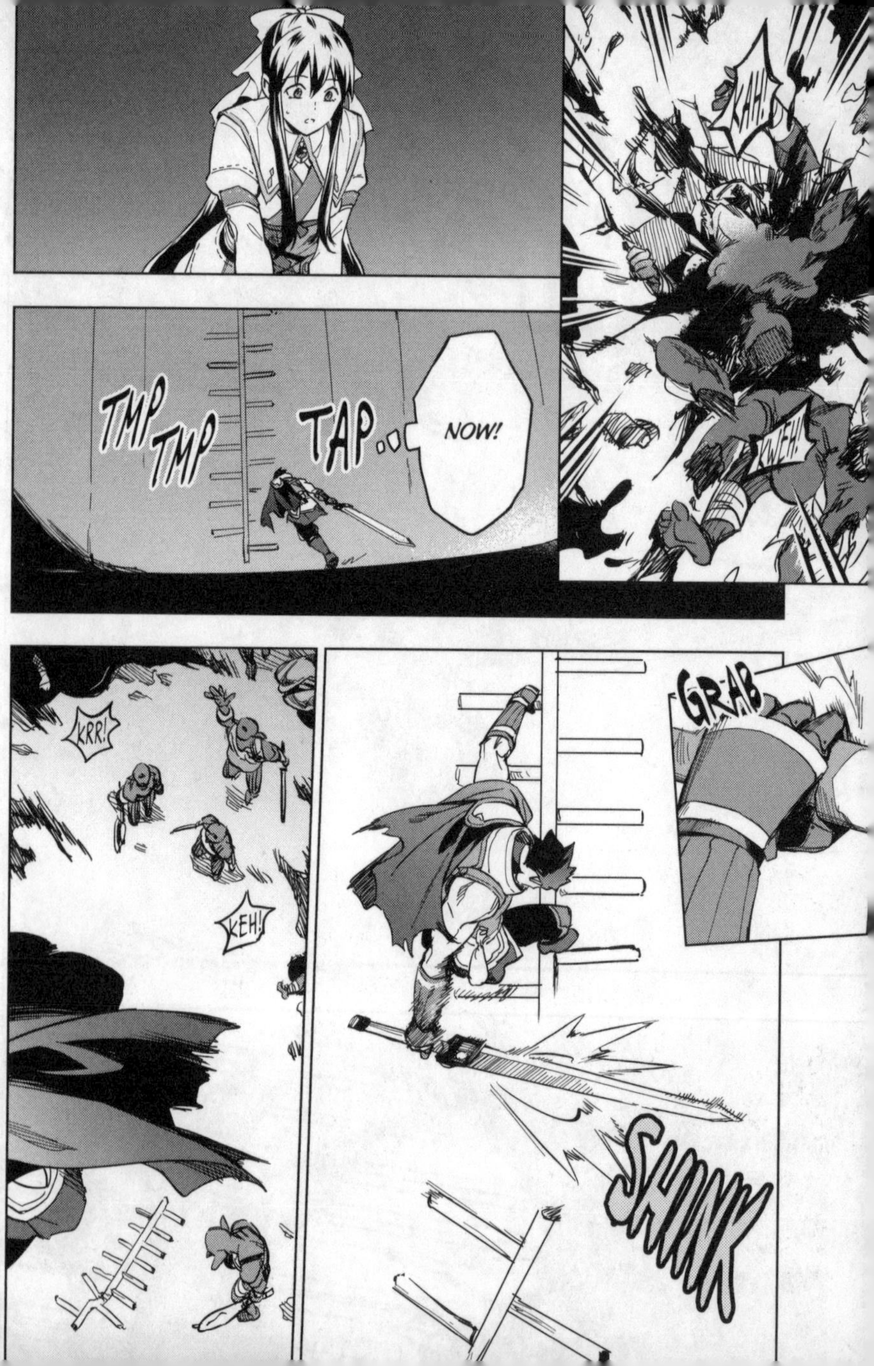
KAH!
KWEH!
TMP TMP
TAP
NOW!
GRAB
SHINK
KRR!
KEH!

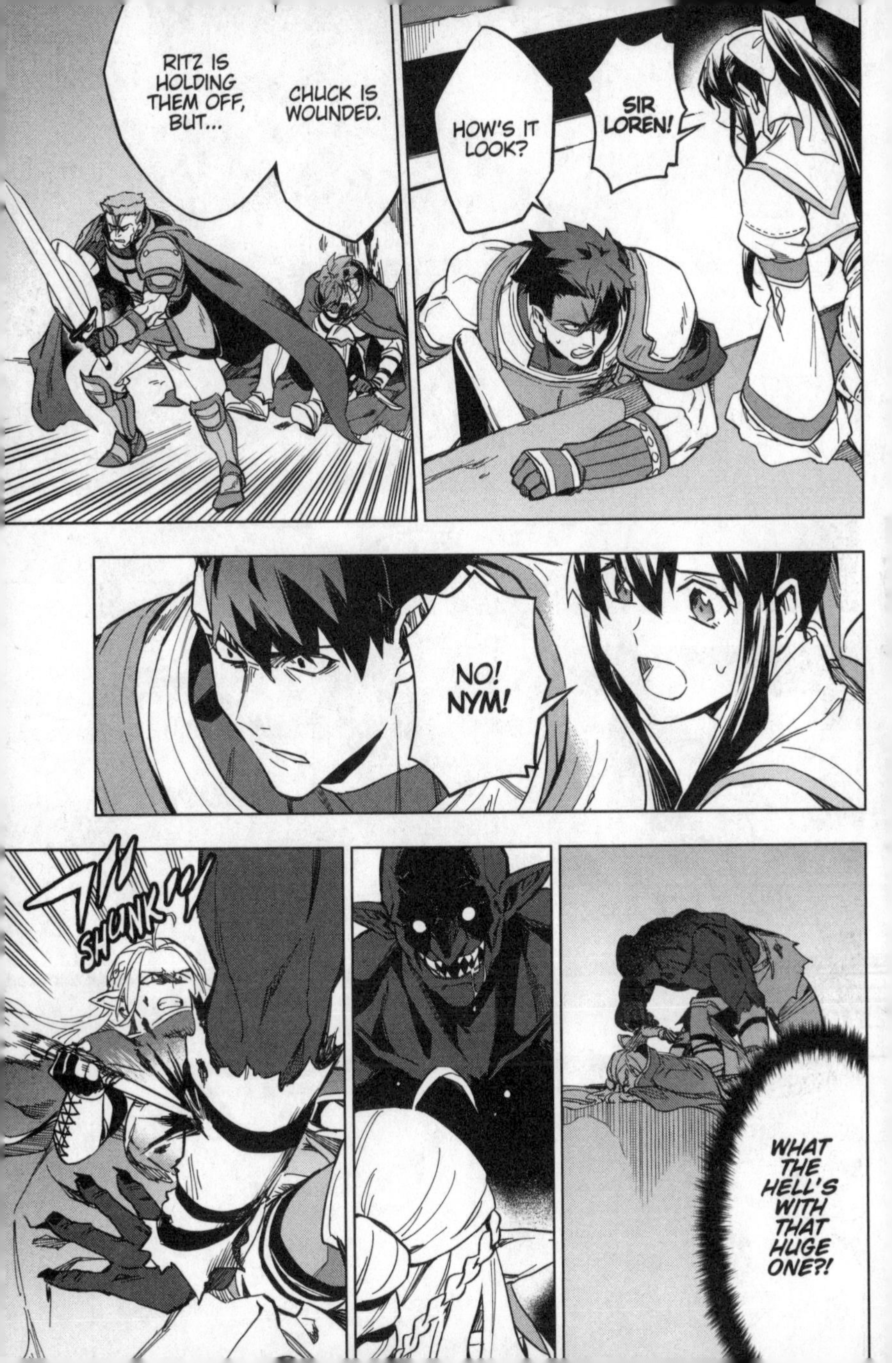
SIR LOREN!
HOW'S IT LOOK?
CHUCK IS WOUNDED.
RITZ IS HOLDING THEM OFF, BUT...
NO! NYM!
WHAT THE HELL'S WITH THAT HUGE ONE?!
SHUNK

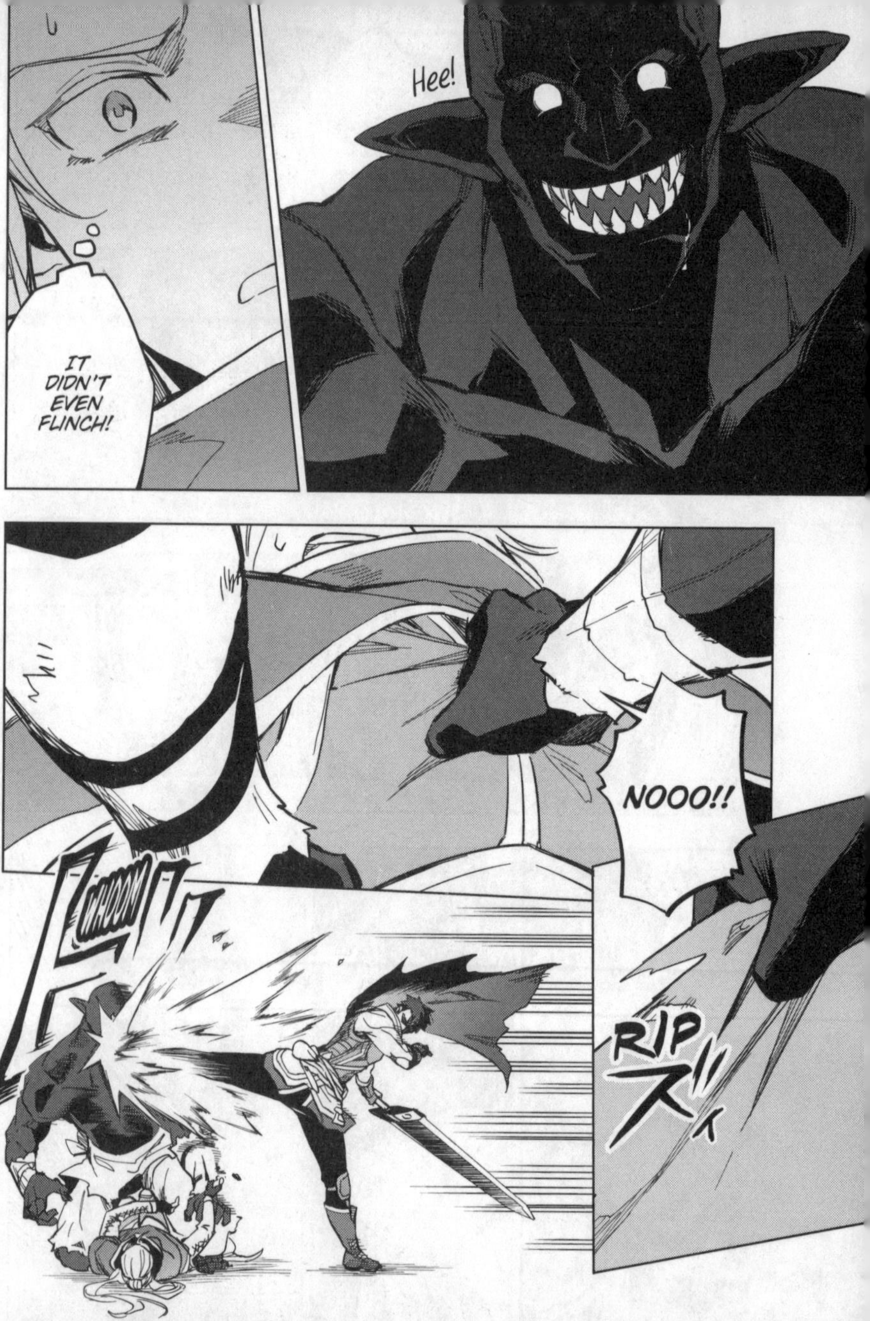
Hee!
IT DIDN'T EVEN FLINCH!
NOOO!!
RIP
WHOOM

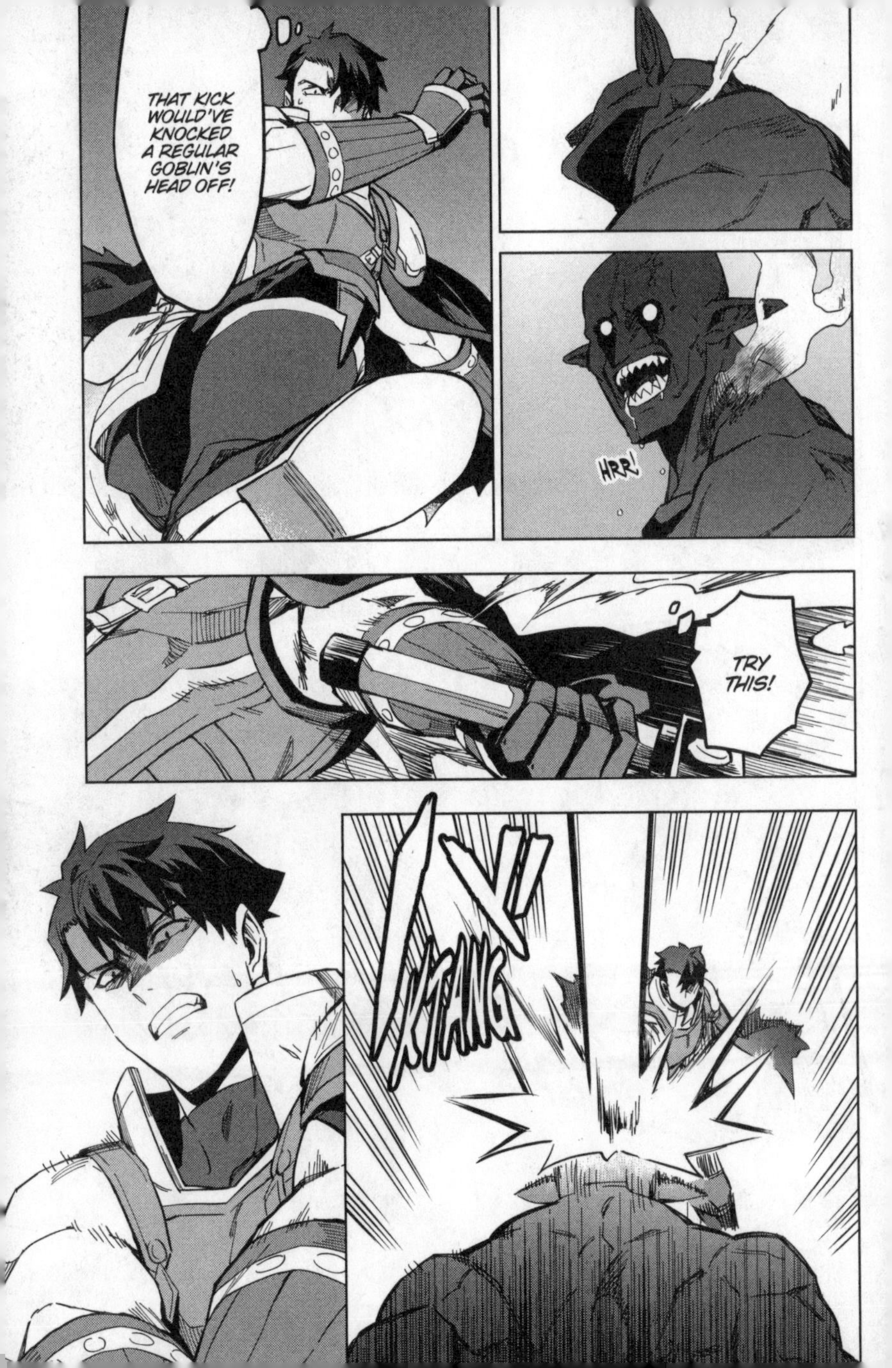
HRR!
THAT KICK WOULD'VE KNOCKED A REGULAR GOBLIN'S HEAD OFF!
TRY THIS!
KTANG

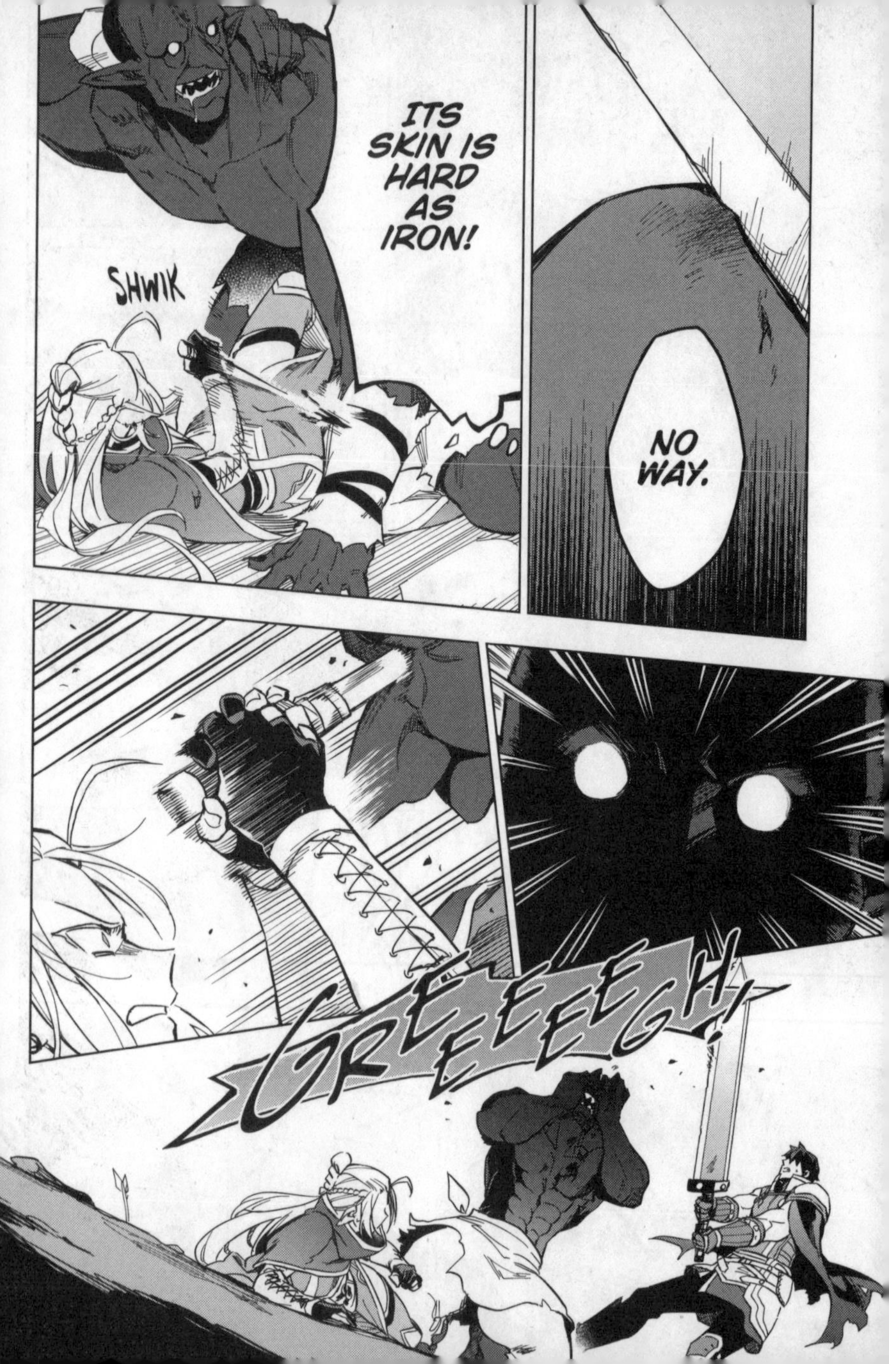
NO WAY.
ITS SKIN IS HARD AS IRON!
SHWIK
GREEEEGH!

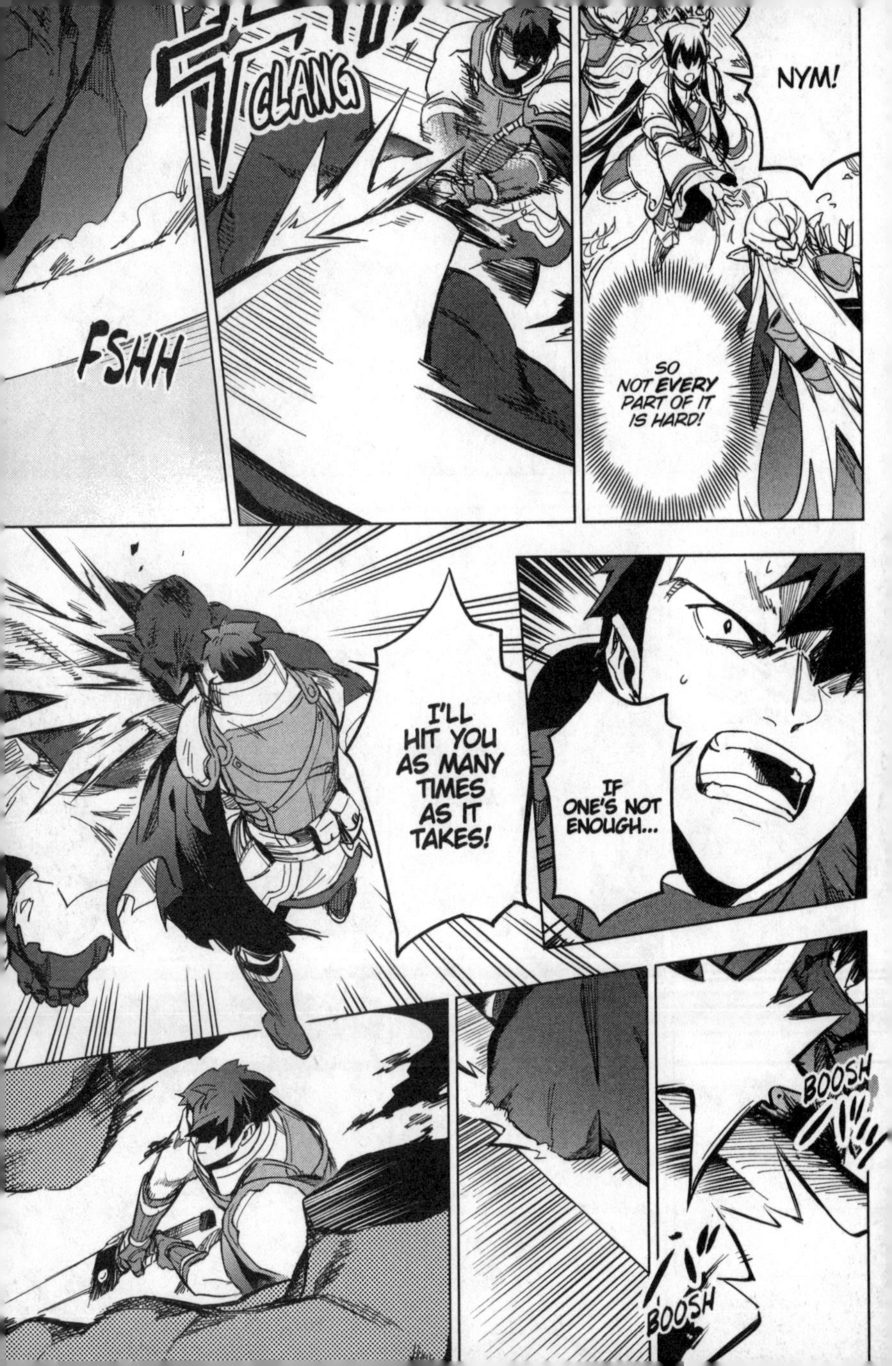
NYM!
SO NOT EVERY PART OF IT IS HARD!
CLANG
FSHH
IF ONE'S NOT ENOUGH...
I'LL HIT YOU AS MANY TIMES AS IT TAKES!
BOOSH
BOOSH

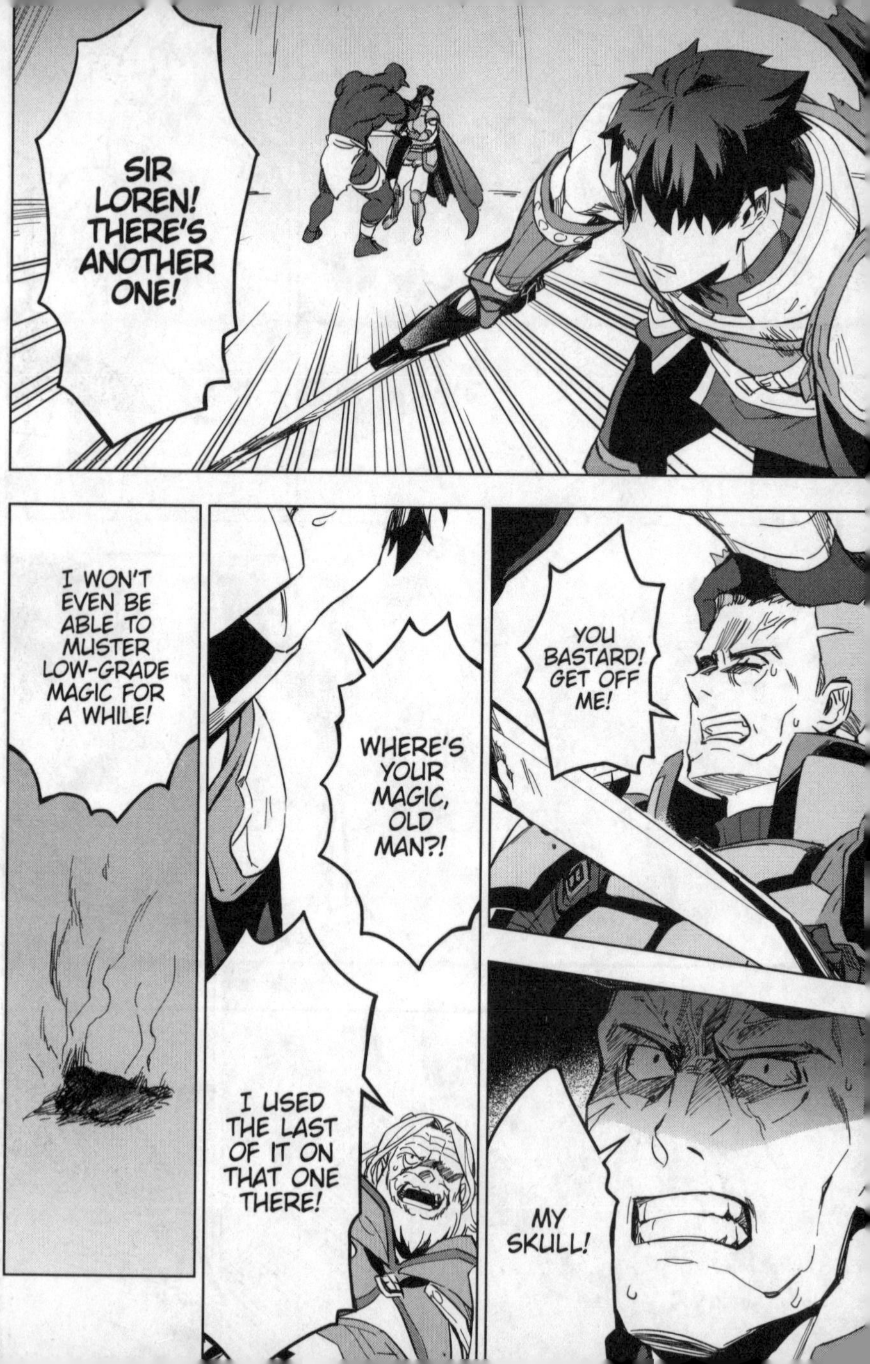
SIR LOREN! THERE'S ANOTHER ONE!
YOU BASTARD! GET OFF ME!
MY SKULL!
WHERE'S YOUR MAGIC, OLD MAN?!
I USED THE LAST OF IT ON THAT ONE THERE!
I WON'T EVEN BE ABLE TO MUSTER LOW-GRADE MAGIC FOR A WHILE!

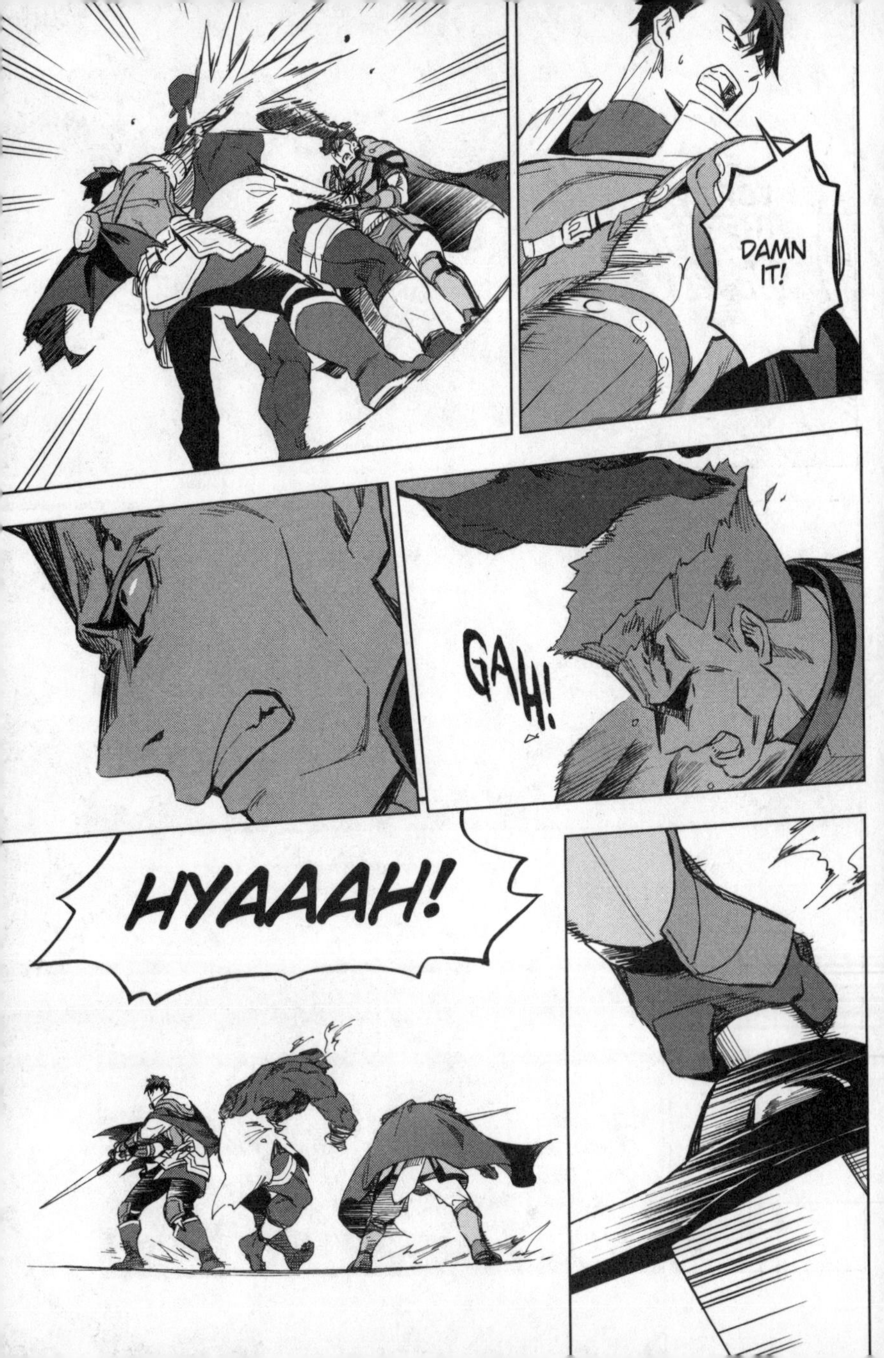
DAMN IT!
GAH!
HYAAAH!

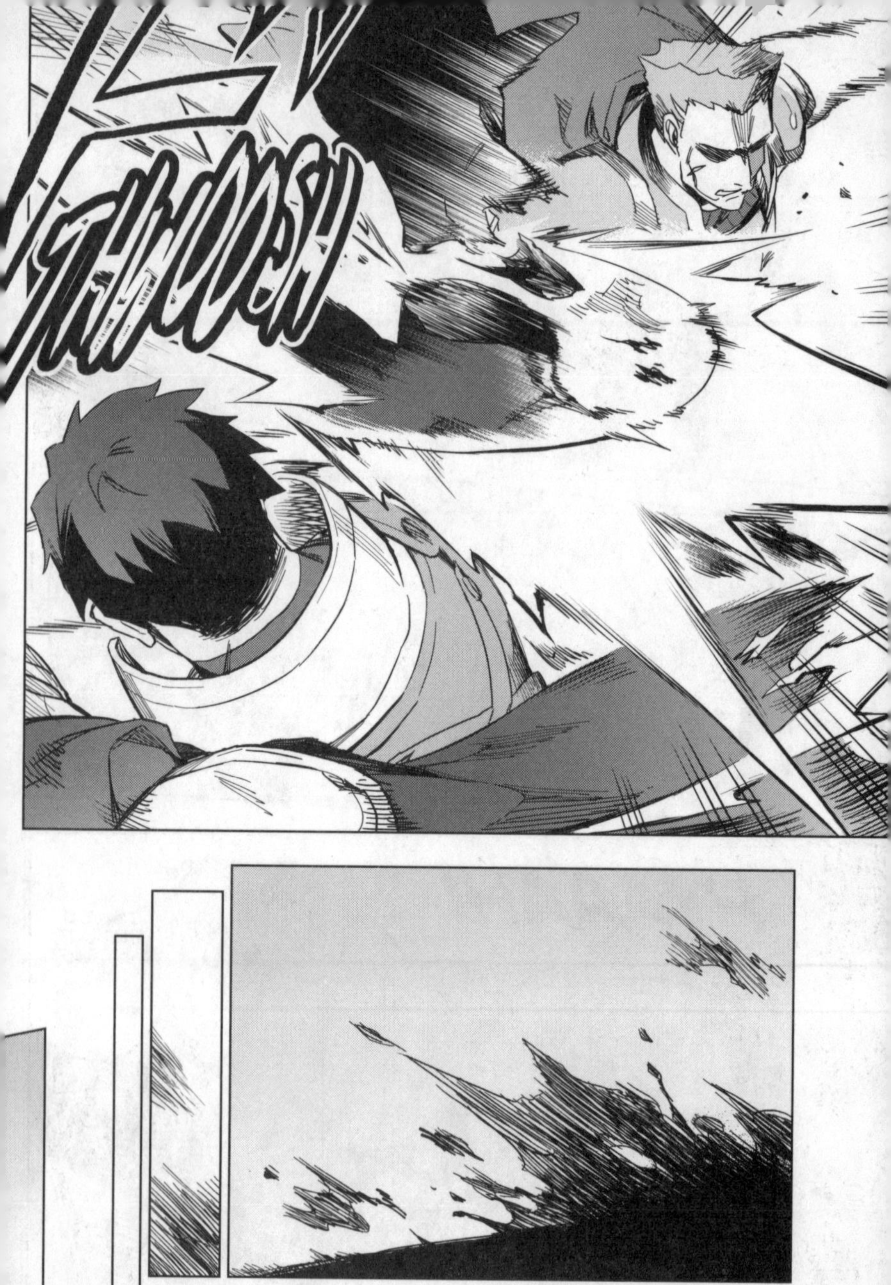
THWOOSH

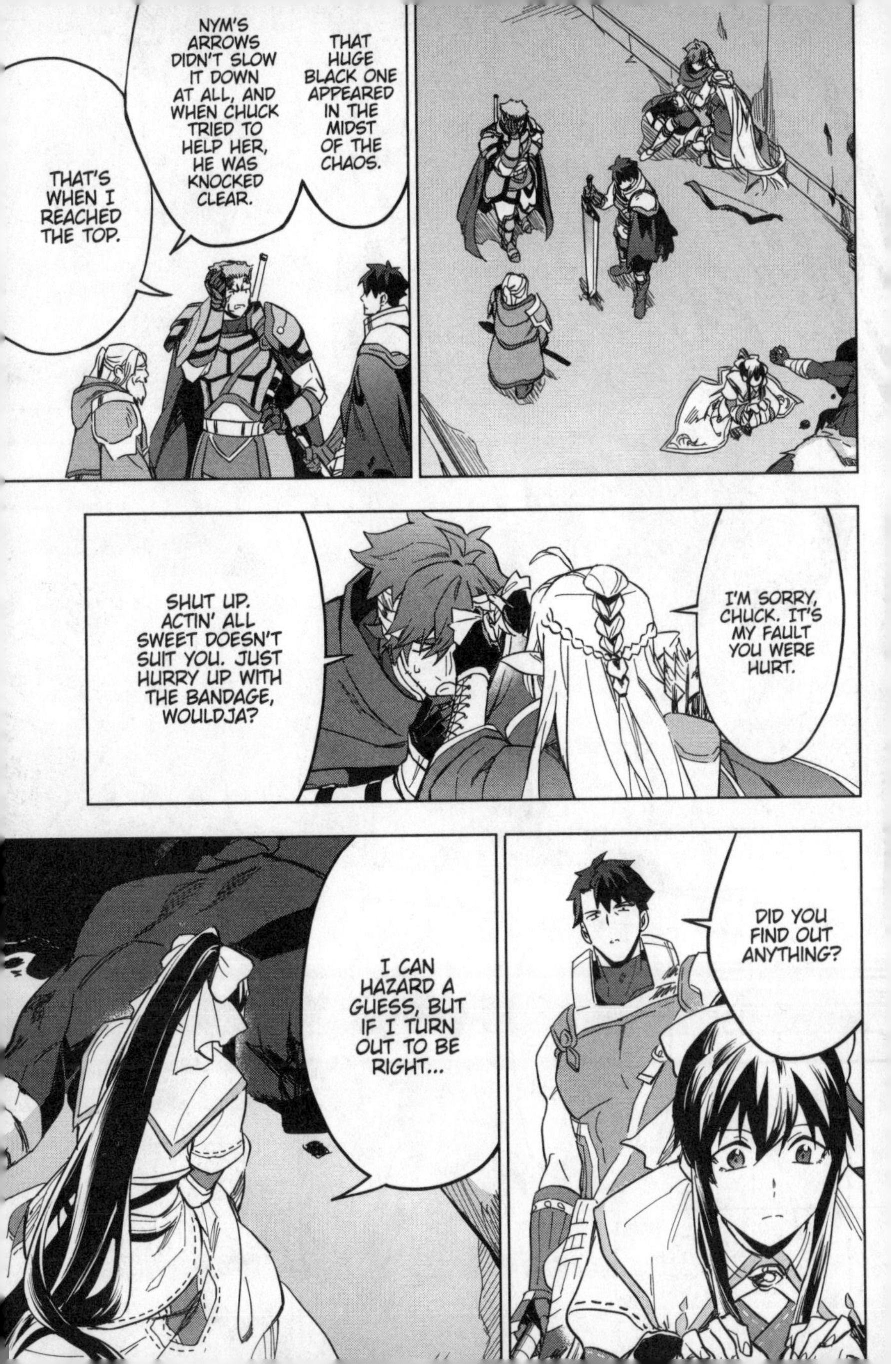
THAT HUGE BLACK ONE APPEARED IN THE MIDST OF THE CHAOS.
NYM'S ARROWS DIDN'T SLOW IT DOWN AT ALL, AND WHEN CHUCK TRIED TO HELP HER, HE WAS KNOCKED CLEAR.
THAT'S WHEN I REACHED THE TOP.
I'M SORRY, CHUCK. IT'S MY FAULT YOU WERE HURT.
SHUT UP. ACTIN' ALL SWEET DOESN'T SUIT YOU. JUST HURRY UP WITH THE BANDAGE, WOULDJA?
DID YOU FIND OUT ANYTHING?
I CAN HAZARD A GUESS, BUT IF I TURN OUT TO BE RIGHT...

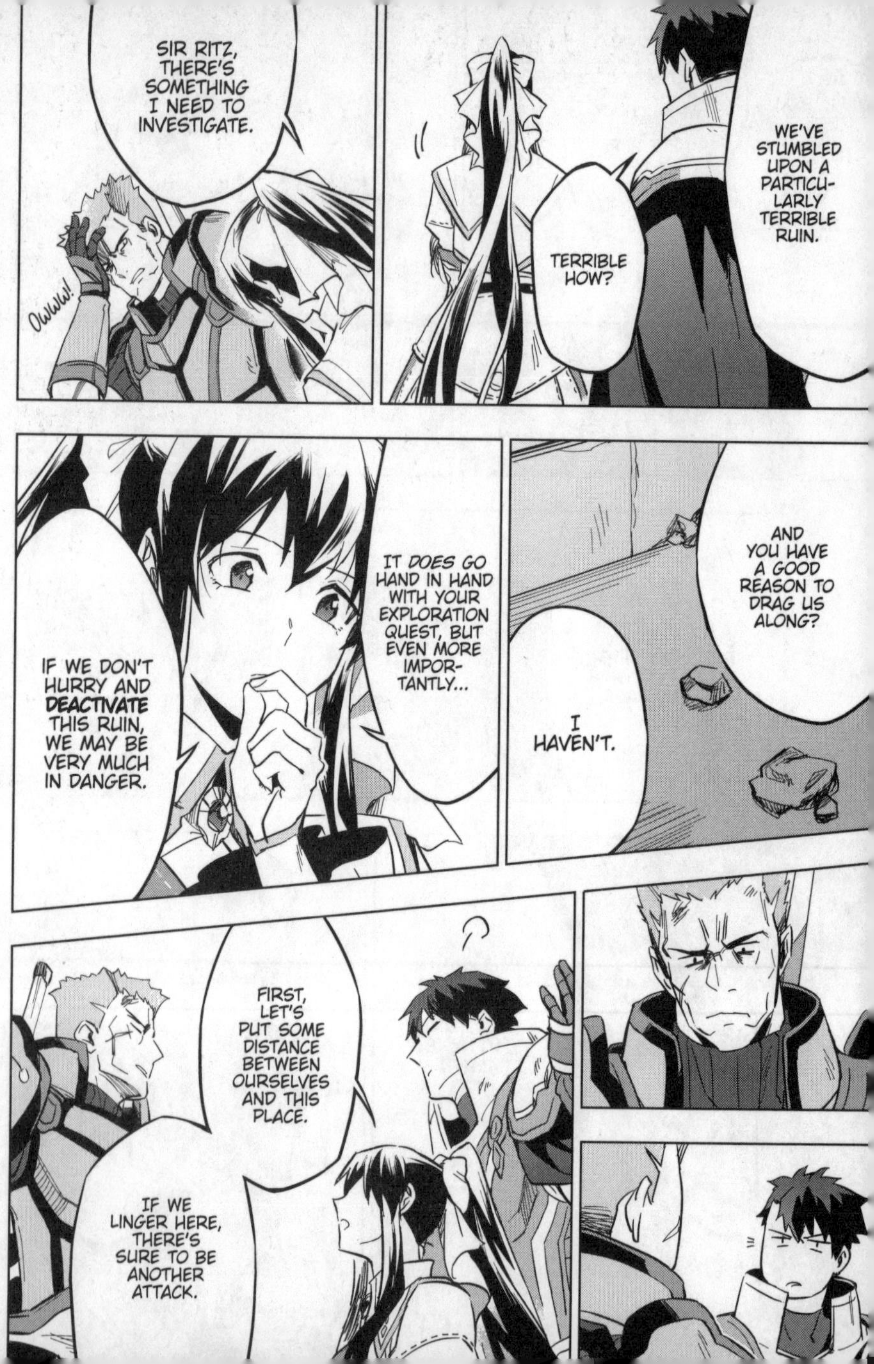
WE'VE STUMBLED UPON A PARTICU-LARLY TERRIBLE RUIN.
TERRIBLE HOW?
SIR RITZ, THERE'S SOMETHING I NEED TO INVESTIGATE.
Owww!
AND YOU HAVE A GOOD REASON TO DRAG US ALONG?
I HAVEN'T.
IT *DOES* GO HAND IN HAND WITH YOUR EXPLORATION QUEST, BUT EVEN MORE IMPOR-TANTLY...
IF WE DON'T HURRY AND **DEACTIVATE** THIS RUIN, WE MAY BE VERY MUCH IN DANGER.
FIRST, LET'S PUT SOME DISTANCE BETWEEN OURSELVES AND THIS PLACE.
IF WE LINGER HERE, THERE'S SURE TO BE ANOTHER ATTACK.

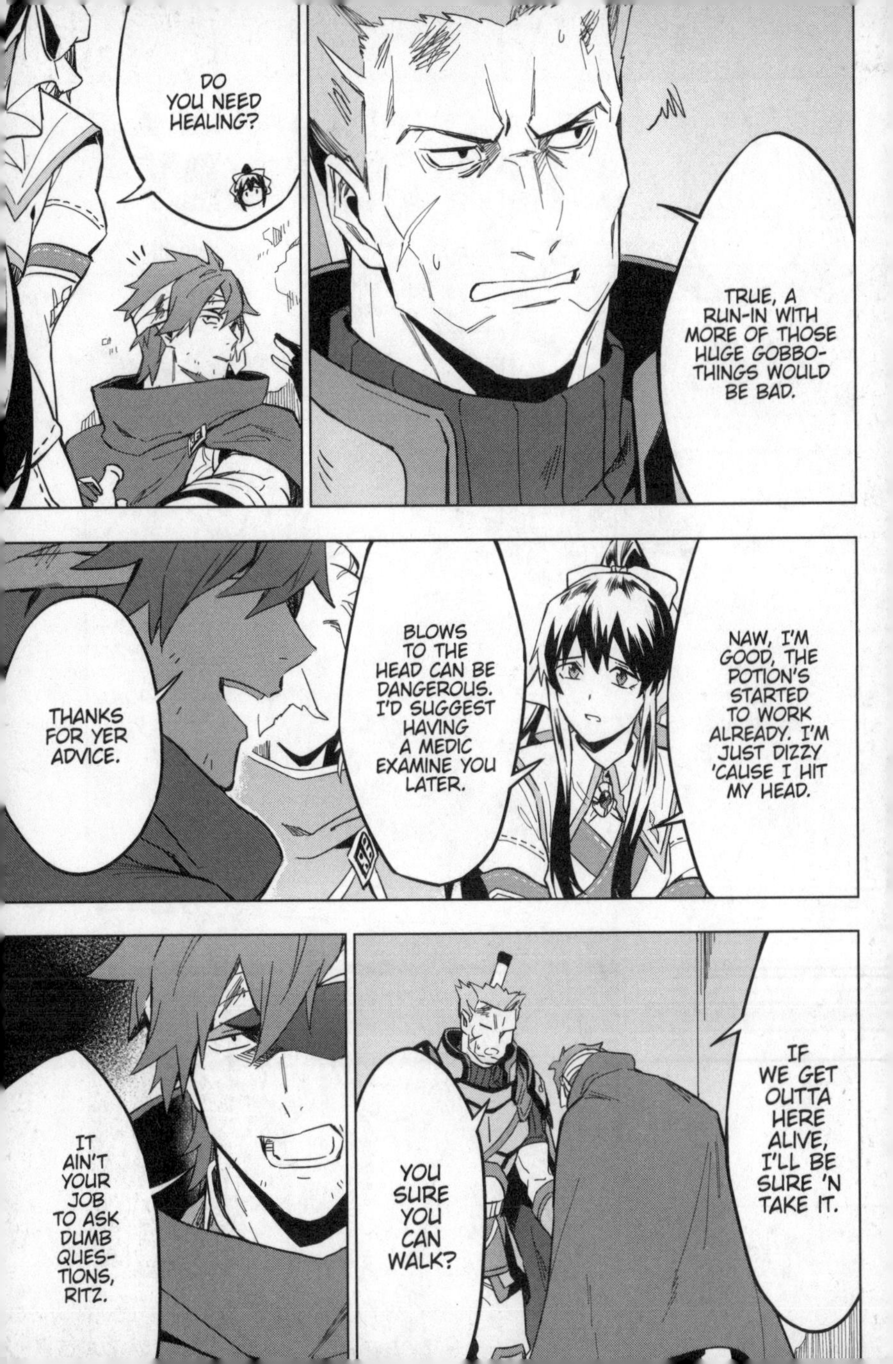
TRUE, A RUN-IN WITH MORE OF THOSE HUGE GOBBO-THINGS WOULD BE BAD.
DO YOU NEED HEALING?
NAW, I'M GOOD, THE POTION'S STARTED TO WORK ALREADY. I'M JUST DIZZY 'CAUSE I HIT MY HEAD.
BLOWS TO THE HEAD CAN BE DANGEROUS. I'D SUGGEST HAVING A MEDIC EXAMINE YOU LATER.
THANKS FOR YER ADVICE.
IF WE GET OUTTA HERE ALIVE, I'LL BE SURE 'N TAKE IT.
YOU SURE YOU CAN WALK?
IT AIN'T YOUR JOB TO ASK DUMB QUES-TIONS, RITZ.

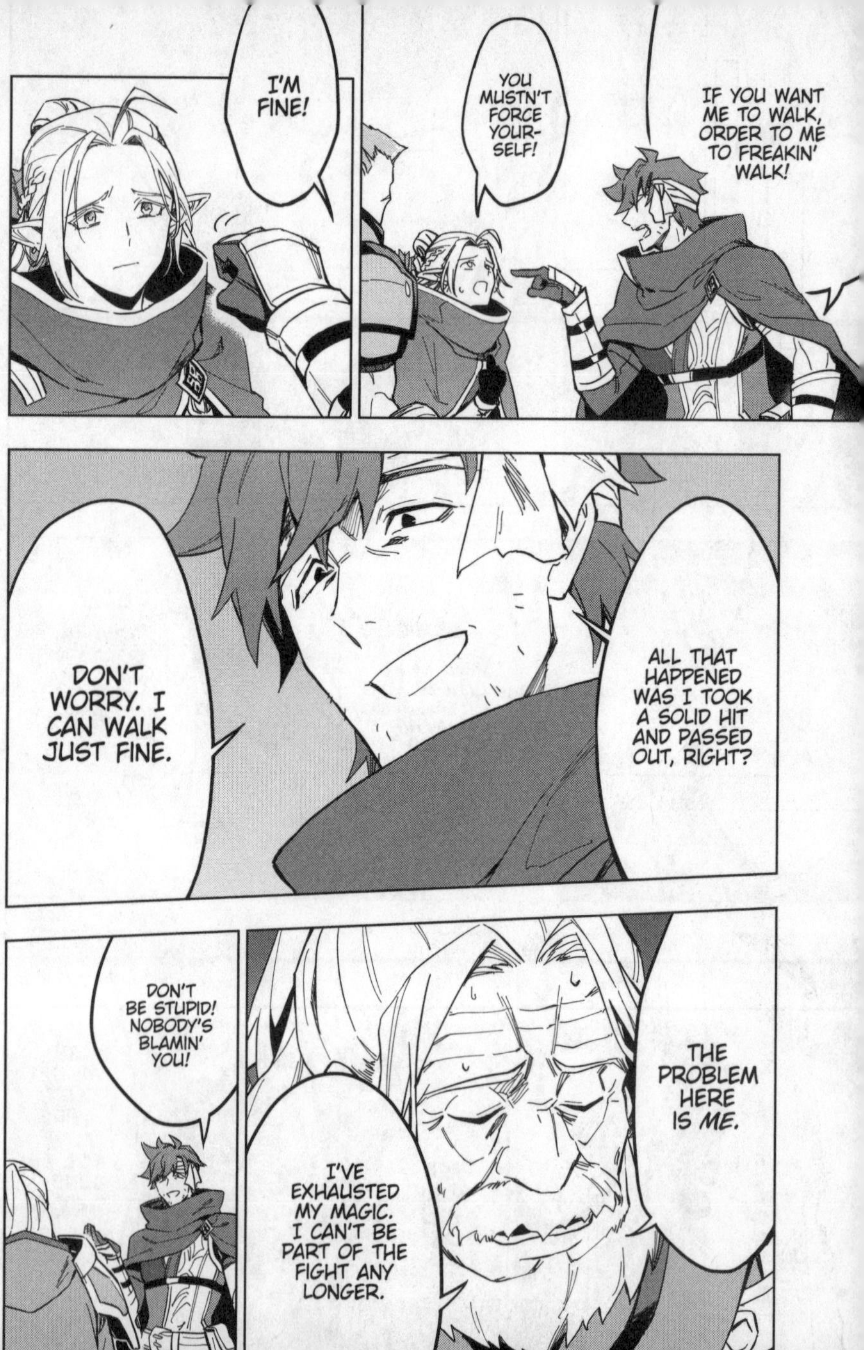
IF YOU WANT ME TO WALK, ORDER TO ME TO FREAKIN' WALK!
YOU MUSTN'T FORCE YOUR-SELF!
I'M FINE!
ALL THAT HAPPENED WAS I TOOK A SOLID HIT AND PASSED OUT, RIGHT?
DON'T WORRY. I CAN WALK JUST FINE.
THE PROBLEM HERE IS *ME.*
I'VE EXHAUSTED MY MAGIC. I CAN'T BE PART OF THE FIGHT ANY LONGER.
DON'T BE STUPID! NOBODY'S BLAMIN' YOU!

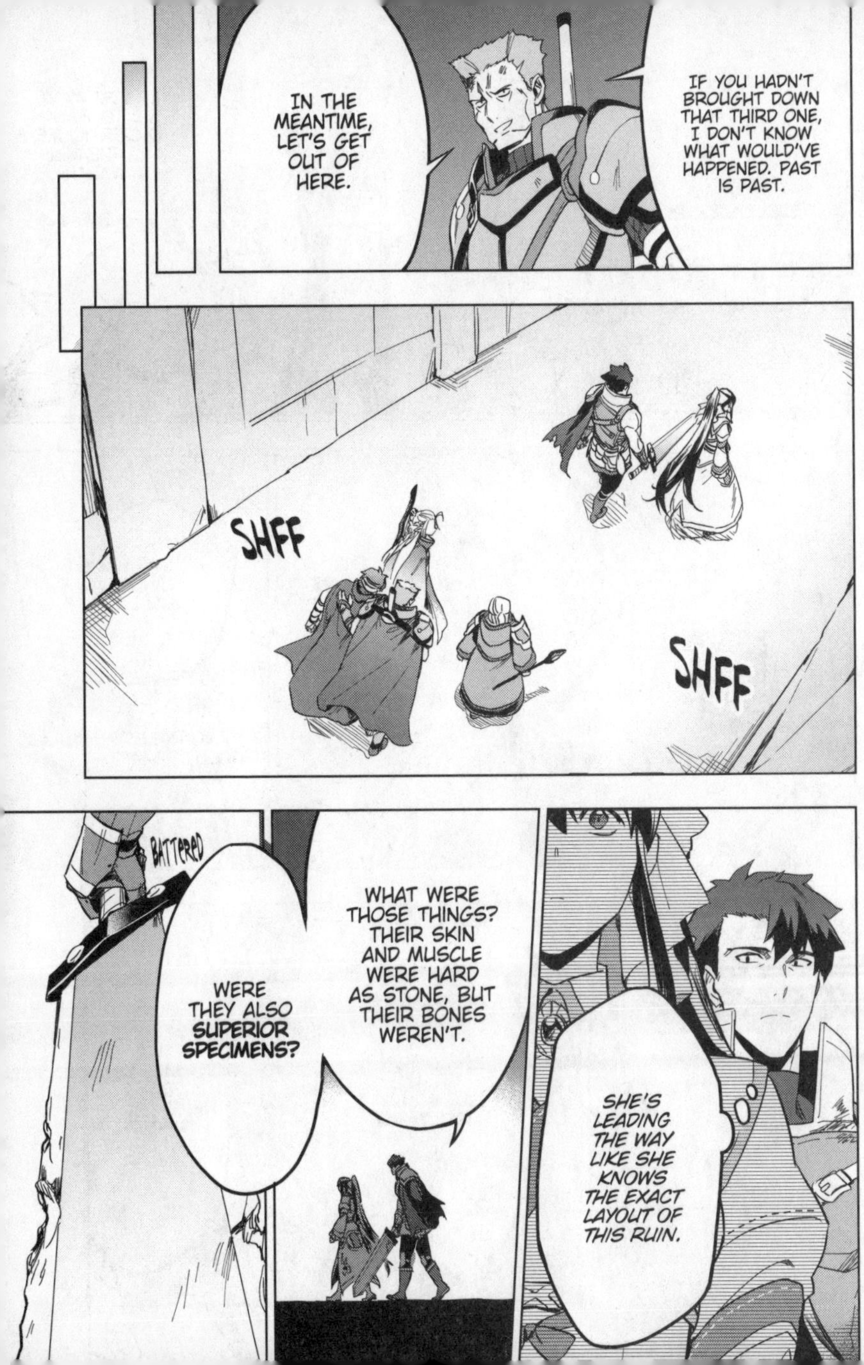
IF YOU HADN'T BROUGHT DOWN THAT THIRD ONE, I DON'T KNOW WHAT WOULD'VE HAPPENED. PAST IS PAST.
IN THE MEANTIME, LET'S GET OUT OF HERE.
SHFF
SHFF
SHE'S LEADING THE WAY LIKE SHE KNOWS THE EXACT LAYOUT OF THIS RUIN.
BATTERED
WHAT WERE THOSE THINGS? THEIR SKIN AND MUSCLE WERE HARD AS STONE, BUT THEIR BONES WEREN'T.
WERE THEY ALSO SUPERIOR SPECIMENS?

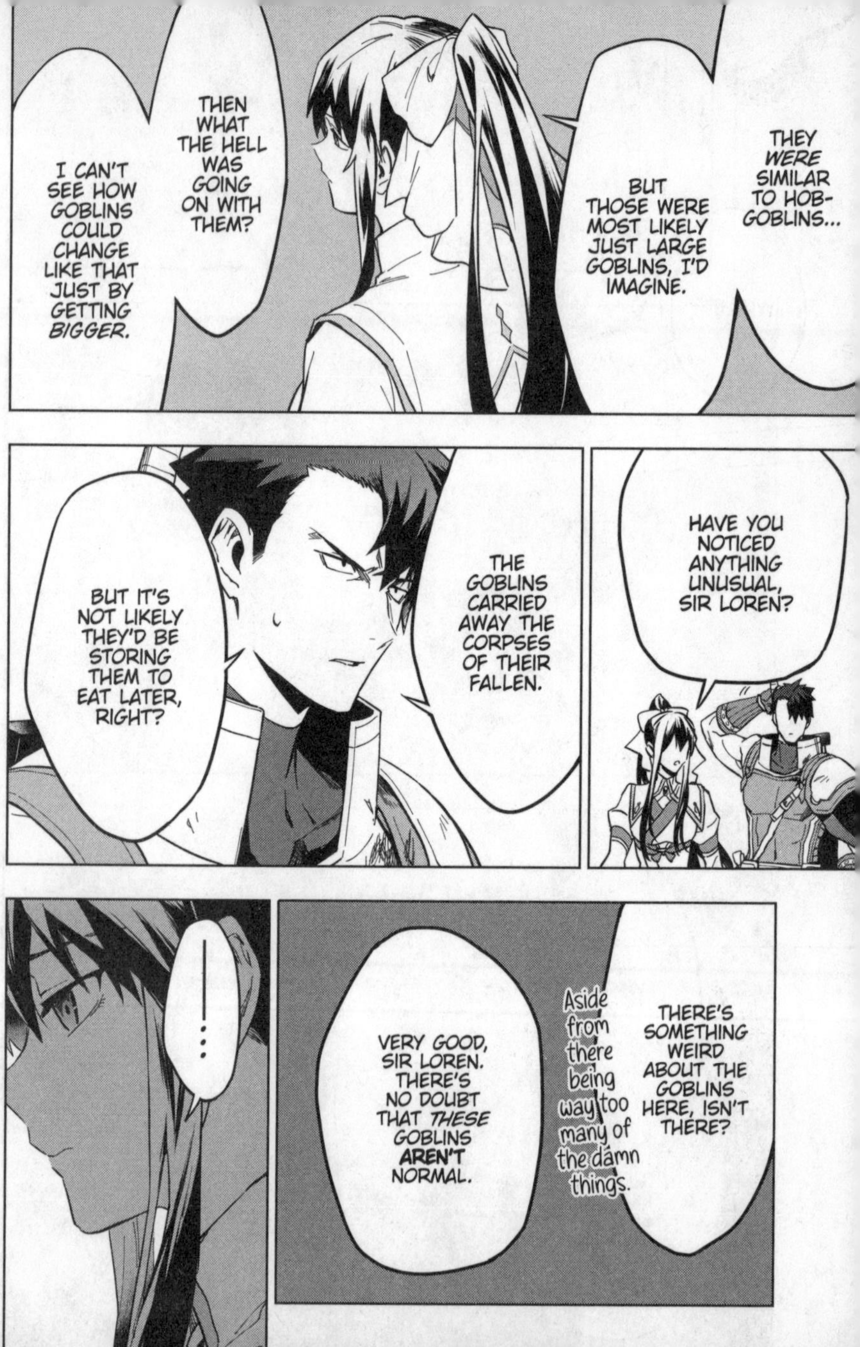
THEY WERE SIMILAR TO HOB-GOBLINS...
BUT THOSE WERE MOST LIKELY JUST LARGE GOBLINS, I'D IMAGINE.
THEN WHAT THE HELL WAS GOING ON WITH THEM?
I CAN'T SEE HOW GOBLINS COULD CHANGE LIKE THAT JUST BY GETTING BIGGER.
HAVE YOU NOTICED ANYTHING UNUSUAL, SIR LOREN?
THE GOBLINS CARRIED AWAY THE CORPSES OF THEIR FALLEN.
BUT IT'S NOT LIKELY THEY'D BE STORING THEM TO EAT LATER, RIGHT?
THERE'S SOMETHING WEIRD ABOUT THE GOBLINS HERE, ISN'T THERE?
Aside from there being way too many of the damn things.
VERY GOOD, SIR LOREN. THERE'S NO DOUBT THAT THESE GOBLINS AREN'T NORMAL.
......

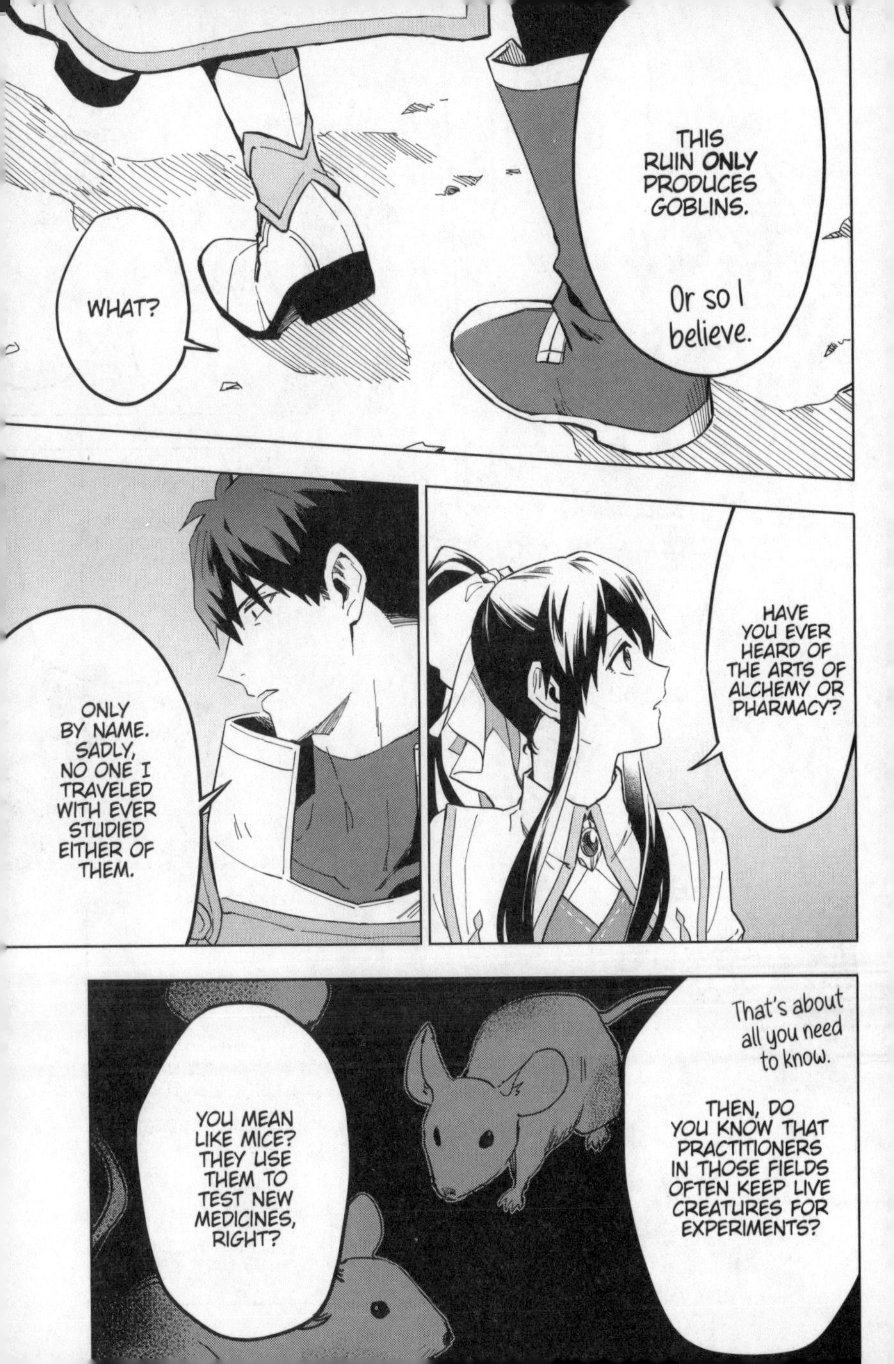
THIS RUIN ONLY PRODUCES GOBLINS.
Or so I believe.
WHAT?
HAVE YOU EVER HEARD OF THE ARTS OF ALCHEMY OR PHARMACY?
ONLY BY NAME. SADLY, NO ONE I TRAVELED WITH EVER STUDIED EITHER OF THEM.
That's about all you need to know.
THEN, DO YOU KNOW THAT PRACTITIONERS IN THOSE FIELDS OFTEN KEEP LIVE CREATURES FOR EXPERIMENTS?
YOU MEAN LIKE MICE? THEY USE THEM TO TEST NEW MEDICINES, RIGHT?

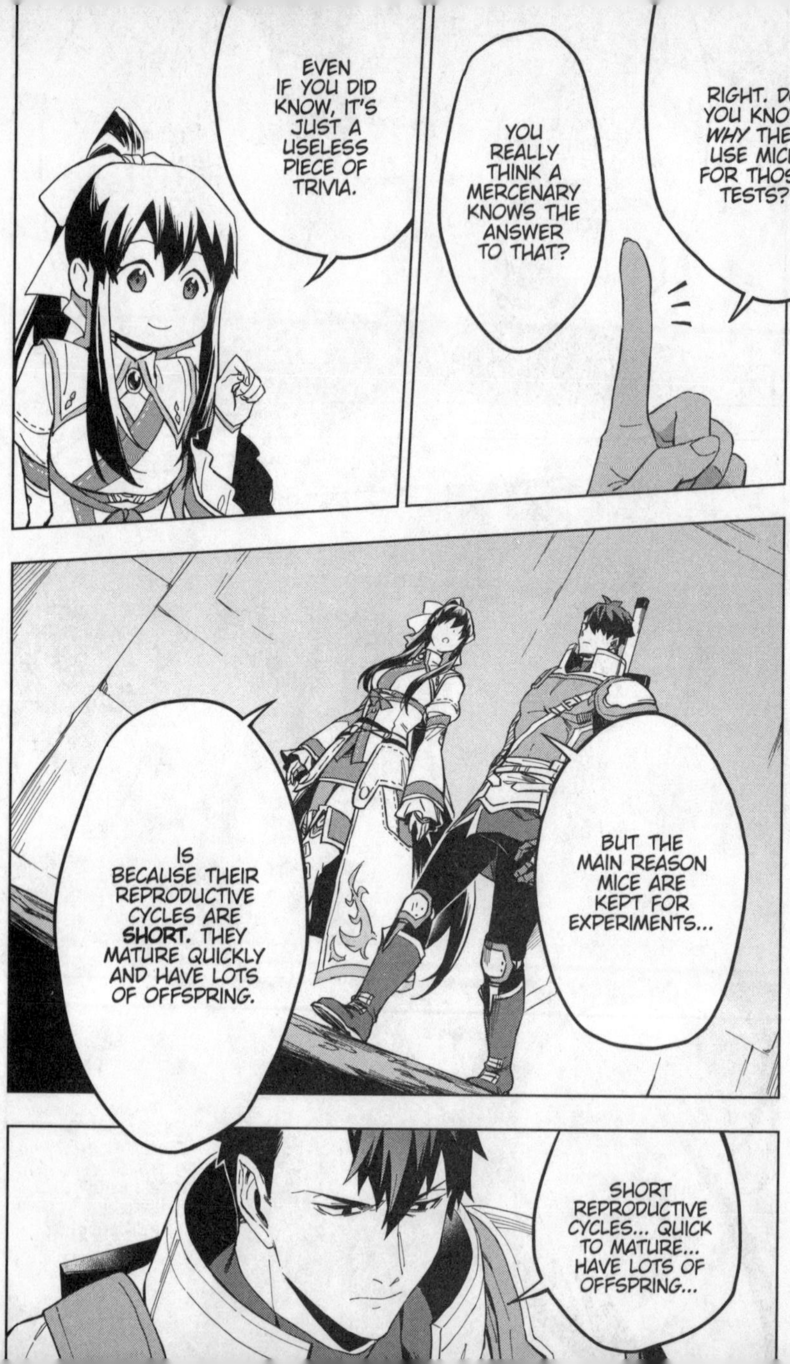
RIGHT. DO YOU KNOW WHY THEY USE MICE FOR THOSE TESTS?
YOU REALLY THINK A MERCENARY KNOWS THE ANSWER TO THAT?
EVEN IF YOU DID KNOW, IT'S JUST A USELESS PIECE OF TRIVIA.
BUT THE MAIN REASON MICE ARE KEPT FOR EXPERIMENTS...
IS BECAUSE THEIR REPRODUCTIVE CYCLES ARE SHORT. THEY MATURE QUICKLY AND HAVE LOTS OF OFFSPRING.
SHORT REPRODUCTIVE CYCLES... QUICK TO MATURE... HAVE LOTS OF OFFSPRING...

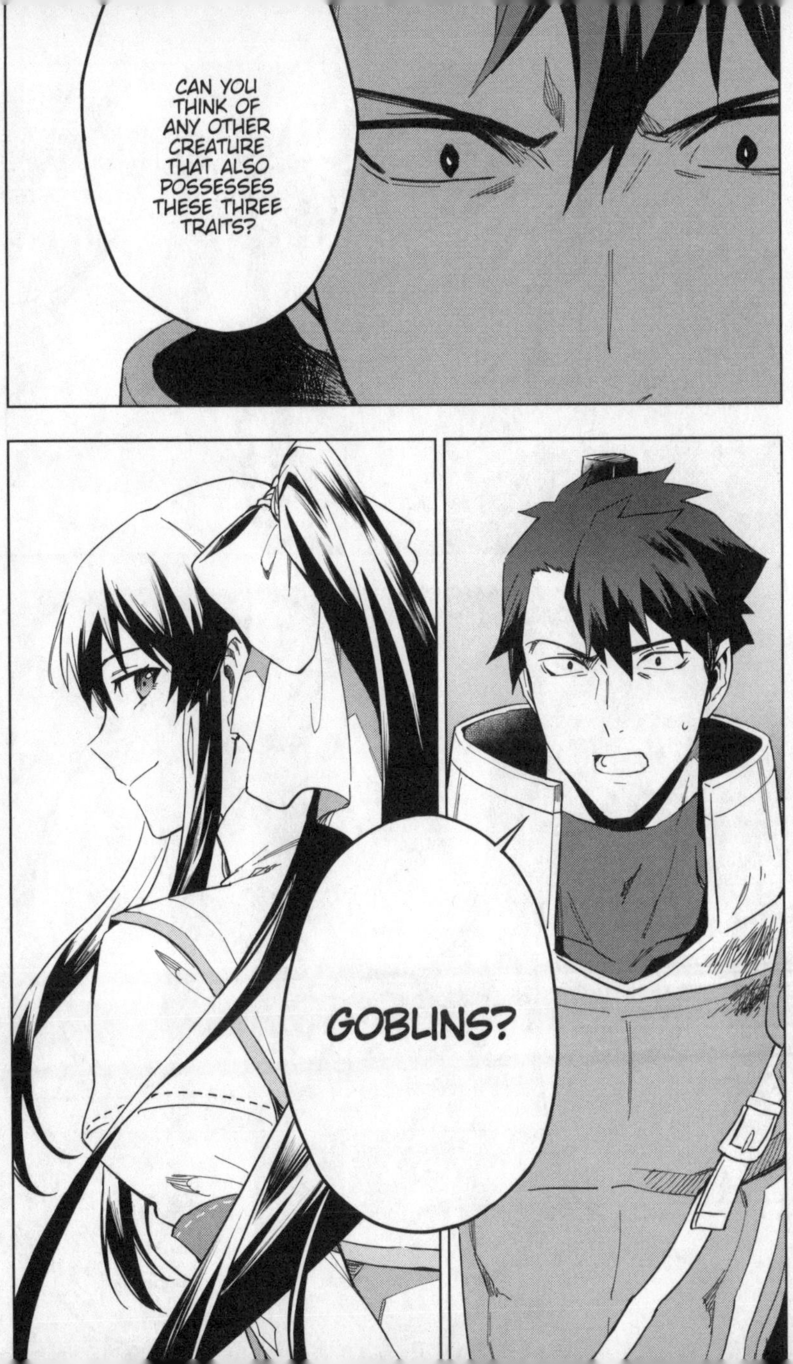
CAN YOU THINK OF ANY OTHER CREATURE THAT ALSO POSSESSES THESE THREE TRAITS?
GOBLINS?

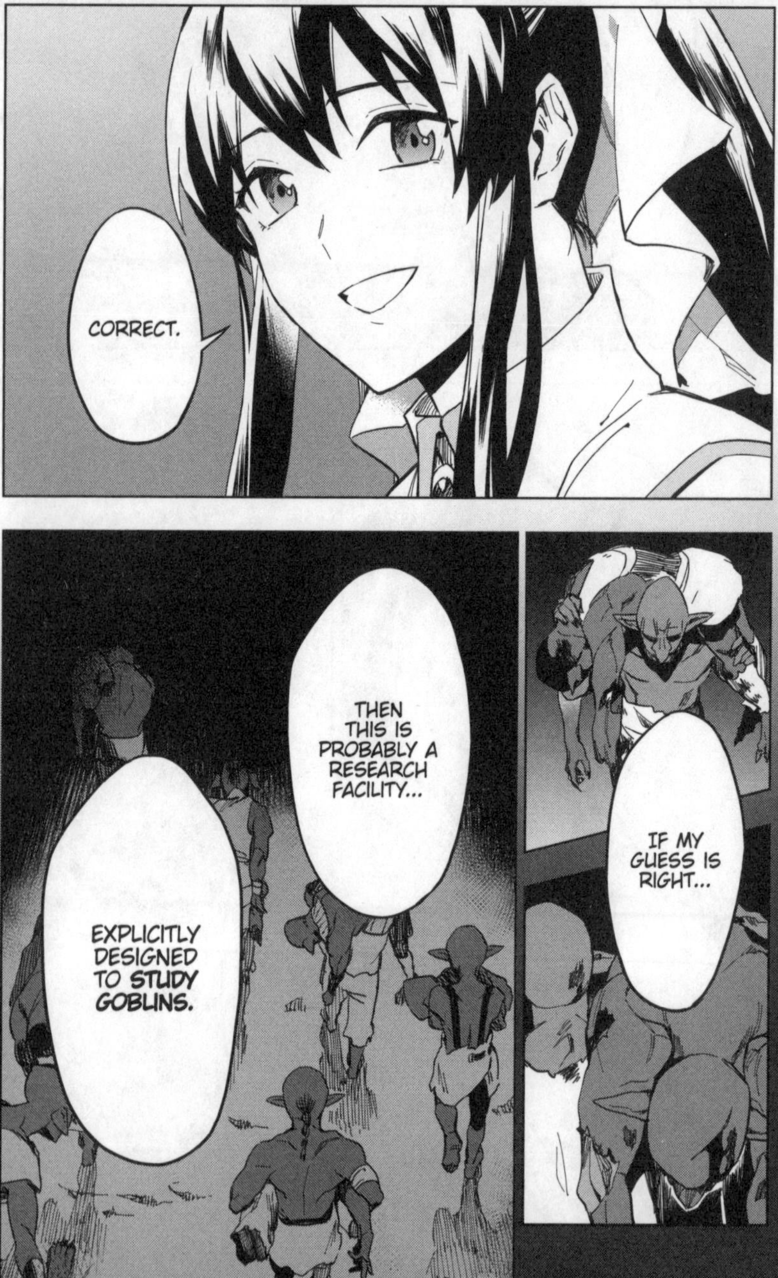
CORRECT.
IF MY GUESS IS RIGHT...
THEN THIS IS PROBABLY A RESEARCH FACILITY...
EXPLICITLY DESIGNED TO STUDY GOBLINS.

THE Strange Adventure OF A Broke MERCENARY

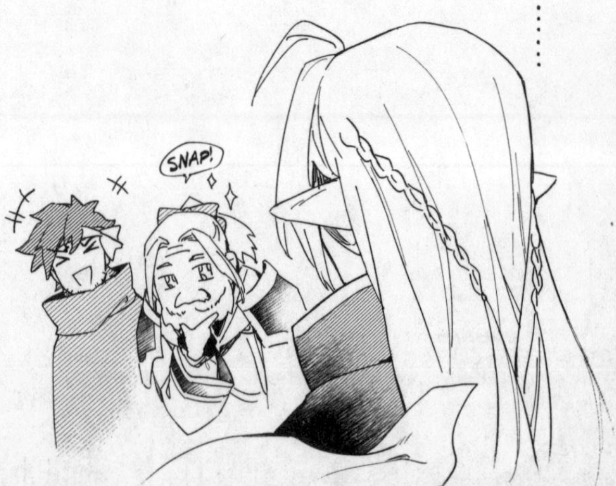
……
SNAP!

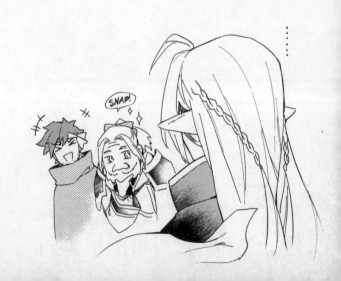

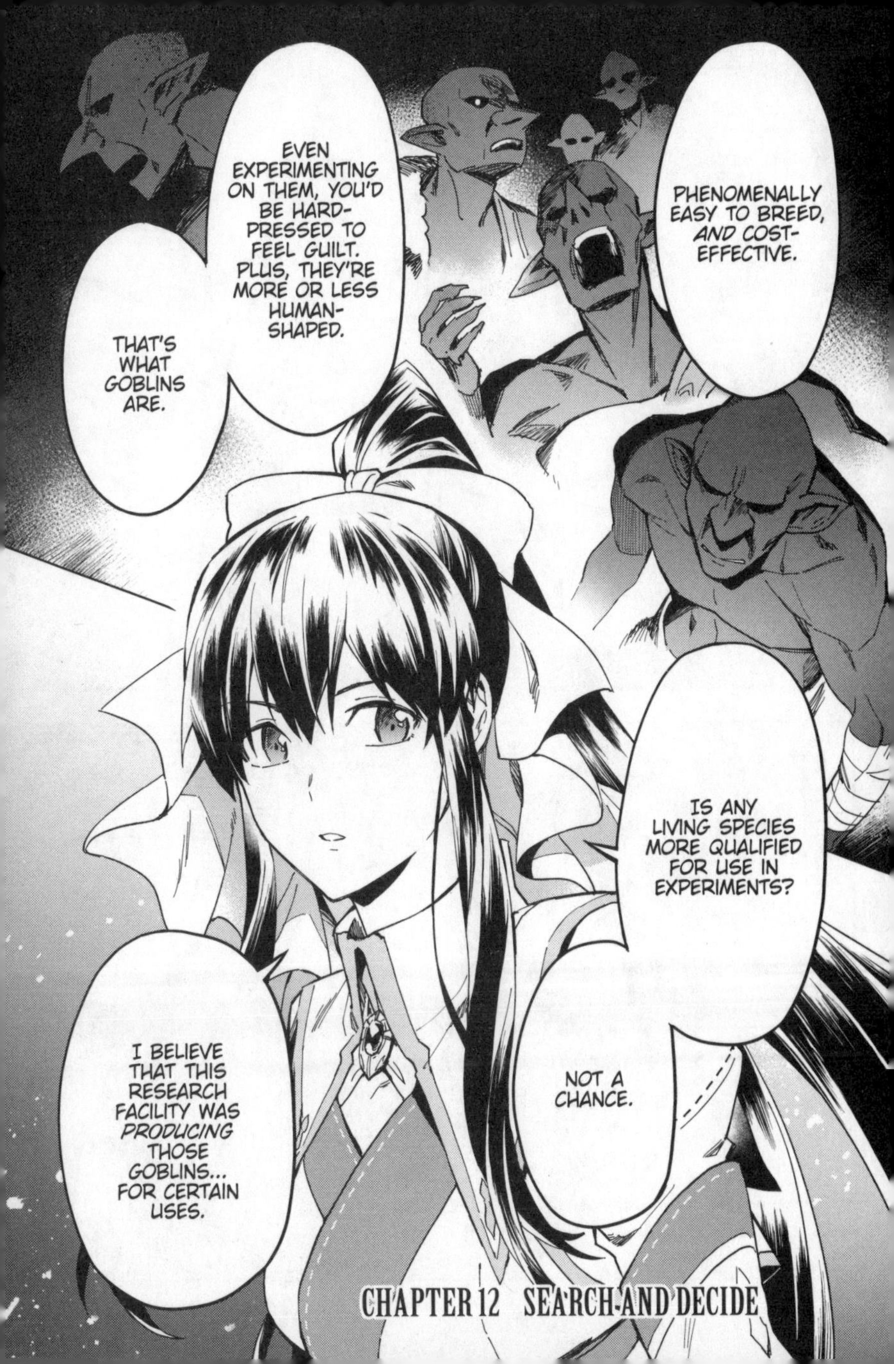
PHENOMENALLY EASY TO BREED, *AND* COST-EFFECTIVE.
EVEN EXPERIMENTING ON THEM, YOU'D BE HARD-PRESSED TO FEEL GUILT. PLUS, THEY'RE MORE OR LESS HUMAN-SHAPED.
THAT'S WHAT GOBLINS ARE.
IS ANY LIVING SPECIES MORE QUALIFIED FOR USE IN EXPERIMENTS?
NOT A CHANCE.
I BELIEVE THAT THIS RESEARCH FACILITY WAS *PRODUCING* THOSE GOBLINS... FOR CERTAIN USES.

CHAPTER 12 SEARCH AND DECIDE

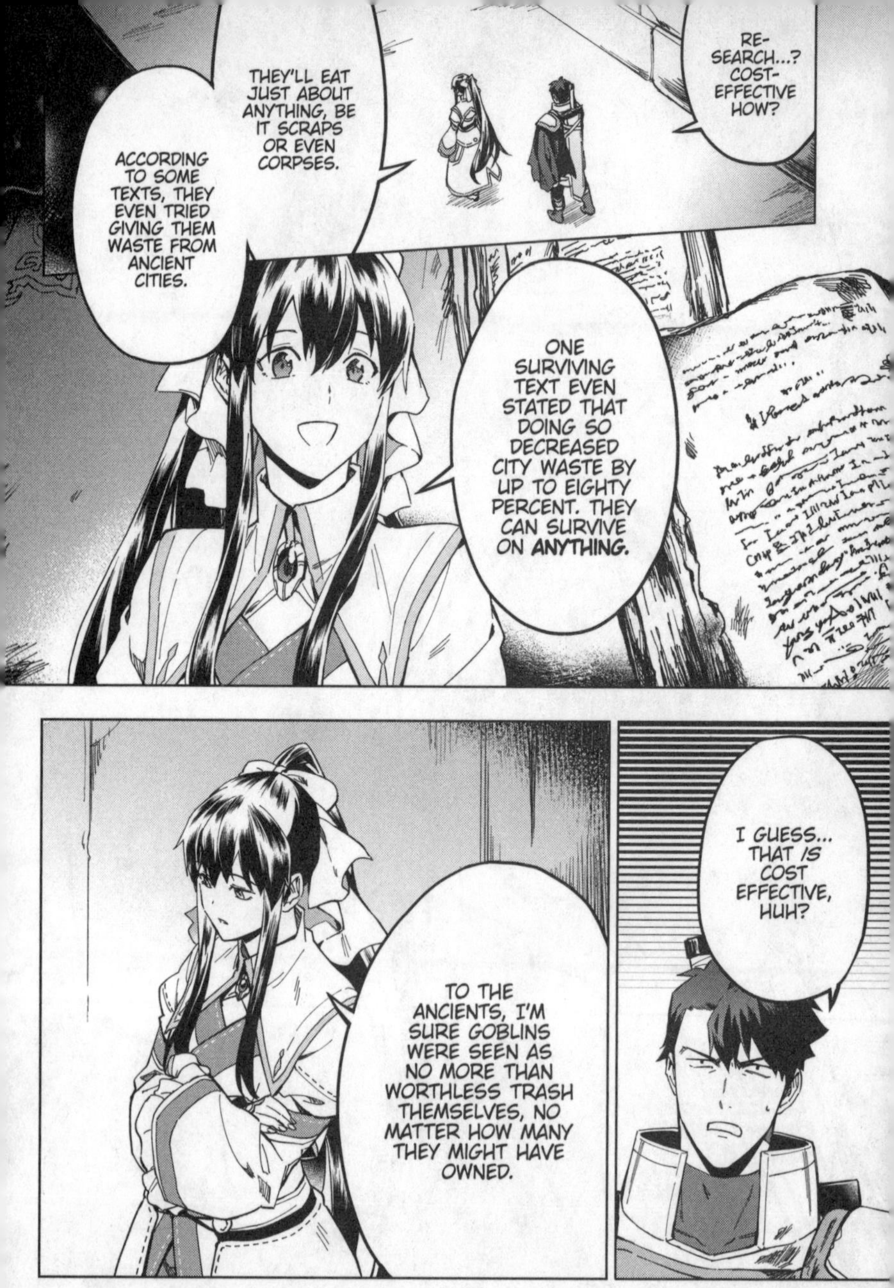
RE-SEARCH...? COST-EFFECTIVE HOW?
THEY'LL EAT JUST ABOUT ANYTHING, BE IT SCRAPS OR EVEN CORPSES.
ACCORDING TO SOME TEXTS, THEY EVEN TRIED GIVING THEM WASTE FROM ANCIENT CITIES.
ONE SURVIVING TEXT EVEN STATED THAT DOING SO DECREASED CITY WASTE BY UP TO EIGHTY PERCENT. THEY CAN SURVIVE ON **ANYTHING.**
I GUESS... THAT *IS* COST EFFECTIVE, HUH?
TO THE ANCIENTS, I'M SURE GOBLINS WERE SEEN AS NO MORE THAN WORTHLESS TRASH THEMSELVES, NO MATTER HOW MANY THEY MIGHT HAVE OWNED.

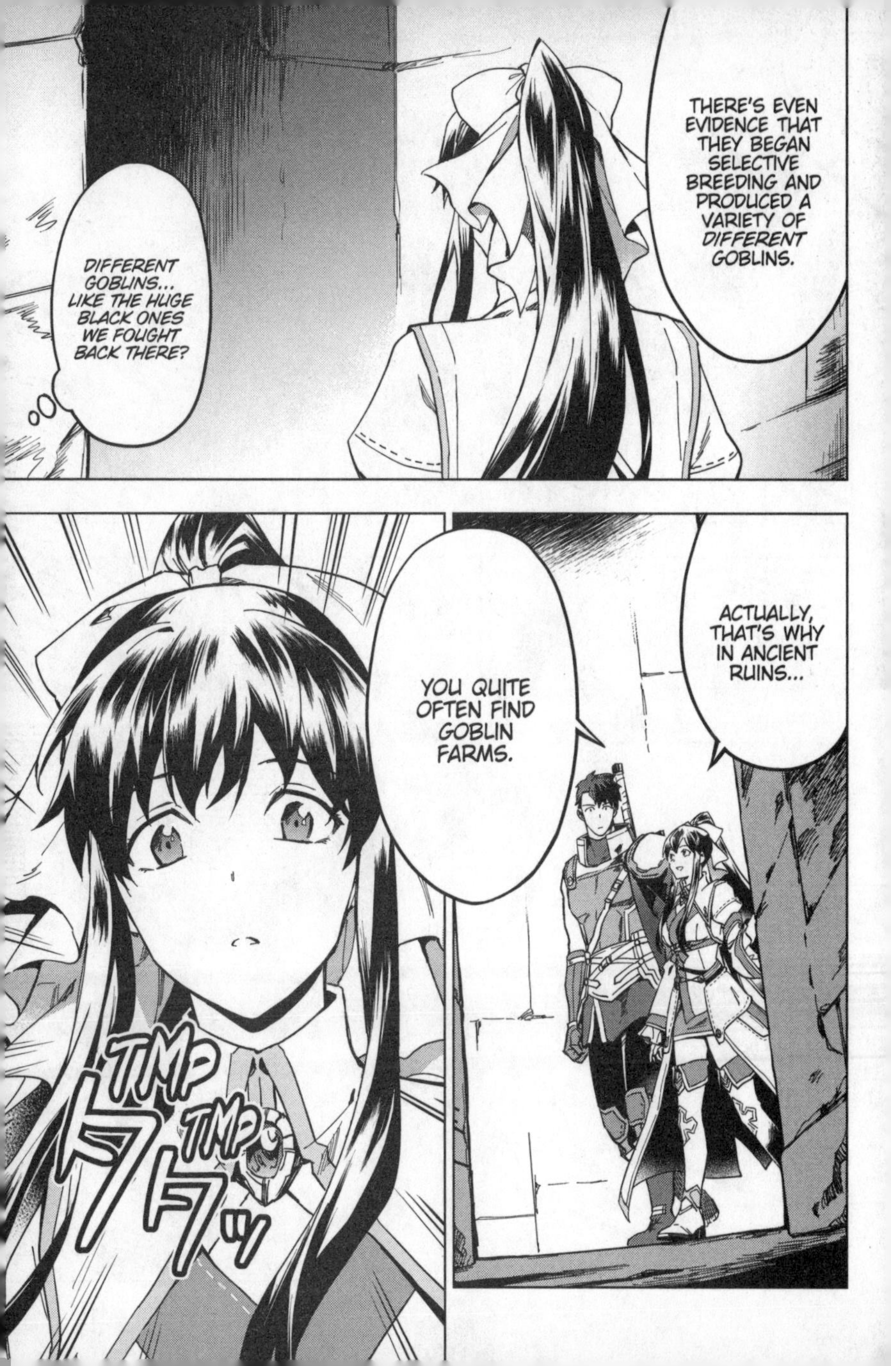
THERE'S EVEN EVIDENCE THAT THEY BEGAN SELECTIVE BREEDING AND PRODUCED A VARIETY OF *DIFFERENT* GOBLINS.
DIFFERENT GOBLINS... LIKE THE HUGE BLACK ONES WE FOUGHT BACK THERE?
ACTUALLY, THAT'S WHY IN ANCIENT RUINS...
YOU QUITE OFTEN FIND GOBLIN FARMS.
TMP
TMP

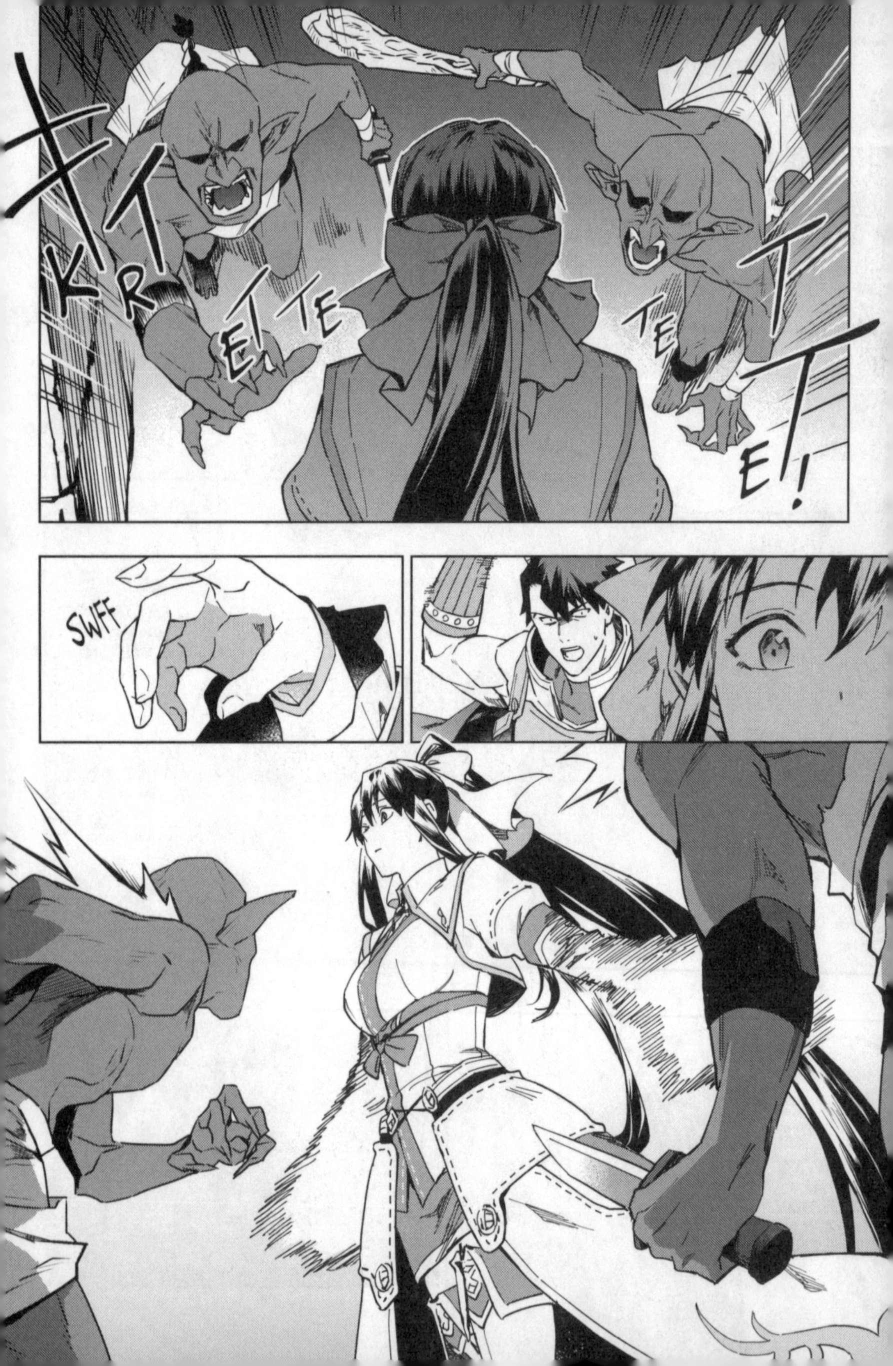
TETTE!
KRTE! TE
SWFF

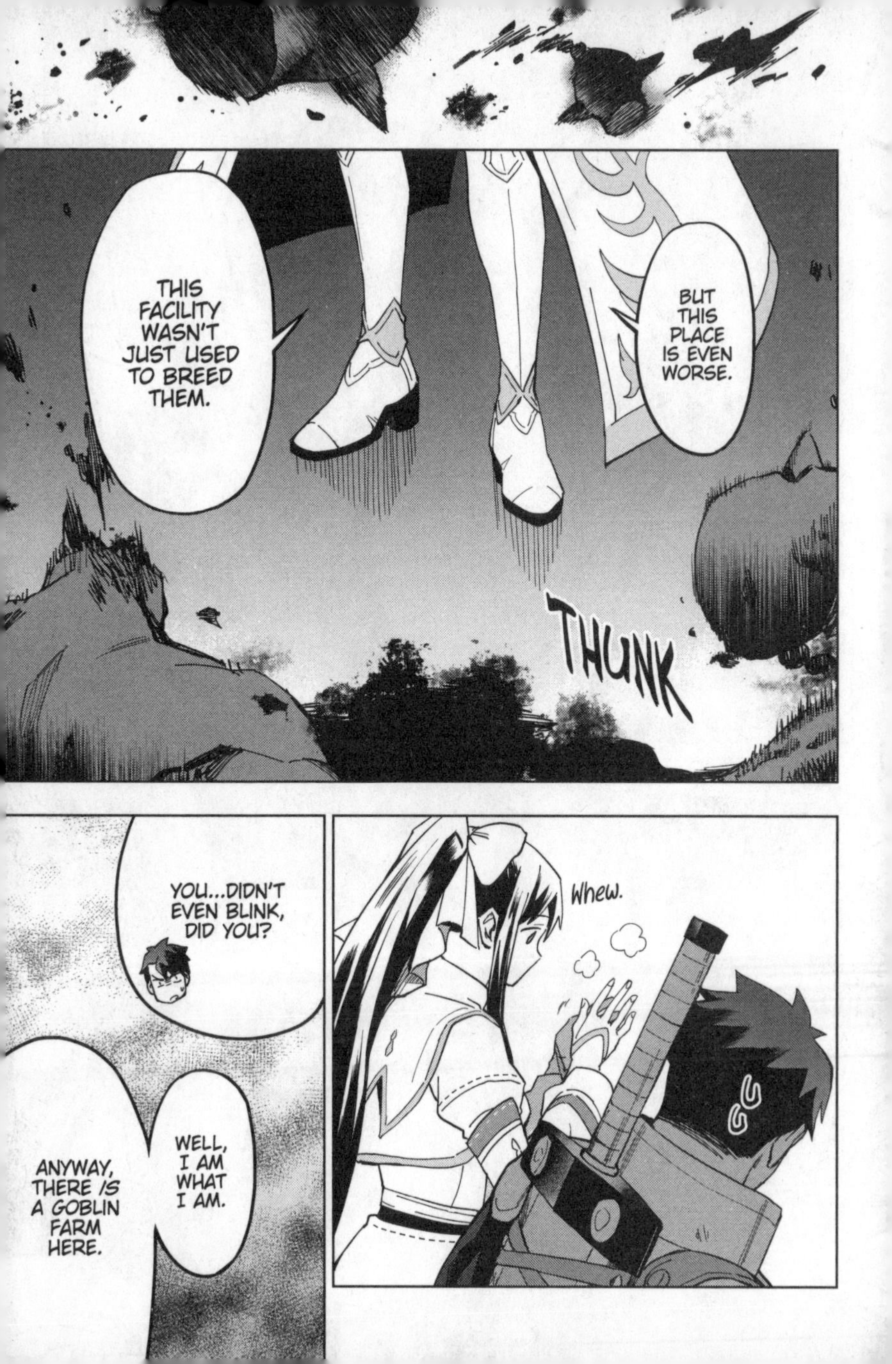
BUT THIS PLACE IS EVEN WORSE.
THIS FACILITY WASN'T JUST USED TO BREED THEM.
THUNK
Whew.
YOU...DIDN'T EVEN BLINK, DID YOU?
WELL, I AM WHAT I AM.
ANYWAY, THERE *IS* A GOBLIN FARM HERE.

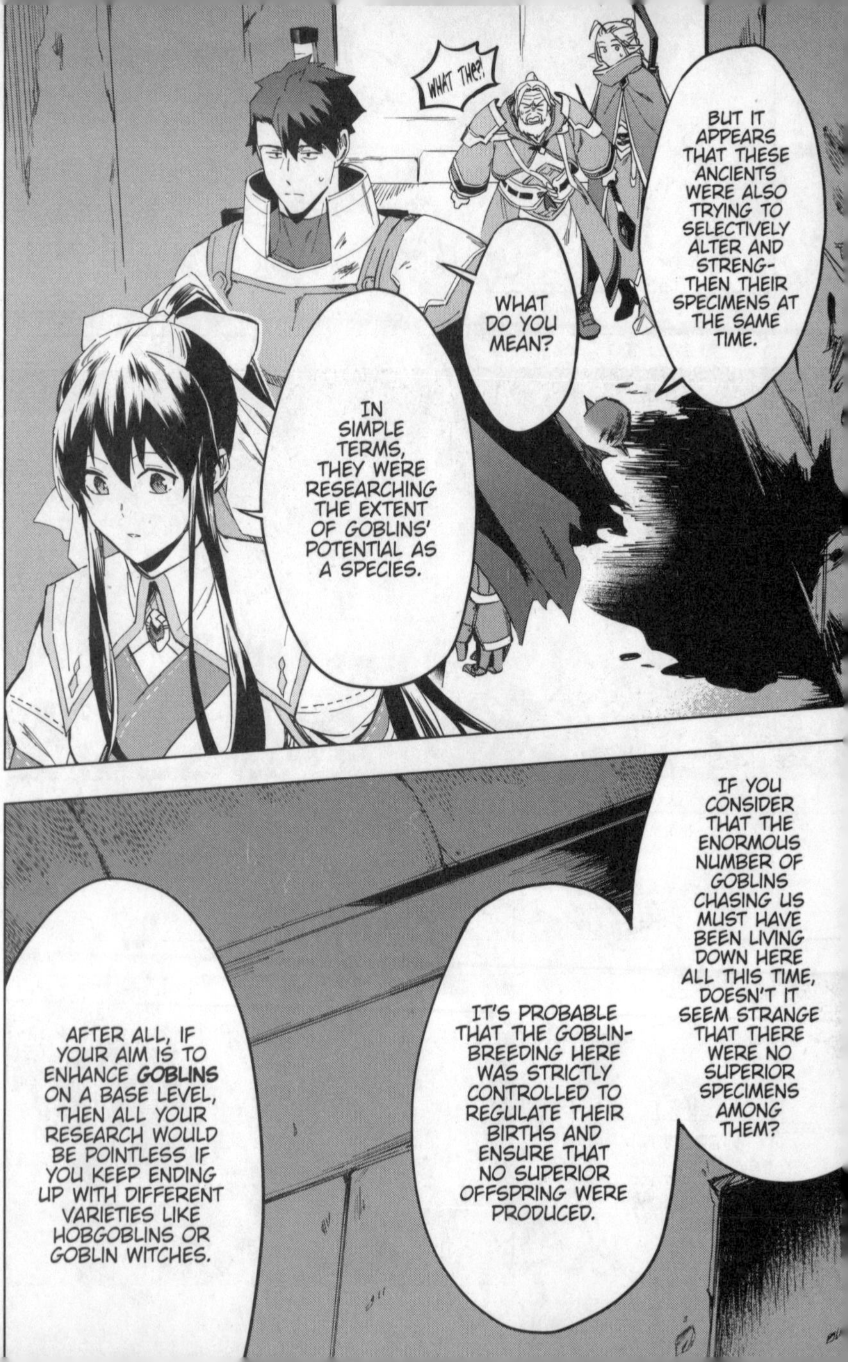
BUT IT APPEARS THAT THESE ANCIENTS WERE ALSO TRYING TO SELECTIVELY ALTER AND STRENG-THEN THEIR SPECIMENS AT THE SAME TIME.
WHAT THE?!
WHAT DO YOU MEAN?
IN SIMPLE TERMS, THEY WERE RESEARCHING THE EXTENT OF GOBLINS' POTENTIAL AS A SPECIES.
IF YOU CONSIDER THAT THE ENORMOUS NUMBER OF GOBLINS CHASING US MUST HAVE BEEN LIVING DOWN HERE ALL THIS TIME, DOESN'T IT SEEM STRANGE THAT THERE WERE NO SUPERIOR SPECIMENS AMONG THEM?
IT'S PROBABLE THAT THE GOBLIN-BREEDING HERE WAS STRICTLY CONTROLLED TO REGULATE THEIR BIRTHS AND ENSURE THAT NO SUPERIOR OFFSPRING WERE PRODUCED.
AFTER ALL, IF YOUR AIM IS TO ENHANCE GOBLINS ON A BASE LEVEL, THEN ALL YOUR RESEARCH WOULD BE POINTLESS IF YOU KEEP ENDING UP WITH DIFFERENT VARIETIES LIKE HOBGOBLINS OR GOBLIN WITCHES.

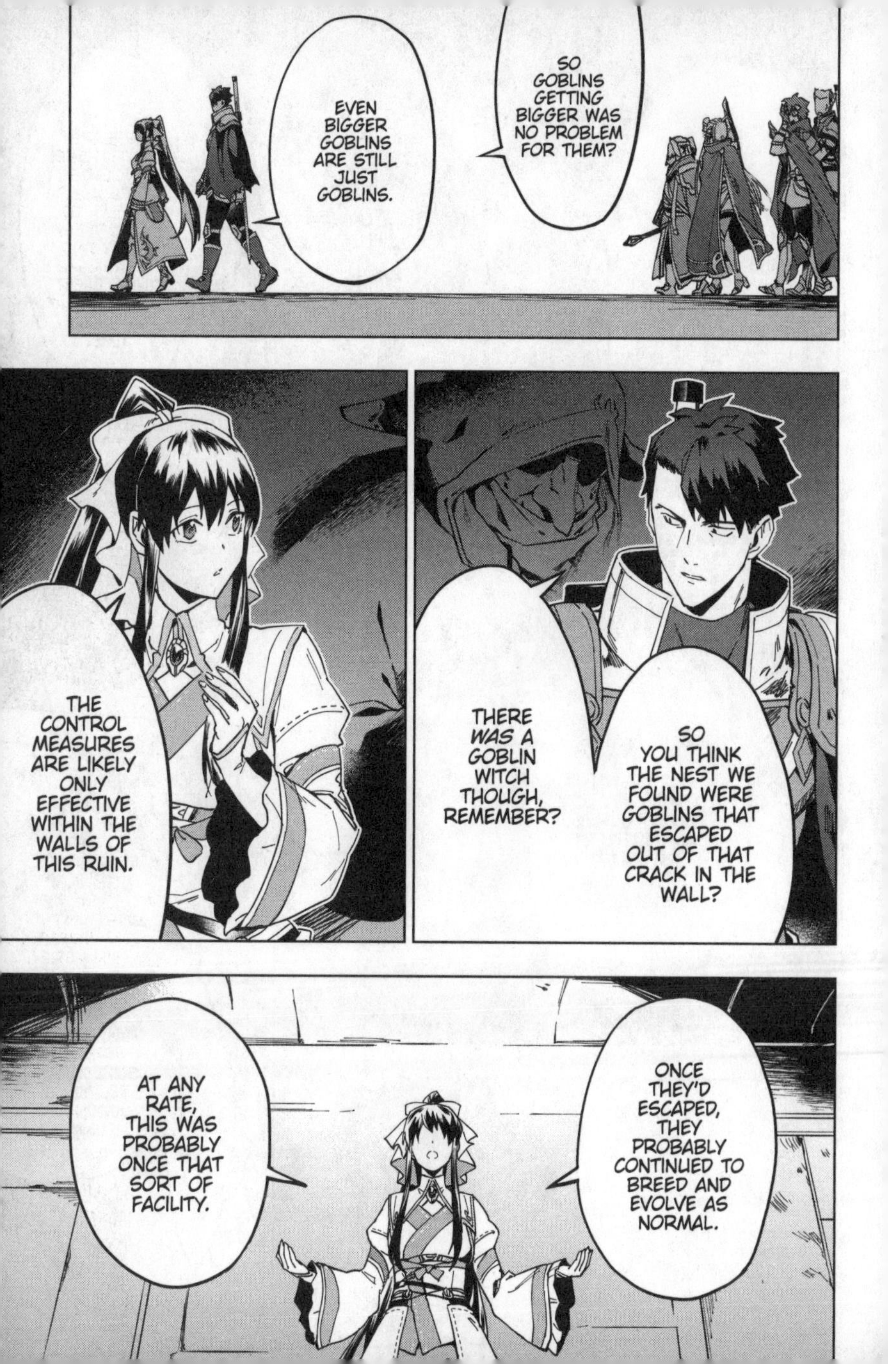
SO GOBLINS GETTING BIGGER WAS NO PROBLEM FOR THEM?
EVEN BIGGER GOBLINS ARE STILL JUST GOBLINS.
SO YOU THINK THE NEST WE FOUND WERE GOBLINS THAT ESCAPED OUT OF THAT CRACK IN THE WALL?
THERE *WAS* A GOBLIN WITCH THOUGH, REMEMBER?
THE CONTROL MEASURES ARE LIKELY ONLY EFFECTIVE WITHIN THE WALLS OF THIS RUIN.
ONCE THEY'D ESCAPED, THEY PROBABLY CONTINUED TO BREED AND EVOLVE AS NORMAL.
AT ANY RATE, THIS WAS PROBABLY ONCE THAT SORT OF FACILITY.

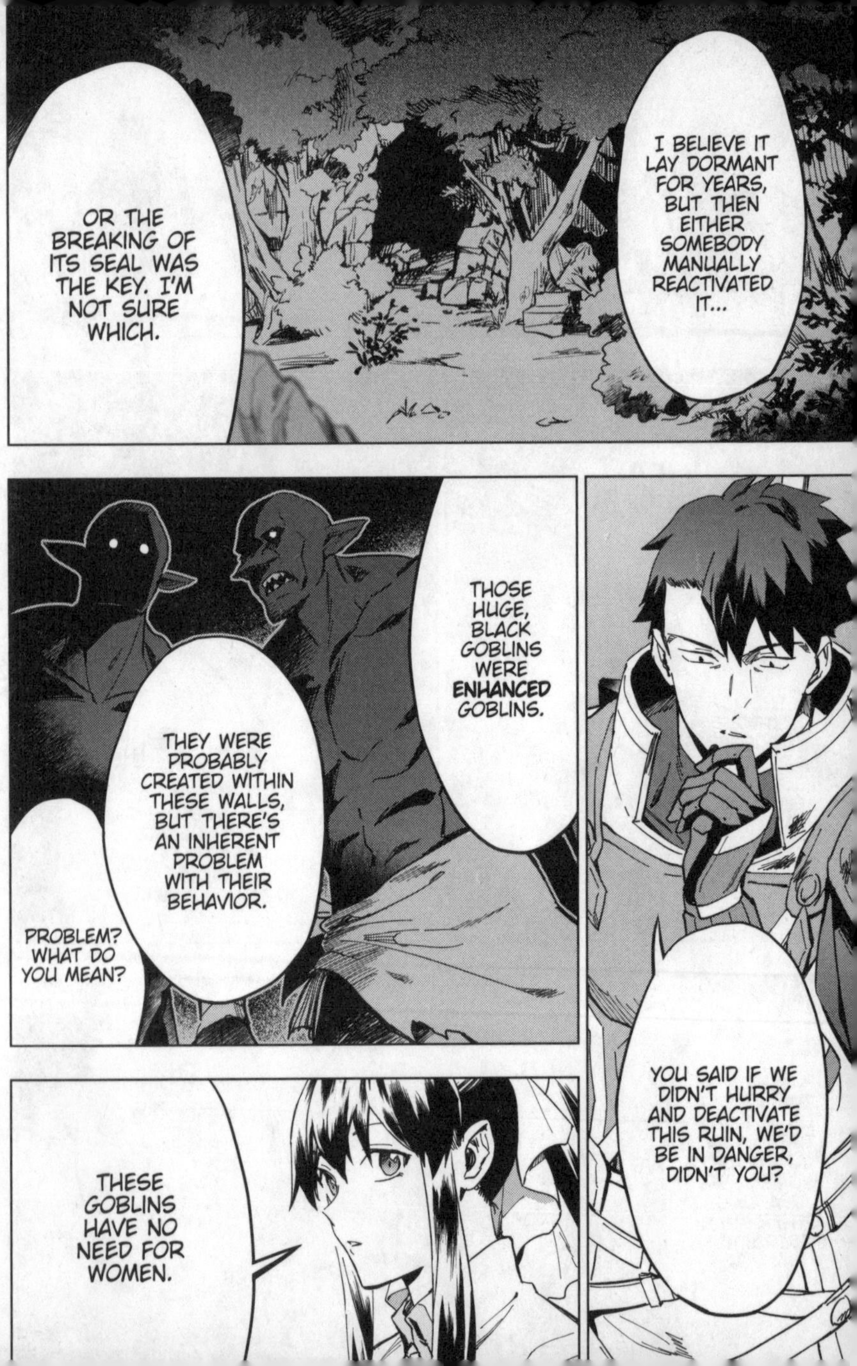
I BELIEVE IT LAY DORMANT FOR YEARS, BUT THEN EITHER SOMEBODY MANUALLY REACTIVATED IT...
OR THE BREAKING OF ITS SEAL WAS THE KEY. I'M NOT SURE WHICH.
YOU SAID IF WE DIDN'T HURRY AND DEACTIVATE THIS RUIN, WE'D BE IN DANGER, DIDN'T YOU?
THOSE HUGE, BLACK GOBLINS WERE **ENHANCED** GOBLINS.
THEY WERE PROBABLY CREATED WITHIN THESE WALLS, BUT THERE'S AN INHERENT PROBLEM WITH THEIR BEHAVIOR.
PROBLEM? WHAT DO YOU MEAN?
THESE GOBLINS HAVE NO NEED FOR WOMEN.

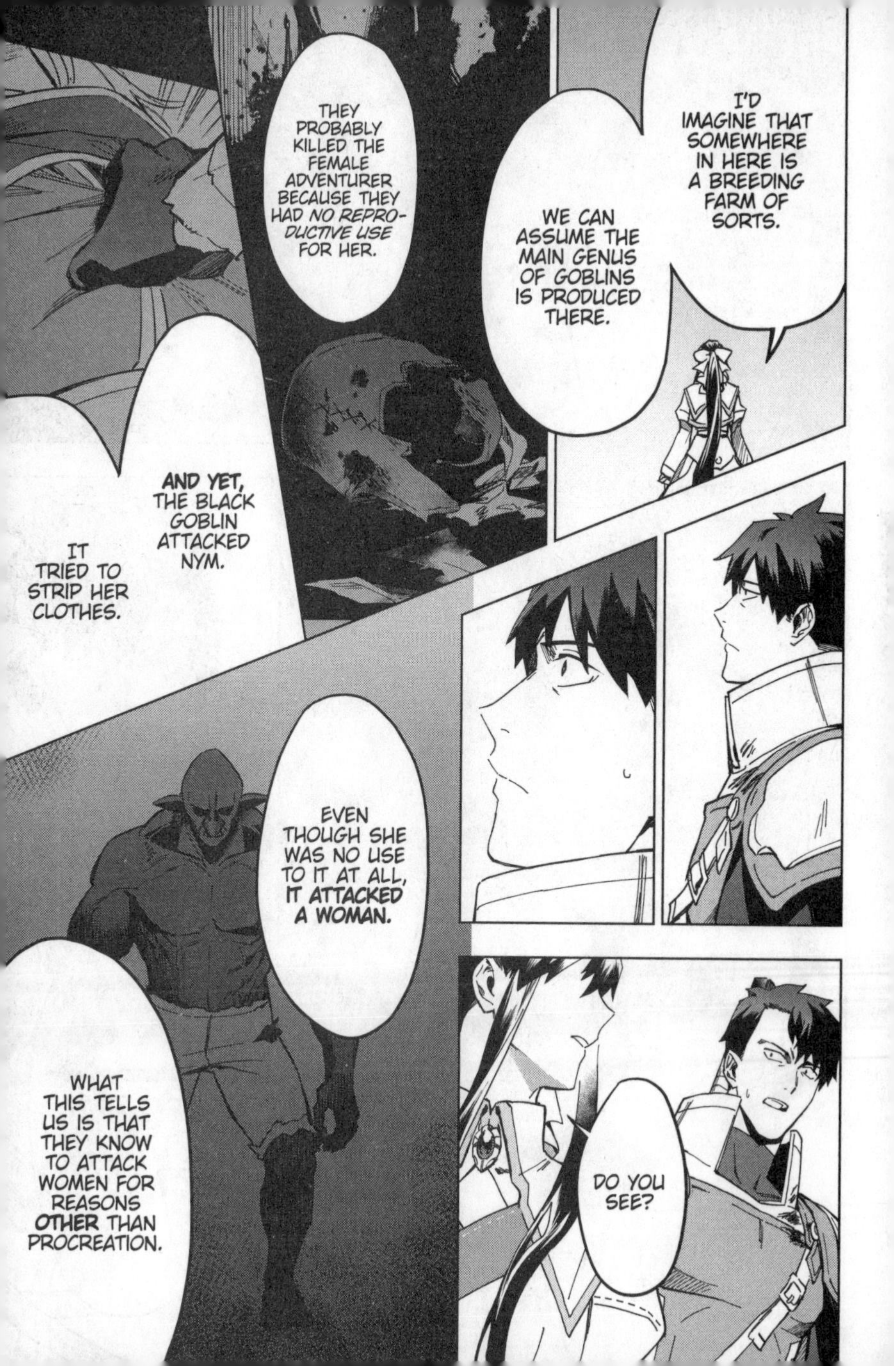
I'D IMAGINE THAT SOMEWHERE IN HERE IS A BREEDING FARM OF SORTS.
WE CAN ASSUME THE MAIN GENUS OF GOBLINS IS PRODUCED THERE.
THEY PROBABLY KILLED THE FEMALE ADVENTURER BECAUSE THEY HAD *NO REPRODUCTIVE USE* FOR HER.
AND YET, THE BLACK GOBLIN ATTACKED NYM.
IT TRIED TO STRIP HER CLOTHES.
EVEN THOUGH SHE WAS NO USE TO IT AT ALL, **IT ATTACKED A WOMAN.**
WHAT THIS TELLS US IS THAT THEY KNOW TO ATTACK WOMEN FOR REASONS **OTHER** THAN PROCREATION.
DO YOU SEE?

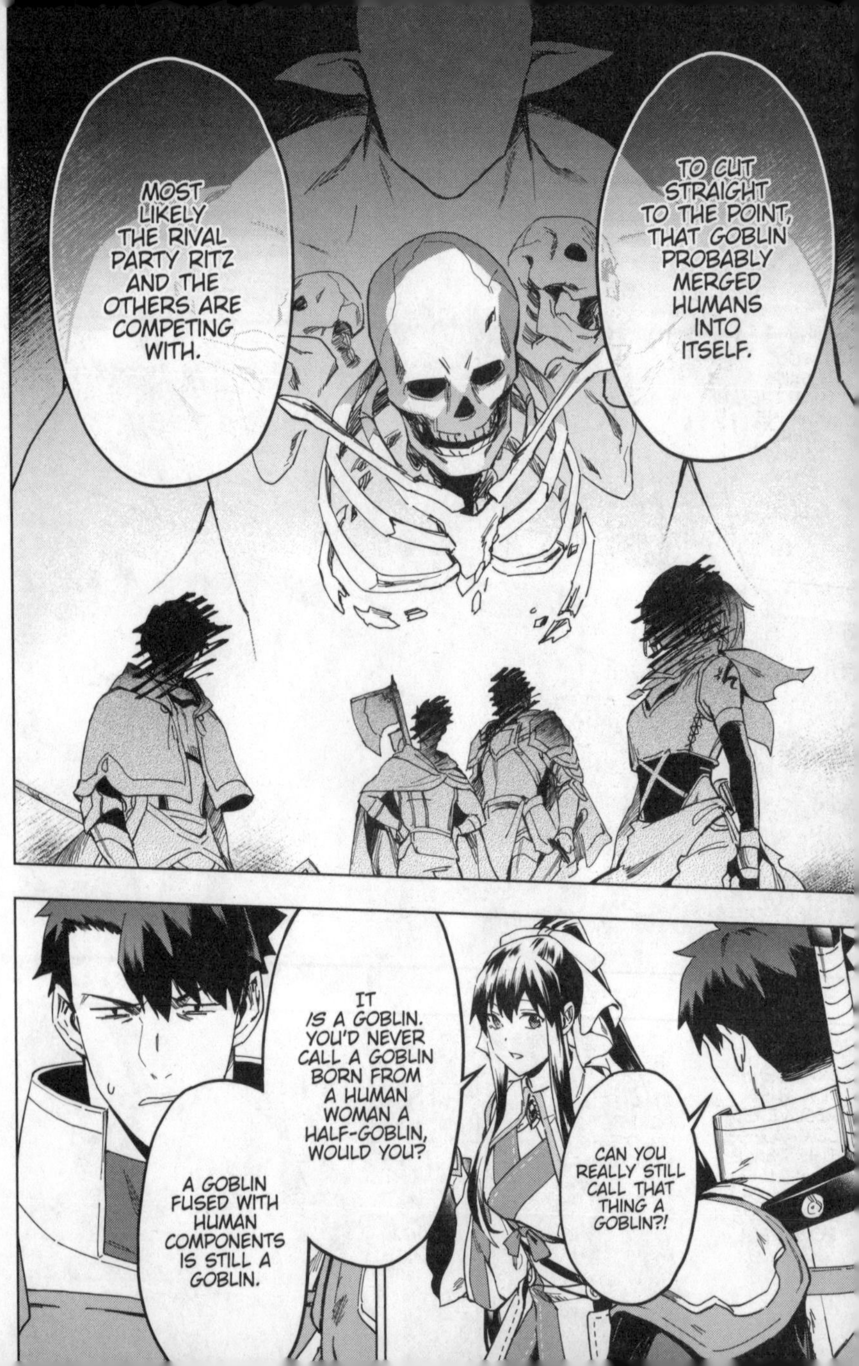
TO CUT STRAIGHT TO THE POINT, THAT GOBLIN PROBABLY MERGED HUMANS INTO ITSELF.
MOST LIKELY THE RIVAL PARTY RITZ AND THE OTHERS ARE COMPETING WITH.
CAN YOU REALLY STILL CALL THAT THING A GOBLIN?!
IT IS A GOBLIN. YOU'D NEVER CALL A GOBLIN BORN FROM A HUMAN WOMAN A HALF-GOBLIN, WOULD YOU?
A GOBLIN FUSED WITH HUMAN COMPONENTS IS STILL A GOBLIN.

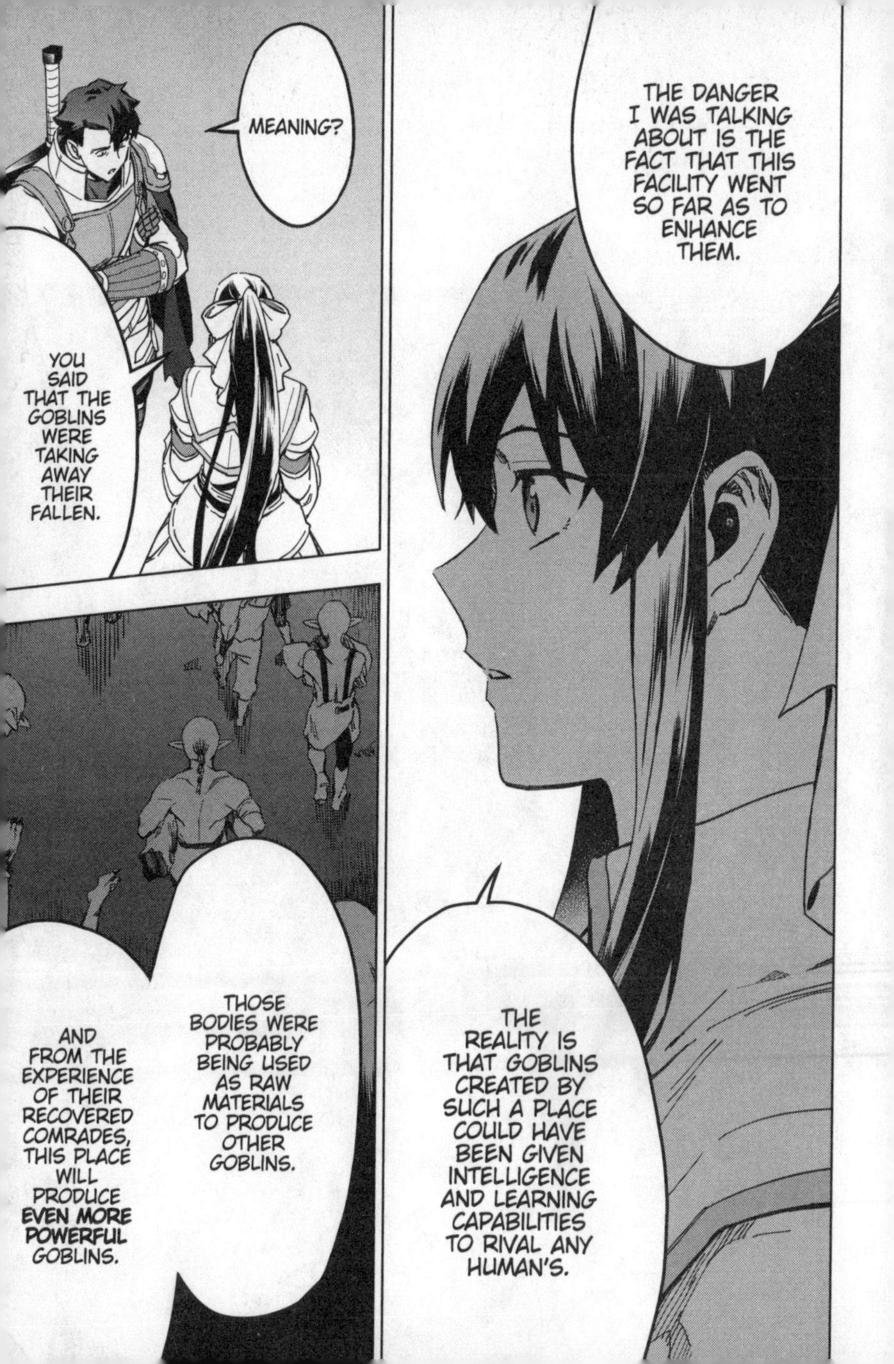
THE DANGER I WAS TALKING ABOUT IS THE FACT THAT THIS FACILITY WENT SO FAR AS TO ENHANCE THEM.
THE REALITY IS THAT GOBLINS CREATED BY SUCH A PLACE COULD HAVE BEEN GIVEN INTELLIGENCE AND LEARNING CAPABILITIES TO RIVAL ANY HUMAN'S.
MEANING?
YOU SAID THAT THE GOBLINS WERE TAKING AWAY THEIR FALLEN.
THOSE BODIES WERE PROBABLY BEING USED AS RAW MATERIALS TO PRODUCE OTHER GOBLINS.
AND FROM THE EXPERIENCE OF THEIR RECOVERED COMRADES, THIS PLACE WILL PRODUCE **EVEN MORE POWERFUL** GOBLINS.

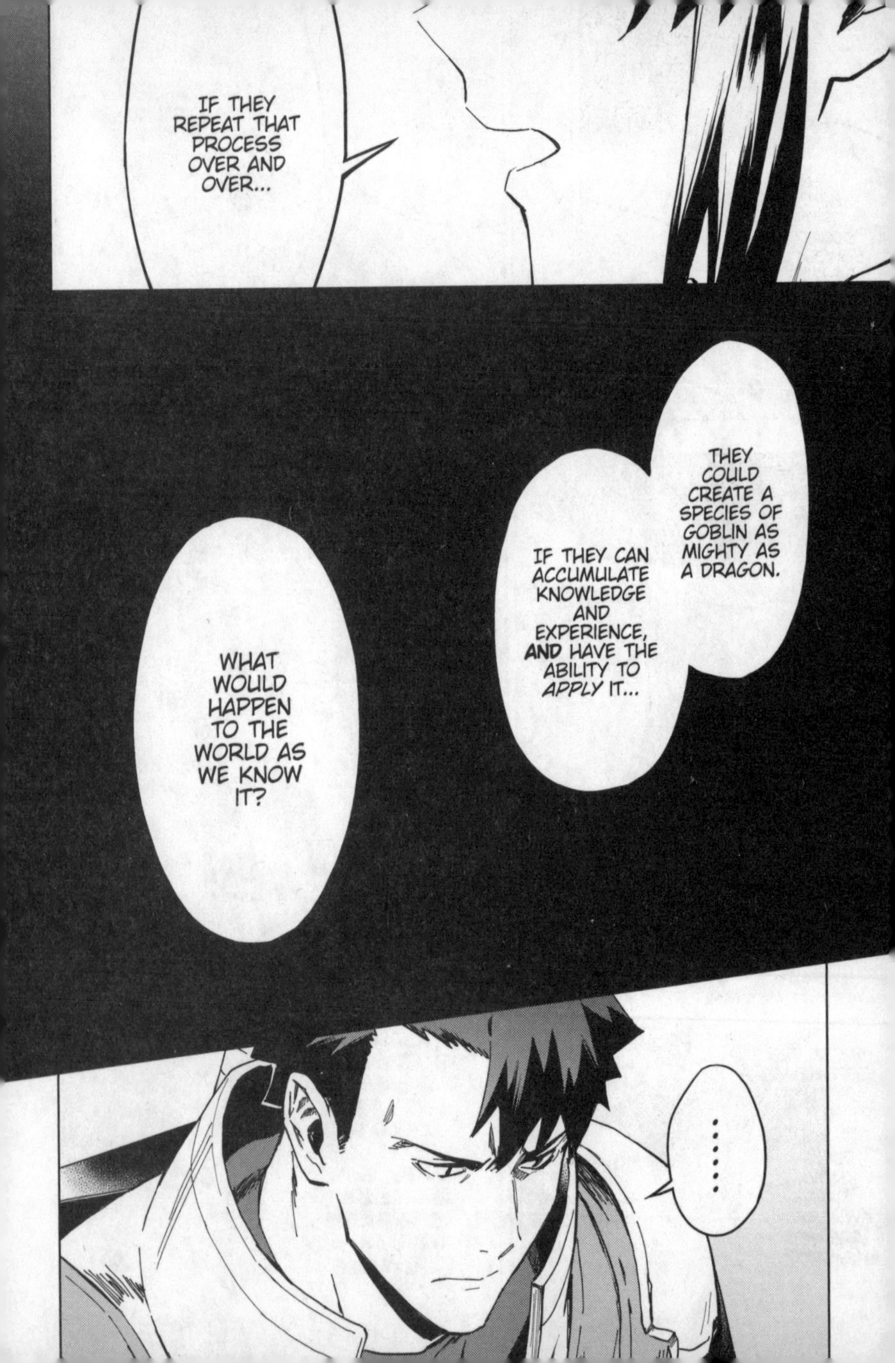
IF THEY REPEAT THAT PROCESS OVER AND OVER...
THEY COULD CREATE A SPECIES OF GOBLIN AS MIGHTY AS A DRAGON.
IF THEY CAN ACCUMULATE KNOWLEDGE AND EXPERIENCE, **AND** HAVE THE ABILITY TO *APPLY* IT...
WHAT WOULD HAPPEN TO THE WORLD AS WE KNOW IT?
......

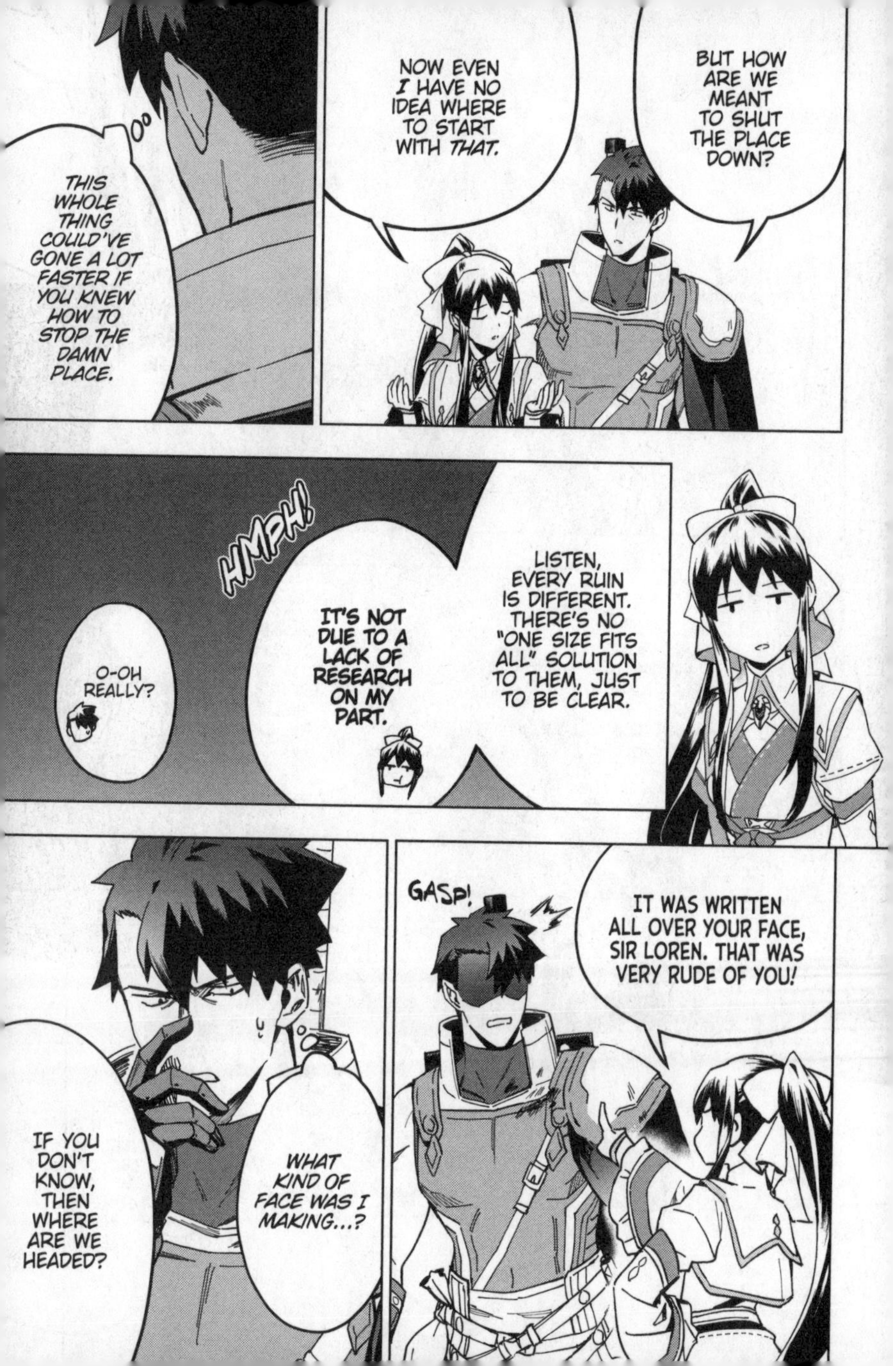
BUT HOW ARE WE MEANT TO SHUT THE PLACE DOWN?
NOW EVEN *I* HAVE NO IDEA WHERE TO START WITH *THAT.*
THIS WHOLE THING COULD'VE GONE A LOT FASTER IF YOU KNEW HOW TO STOP THE DAMN PLACE.
LISTEN, EVERY RUIN IS DIFFERENT. THERE'S NO "ONE SIZE FITS ALL" SOLUTION TO THEM, JUST TO BE CLEAR.
IT'S NOT DUE TO A LACK OF RESEARCH ON MY PART.
HMPH!
O-OH REALLY?
IT WAS WRITTEN ALL OVER YOUR FACE, SIR LOREN. THAT WAS VERY RUDE OF YOU!
GASP!
WHAT KIND OF FACE WAS I MAKING...?
IF YOU DON'T KNOW, THEN WHERE ARE WE HEADED?

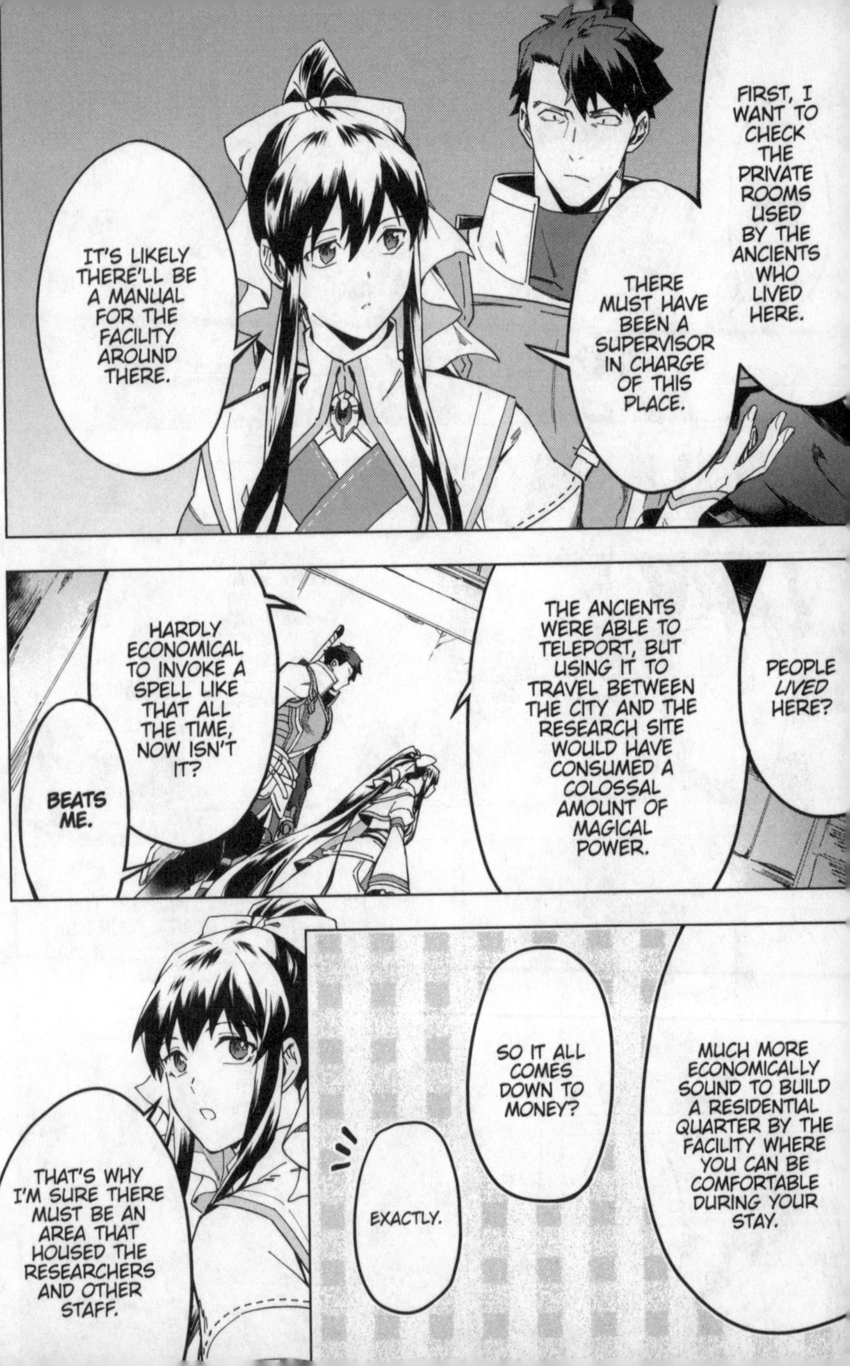

FIRST, I WANT TO CHECK THE PRIVATE ROOMS USED BY THE ANCIENTS WHO LIVED HERE.
THERE MUST HAVE BEEN A SUPERVISOR IN CHARGE OF THIS PLACE.
IT'S LIKELY THERE'LL BE A MANUAL FOR THE FACILITY AROUND THERE.
PEOPLE *LIVED* HERE?
THE ANCIENTS WERE ABLE TO TELEPORT, BUT USING IT TO TRAVEL BETWEEN THE CITY AND THE RESEARCH SITE WOULD HAVE CONSUMED A COLOSSAL AMOUNT OF MAGICAL POWER.
HARDLY ECONOMICAL TO INVOKE A SPELL LIKE THAT ALL THE TIME, NOW ISN'T IT?
BEATS ME.
MUCH MORE ECONOMICALLY SOUND TO BUILD A RESIDENTIAL QUARTER BY THE FACILITY WHERE YOU CAN BE COMFORTABLE DURING YOUR STAY.
SO IT ALL COMES DOWN TO MONEY?
EXACTLY.
THAT'S WHY I'M SURE THERE MUST BE AN AREA THAT HOUSED THE RESEARCHERS AND OTHER STAFF.

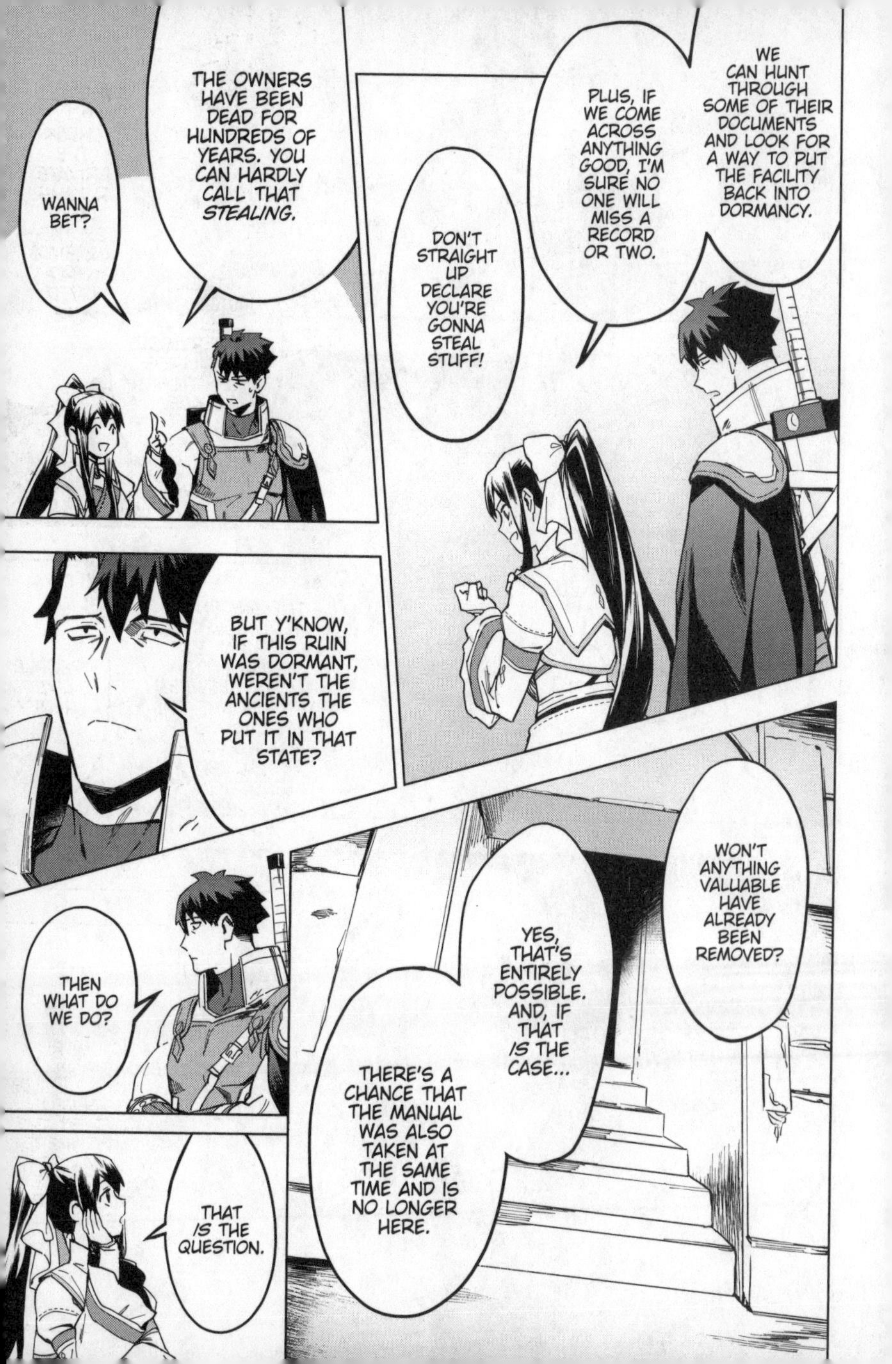
WE CAN HUNT THROUGH SOME OF THEIR DOCUMENTS AND LOOK FOR A WAY TO PUT THE FACILITY BACK INTO DORMANCY.
PLUS, IF WE COME ACROSS ANYTHING GOOD, I'M SURE NO ONE WILL MISS A RECORD OR TWO.
DON'T STRAIGHT UP DECLARE YOU'RE GONNA STEAL STUFF!
THE OWNERS HAVE BEEN DEAD FOR HUNDREDS OF YEARS. YOU CAN HARDLY CALL THAT *STEALING*.
WANNA BET?
BUT Y'KNOW, IF THIS RUIN WAS DORMANT, WEREN'T THE ANCIENTS THE ONES WHO PUT IT IN THAT STATE?
WON'T ANYTHING VALUABLE HAVE ALREADY BEEN REMOVED?
YES, THAT'S ENTIRELY POSSIBLE. AND, IF THAT *IS* THE CASE...
THERE'S A CHANCE THAT THE MANUAL WAS ALSO TAKEN AT THE SAME TIME AND IS NO LONGER HERE.
THEN WHAT DO WE DO?
THAT *IS* THE QUESTION.

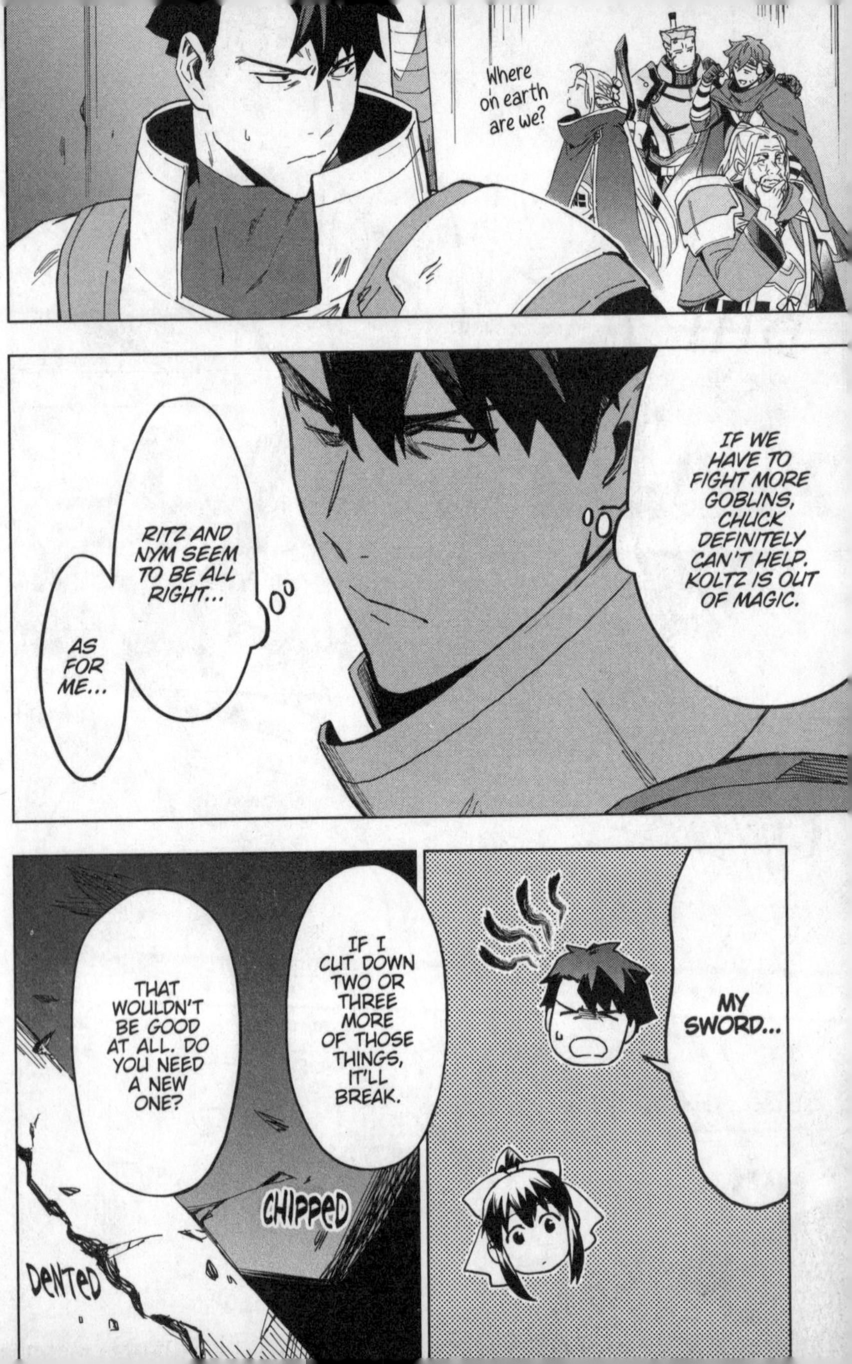
Where on earth are we?
IF WE HAVE TO FIGHT MORE GOBLINS, CHUCK DEFINITELY CAN'T HELP. KOLTZ IS OUT OF MAGIC.
RITZ AND NYM SEEM TO BE ALL RIGHT...
AS FOR ME...
MY SWORD...
IF I CUT DOWN TWO OR THREE MORE OF THOSE THINGS, IT'LL BREAK.
THAT WOULDN'T BE GOOD AT ALL. DO YOU NEED A NEW ONE?
CHIPPED
DENTED

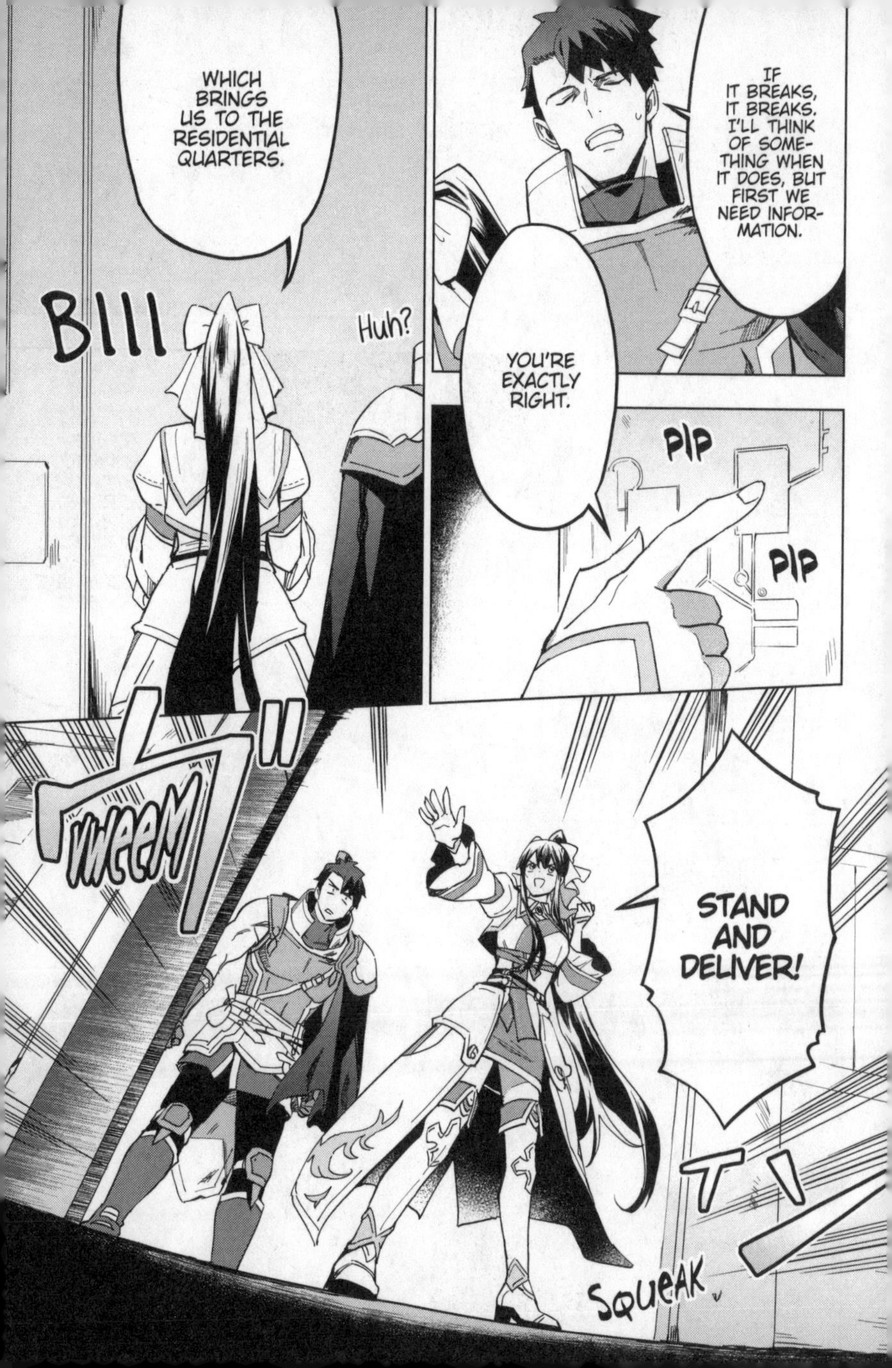
IF IT BREAKS, IT BREAKS. I'LL THINK OF SOME-THING WHEN IT DOES, BUT FIRST WE NEED INFOR-MATION.
YOU'RE EXACTLY RIGHT.
PIP
PIP
WHICH BRINGS US TO THE RESIDENTIAL QUARTERS.
Huh?
BIII
STAND AND DELIVER!
vweem
Squeak

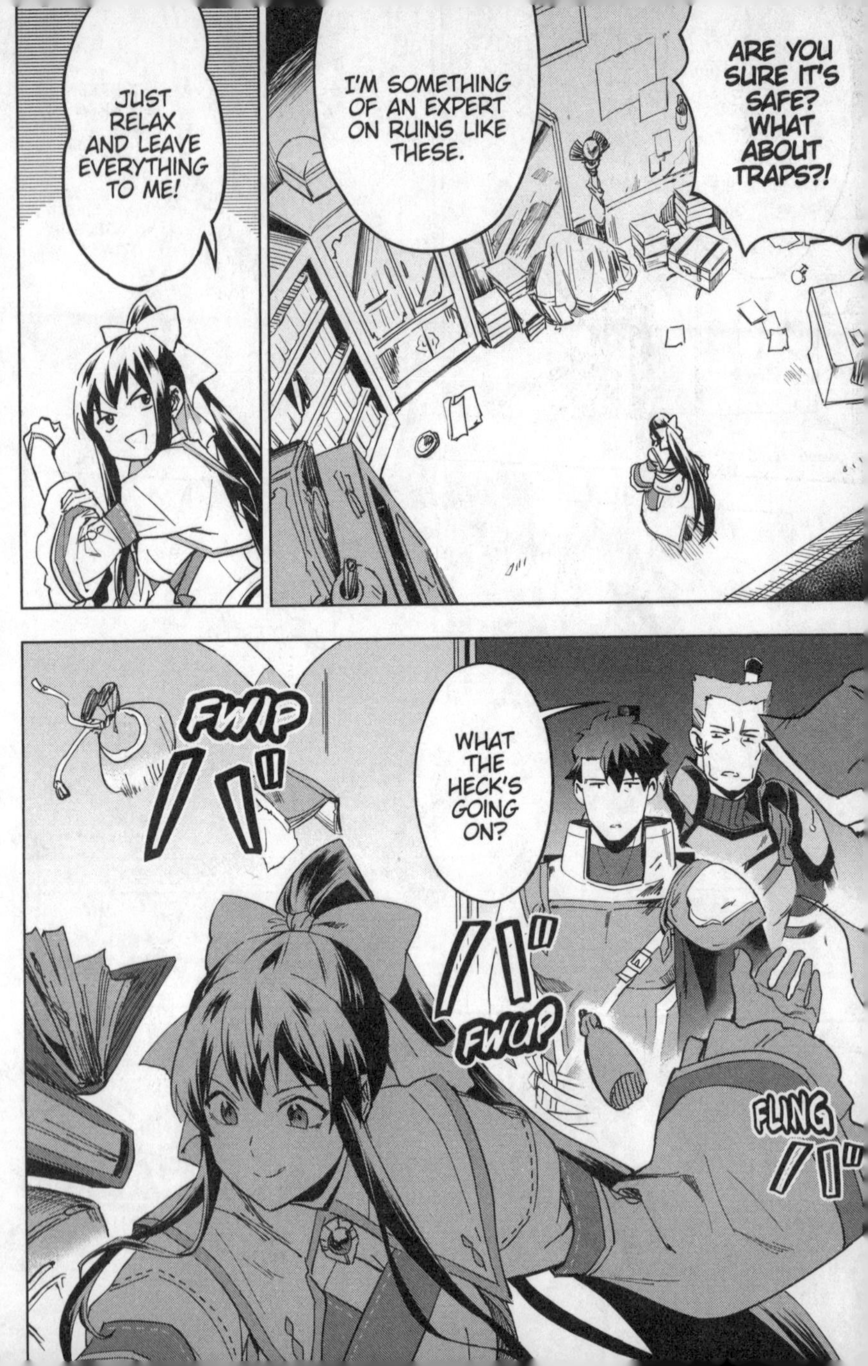
ARE YOU SURE IT'S SAFE? WHAT ABOUT TRAPS?!
I'M SOMETHING OF AN EXPERT ON RUINS LIKE THESE.
JUST RELAX AND LEAVE EVERYTHING TO ME!
WHAT THE HECK'S GOING ON?
FWIP
FWUP
FLING

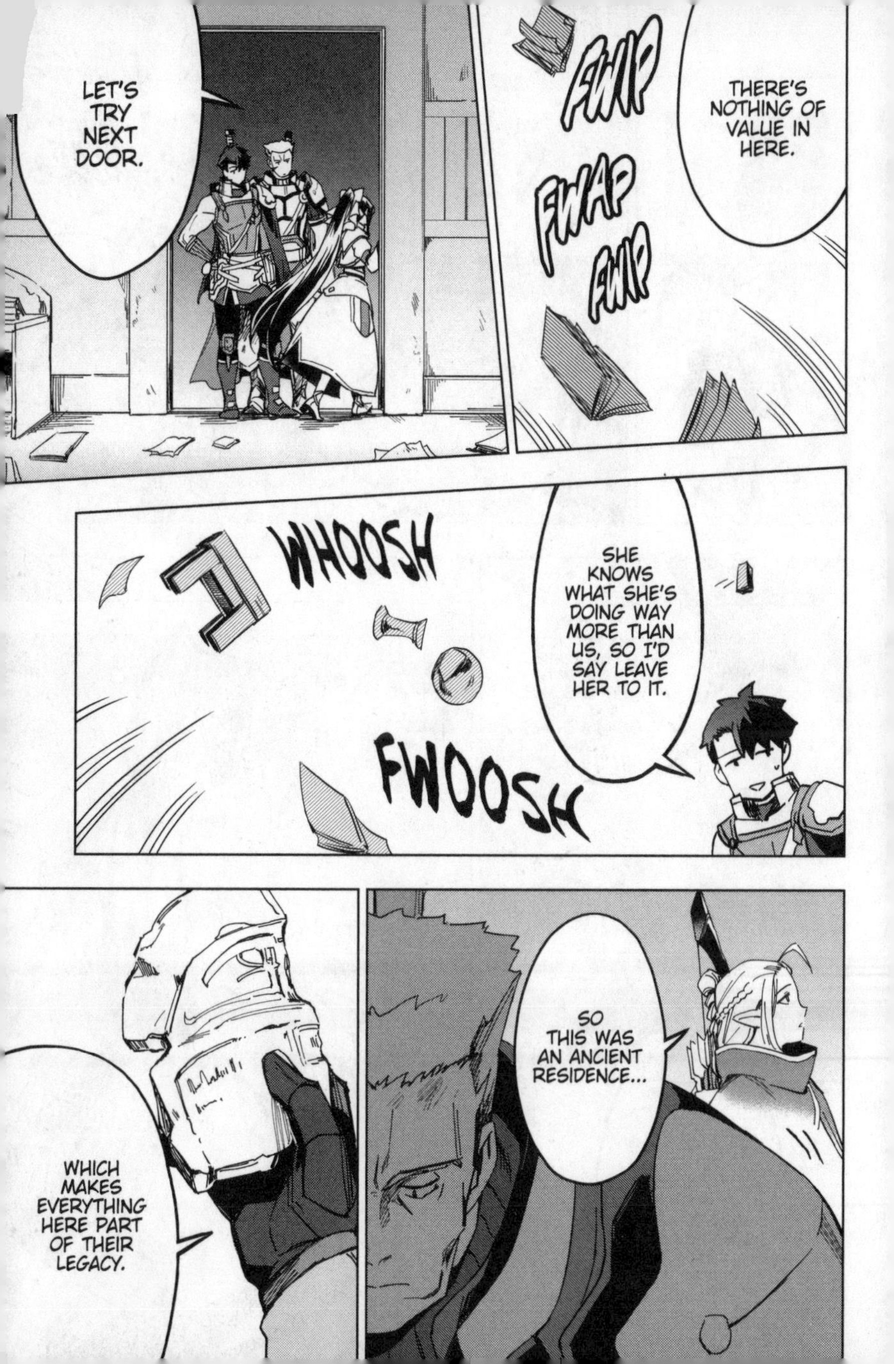
FWIP
FWAP
FWIP
THERE'S NOTHING OF VALUE IN HERE.
LET'S TRY NEXT DOOR.
SHE KNOWS WHAT SHE'S DOING WAY MORE THAN US, SO I'D SAY LEAVE HER TO IT.
WHOOSH
FWOOSH
SO THIS WAS AN ANCIENT RESIDENCE...
WHICH MAKES EVERYTHING HERE PART OF THEIR LEGACY.

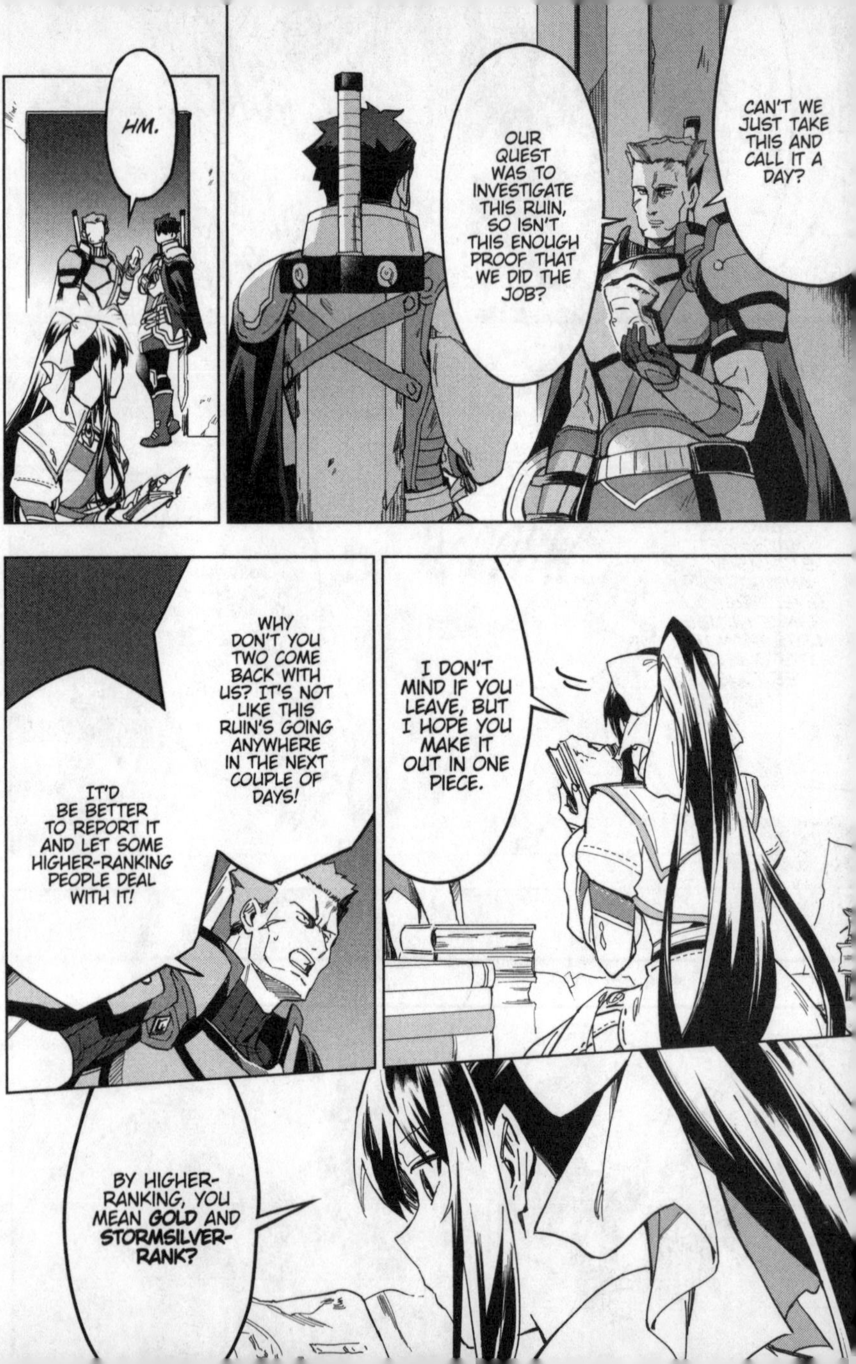
CAN'T WE JUST TAKE THIS AND CALL IT A DAY?
OUR QUEST WAS TO INVESTIGATE THIS RUIN, SO ISN'T THIS ENOUGH PROOF THAT WE DID THE JOB?
HM.
I DON'T MIND IF YOU LEAVE, BUT I HOPE YOU MAKE IT OUT IN ONE PIECE.
WHY DON'T YOU TWO COME BACK WITH US? IT'S NOT LIKE THIS RUIN'S GOING ANYWHERE IN THE NEXT COUPLE OF DAYS!
IT'D BE BETTER TO REPORT IT AND LET SOME HIGHER-RANKING PEOPLE DEAL WITH IT!
BY HIGHER-RANKING, YOU MEAN **GOLD** AND **STORMSILVER**-RANK?

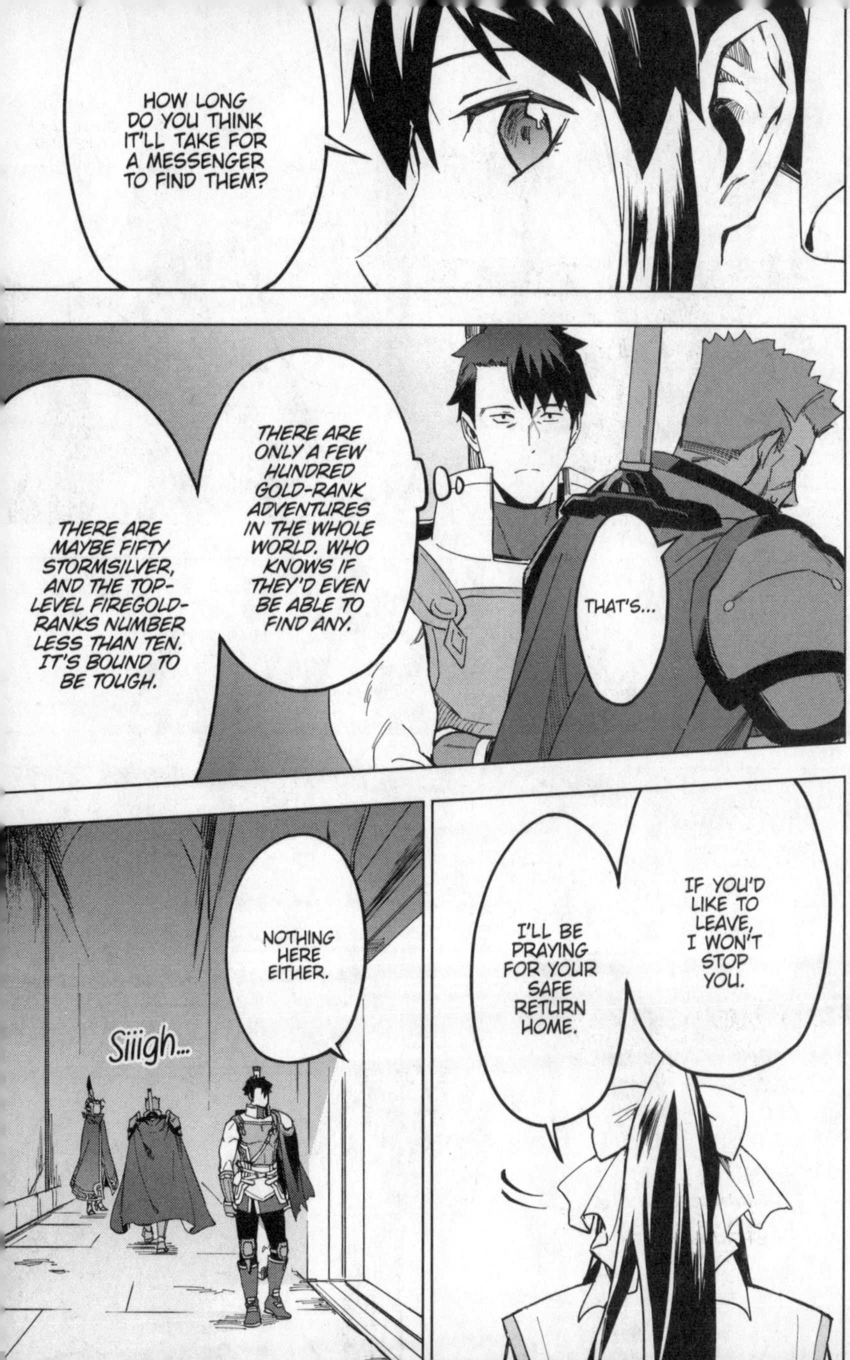
HOW LONG DO YOU THINK IT'LL TAKE FOR A MESSENGER TO FIND THEM?
THAT'S...
THERE ARE ONLY A FEW HUNDRED GOLD-RANK ADVENTURES IN THE WHOLE WORLD. WHO KNOWS IF THEY'D EVEN BE ABLE TO FIND ANY.
THERE ARE MAYBE FIFTY STORMSILVER, AND THE TOP-LEVEL FIREGOLD-RANKS NUMBER LESS THAN TEN. IT'S BOUND TO BE TOUGH.
IF YOU'D LIKE TO LEAVE, I WON'T STOP YOU.
I'LL BE PRAYING FOR YOUR SAFE RETURN HOME.
NOTHING HERE EITHER.
Siiigh...

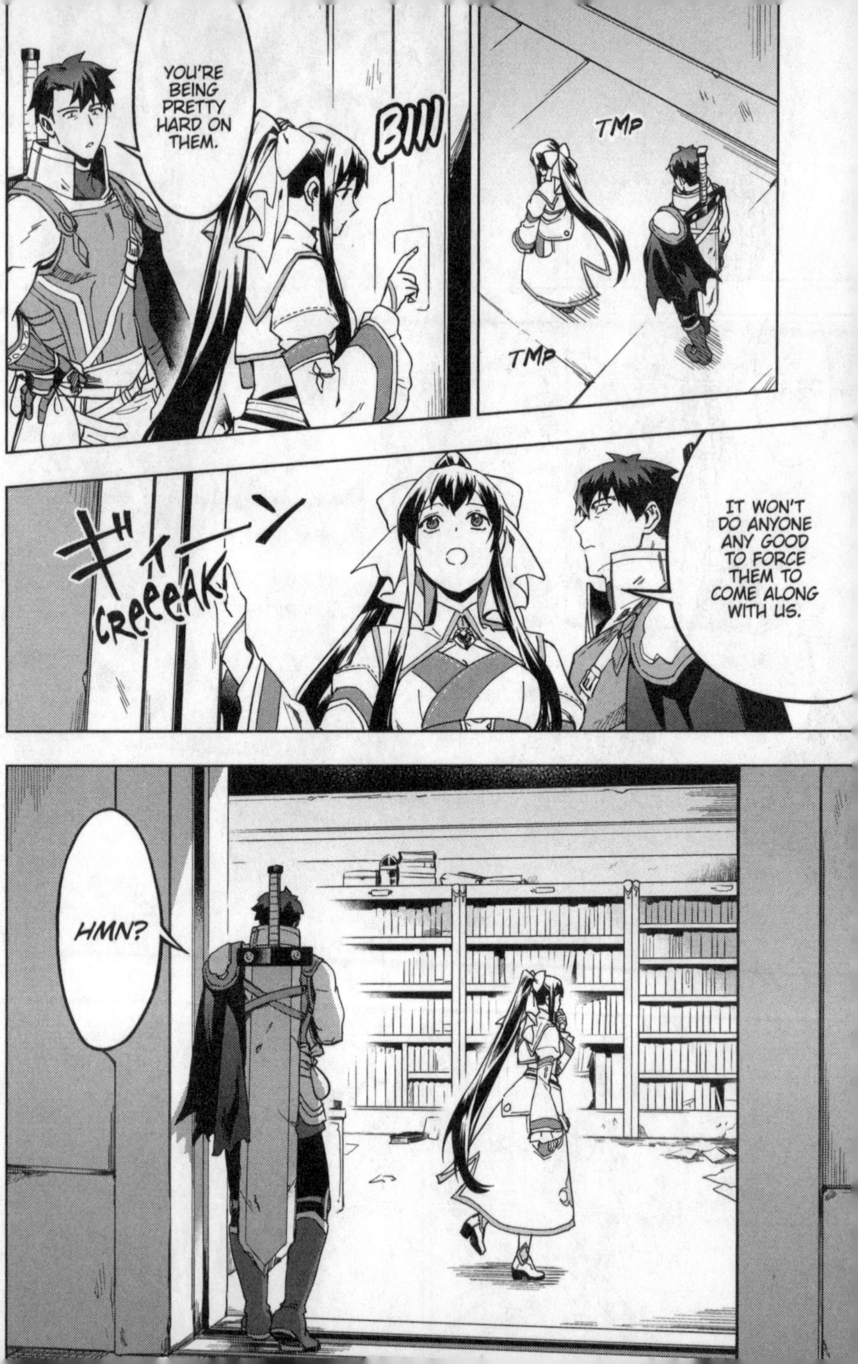
TMP
TMP
YOU'RE BEING PRETTY HARD ON THEM.
BIII
IT WON'T DO ANYONE ANY GOOD TO FORCE THEM TO COME ALONG WITH US.
ギィーン
CREEEAK
HMN?

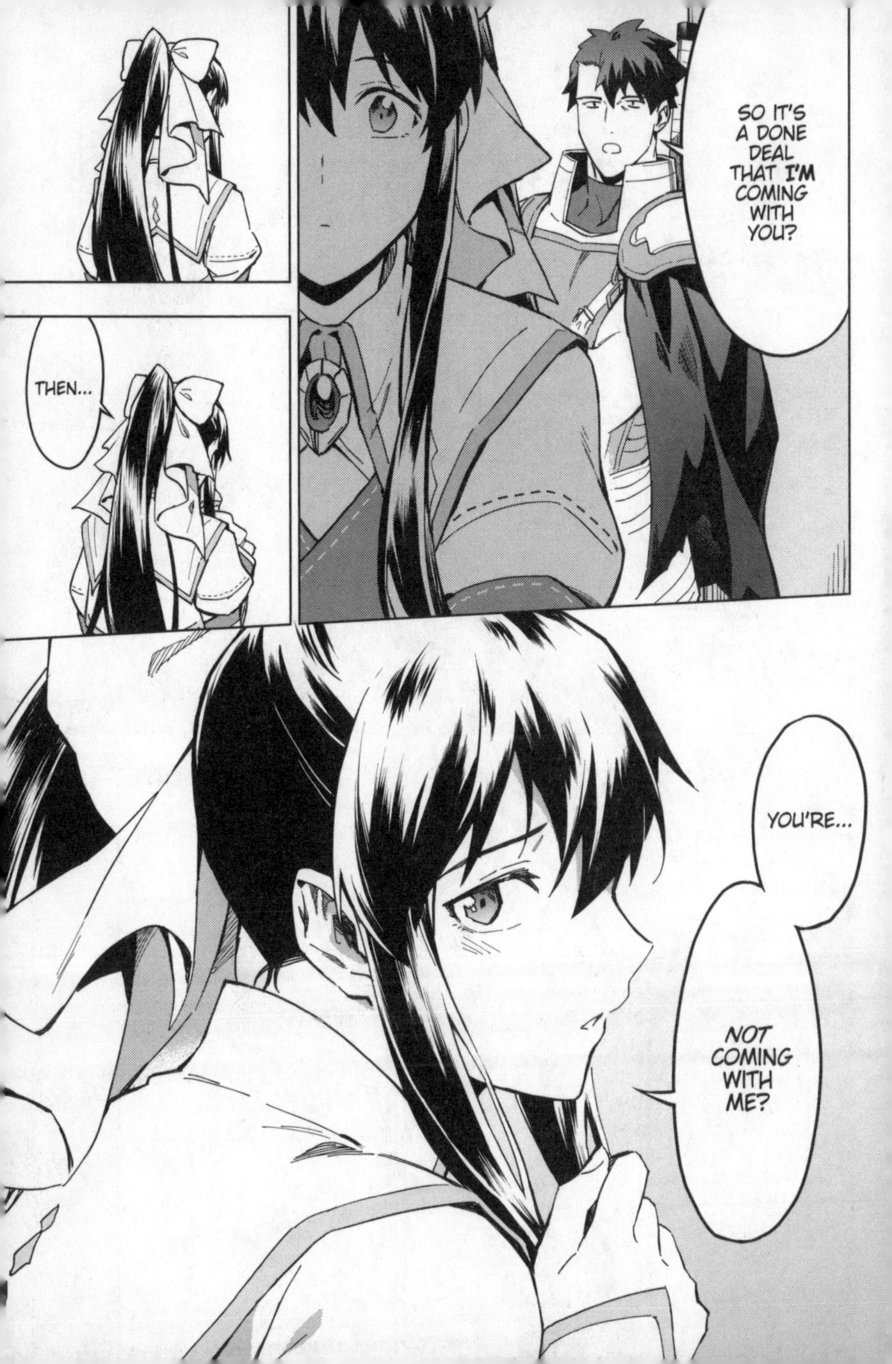
SO IT'S A DONE DEAL THAT I'M COMING WITH YOU?
THEN...
YOU'RE...
NOT COMING WITH ME?

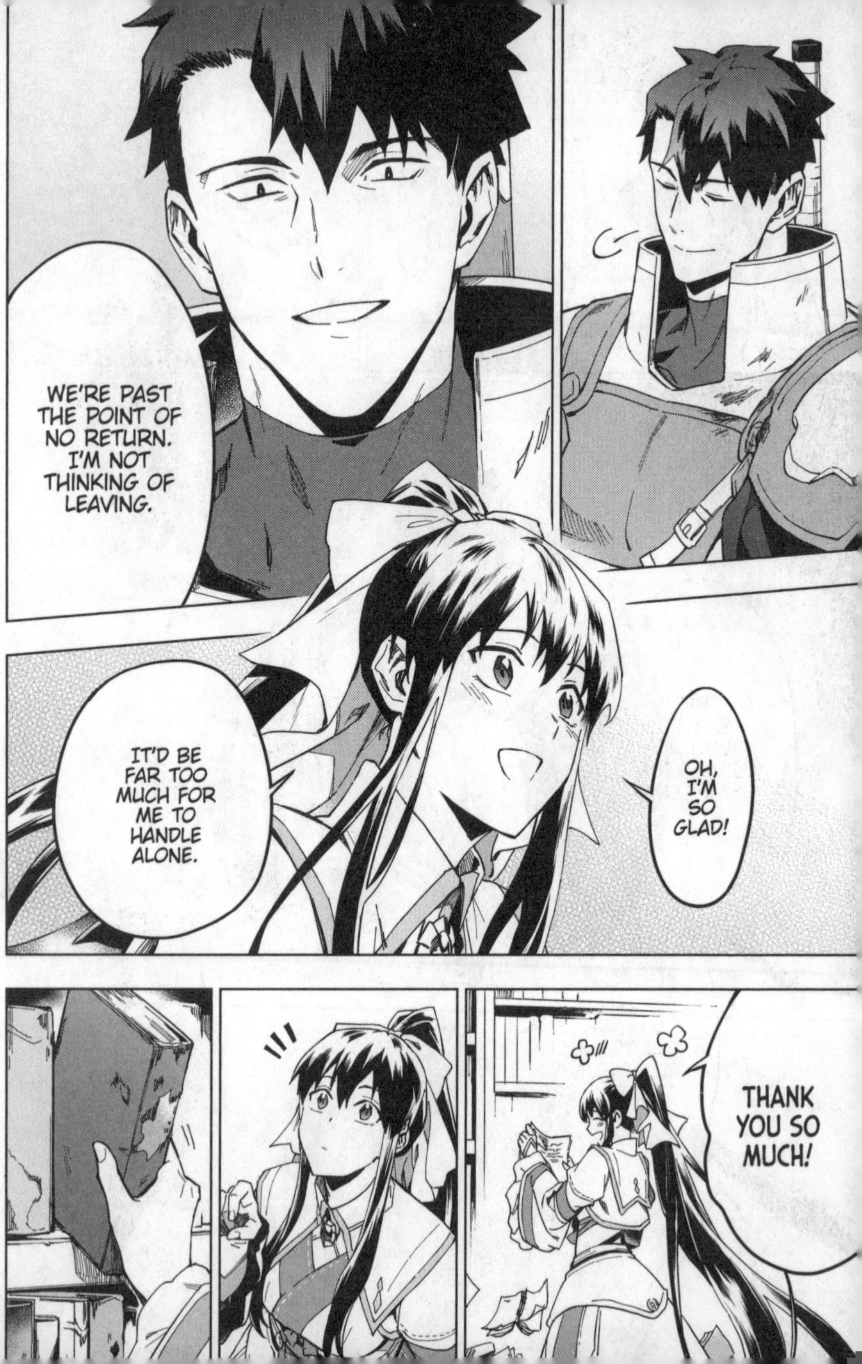
WE'RE PAST THE POINT OF NO RETURN. I'M NOT THINKING OF LEAVING.
OH, I'M SO GLAD!
IT'D BE FAR TOO MUCH FOR ME TO HANDLE ALONE.
THANK YOU SO MUCH!

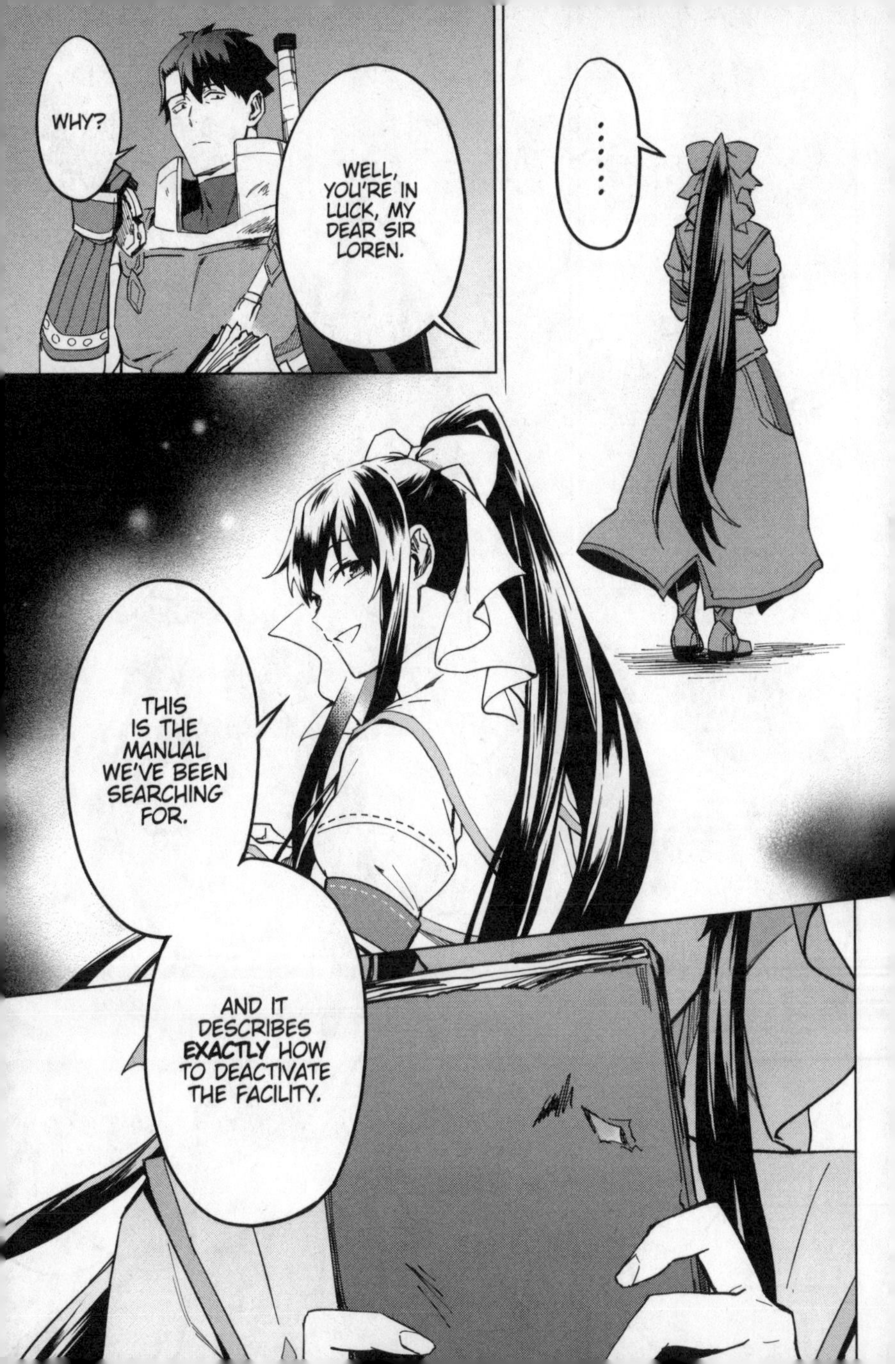
......
WHY?
WELL, YOU'RE IN LUCK, MY DEAR SIR LOREN.
THIS IS THE MANUAL WE'VE BEEN SEARCHING FOR.
AND IT DESCRIBES EXACTLY HOW TO DEACTIVATE THE FACILITY.

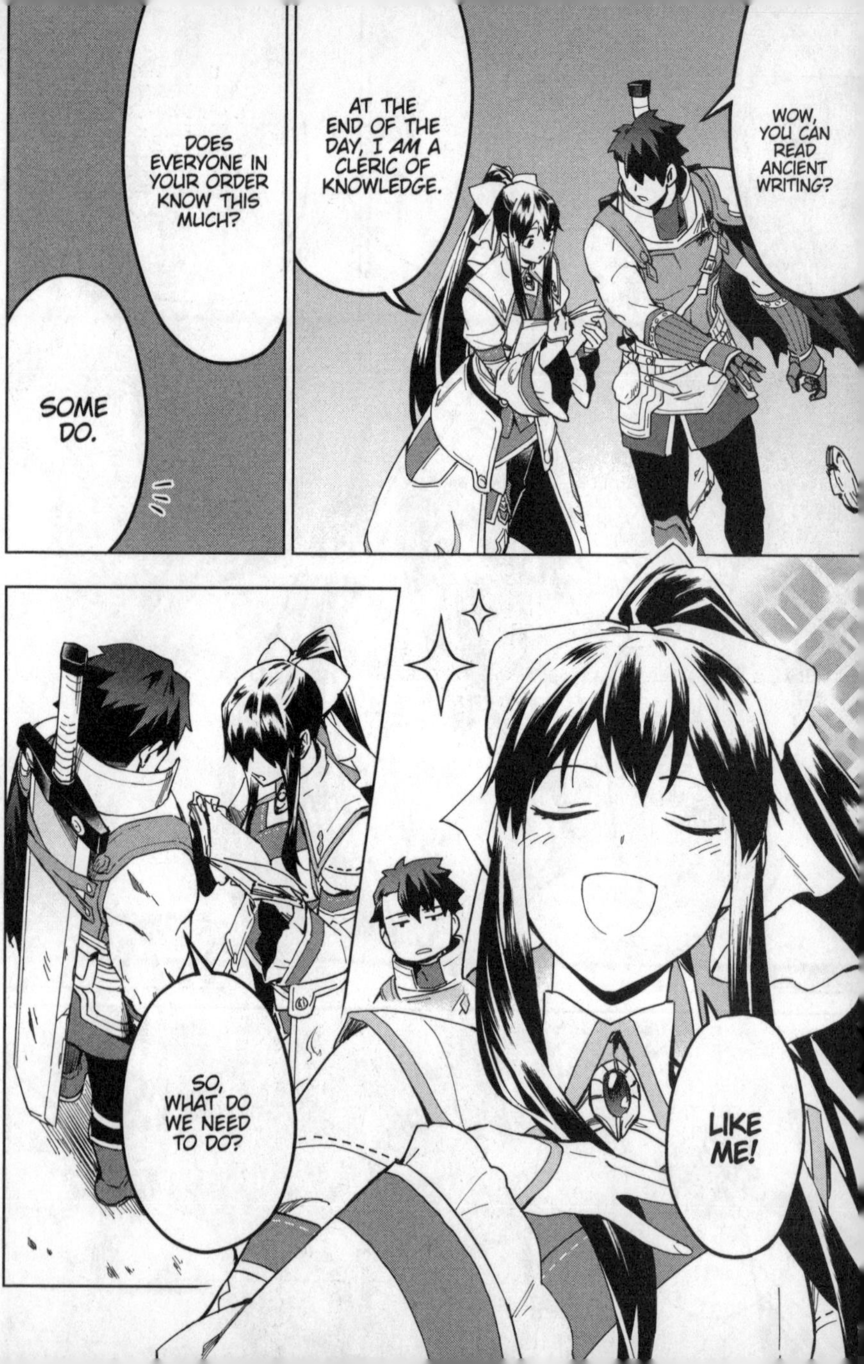
WOW, YOU CAN READ ANCIENT WRITING?
AT THE END OF THE DAY, I *AM* A CLERIC OF KNOWLEDGE.
DOES EVERYONE IN YOUR ORDER KNOW THIS MUCH?
SOME DO.
LIKE ME!
SO, WHAT DO WE NEED TO DO?

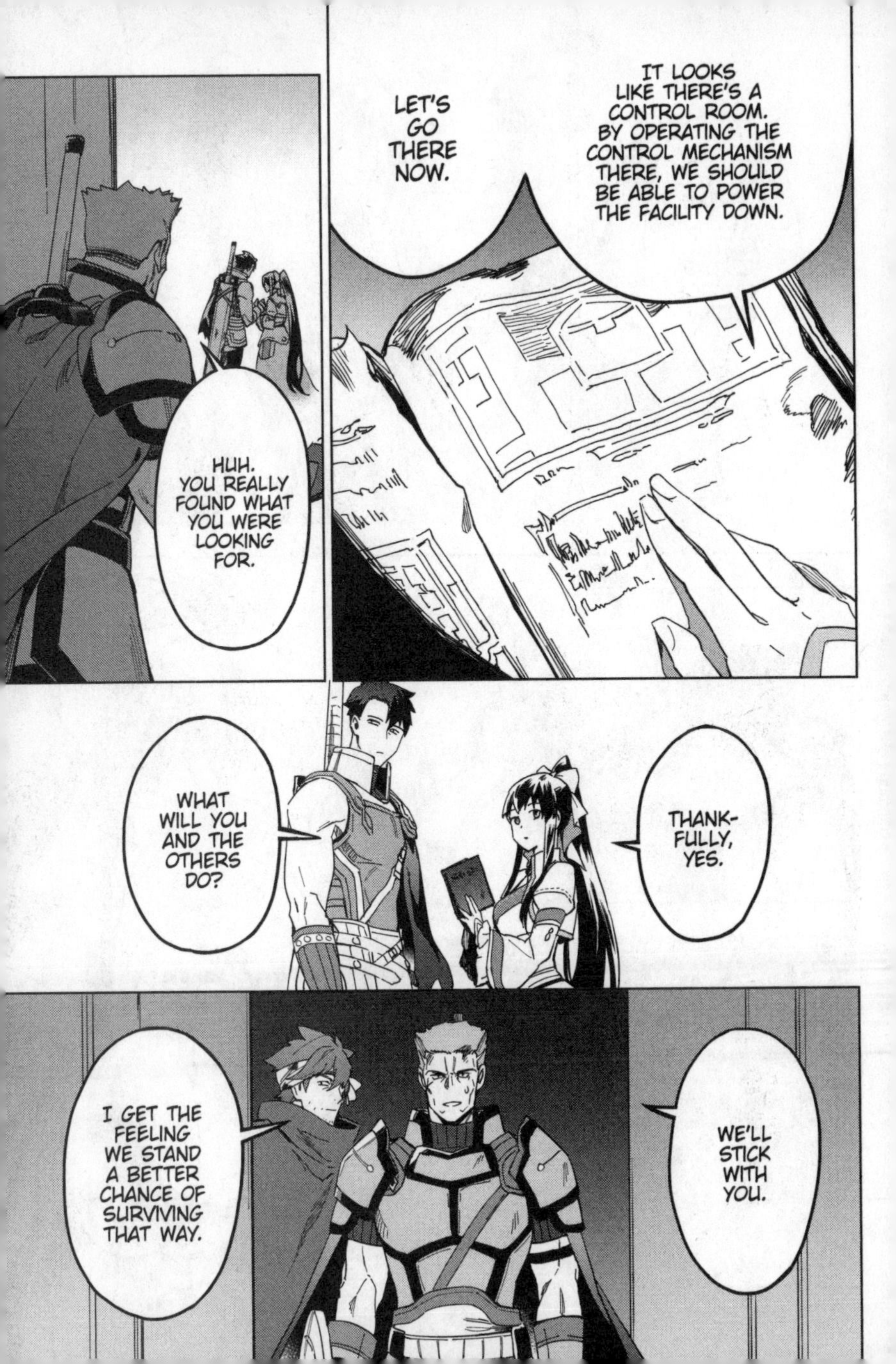
IT LOOKS LIKE THERE'S A CONTROL ROOM. BY OPERATING THE CONTROL MECHANISM THERE, WE SHOULD BE ABLE TO POWER THE FACILITY DOWN.
LET'S GO THERE NOW.
HUH. YOU REALLY FOUND WHAT YOU WERE LOOKING FOR.
THANK-FULLY, YES.
WHAT WILL YOU AND THE OTHERS DO?
WE'LL STICK WITH YOU.
I GET THE FEELING WE STAND A BETTER CHANCE OF SURVIVING THAT WAY.

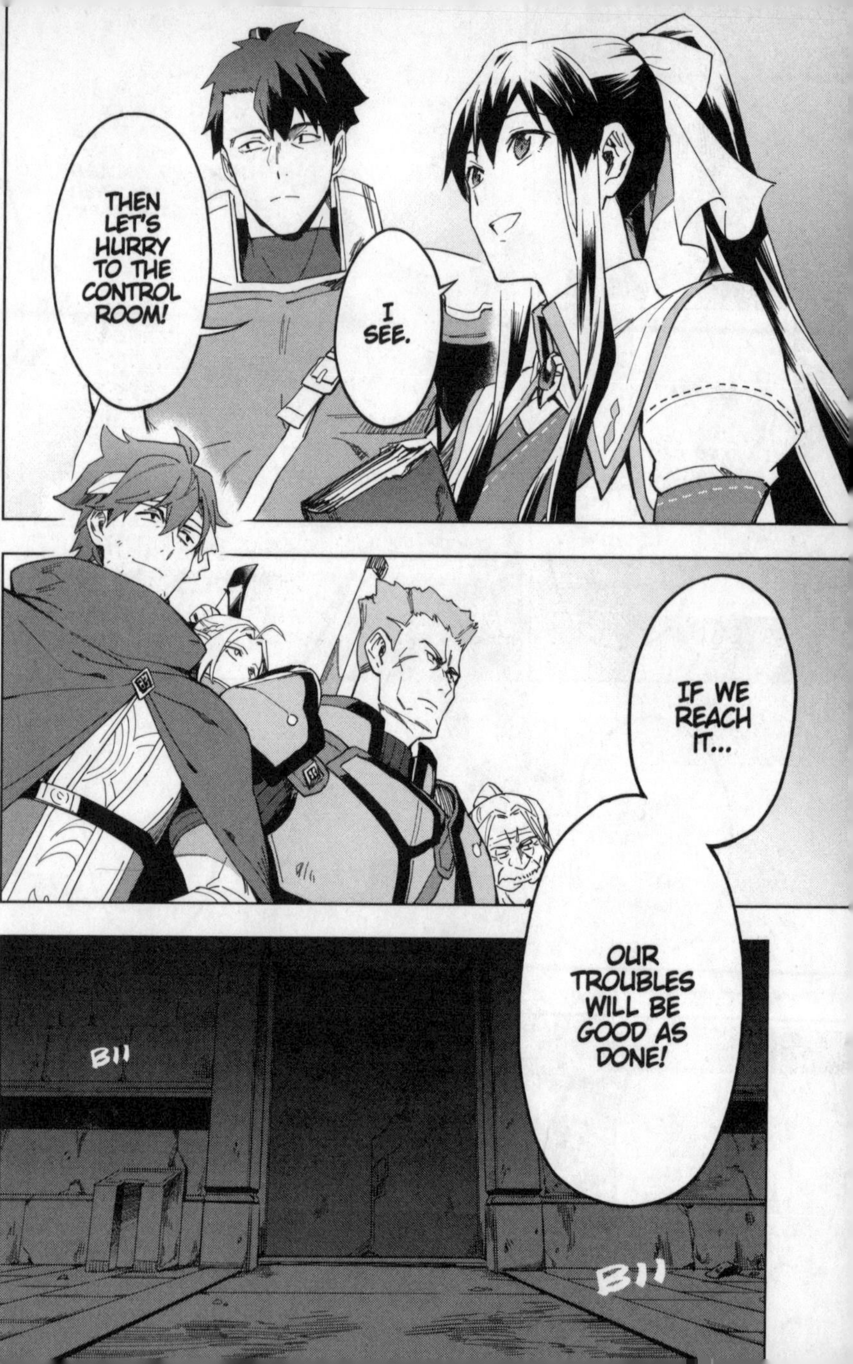
I SEE.
THEN LET'S HURRY TO THE CONTROL ROOM!
IF WE REACH IT...
OUR TROUBLES WILL BE GOOD AS DONE!
BII
BII

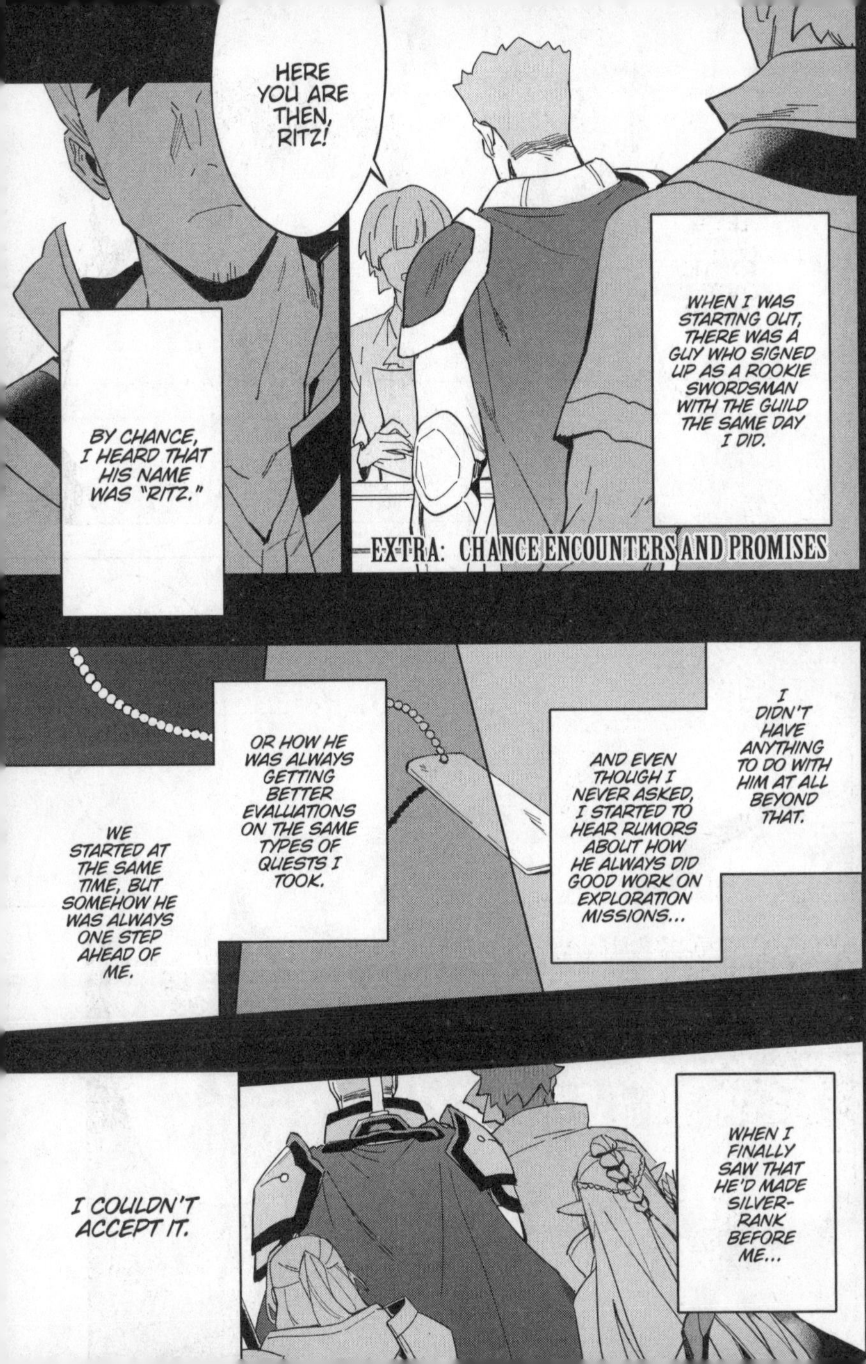
WHEN I WAS STARTING OUT, THERE WAS A GUY WHO SIGNED UP AS A ROOKIE SWORDSMAN WITH THE GUILD THE SAME DAY I DID.
EXTRA: CHANCE ENCOUNTERS AND PROMISES
HERE YOU ARE THEN, RITZ!
BY CHANCE, I HEARD THAT HIS NAME WAS "RITZ."
I DIDN'T HAVE ANYTHING TO DO WITH HIM AT ALL BEYOND THAT.
AND EVEN THOUGH I NEVER ASKED, I STARTED TO HEAR RUMORS ABOUT HOW HE ALWAYS DID GOOD WORK ON EXPLORATION MISSIONS...
OR HOW HE WAS ALWAYS GETTING BETTER EVALUATIONS ON THE SAME TYPES OF QUESTS I TOOK.
WE STARTED AT THE SAME TIME, BUT SOMEHOW HE WAS ALWAYS ONE STEP AHEAD OF ME.
WHEN I FINALLY SAW THAT HE'D MADE SILVER-RANK BEFORE ME...
I COULDN'T ACCEPT IT.

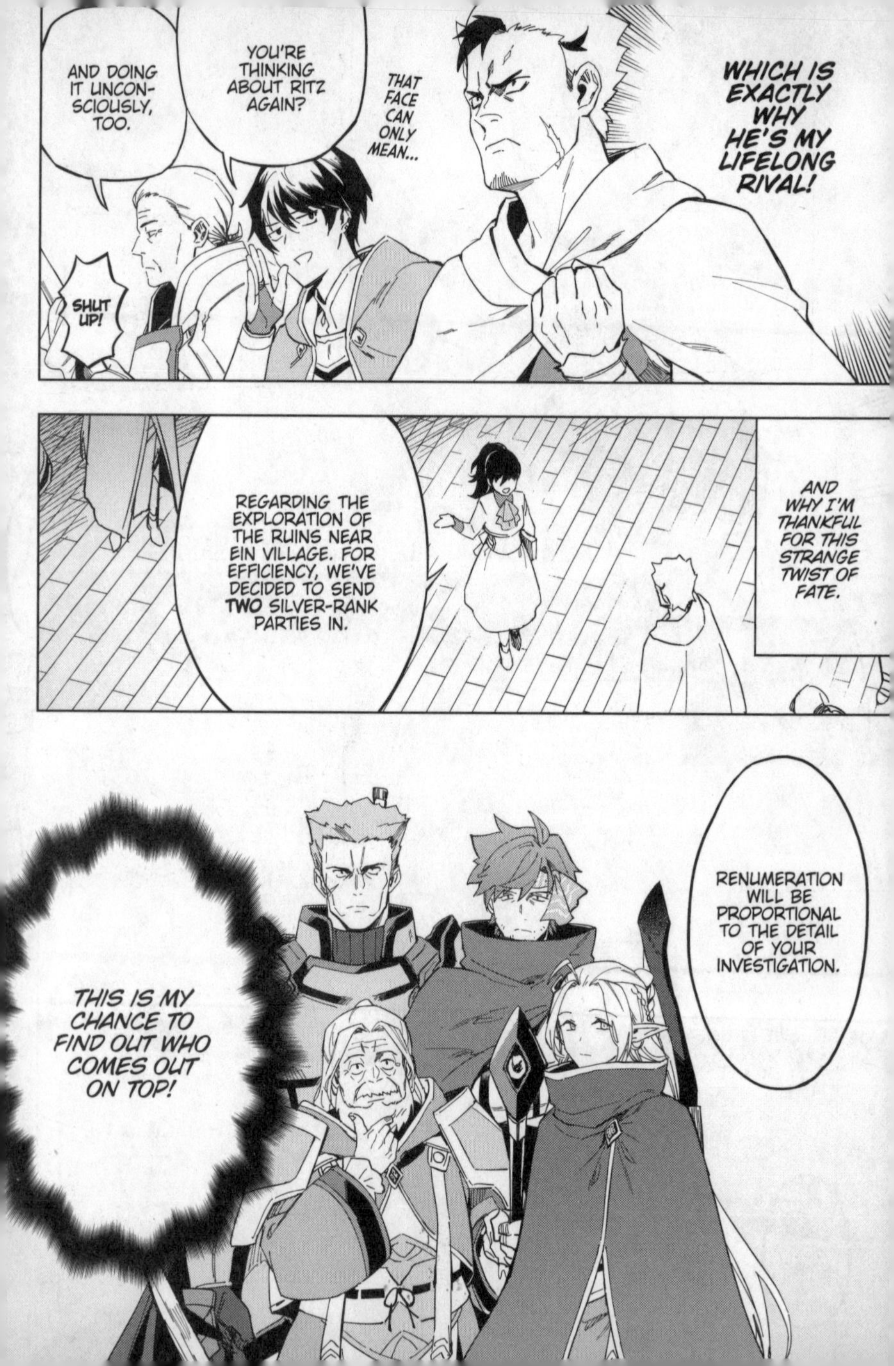
WHICH IS EXACTLY WHY HE'S MY LIFELONG RIVAL!
THAT FACE CAN ONLY MEAN...
YOU'RE THINKING ABOUT RITZ AGAIN?
AND DOING IT UNCONSCIOUSLY, TOO.
SHUT UP!
AND WHY I'M THANKFUL FOR THIS STRANGE TWIST OF FATE.
REGARDING THE EXPLORATION OF THE RUINS NEAR EIN VILLAGE. FOR EFFICIENCY, WE'VE DECIDED TO SEND **TWO** SILVER-RANK PARTIES IN.
RENUMERATION WILL BE PROPORTIONAL TO THE DETAIL OF YOUR INVESTIGATION.
THIS IS MY CHANCE TO FIND OUT WHO COMES OUT ON TOP!

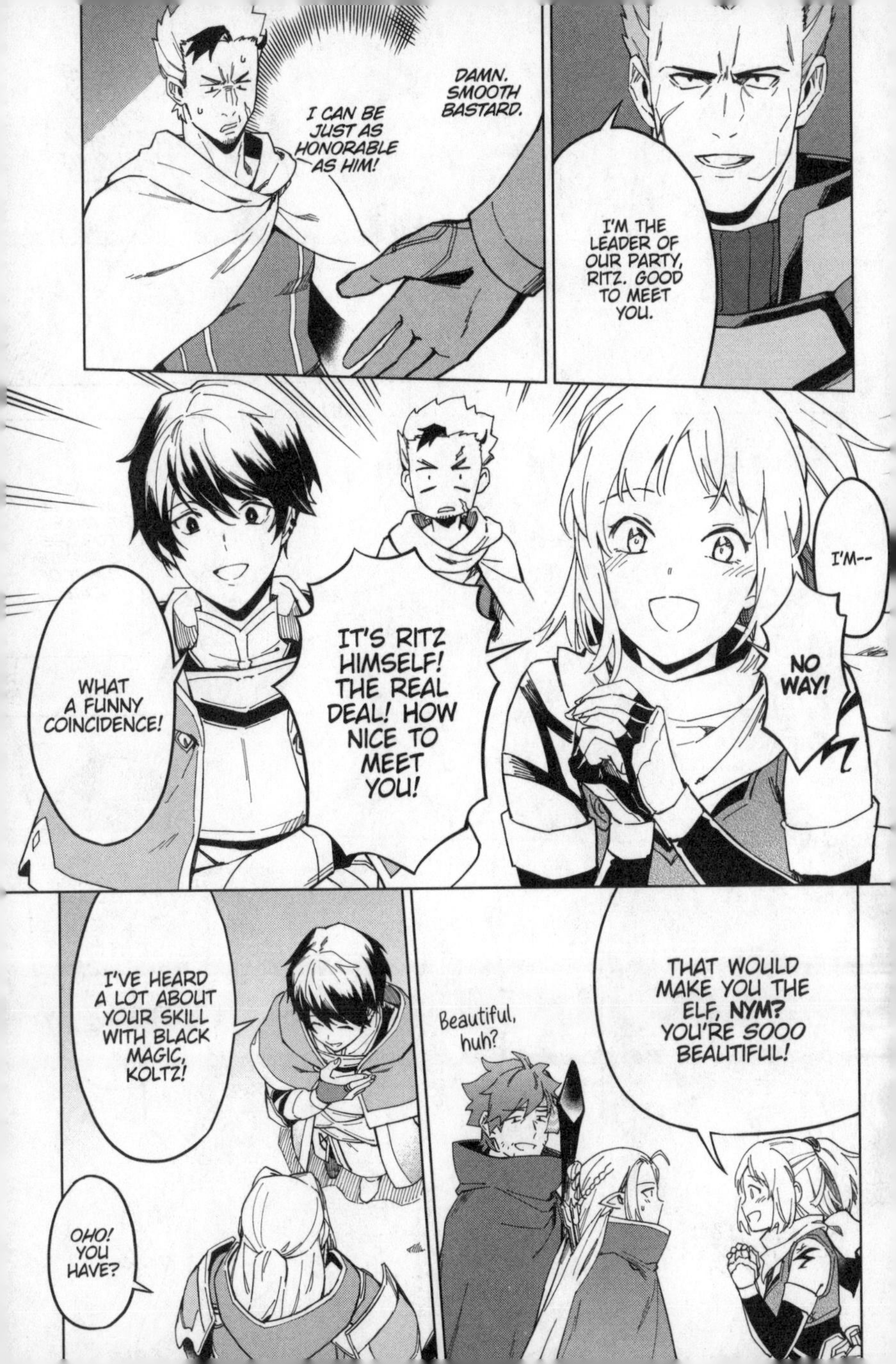
I'M THE LEADER OF OUR PARTY, RITZ. GOOD TO MEET YOU.
DAMN. SMOOTH BASTARD.
I CAN BE JUST AS HONORABLE AS HIM!
I'M--
NO WAY!
IT'S RITZ HIMSELF! THE REAL DEAL! HOW NICE TO MEET YOU!
WHAT A FUNNY COINCIDENCE!
THAT WOULD MAKE YOU THE ELF, NYM? YOU'RE SOOO BEAUTIFUL!
Beautiful, huh?
I'VE HEARD A LOT ABOUT YOUR SKILL WITH BLACK MAGIC, KOLTZ!
OHO! YOU HAVE?

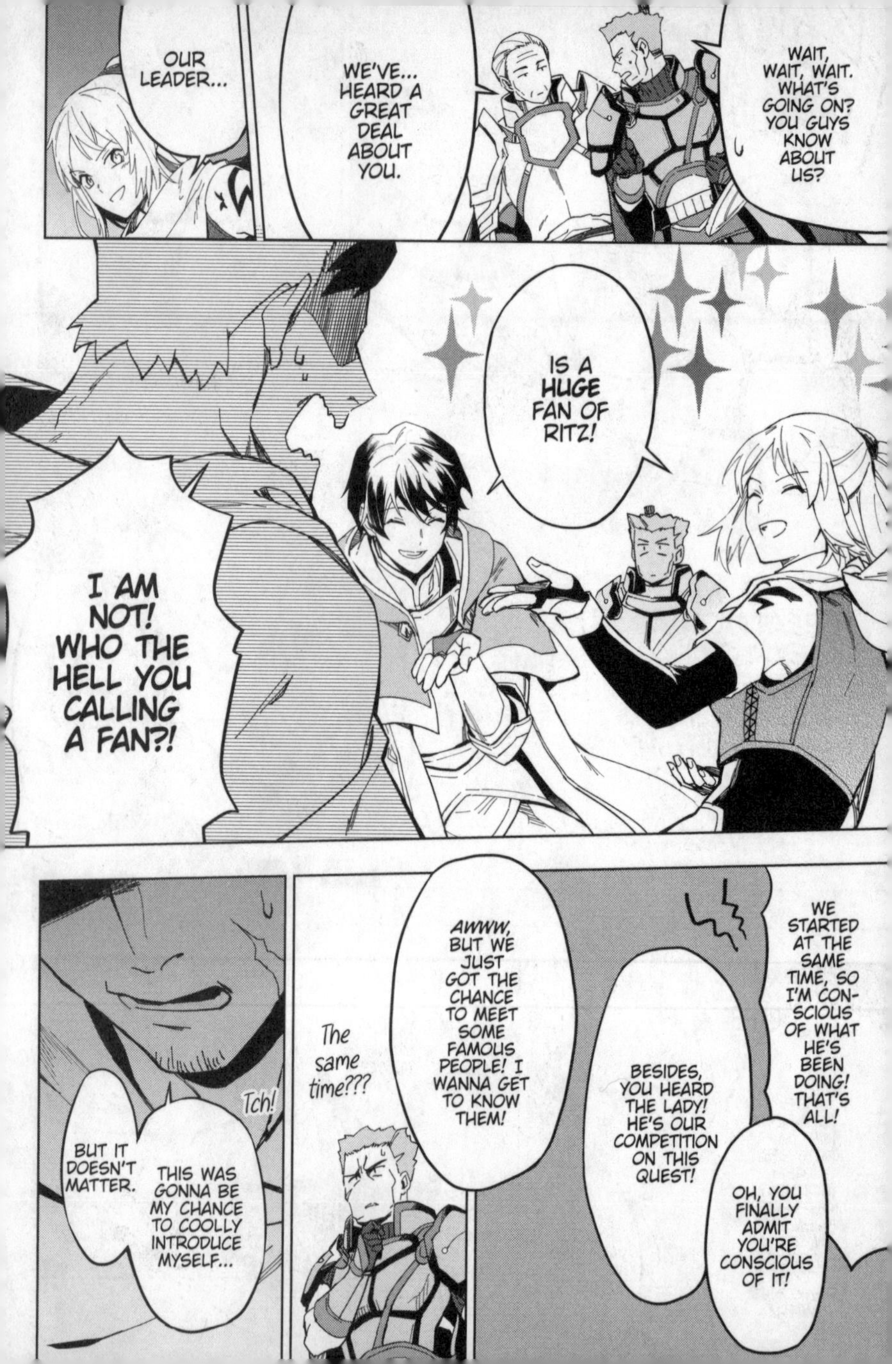

WAIT, WAIT, WAIT. WHAT'S GOING ON? YOU GUYS KNOW ABOUT US?
WE'VE... HEARD A GREAT DEAL ABOUT YOU.
OUR LEADER...
IS A HUGE FAN OF RITZ!
I AM NOT! WHO THE HELL YOU CALLING A FAN?!
WE STARTED AT THE SAME TIME, SO I'M CONSCIOUS OF WHAT HE'S BEEN DOING! THAT'S ALL!
OH, YOU FINALLY ADMIT YOU'RE CONSCIOUS OF IT!
BESIDES, YOU HEARD THE LADY! HE'S OUR COMPETITION ON THIS QUEST!
AWWW, BUT WE JUST GOT THE CHANCE TO MEET SOME FAMOUS PEOPLE! I WANNA GET TO KNOW THEM!
The same time???
Tch!
BUT IT DOESN'T MATTER.
THIS WAS GONNA BE MY CHANCE TO COOLLY INTRODUCE MYSELF...

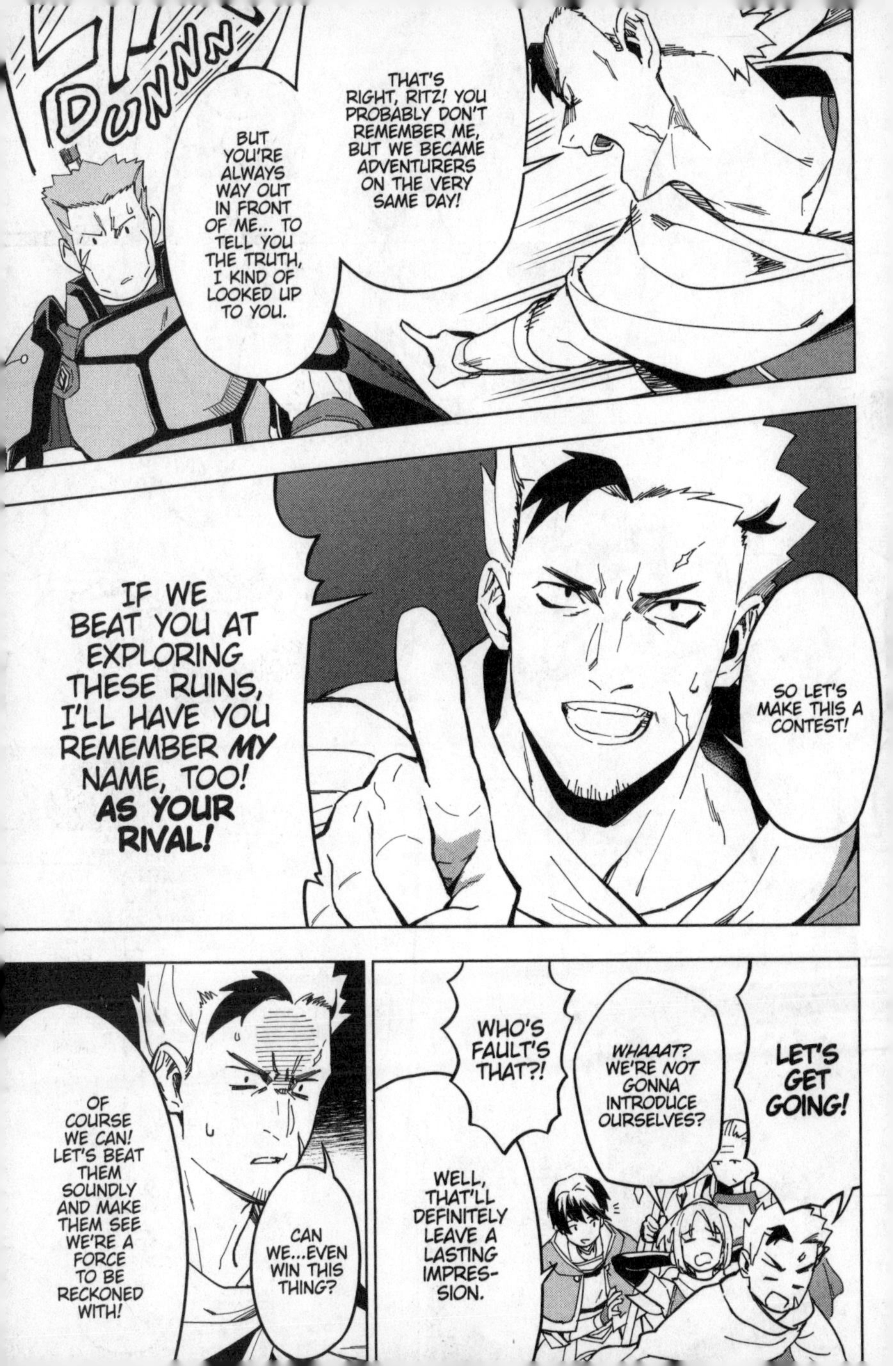

THAT'S RIGHT, RITZ! YOU PROBABLY DON'T REMEMBER ME, BUT WE BECAME ADVENTURERS ON THE VERY SAME DAY!
BUT YOU'RE ALWAYS WAY OUT IN FRONT OF ME... TO TELL YOU THE TRUTH, I KIND OF LOOKED UP TO YOU.
DUNNN
SO LET'S MAKE THIS A CONTEST!
IF WE BEAT YOU AT EXPLORING THESE RUINS, I'LL HAVE YOU REMEMBER *MY* NAME, TOO! **AS YOUR RIVAL!**
LET'S GET GOING!
WHAAAT? WE'RE *NOT* GONNA INTRODUCE OURSELVES?
WHO'S FAULT'S THAT?!
WELL, THAT'LL DEFINITELY LEAVE A LASTING IMPRES-SION.
CAN WE...EVEN WIN THIS THING?
OF COURSE WE CAN! LET'S BEAT THEM SOUNDLY AND MAKE THEM SEE WE'RE A FORCE TO BE RECKONED WITH!

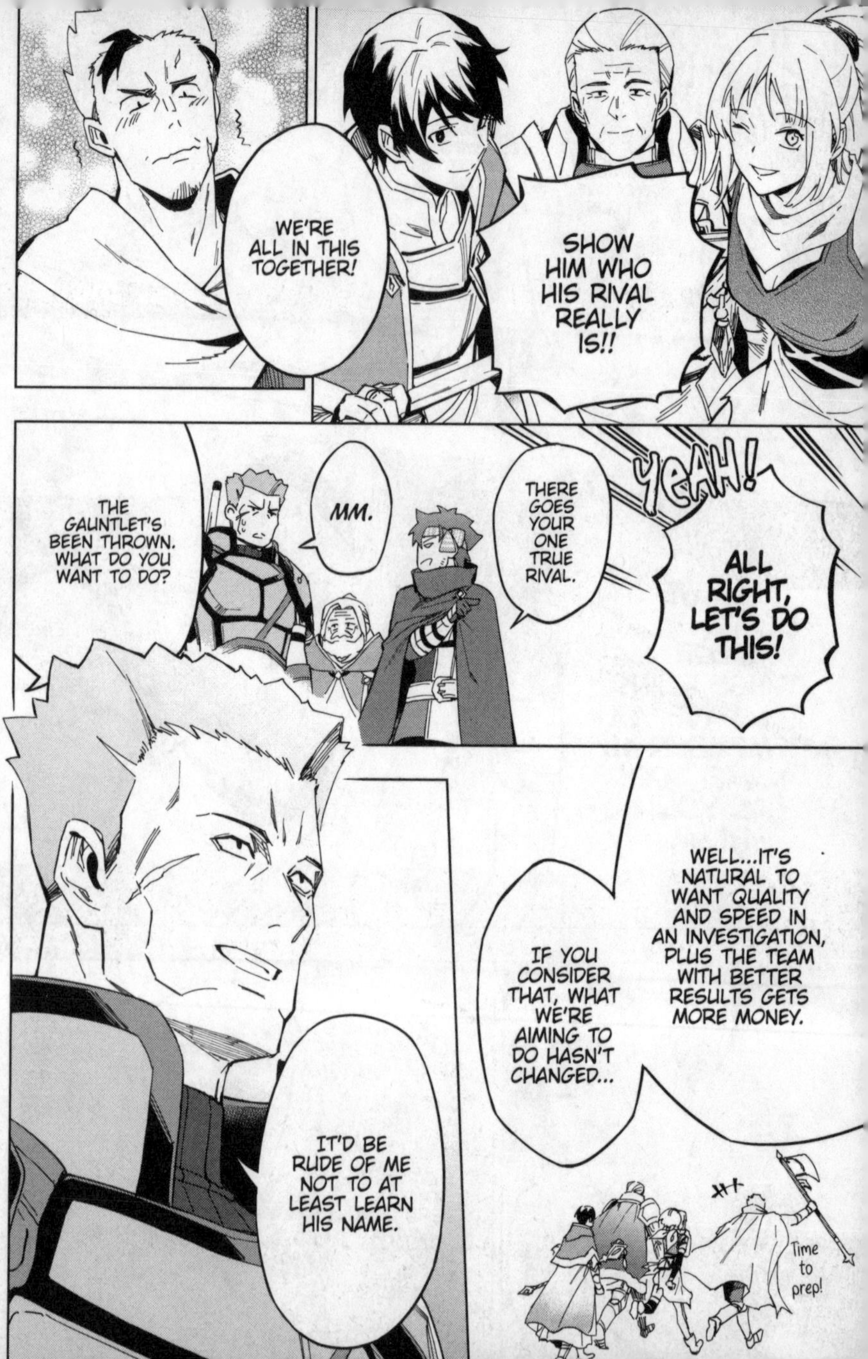
SHOW HIM WHO HIS RIVAL REALLY IS!!
WE'RE ALL IN THIS TOGETHER!
YEAH!
ALL RIGHT, LET'S DO THIS!
THERE GOES YOUR ONE TRUE RIVAL.
MM.
THE GAUNTLET'S BEEN THROWN. WHAT DO YOU WANT TO DO?
WELL...IT'S NATURAL TO WANT QUALITY AND SPEED IN AN INVESTIGATION, PLUS THE TEAM WITH BETTER RESULTS GETS MORE MONEY.
IF YOU CONSIDER THAT, WHAT WE'RE AIMING TO DO HASN'T CHANGED...
Time to prep!
IT'D BE RUDE OF ME NOT TO AT LEAST LEARN HIS NAME.

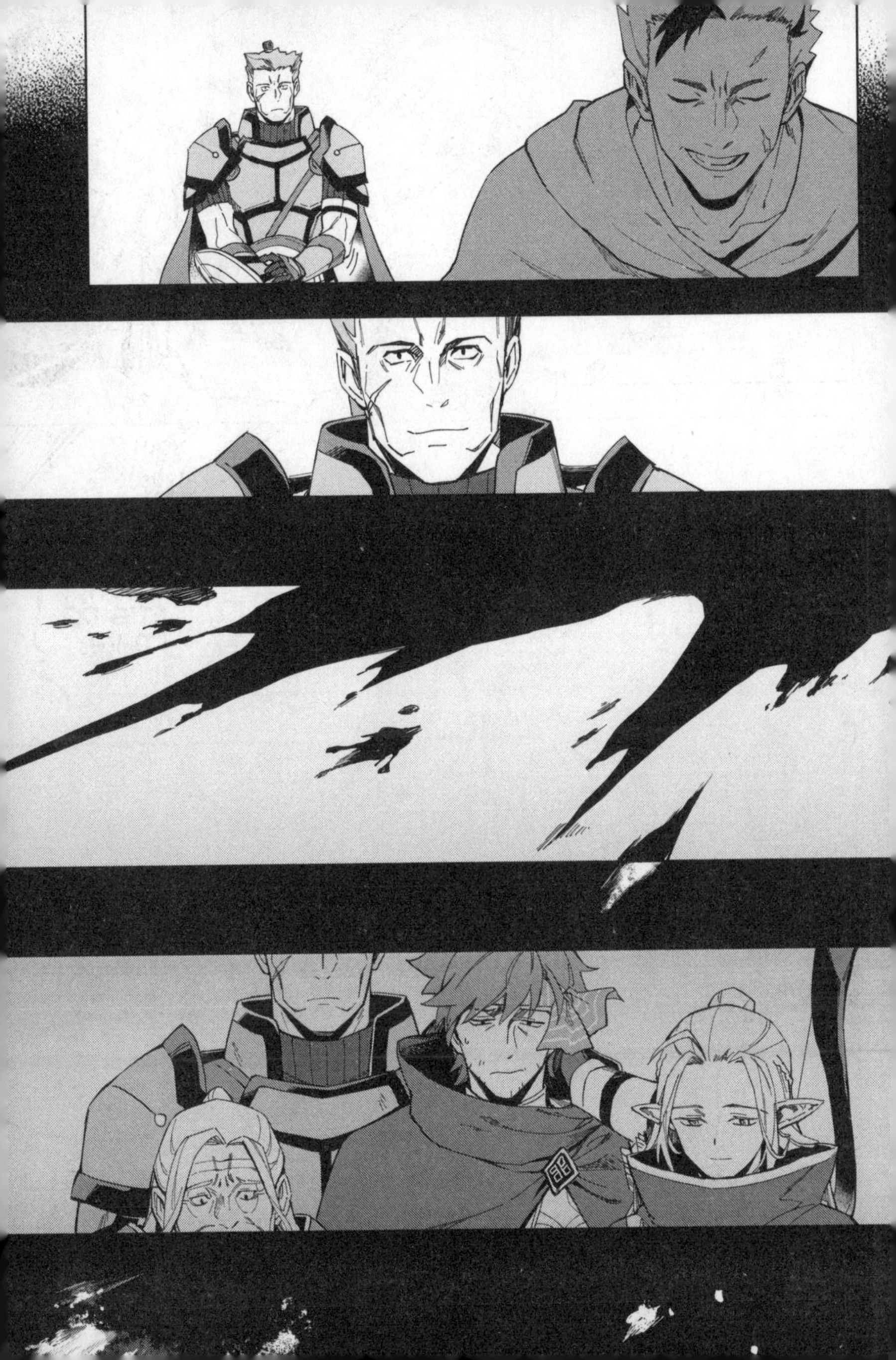

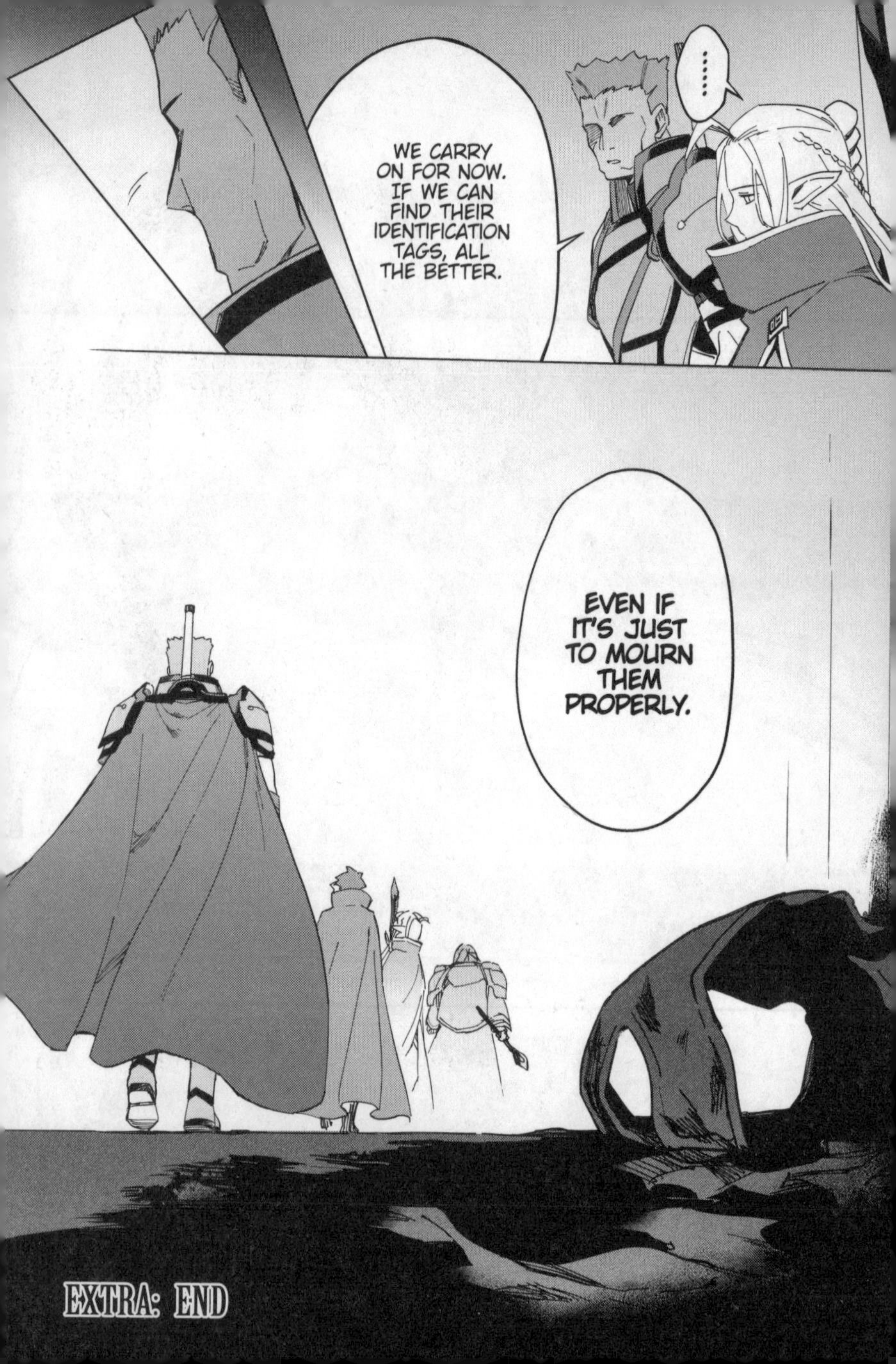
......
WE CARRY ON FOR NOW. IF WE CAN FIND THEIR IDENTIFICATION TAGS, ALL THE BETTER.
EVEN IF IT'S JUST TO MOURN THEM PROPERLY.
EXTRA: END

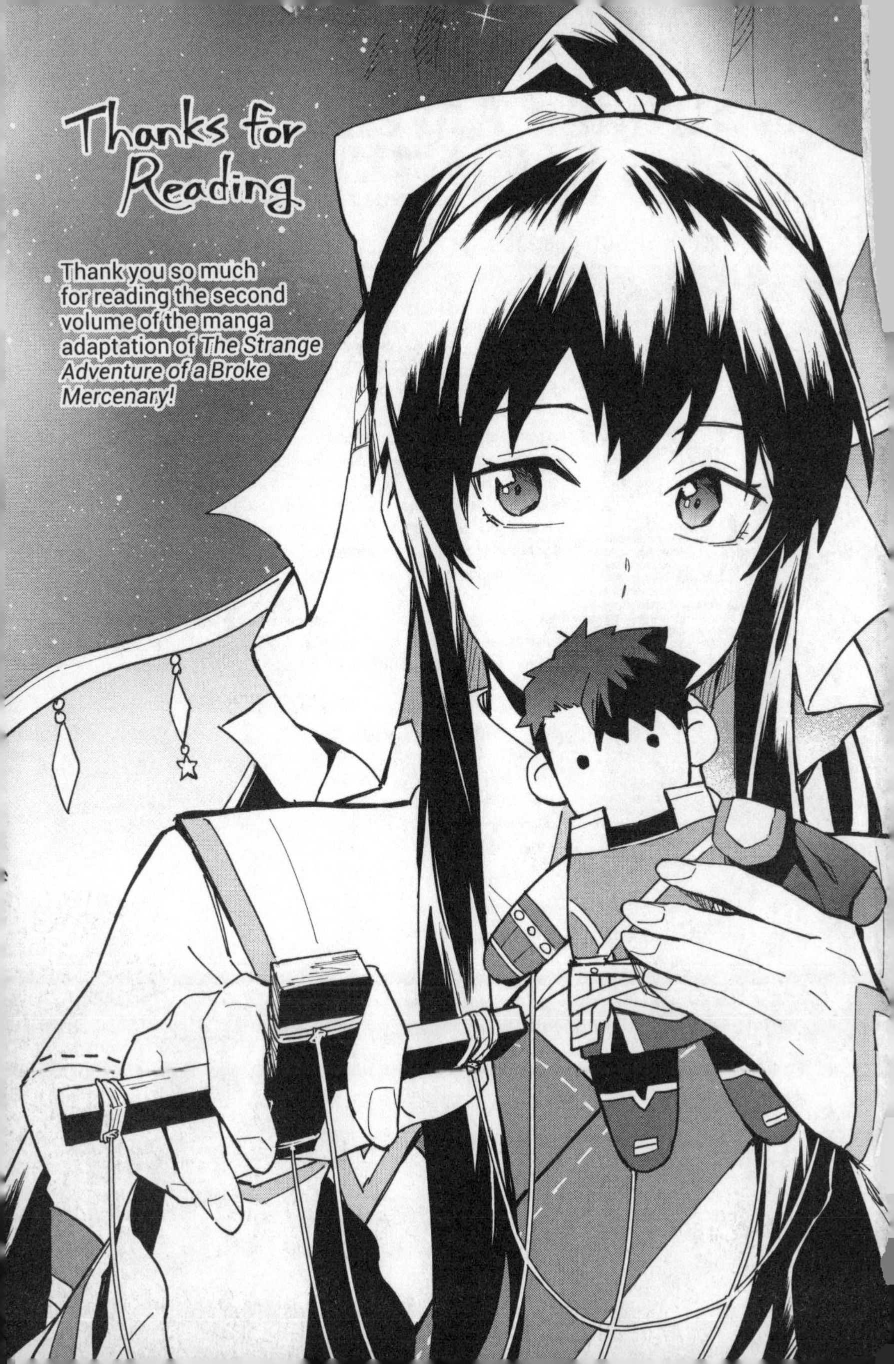
Thanks for Reading
Thank you so much for reading the second volume of the manga adaptation of *The Strange Adventure of a Broke Mercenary!*

SEVEN SEAS ENTERTAINMENT PRESENTS

THE Strange Adventure OF A Broke MERCENARY Vol. 2

story: **Mine**   art: **Araea Ikemiya**   character design: **peroshi**

TRANSLATION
Kat Skarbinec

LETTERING
Kai Kyou

COVER AND LOGO DESIGN
Hanase Qi

COPY EDITOR
Dawn Davis

EDITOR
J.P. Sullivan

PREPRESS TECHNICIAN
Rhiannon Rasmussen-Silverstein

PRODUCTION ASSOCIATE
Christa Miesner

PRODUCTION MANAGER
Lissa Pattillo

MANAGING EDITOR
Julie Davis

ASSOCIATE PUBLISHER
Adam Arnold

PUBLISHER
Jason DeAngelis

KUITSUME YOHEI NO GENSO KITAN Volume 2
©Mine / Araea Ikemiya / peroshi
Originally published in Japan by HOBBY JAPAN, Tokyo.
English translation rights arranged with HOBBY JAPAN, Tokyo,
through TOHAN CORPORATION, Tokyo.

Seven Seas press and purchase enquiries can be sent to Marketing Manager Lianne Sentar at press@gomanga.com. Information regarding the distribution and purchase of digital editions is available from Digital Manager CK Russell at digital@gomanga.com.

ISBN: 978-1-64827-450-3
Printed in Canada
First Printing: November 2021
10 9 8 7 6 5 4 3 2 1

////// READING DIRECTIONS //////

This book reads from *right to left*, Japanese style. If this is your first time reading manga, you start reading from the top right panel on each page and take it from there. If you get lost, just follow the numbered diagram here. It may seem backwards at first, but you'll get the hang of it! Have fun!!

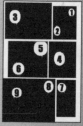

Follow us online: www.SevenSeasEntertainment.com